Songs of Seoul

Songs of Seoul

*An Ethnography of Voice and Voicing
in Christian South Korea*

Nicholas Harkness

UNIVERSITY OF CALIFORNIA PRESS

Berkeley · Los Angeles · London

University of California Press, one of the most
distinguished university presses in the United States,
enriches lives around the world by advancing scholarship
in the humanities, social sciences, and natural sciences. Its
activities are supported by the UC Press Foundation and
by philanthropic contributions from individuals and
institutions. For more information, visit www.ucpress.edu.

University of California Press
Berkeley and Los Angeles, California

University of California Press, Ltd.
London, England

Library of Congress Cataloging-in-Publication Data

Harkness, Nicholas.
   Songs of Seoul : an ethnography of voice and voicing
in Christian South Korea / Nicholas Harkness.
      pages cm
   Includes bibliographical references and index.
   ISBN 978–0-520–27652–9 (cloth : alk. paper)
   ISBN 978–0-520–27653–6 (pbk. : alk. paper)
      1. Church music—Korea (South)   2. Singing—Korea
(South)   3. Music—Religious aspects—Korea
(South)   I. Title.
   ML3151.K6H37 2013
   782.2'2095195—dc23   2013018595

23 22 21 20 19 18 17 16 15 14
10 9 8 7 6 5 4 3 2 1

In memory of Martha, Orlo, and Maxine

Contents

Illustrations

Acknowledgments

I am grateful to my teachers, colleagues, and students for the important roles they have played in the life of this book. This project began at the University of Chicago, where I was fortunate to be trained by Michael Silverstein, Judith Farquhar, Susan Gal, and Kyeong-Hee Choi. Robert E. Moore deserves special thanks for first suggesting that I go to Chicago to study semiotics and anthropology. Other faculty at the University of Chicago who dedicated time and energy to this project included Bruce Cumings, Danilyn Rutherford, William Mazzarella, John Kelly, Robin Shoaps, Raymond Fogelson, Nancy Munn, George Stocking, and Martin Stokes. I am especially grateful to Hisun Kim and Jung Hyuck Lee for teaching me Korean. Parts of this book benefited from the comments of a number of people who were students with me at Chicago: Filipe Calvão, Kiho Kim, Eitan Wilf, Lily Hope Chumley, Shunsuke Nozawa, Kerry Chance, Laurence Ralph, Courtney Handman, Chris Ball, Kate Goldfarb, Joshua Pilzer, Gretchen Pfeil, Yongjin Kim, Anup Grewal, and Max Bohnenkamp.

A Korea Foundation Postdoctoral Fellowship made it possible for me to work with Nancy Abelmann at the University of Illinois Urbana-Champaign from 2010 until 2011. Nancy and the graduate students at the U of I's Korea Workshop were crucial during the process of revising this manuscript.

Most recently, my colleagues and students in the Department of Anthropology at Harvard University have provided an inspiring intellectual environment for me to finish the book. I especially want to thank Steve Caton, who read and commented on the entire manuscript at a late stage, as did two extremely insightful graduate students: Vivien Chung and Andrew Ong. Many of the arguments put forth in this book were discussed at length with participants in my Voice and Voicing seminar: Dilan Yildirim, Esra Gokce Sahin, Jonathan Withers, and Marianne Fritz. I have benefited greatly from conversations with Asad Ahmed, Naor Ben-Yehoyada, Anya Bernstein, Ted Bestor, Lucien Castaing-Taylor, Kerry Chance, Jean Comaroff, John Comaroff, Rowan Flad, Byron Good, Susan Greenhalgh, Michael Herzfeld, Ernst Karel, Arthur Kleinman, Julie Kleinman, Smita Lahiri, Matt Liebmann, Laurence Ralph, Mary Steedly, Ajantha Subramanian, Kimberly Theidon, Jason Ur, and Gary Urton. Susan Farley, Monica Munson, and the rest of the departmental staff were a great help to me while I compiled the final manuscript.

At Harvard I have had the great privilege of working alongside and learning from my colleagues at the Korea Institute: Sun Joo Kim, Carter Eckert, David McCann, and Ed Baker. And it has been a real pleasure to work with the KI's outstanding staff, Susan Laurence, Jina Kim, and Myung-suk Chandra; Harvard's librarian specializing in Korean materials, Mikyung Kang; and my graduate research assistant, Yaejin Cho.

Other colleagues and friends whose generous intellectual engagement has helped shape this book include Asif Agha, Donald Brenneis, David Chung, John Duncan, Olga Fedorenko, Adi Hastings, Miyako Inoue, Jiyeon Kang, Laurel Kendall, Jaeeun Kim, Ju Yon Kim, Ross King, Doreen Lee, Adrienne Lo, Paul Manning, Janet McIntosh, Seungsook Moon, Saeyoung Park, Michael Prentice, Sophia Roosth, and Jesook Song.

I am grateful for the confidence that my colleagues and mentors in Korea had in me and in this project: Kim Kwang-ok, Wang Hahn-Sok, Oh Myung-seok, Kweon Sug-in, and Jung Hyang-jin in the Department of Anthropology at Seoul National University, where I was in residence as a Research Fellow with the Institute for Cross-Cultural Studies; Kim Moonyoung, Pak Kwang-u, Kim Ki-hwa, and the voice students in the Department of Music at Seoul National University; Kim Yŏng-mi at the Korea National University of Arts; and Ha Kyŏng-mi at the National Center for Korean Traditional Performing Arts.

The singers at Somang Presbyterian Church warmly welcomed me into their ensemble. I especially want to thank Hwang Jee-hee, Koh Han-na, Kim Mun-ja, Lee Kwŏn-t'ae, Lee Sŏng-ja, An Yong-ch'an, Pak Yun-gyŏng, Sŏ Yong-jin, Chŏng Chi-yŏn, Lee Yŏn-jŏng, Ch'oe Chu-hŭi, Woo Sŭng-hyŏn, Kim Ae-ri, and Lee Chae-hwan.

During my fieldwork in Seoul, I also benefited from the help and friendship of Kim Yoojung, Kim Hyeyoung, Kim Young Ah, Kim Jihyun (ziihiion), Chang Ŭn-hwa, Arhm Choi, Donald Park, and John Lee. In Germany, Youn Kwangchul, Julie Kaufmann, and Elizabeth Weres were generous with their time and thoughts.

Since 2011 I have worked with and learned a great deal from a team of colleagues studying religion and urban aspiration in Seoul through the Max Planck Institute for the Study of Religious and Ethnic Diversity, funded by the Academy of Korean Studies: Peter van der Veer, Ju Hui Judy Han, Song Doyoung, Kim Hyun-mee, Jin-heon Jung, and Angela Heo.

While I take full responsibility for any errors in this book, I must give much credit to Heejin Kim, who proofread my Korean translations, and to Yun-hee Lee, who proofread my McCune-Reischauer Romanization. Arum Kang, Jin Song, and Youn Ki also helped with early transcriptions of many of my interviews.

At the University of California Press, senior editor Reed Malcolm provided excellent guidance as I prepared the manuscript for publication. Stacy Eisenstark (editorial assistant), Robin Whitaker (copy editor), Francisco Reinking (senior project editor), and Sharon Sweeney (indexer) all contributed much to the preparation and production of the book.

I have presented parts of this manuscript in its earlier stages at the University of Chicago, the University of Illinois Urbana-Champaign, Harvard University, the University of Pennsylvania, the University of Toronto, the University of Michigan, Dartmouth College, Brown University, Seoul National University, Social Science Research Council Korean Studies Dissertation Workshop, and meetings of the American Anthropological Association and of the Association for Asian Studies.

Chapter 6 was published previously in slightly altered form as "Encore! Homecoming Recitals in Christian South Korea" in the *Journal of Korean Studies* 17, no. 12 (2012): 351–81. I gratefully acknowledge permission granted by Professor Hong Ki-hwan of Chŏnbuk National University Hospital to reproduce his images of vocal cords in figures 8 and 9, and from Sage Publications to reproduce Max Noah's photograph in figure 10.

Most recently, the research and writing for this book has been supported by the Academy of Korean Studies Grant funded by the Korean government (MEST) (AKS-2011-AAA-2104), a faculty grant from Harvard University's Asia Center, and a Korea Foundation Postdoctoral

Fellowship at the University of Illinois. At the University of Chicago, my research was supported by a Mellon Foundation/Hanna Holborn Gray Fellowship; numerous FLAS Title VI scholarships for Korean; travel grants from the University of Chicago Center for East Asian Studies, the Janco/Orrin Williams Fund, the Lichtstern Fund, and the Leiffer Fellowship.

I want to thank my voice teachers, Jane McMahan, Adalbert Kraus, and Tom Wikman.

Alaina Jasinevicius witnessed this project's beginnings and offered support and encouragement as it evolved.

And finally I want to thank Daniel Harkness and Harriet Hensley; Julie, Mark, Nathan, and Adelyn Amor; Geoff, Laura, and Benjamin Harkness; Sam Harkness; and all of the people who made the annual pilgrimage to Lawrence, Kansas.

Note on Romanization

I have followed the McCune-Reischauer system of Romanization for Korean. I did not make changes to the spelling of Korean names or proper nouns if quoted from a different publication or if circulated widely following a different Romanization system (e.g., "Seoul" and "Lee Myung-bak"). In general, personal names appear in Korean order, with the surname first and the given names hyphenated (e.g., "Pak Tong-jin"), unless the person has specified a different order. However, for consistency, Korean names in the bibliography occur with a comma between the surname and the given name, and in the note citations they occur with the given initials preceding the surname. I refer to the Republic of Korea as "Korea" or "South Korea" unless otherwise noted.

Introduction

Pudae tchigae is a bubbling, reddish stew consisting of chunks of processed meat, vegetables, spices, and red pepper paste. Often translated as "army base stew," "GI stew," or even "Yankee stew," the dish takes its name from the way hungry Koreans in the 1950s boiled leftover food from U.S. Army bases—some donated, some pulled from the trash—to feed themselves and their families.[1] Although an unscavenged form of *pudae tchigae* is popular today and continues its flexible model of culinary integration by incorporating contemporary consumer products such as ramen noodles and thinly sliced American cheese into its spicy broth, its origins in South Korea's (hereafter Korea's) impoverished, war-torn past are not lost on those who consume it.

In November 2008 I shared a pot of *pudae tchigae* with Su-yŏn, a soprano and church choir director in Seoul. As we dined, she explained that when she ate this stew, she was reminded of Korea's history and occasionally felt sad. She said that Korea's history was extremely sad and that the dish was obviously associated with that fact. For her, it still had the taste of poverty. Then she added, with a characteristic chuckle, "We still like to eat *pudae tchigae*, even though these days we should not be sad." "Why should you not be sad?" I asked. She replied, "Because we have God's grace *[ŭnhye]*."

After dinner, we walked to the nearby Seoul Arts Center to hear her friend sing. The scene at the massive performing arts and education complex, which was completed in 1993, was a stark contrast to that conjured up by our dinner: children played by a fountain with moving spigots synchronized to well-known classical music tunes; families peacefully strolled the concrete grounds, laughing and eating; well-dressed patrons walked across the plaza from Café Mozart to the concert hall to hear European classical music sung in foreign languages. Su-yŏn's friend had recently returned from study and professional work in Germany and was giving a "homecoming recital" *(kwiguk tokch'anghoe)* of songs and arias by Bach, Brahms, Mozart, Strauss, Verdi, and Puccini. At the end of the recital, for her final encore, the soprano sang a Christian hymn, known in English as "Higher Ground" or "I'm Pressing on the Upward Way." The Korean lyrics of the song are as follows:

Chŏ nop'ŭn kot ŭl hyanghayŏ nalmada naa kamnida.
Nae ttŭt kwa chŏngsŏng moduŏ nalmada kido hamnida.
Nae Chu yŏ nae pal puttŭsa kŭ kot e sŏge hasosŏ
Kŭ kot ŭn pit kwa sarang i ŏnjena nŏmch'iomnida.

I look to that high place, and every day I go forward.
Every day I pray with all my mind, heart, and soul.
"My Lord, seize my feet and let me stand there."
In that place light and love always overflow.[2]

As the soprano sang the hymn, Su-yŏn clasped her hands together, closed her eyes, and bowed her head in prayer. Others in the audience did the same. Had we not been in a concert hall, the appearance of the audience and sound of the music emanating from the stage would have suggested that a church service was taking place. After the hymn, some members of the audience even called out, "Amen!"

This is a standard format for classical vocal music in Korea: a recital of classical songs and arias that ends with a hymn delivered as a final encore. The hymn makes explicit for the singer and the audience alike that European-style classical singing in Korea is basically a Christian form of vocal practice. The final hymn makes this social fact clear by framing the recital as an inherently Christian event. Furthermore, the qualities perceived in the European-style classical voice are precisely those of the "higher ground" described in the hymn above—the sound of light and love, the sound of grace. For many Korean Christians, the transformation from memories evoked by *pudae tchigae* to the experience of the prosperous present is embodied and expressed by the cultivation of this kind of voice. It is the voice of Korean Christian aspiration.

This book is an ethnographic study of the human voice in a particular stratum of Korean Christian culture. At the heart of my analysis is the way the European-style classical voice is a privileged nexus of phonic and sonic practice for Christians. This voice is treated as a qualitative emblem of a broader cultural transformation from a suffering, war-torn nation to one that has received "God's grace." While many are still drawn to the qualities of sadness and roughness as familiar, if now somewhat quaint, features of past expressive forms—indeed, of past culinary forms, if we consider Su-yŏn's account of *pudae tchigae*—they nonetheless hold as their ideal a Korean social world in which ethnonational sadness and suffering may be remembered, even memorialized, but not experienced directly. This ideal world is captured in the moment when an audience listens to a hymn sung in a Western classical style (*sŏngak*) and utters, "Amen."[3] In the following pages, I show how the cultivation of the human voice—specifically, the ideal qualities of the voice as a *phonosonic nexus* (see below)—in churches and music schools throughout Seoul instantiates this transformation.

The empirical questions that led to my ethnographic research began five thousand miles away in Germany. In the winter of 2002, I flew from Munich to Berlin to audition for two music conservatories: the Universität der Künste (UdK), in western Berlin, and the Musikhochschule Hanns Eisler, in eastern Berlin. I was working as a writer and editor for a technology services company in Munich and was taking voice lessons on the side. On the suggestion of my teacher at the Hochschule für Musik und Theater München, I joined singers from around the world in trying to get one of a handful of spots at one of these schools. I was not accepted. I was disappointed. But besides my own disappointment, perhaps the strongest impression I took from that experience was that more than half of the people auditioning with me were from South Korea.

The presence of Korean singers at a European audition was no surprise. I had encountered many Korean musicians, both Korean nationals and Korean Americans, in New York City (where I had gone to college) and elsewhere in the United States.[4] The numbers were remarkable, but beyond that, two things astonished me. The first was how well all of the Korean singers seemed to know one another and how comfortable they seemed in this competitive environment. While many prospective students stood alone in the hallway, nervously awaiting (and perhaps dreading) our turn to sing, the Korean students walked in large convivial groups through the hallways of the music building, chatting and even laughing. They seemed—to me, at least—to be at ease. The second was how well the Korean singers performed in the auditions.

Many of the singers called back for the second round of auditions were Korean. And, after listening to a few of them, my surprise turned into admiration and respect. I remember standing with other singers in the hallway at the UdK during one Korean tenor's audition and looking at one another, amazed at the size and beauty of the voice that emanated from the room.

What I observed in 2002 was not a quirk. For example, in the first round of the 2007 auditions for the voice department of Berlin's Hochschule für Musik Hanns Eisler, 104 out of 164 applicants were from Korea.[5] And the successes of Korean singers have not stopped at conservatories. At the Rocca delle Macìe International Opera Competition, fifteen of the thirty finalists between 1999 and 2006 were from Korea.[6] In 2009, the first-, second-, and third-prize winners at the biennial Neue Stimmen International Voice Competition were also Korean.[7] Given the obvious interest in this genre of vocal arts, I assumed at first that there must be a thriving public arts scene that supported and encouraged this type of music. But when I arrived in Korea in 2005 for my first research trip to explore this phenomenon, I was surprised to find that concert halls were basically empty at each of the performances I attended. Why were these singers flying across the world to learn to sing if there was no one to listen to them in Korea? Why put in so much effort abroad and then return home if there was no work at home? Why spend time, money, and other resources on cultivating this particular kind of vocal sound if there was no clear public appreciation for it?

In 2005, I went to Seoul looking for an explanation for the wild successes of Korean opera singers in conservatories and at competitions around the world. I expected to find a culture of rigorous, disciplined practice organized by discourse about vocal technique: a system of semiotic awareness and control that allows singers to manipulate their bodies to produce particular kinds of sounds. What else could account for their successes? I expected to arrive in Seoul and find the singers there already able to explain the ways they produced the sounds I had heard years before in Berlin. But this was not the case. Although the singers I met on this early trip had a few things to say about how they sang and how much time they spent in the practice room, many were much more interested in talking about another set of motivations: Christianity, God, Jesus Christ, church, faith, and evangelism.

It wasn't until 2006, when I returned for a second research trip, that I realized how central the church was to the lives of these singers of *sŏngak*. Just as these singers demonstrated no pervasive or detailed or even consistent technical register for talking about singing or the voice, so too was a register of connoisseurship among audiences absent. Although there were numerous *sŏngak* performances throughout the city, the audiences were rarely full, and those who attended seemed hardly engaged in the performance (except, as above, when there was a Christian hymn). In contrast to Japan, where the arts market for operatic singing is quite developed and the fans are known to be very passionate (despite the fact that there are far fewer world-famous Japanese opera singers), in Korea there is not much of a "public" for *sŏngak*. I learned that most members of concert audiences had some kind of first- or second-degree institutional relation to the performer—family members, church members, or school friends. Their attendance was motivated primarily by personal obligation, and these listening audiences demonstrated no great interest in the cultural categories of aesthetic judgment and critique that one encounters in the United States, Europe, and elsewhere, such as technical virtuosity or artistry or intelligence of singing. If people happened to be interested in the music, this interest was expressed primarily in terms of the way the singing made them *feel*. And this feeling was largely related to the role of *sŏngak* as an overwhelmingly, if still somewhat implicit, Christian register of communication in Korea. And so for a year of fieldwork beginning in early 2008, I sang with one of the choirs at the large, wealthy, powerful Somang Presbyterian Church and attended classes in Seoul National University's (SNU) Department of Voice, one of the most selective programs in the country.

The vast majority of students and professionals of *sŏngak* not only described themselves as Evangelical Christians but also characterized *sŏngak* in both direct and indirect ways as a mode of evangelical training and Christian activity. Singers repeatedly told me that they were singing for God, that even secular art music could be used for evangelism, and that the *sŏngak* method of sound production was chosen explicitly to bring out the natural, and therefore "God-given," voice in each person. My informants consistently told me that 99 percent of university students majoring in *sŏngak* were Christian and mostly Presbyterian—in a country where Protestant Christians usually are estimated to account for only about 20 percent of the population of around 50 million. In my own interviews I found the numbers to be a bit lower: at least four out of five were Protestant and the remaining were mostly Catholic. But it is telling that the singers themselves see their own field of *sŏngak* as dominated by Protestant Christians. According to these same informants, just over half of the classically trained instrumentalists at universities are practicing Christians. This difference between the study of *sŏngak* and the study of Western musical instruments—both the rough statistical difference and people's perceptions of difference—disrupts the easy sociological notion that Christianity and classical music are connected in Korea simply because both are "Western" and therefore status-raising, modern, and instrumental in Korea for social mobility and class reproduction, or that the thousands of Korean students who study Western music in Korea or abroad all do so for the same reasons.

Although class and gender do play important roles in shaping the social landscape of *sŏngak* singing, I have chosen to weave the treatment of these categories into my broader argument regarding the relationship between Christianity and *sŏngak*.[8] I have found the explicit role of faith and its institutionalization through particular communicative practices illuminating for an understanding of voice in this context, in large part because some relationship between religion and vocal style was clearly understood and articulated by the singers I met, Christian or not. This was profoundly different from my own experience in singing classical music in the United States, where I have participated in it since childhood in the completely agnostic way in which I was raised. My contact with music in church came only much later, when I was hired as a paid member of an all-professional choir in an Episcopal church during graduate school in Chicago. While the professional experience with the church choir prepared me—to a point—for fieldwork, singing in these two religious environments was dramatically different. In the church in Chicago, there was no expectation on the part of the church that the classically trained singers in the choir be members of the church, let alone profess any particular faith. We were paid to sing well, plain and simple. In the churches I observed in Seoul, however, Christianity provided a specific ideological frame precisely in terms of which singers cultivated their classical voices and thereby shaped the voices and influenced the uses to which such voices were put.

In this book, I examine the way Christians in South Korea treat the human voice as a God-given tool for praise and evangelism. I argue that these Christians strive through vocalization to exhibit certain idealized qualities of contemporary Christian personhood, using European-style classical singing as their model. I show how their aim is to cultivate a "clean" voice, a specific cultural form of aesthetics and ethics, expression and embodiment, which comes to stand for Christian progress more broadly. In this framework of cultivation, progress is achieved by purifying the nation of residual elements of a superstitious, unenlightened Korean past and by softening the feelings of suffering and hardship that can be heard in the voices of older generations. An advanced nation is joyful, healthy, stable, and clean—and so should its voice be. But this book is much more than a study of singers. In the pages that follow, I trace the voice through multiple sites, some not explicitly religious or musical, to offer an ethnographic view into South Korean Christianity, its linked institutions, its rituals and practices, and the people for whom it is a raison d'être. Additionally, this book offers an ethnographically grounded and semiotically informed theorization of voice that accounts for the relationship of sound to body, speech to song, and everyday vocalization practices to higher-order social voicings of perspective and personhood. A major piece of this account is organized around locating the *sŏngak* voice in the cultural time and space of Christian Korea and examining the kinds of social relations that are mediated by this voice and framed by this cultural model of ethnonational time-space.

A CHRISTIAN AESTHETIC OF PROGRESS

After the devastation of the Korean War (1950–53), South Korea went from being one of the poorest countries in the world to being one of the richest. This transformation followed half a millennium of rule by the Yi royal house and a neo-Confucian elite formed of scholarly bureaucrats, the *yangban,* during the Chosŏn dynasty (1392–1910) and decades of colonial rule by Japan during the first half of the twentieth century (1910–45). For South Korea, the second half of the twentieth century was a period of painful national division, combined with rapid industrialization, urbanization, economic growth, and political transformation from military dictatorship to democracy.[9] Korean Christians take much credit for this transformation and see individual conversions, widespread spiritual enlightenment, and ethnonational advancement as part of the history and influence of Christian institutions.[10] The story usually begins with Protestant missions to Korea in the late nineteenth century. It emphasizes the role Christians played in establishing schools and hospitals, their participation in nationalist efforts under Japanese colonial rule, and their staunch anti-communism. The story culminates with the rapid growth in the number of Protestants after the Korean War, the membership numbers of contemporary Korea's Protestant churches, and the global reach of Korean evangelical missions. Newspapers regularly report that some of the largest Christian congregations in the world are located in Seoul, including the largest single congregation in the world— the Yoido Full Gospel Church (Yŏŭido Sun Pogŭm Kyohoe), with an alleged membership of more than eight hundred thousand. And with estimates upward of twenty thousand evangelists working around the world, Korea is said to be outnumbered only by the United States in sending missionaries abroad.[11]

The triumphalist narrative of Korea's Christianization celebrates a number of fundamental shifts in Korean society: the shift from Confucianism, shamanism, and Buddhism to Christianity; from superstition to enlightenment; from dictatorship to democracy; from suffering to grace; from sickness to health; from poverty to wealth; and from dirtiness to cleanliness. As I show throughout this book, these shifts are expressed in music schools and the wealthy Presbyterian churches of Seoul through a particular kind of singing voice—a European-style classical voice, the *sŏngak* voice—and are embodied in professional and semiprofessional soloists as well as in the members of church choirs. The aesthetics of this singing voice are also related to styles of speaking, praying, and preaching, thus shaping the overall soundscapes of Christian environments.

Each week, *sŏngak* singers perform for audiences of tens of thousands at various churches throughout Seoul. A typical singer's Sunday might begin early in the morning to prepare for the first service of the day, followed by travel to other churches in the city, and last well into the afternoon or evening. At school and elsewhere, Christian singers form mission groups and raise money to travel outside Korea and evangelize through song. By the time they go abroad for study—a necessary step in the legitimization of a *sŏngak* singer in Korea—some of them will have given performances of both secular and Christian songs in multiple languages for hundreds of thousands if not millions of people. By generalizing from these specialists, I draw on one of the great strengths of ethnography, which is to penetrate such powerful, influential points of cultural orientation in order to explain broader social phenomena. Although I do not claim to tell a story of absolute cultural coherence—certainly my account does not apply to all churches, all Christians, or all singers—I do understand these highly specialized voices to be saturated with a particular Christian aesthetic, serving as emblems to which many people orient and for which they aspire.

In their ritual instantiations of explicitly Christian soundscapes, churches serve as aesthetic sites, as well as affective and ethical sites, of authorization for singers as they evaluate their own voices and the voices of others. By aesthetics, I mean the institutionally anchored and ideologically distilled systems of judgment immanent in the use, apperception, and evaluation of, in this case, vocal sound. Aesthetics concern the way experiences of qualities are shaped and structured by semiotically mediated frameworks of value.[12] For the singing style that has emerged as a standard in many Christian churches in Korea, what is at stake in this Christian aesthetic is not just the problem of beauty but also more generally the successful performance and reproduction of the naturalized values of powerful institutions and their members through sensuous vocal form. One of these values is progress, which for many Korean Christians is both beautiful and natural.

In the Christian churches of Seoul (as in contemporary Korean society more generally), everyone is expected to sing, regardless of technical or musical ability. And as specialists among millions of Christians—all of whom sing in some respect—trained *sŏngak* singers strive to produce a clean voice. Vocal cleanliness refers to the suppression and removal of two types of unwanted sounds: the "fuzz" caused by pressed vocal cords, abrasions on the vocal cords, or other forms of what we might call "obstruence" along the vocal tract; and the "wobble" of unstable vocal adduction, "shakiness" from habituated muscle tension, or an "artificial" vibrato. Such "unclean" sounds are associated with the voices of the past—someone from the older generation who has lived through the suffering of Korea's recent history and lives on as an embodied representation of it. In these churches, classical singing often combines with preaching and prayer to materialize as the veritable voice of modern Korea. As a key part of the Christian soundscape, the clean voice is an emblem of personal and national advancement, an aesthetic horizon against which singers judge their personal development and the development of their country. To be clear, my aim is not to reproduce well-known arguments about cleanliness and modernity, colonial sanitation projects, or purified sacred spaces. Instead, I aim to understand thoroughly the significance of "cleanliness" in the Korean context by demonstrating ethnographically how cleanliness as an aspirational quality is linked with other valuable qualities via the semiotics of vocalization within Korean Christian culture.

The Christian aesthetic of progress also reveals a basic contradiction: although Koreans are supposed to have "in-born" *(t'agonan)* or "God-given" voices, precisely the attributes seen as most "traditionally" Korean (e.g., a "harsh"-sounding singing style) must be removed in the process of cleaning the voice. (Ultimately, singers are expected to study and work abroad in order to truly clean the voice.) In the same way, contemporary conservative Presbyterian Christianity cultivates Koreans' purportedly in-born tendency toward spirituality by seeking to expunge from believers' religious faith and practice all traces of a superstitious, unenlightened Korean past. Yet these Christian ideals often seem to evade the grasp of singers whose voices, lives, and country aim toward a future horizon that cunningly recedes from view, while the residue of Korea's troubled past stubbornly persists. The following ethnographic portrait of singers as they move through different institutional contexts—especially the church and the school—illuminates the central tension inherent in their position, namely, that their great success as Christian singers is attributed to the Koreanness of their voices, while residual Korean sociocultural traits seem to hold them back from their Christian aims.

This book centers around the anxieties, successes, and failures of singers who strive to achieve the idealized voice of an advanced Christian nation. I explore the semiotics of vocal communication, ranging from the linguistic and musical to the material and anatomical dimensions of voice. I follow singers as they negotiate the soundscapes and bodily practices that are part and parcel of modern Korean Christianity. And I explore ethnographically how the clean voice emerges in a postcolonial, postwar, postdictatorship Korean society; through institutionalized Christianity on a massive scale; as a part of the globalization of the culture industry; and as a product of and catalyst for shifting expressive forms in contemporary Korea. In this way, I show how a Christian aesthetic of progress is powerfully exhibited through the human voice.

VOICE AND VOICING

My central ethnographic concern in this book is the human voice as a medium of communication, an object of cultivation, and a qualitative emblem of ethnonational advancement for Protestant Christians in Korea. This ethnographic concern poses the analytical, and hence methodological, challenge of positing the voice as an anthropological domain of inquiry. Whenever I introduced myself in Korea as an anthropologist doing research on the voice, most people responded positively. I usually began by touching my throat and saying something general, such as *"Moksori e taehan yŏn'gu rŭl hago issŏyo"* (I am doing research on the voice) or, even vaguer, *"Moksori e kwansim i issŏyo"* (I am interested in the voice). My Korean interlocutors generally replied as if I had said I was studying the weather, Korean history, or mechanical engineering. And they often followed with a statement about how Koreans love to sing. Then they would ask if I knew about *p'ansori* (Korean story singing), if I had ever heard of Jo Sumi (Cho Su-mi), the famous soprano, or if I had ever been to a *noraebang,* the ubiquitous song rooms where friends and colleagues meet to drink and sing together.[13] To most people I talked to in Korea, my research interest in the voice was no surprise.

In North America, this has not been the case. When I have told people that I am an anthropologist doing research on the voice, I have met confusion, puzzled expressions, and sometimes hostility, as if I were being intentionally opaque. There are almost always further questions about what exactly I "mean" by *voice.* The metaphorical productivity of the term in English—and its appropriation in both everyday usage and social and literary theory—makes my fairly literal usage of the word seem threateningly vague. People often ask, "Do you mean a political voice?"; "Do you mean finding one's own individual voice?"; "Do you mean a literary voice?"; "Do you mean the voice of a people?" My normal response has been: "No, I mean the voice voice," hoping that reduplication will suffice to clarify my usage of the term. More often than not, it fails to do so.

There are actually two words for "voice" in Korean. The most common term is the native Korean word *moksori,* which is a compound of the words for "throat" *(mok)* and "sound" *(sori).* The Sino-Korean term, *ŭmsŏng,* is usually used in technical registers (e.g., phonology, voice pathology, etc.) or as an honorific term to refer to the voice of someone of relatively high social standing, such as an elder relative, a teacher, or a god. While the word *voice* in Korean can be used tropically in the same way it is used in English, members of the native stratum of the Korean lexicon are more metaphorically productive than those of the Sino-Korean stratum that belong to more restricted technical registers. Therefore, the tropic uses of the word *voice* in Korean are built upon *moksori,* not *ŭmsŏng* (e.g., *minjung ŭi moksori,* "voice of the people"; *munhak ŭi moksori,* "literary voice"). Yet despite these usages, the word *moksori*—perhaps because of its rather clear compound of the existent lexemes *throat* and *sound*—generally did not generate further questions from my Korean interlocutors as to my meaning. Not only was the term referentially clear, it was also rather unsurprising. It seemed self-evident to most Koreans I met that if I was interested in the voice and vocalization I might come to Korea to study it. Some even insisted that to talk about Korea and Koreans, one must talk about the cultural importance of the human voice.

But let us ask: What is the voice as an object of anthropological study? Or rather, what *ought* it to be for the purpose of sociocultural analysis? In the pages that follow, I treat the voice as an ongoing intersection between the phonic production, shaping, and organization of sound, on the one hand, and the sonic uptake and categorization of sound in the world, on the other. I give this practical, processual intersection the name *phonosonic nexus*. As I show throughout this book, the pragmatically productive concept of a phonosonic nexus allows us to analyze systematically two important facts: that the voice concerns both sound and body, and that it links speech and song. Furthermore, this concept clarifies the relationship between literal understandings of "voice" (e.g., a laryngeal setting involving vocal cord adduction, a material locus of human sound production, an instantiation of a speaking or singing individual, etc.) and more tropic understandings of "voicing" (e.g., a metonym of political position and power, a metaphor for the uniqueness of an authentic self or collective identity, an expression of a typifiable persona, etc.). These two related views consider voice as a ubiquitous medium of communicative interaction and channel of social contact and as the positioning of a perspective within a culturally meaningful framework of semiotic alignments.[14]

By organizing this ethnography around the concept of the phonosonic nexus, I show how voice in the concrete sense and voicing in the tropic sense are scalar relations of the same thing from the point of view of semiotic function. Voice as phonosonic nexus and voicing as the discursive alignment to a socially identifiable perspective are linked semiotic phenomena by which persons and groups situate themselves in worlds of significance.

There is a persistent fantasy that there might be something we can call "voice" prior to, apart from, or beneath the semiotic, communicative, social, or cultural. An otherwise ethnographically grounded Edward Sapir indulged in this philosophical fantasy when he wrote, nearly a century ago, "What we ordinarily call voice is voice proper plus a great many variations of behavior that are intertwined with voice and give it its dynamic quality."[15] Despite positing a voice proper, Sapir admitted, "The voice is a complicated bundle of reactions and, so far as the writer knows, no one has succeeded in giving a comprehensive account of what the voice is and what changes it may undergo."[16]

The voice proper with which Sapir was concerned has continued to serve as a prized but elusive object of research. His notion begins with the problem of sound as an isolable medium of communication and its locus of origin. This anticipates a common definition of voice in linguistic phonetics, namely, that "voiced" sounds are "sounds produced when the vocal folds are vibrating."[17] This understanding is the basis for determining glottal phonation as a distinctive feature in languages.[18] The various modulations of this act of glottal phonation according to laryngeal setting ("modal voice," "creaky voice," etc.)—normally called "voice quality"—Sapir called "voice dynamics" and treated them as the first step from a voice proper into the sociality of voice.[19]

But the sounds produced when vocal cords vibrate are not limited to a simple fundamental pitch, nor are they determined merely by the vibrating vocal cords. A focus on the vocal cords alone is reasonable within a systematic study of the anatomical components of phonation.[20] However, the voice that is heard and made meaningful to researchers and everyday listeners alike—the "voice voice," as I put it earlier—is a processually achieved complex of a fundamental pitch and peaks of acoustic energy, called formants, which are shaped by the resonating surfaces and points of articulation along the vocal tract, the entailments of which are perceived by listeners within, and in terms of, a particular acoustical space where certain kinds and arrangements of vocal sounds are the norm (e.g., preaching in a megachurch in Seoul, chatting in a subway in New York, yelling in a park in Lawrence, Kansas).[21]

The problem of where the voice as sound begins and ends is further exacerbated when we look at various singing practices and their attendant phonic requirements. Let us take an example that is relevant to the rest of this book. At its most basic anatomical level, the European-style classical vocal technique employed for the performance of opera, oratorio, art song, and choral singing (accounting for the different demands of these different compositional genres) is based on a combination of low subglottic pressure, a lowered larynx, reduced muscle tension in the throat, tongue, and face, and an expanded pharyngeal cavity.[22] The basic formula for this coordination involves two main actions that redirect local effort from the site of phonation (the glottis), to the sites of respiration and articulation. When a singer reduces air pressure beneath the glottis, it allows the larynx to relax and descend in the throat, a position from which the vocal folds can phonate without also "holding back" air from the lungs. The singer also must expand and shape the resonators in the pharyngeal and oral chambers to create certain combinations of vowels, pitch, timbre, and amplitude. The lower the breath pressure, the lower and more relaxed the larynx, the more agile and enduring the vocal cords, the more space for resonation, the more "efficient" the singing will be. The corresponding aesthetic norms demand a "concentrated" tone, "unforced" production, "free" movement, and "legato" phrasing.[23] An important feature of European-style classical technique is its cultural emphasis on a kind of vocal economy: it is designed to produce the most prosthetically unamplified sound in an acoustically favorable environment with the least amount of stress on the bodily sources of that sound. And so to phonically engage with, align with, and contribute to the aesthetic values of *sŏngak* is to align one's body to sound. The values associated with corporeal and acoustic sensations become linked indexically through specific modes of phonic-sonic engagement, alignment, and contribution.

Many have noted that what we call "voice" is not sound alone. In particular, Roland Barthes, in his essay "The Grain of the Voice," famously discussed the auditory perception of anatomico-material processes in the singing of classically trained European baritones—one of whom had been his own teacher.[24] That "voice is among the body's first mechanisms of difference" is an important concluding point of a programmatic article on vocal anthropology by Steven Feld and three colleagues.[25] In the final paragraphs of the piece, the authors introduce the notion of the body to argue that "the physical grain of the voice has a fundamentally social life."[26] If so, then how should we study this social life? How should we carry out a sociocultural anthropology of the bodily aspects of the voice in its thoroughly social, interactional role in communication?[27]

Regarding the bodily aspects of the phonosonic nexus, my approach in this book has been to focus, on the one hand, on the anatomical dimensions of vocalization as well as on reported corporeal or sensorial experiences of what Charles S. Peirce termed "firstness," the realm of "feeling" and its empirical form, "qualia." In using the term *qualia*, I am not referring to the subjective, mental experiences of quality, the status of which has long been debated in Western philosophy. My use of the term *qualia* refers to the actual instantiations of culturally conceptualized sensuous qualities that people orient to, interact in terms of, and form groups around.[28] The term *quality* refers to abstract attributional categories of qualitative experience (e.g., "softness" or "roughness," which can transcend specific modalities or sensory channels), while the term *qualia* refers to actual instantiations of sensuous quality, such as the particularly soft give of a pillow or the particular style and decibel level of a performance of music. Whereas a quality like cleanliness becomes valuated as an overarching abstract property attributed to multiple objects, events, and experiences, the qualia of one's individual voice are tuned and manipulated phonically to align with a sonically experienced framework of value. (I call this "qualic tuning" in chapter 5.)

On the other hand, I examine processes of bringing the voice in its various qualitative dimensions into awareness as "embodied principles."[29] And I do so both in the sense of materialization in observable bodily practice and reported qualitative experience of individuals (e.g., vocal cleanliness), as well as in the emblematic forms of higher-order categories of value that can be embodied in a voice and, by extension, the person or people who emit it (e.g., cleanliness as an emblem of advancement). The voice is revealed to be as much body as it is sound, as much inalienable and personal as it is shared and social, as much private and interoceptive as it is public and exteroceptive, and as much a medium of communication as it is an object of cultural reflection that can lie beyond the realm of denotational representation even while it serves as an object of conscious manipulation and cultivation. Because the voice, as a materially achieved intersubjective point of mutual orientation is inherently bound to, produced through, and culturally conceptualized in terms of communicative interaction, this is where I begin the investigation.[30]

Any quest for Sapir's voice proper (wherever it is thought to lie) leads only to obscurity.[31] Such an investigation forces one to strip so much from the voice that it no longer resembles the object that one originally intended pursue.[32] My initial bumbling ethnographic steps in Seoul, when I looked solely for vocal technique and was blind to other cultural dimensions, were an example of precisely this problem. As a channel for human communication and sociality, as a thoroughly bodily process with anatomical regularities, as a means of self-reflexive personal and collective expression, the practical social action of the voice cannot be divorced from its ongoing cultural conceptualization. The bodily dimension of voice, much of which flies far under the radar of awareness, is anchored to the communicative dimension of voice, which itself provides the framework in terms of which vocal expression finds a meaningful form between people. By viewing vocal communication in terms of semiotic registers, that is, as cultural models of social behavior, we can see how the relatively more "embodied" or more "expressive" dimensions of voice are really two sides of the same semiotic token—and this token is inherently social.[33] Voice is not merely a sonorous extension of an embodied individual or the natural expressive outlet or externalization of interior emotions, but also, and centrally, a channel-emphasizing phatic mode of social contact.[34] Whereas sound may be delinked logically from the social (as a tree falling in the forest), voice, as I understand it, never can be.

With this in mind, I proceed by accepting the fullness of the anthropological problem: there is a culturally conceptualized, sociohistorically normative, prototype-based voice that has to do with sounds produced when the vocal folds are vibrating but also has to do with the shaping of these sounds along the vocal cavity, with the coordinated role of the body in respiration, phonation, and articulation, with the acoustic space in which voice is emitted, with culturally meaningful soundscapes into which such emissions are supposed to fit, with formal genres in which it is expected to be used, with ritual sites in which these forms and genres are authorized and from which they emanate, with the ideological frames in terms of which vocal sound and its processes of sound making are evaluated and categorized, and with the various conceptually anchored analogies that it generates. It is on account of these multiple interacting layers that people describe the activity of making certain sounds with the body as "a" voice, or "someone's" voice, or "the" voice, or "a type of" voice, with respect to the other sounds in the world (those that it resembles and those from which it can be distinguished), as meaningful activity that, in one way or another, establishes or is modeled on social contact.

We now can see how what we call the voice is, as Sapir noted, indeed the product of "a great many variations of behavior" as well as interacting acoustic spaces of different sorts (the vocal tract as well as the space in which a person is vocalizing, etc.). Furthermore, when a voice is identified as such, when we extend the referent, *voice*, we normally do so through metapragmatic framings of communicational acts.[35] That is, we do not normally refer to the voice as the vibrating of vocal cords or even as a decontextualized sound; rather, we identify a person's voice and interpret its sound in terms of particular kinds of social acts, in terms of descriptive labels such as "to speak" or "to sing," "to yell" or "to whimper."[36] Socioculturally speaking, conceptualizations of voice emerge from participation in, anchoring to, and reflection upon events of communicative interaction. And such acts are interpreted in terms of their indexical relation to context. So although it might be tempting to deconstruct the various dimensions of voice to arrive at the voice proper, as Sapir and others hoped to do, we can see that in fact this voice proper does not exist as such. It is not merely that the voice is always "intertwined" with something. Rather, the voice itself is a constant intertwining.

This intertwining is continually articulated as a combination of formants (which affect everything from the perception of vowels to the qualia of voice), conditioned by the shape and resonant surfaces of the vocal cavity, sustained by the coordination of bodily activity, emitted in a particular acoustic space, linked to particular forms of semiotic production, locatable in social activity of all kinds, and culturally conceptualized, experienced, and reportable *as voice*. When we look closely at voice as sound, it is not clear where the voice begins and ends. Likewise, when we look closely at voice as a bodily mechanism or an act of sound production, it also is not clear where the voice begins and ends. This leaves us then with the view of voice as an ongoing intersection between the phonic production, shaping, and organization of sound, on the one hand, and the sonic uptake and categorization of sound in the world, on the other. The voice as phonosonic nexus is a medium through which we orient to one another, not directly, but through phonic engagements with sonically differentiated frameworks of value that shape our social interactions.[37]

The question for the ethnographer of voice is how to view the intersection of particular phonic and sonic dimensions in terms of a broader sociocultural analysis. The voice as sound is related to other kinds of sounds in the world (a human voice versus the sound of a tractor's engine), different vocal sounds are related to other vocal sounds within a phonological system of differentiation (vowels versus consonants), types of vocal activity are related one to another (singing versus speaking), and so on, all at different levels, and in different dimensions, of cultural meaningfulness. In its more expressive dimensions, the voice serves as a locus of signal forms available to the perceptual fields of people beyond the agent or agents of sound production. In its more embodied dimensions, the voice is understood to reside in or emanate from a body or bodies, to have a material site of origin or instantiation, or to be experienced corporeally but not always directly available to the sensorial experiences of others. By examining the sociocultural intertwining of the phonic and the sonic, we make available for systematic analysis the voice as a practical channel mediating the social world.

The voice, when conceptualized as a phonosonic nexus, becomes a lens through which we can view these different inner configurations of sound and sound production. This conceptualization allows us to view the voice as linking related forms of communication like speech and song and culturally relevant ontic dimensions like sound and body. Furthermore, it helps us better understand how the more literal "voice voice" can afford more tropic extensions of "voicing" that project cultural notions of the authenticity, particularity, authority, subjectivity, political position, or intentionality of singing or speaking bodies onto distinct, potentially generalizable identities.

The literal voice is a phonosonic medium through which a discursively engaged individual can place herself within and in relation to a number of meaningful semiotic realms at a number of different scales, both explicitly linguistic and nonlinguistic. It is a primary medium through which a person situates herself in worlds of significance, which makes the configuration of social lives, in all of their acoustic and corporeal dimensions, congruent and in dialogue with presupposable social configurations of some sort, at different scales. As I show throughout this book, individuals and groups align themselves with and adjust to the different contexts of their social worlds through the phonosonics of vocalization.

From this semiotic recasting of the human voice as phonosonic nexus, we can now move to the question of how this nexus can serve as a kind of representational trope. In Korea, as elsewhere, certain kinds of voices, or vocal attributes, can lead people to make characterological assumptions about the speaker or singer.[38] The assumptions usually equate the qualia perceived in the semiotic form with the qualities thought to belong to the agent of semiotic production.[39]

I will give empirical evidence for this phenomenon in chapter 2, when I analyze the sermon of a Korean Presbyterian pastor, in which he pitted the voices of the Pharisees against the voice of Jesus. Through the qualic tuning of voice, the pastor set up a duality of positions, as social types in a social universe that members of the congregation would be able to experience as real.[40] In this manner, the literal "voice voice" as a phonosonic nexus can be related to its various tropic extensions by considering voicing as a manifestation of the inherent relationality of utterances and semiotic forms representing ascriptive intentionalities.[41] The congruent alignment of the voice as phonosonic nexus and the voicing structure of a pastor's reported speech positions the perspective of the narrator (the pastor) within a social world of competing perspectives. By manipulating the qualitative features of the phonosonic voice in his performance of these different perspectives and by reducing the prosodic differentiation between his own sermonic voice and one of the narrated voices, the pastor is able to align his own perspective with that of one of the voices he is narrating (Jesus)—and thereby instruct his congregation to do the same. The phonosonics of vocalization in this event of voicing link particular qualities or attributes to different moral perspectives.

Insofar as voicing describes the relations among, and interpenetrations by, different perspectives indexed by semiotic form, we can see then how one is not merely a speaker or an addressee, a singer or an audience, in an isolated communicative event. Rather, one is summoned to roles within an inner configuration of role possibilities, which then are further linked to a higher indexical order of social positions within a cultural framing of generalizable forms of personhood.[42] These roles have indexical relations one to another and may also be understood to possess specific attributes.[43] These roles are inhabited interdiscursively; we inhabit previous communications in which we have engaged or that we have observed. This inhabitance takes place through the location of the self with respect to denotational, musical, or other textual forms produced during communicative situations.[44] What appears as a system or an array or a repertoire of social voices is really a model for observing the sociohistorically situated and morally saturated interdiscursivity of such semiotic alignments in particular cultural contexts, in which "identity" can be seen as interdiscursive continuity and "alterity" as interdiscursive contrast.[45] Just as the phonosonic nexus is known in part by its acoustic overtones in particular spaces, the interdiscursive histories of utterances and reported speech can also be said to result in their giving off "contextual overtones."[46]

As I show through numerous examples throughout this book, the scalar relationship between the voice, as phonosonic nexus, and voicing, as semiotic alignment to perspective within an immanent narrative structure, is made evident by the way the phonosonic nexus facilitates the inhabitance of roles within a culturally framed social world of discursive interaction.[47] Sociality is unavoidably semiotically mediated, and this semiotic mediation, as a material presence in the world, continually compels people to repeat and revise themselves and others as they interact with one another. In interaction, we are confronted by and are potentially always ready to report on our own events of communication (speech, song, etc.) as well as those of others; in so doing, we align with, or distance ourselves from, the perspectives indexed by these communicative forms. That is, we are continually confronted with narratable voicing structures as metapragmatic framings that situate our own selves in relation to and in terms of the pragmatically inhabitable roles available to us through meaningful social behavior.

This book is in large part about apperception—the landmarks of perception that bias one's classificatory abilities and assimilation of experience.[48] Specifically in the case of voice and voicing, culturally shaped apperception conditions not only what is heard but also how it is heard. Sapir recognized that sound shapes have a "psychological background" for speakers, which makes them recognizable and interpretable as a meaning-differentiating signal within the inner configuration of a system of indexical relations and distinctions.[49] In a similar manner, Bakhtin observed that "every utterance is oriented toward [an] apperceptive background of understanding, which is not [merely] a linguistic background but rather one composed of specific objects and emotional expressions."[50] From the level of voice as phonosonic nexus to the level of voicing as perspectival alignment with respect to communicative media (denotational, musical, or otherwise), these different scales of semiotic production both figure into and gain meaningfulness in terms of some culturally stipulated inner configuration—whether it be a phonological or a musical framework of sonic values or a social universe of positional values. Voice and voicing are thus scalar relations of the same thing from the point of view of semiotic function. In the social world of Korean Christianity depicted in the present ethnography, the former is framed by aesthetic discourse and the latter by ethical discourse— although these two discursive areas often bleed into one another.[51]

Seen this way, it becomes clear why the voice as phonosonic nexus should be capable of such powerful metonymical and metaphorical extensions in the form of political position and power, communicative agency and recognition, authenticity and individuality, personal attributes and expressive style, in particular sociohistorical contexts. These extensions are different ways of looking at an ongoing and emergent self-location in sociosemiotic space, whether this reflexive self is shaped by an emphasis on personal individuation or group-level identification and differentiation. Structures of voicing give a psychological or apperceptive background—a cultural background—to meaningful, recognizable social behavior.

Just as there is no pure or isolable "voice proper" at the level of the phonosonic nexus and its psychological background, there is no "neutral utterance" at the level of voicing and an utterance's apperceptive background.[52] In considering how each phonosonic token or uttered phrase or social act can have a specific richness, a particular character, a powerful cultural significance, a notable social effect, and yet be recognizable as "like" something else, we return via voicing to where we began with the phonosonic voice—by considering the play of overtones that constitute both voice dynamics and the dynamics of culture.

My aim in the present analysis is to explore the semiotic overtones—both acoustic and sociocultural—produced by Christians in South Korea to elucidate the relationship between the everyday phonosonic voice and a higher-order cultural narrative revealed by structures of voicing. By focusing in particular on the European-style *sŏngak* voice in Korean megachurches and schools of music as a normative voice for these institutions and their members, I systematically explore how the discursively engaged, qualically tuned voice becomes a medium through which the qualities and interests of Korean Presbyterian Christianity are expressed and embodied by individuals, groups, and entire institutions. From the body to sound, from sound to society, and back to the socialized body, I show how *sŏngak* singing as a phonosonic register of communication mediates the invocation of a particular form of Christian identity and instantiates its value within a pervasive and powerful Christian aesthetic of progress.

CHAPTER OVERVIEW

This book consists of two parts. Part one, "The Qualities of Voice" (chapters 1 through 4), deals with the features and practices of the voice and their moral backing in Christian South Korea. Part two, "The Sociality of Voice" (chapters 5 through 7), deals with the role of the voice in mediating social relations in Christian South Korea.

Chapter 1 is an ethnographic introduction to the central themes and theoretical claims of the book. It focuses primarily on the transformation of the qualia of voices and the relation of this transformation to coded emotionality. The aesthetic dimension of sound and the ethically charged treatment of the body become points of orientation within a Christian ideology of progress. Specifically, I explore the way an aspiration for a voice that does not sound like suffering engenders new forms of sociality, ideally created around the absence of pain as a departure from the past, but also produces nostalgia in those who cannot access the voices of the past. The ethnographic glimpses offered in this first chapter serve as concrete examples of the relationship between voice and voicing that I explore in greater detail in later chapters.

In chapter 2, I show the specific ways in which a Christian narrative of progress in Korea combines a story of ethnonational advancement with one of spiritual enlightenment. In 2008 these two dimensions were amplified by two major events. First, when Lee Myung-bak (Yi Myŏng-bak), an elder at Somang Presbyterian Church, assumed the office of the Korean presidency, he announced that South Korea had finally reached the status of an "advanced nation" *(sŏnjin'guk)*. And then, months later, when large-scale public protests erupted against his government, the head pastor of Somang Church, in a series of sermons, characterized the protests as holding on to the frustrations and lamentations of the past and indirectly reprimanded the protesters for discounting the vital role of Christian institutions in bringing democracy and social progress to the country. Using these events and their discursive entailments, I show how this narrative of progress can be "heard" in the human voice: both in terms of the voice itself and in terms of the way Christians are instructed to voice themselves in respect of (i.e., align themselves to) the narratives of their political and spiritual leaders.

Chapter 3 builds on the link between the sensuous qualities of voice and the institutional values of voicing by demonstrating the way in which *sŏngak* singing constitutes a semiotic register of communication. I detail the phonic and sonic specifics of *sŏngak* in terms of the Korean Christian culture that I encountered and show how it was anchored to the broader practice of evangelism that was being forged in the church. I do this in three parts. First, I locate the role of singing for Korean Christians, both historically and institutionally, as a privileged form of social action, focusing on how *sŏngak* sits at the intersection of singing and evangelism, serving the parallel claims of Koreans' supposed "in-born" capacity for song and for spirituality. Second, I explore how the systematic differentiation of voice qualities between *sŏngak* and sounds considered to be more traditional relies on and produces higher-order social categories that belong to the Christian narrative of progress described in chapter 2. Finally, I look at aspects of variation and change in vocal aesthetics that connect the relatively more expressive or audible dimension of voice to the relatively more embodied or proprioceptive dimensions of voice in the contexts of its Christian enregisterment. The voice becomes an emblem of progress for these Christians, a communicative medium spanning bodily manipulation and sonic entailment to exhibit the idealized qualities of larger-scale social change in Korea.

Chapter 4 focuses on a core aesthetic and ethical quality of the *sŏngak* voice: cleanliness. In Korea, people commonly use the notion of a clean voice in their descriptions of singing and speech. I trace the attribute of cleanliness and related notions of sanitation, hygiene, and health in Korean social history to illuminate this metaphor's place in Korean Christian culture and history. My discussion hinges on the way the concrete qualia of vocal sound are linked to the more abstract quality of cleanliness (and healthfulness) of bodily practice. Expanding the discussion of expression and embodiment to a broader Christian aesthetic of progress, I show how these qualitative attributes are related and polarized according to a narrative of development that positions the unclean, murky, unhealthy voice at an undeveloped stage (most clearly represented by markedly traditional forms of singing) and the clean, clear, healthy voice at the more developed stage.

Moving to the sociality of voice in chapter 5, I show ethnographically how the lives of Christian singers in Korea are anchored institutionally to the church and the university (or, simply, the school, *hak-kyo*). The school provides the credentials and authorizes individuals to sing; the church provides the audience and authorizes the performance events. Despite this complementary relationship, there is an enormous contrast between the two institutions, which presents challenges for singers as they move between them and "tune" their voices accordingly. At church, singers are expected to be disciples of Jesus Christ, exemplifying Christian service and modeling Christian personae through their voices in praise and worship, as well as in secular classical music. At school, in contrast, singers are expected to be disciples whose vocalization should always be performed in emulation of and deference to their professors. At church, then, they cultivate what they consider to be the God-given voice as Christian service; at school, they emulate the voices of their teachers as a kind of filial servitude. Although school ostensibly is where singers are transformed into specialists of voice, the impetus to sing classical music usually comes from the church. And although the school is the authoritative site of European-style classical singing, its pedagogical framework is considered to be backward and destructive for singing—more focused on teachers' status and income than on students' personal development. As students and professionals move between these competing and complementary sites of social interaction, their voices become key loci of contestation, with a "grain," so to speak. The qualic tuning of their voices expresses and embodies competing institutional identities and ideologies and reproduces in social space a temporal narrative of progress that links a seemingly corrosive past to an idealized, aspirational future.

Chapter 6 is an analysis of the "homecoming recital" *(kwiguk tokch'anghoe)*, a ritual that reincorporates singers into Korean society after an enforced separation abroad for study and professional experience. By recasting "private" relations (kin, school, church, or otherwise) within a "public" setting, singers are presented as public professionals to an audience of intimates and institutional relations. And by ending these recitals of secular art music with an unscripted (but expected) Christian encore (e.g., a hymn), the markedness of Christian faith and worship—something nearly all those involved in the recital share—is erased and presented as a general, unmarked feature of public life in South Korea. In so doing, the ritual characterizes contemporary South Korean Christianity as an inherent attribute of modern Korean publicity.

Finally, chapter 7 deals with the way Christian conceptualizations of *маŭm* (heart-mind) are central to practices of faith and voice among Korean singers. I explore the notion of *маŭm* to understand what it means to have a clean voice and sing "with feeling" in Christian Korea, that is, to align personally felt emotional experiences with culturally meaningful modes of expression and communication. In this model, a *маŭm* that is stably and sincerely directed toward God allows one to emit a voice that is consistently in the service of God. In this way Christian singers aim to achieve a kind of calmness and maturity of presence that they say affords them the capacity to stir the emotions of others. According to these singers, this is a shift from earlier forms of emotional expression, in which the pain and torment of individual performers were channeled directly into the laments that they performed and then passed on to audiences—leading to an overall aesthetics of suffering. For contemporary Presbyterians featured in this book, a new framework of emotional expression has emerged in which a joyful *маŭm*, reflected by a clean voice, is central to leading a modern life, contributing to worldwide evangelism, and placing Korea at the spiritual center of the Christian world.

In the conclusion, I return to the problem of aspiration as it both fuels and frustrates the Christian culture of *sŏngak* in Korea. For those determined to achieve a clean voice, there remains both a stubborn history to be overcome and a horizon of progress toward which they constantly strive. Increasingly, in the short memories of Korea's younger generations, the stubborn history is not just of poverty, hunger, and war but also of striving itself—of the "pushing" and "struggle" toward advancement. These aspirational practices can work against the idealized qualities of the stable, mature, naturally emergent *sŏngak* voice. For those who have achieved this voice, as with those who would rather not achieve it at all, there is an unsettling feeling of something missing, of something passing by, of something lost when they can hear but no longer produce the sounds of the past.

PART ONE

The Qualities of Voice

CHAPTER I

Transformations of Voice

An obvious point regarding the transformation of voice is that it involves a change in sound. For the analyst of such a transformation, sound is the low-hanging fruit. The far more difficult question asks: What is the relationship between a change in sound and a change in meaning? Another way—an ethnographic way—to ask this question is: Are groups that are mediated by changing vocal sound also changed by a new orientation to meaning? Is the change in sound significant for the group? Does it have consequences for groupness? While these questions might seem overly abstract, they are nonetheless central to understanding not only the stereotypical association of types of vocal sounds with sociological types of persons but also the way in which members of groups, whether short-lived or relatively perduring, orient to one another via, and conceptualize the group in some respects in terms of, types vocal sound. An obvious example is the choir or music ensemble, in which vocal sound is a reflexively acknowledged channel of social mediation. But the same principle of phonosonic normativity holds true at some level in classrooms, political proceedings, blind dates, and everyday service interactions. Despite the differing levels of explicit ritual formality, vocal sound serves as a salient dimension of different interactional genres and registers. For the ethnographer, what is at stake is the pragmatically realized meaning of the normativity, variation, or change.

In this first chapter, I use three different ethnographic angles to illustrate and make concrete the vocal transformation in Korea that I have briefly introduced. These examples show how people orient to the different qualities of the voice and in so doing orient to one another in terms of these qualities. In this way new kinds of voices serve as mediators of new kinds of social relations (and the perspectives they invoke). These three glimpses also exemplify the linkage between the phonosonic voice and higher-order voicings, between practical engagements with particular structures of meaningful differentiation and moral stances on such engagements. In the first glimpse, we are confronted with a man who can hear this new kind of voice but cannot access or produce it himself. In the second, I introduce an accomplished opera singer, a specialist of this new, transformed voice, who is unable to access or produce a voice she associates with the past. And in the third, I look at performance events and personal anecdotes to begin to discern the complicated sociocultural life of this new voice as phonosonic practice is linked up with coded emotionality and other affectively charged forms of sociality within a Korean Christian ideology of progress. Across these three sections, I show how the change in sound is meaningful, principally, because of the specific kind of sadness that it silences.[1]

A VOICE IN TIME AND SPACE

This is a story about a taxi ride I took to the airport in the summer of 2008.[2] I was waiting for the airport bus near my apartment in Seoul when a taxi pulled up in front of me and the driver offered me a ride. He told me he was already headed to the airport and would take me with him for a nominal fee. (The regular fare would have exceeded my research budget.) I agreed. Our brief, painless negotiation in Korean must have sparked his interest in me, because just as we drove off he asked me why I spoke Korean and what I was doing in Korea. I told him about my research on the voice, and he began asking questions about my research. Which voices? What sorts of singing? Which kinds of people? What kinds of sounds? I explained how I had made the decision to do research in Korea when I started counting the number of Korean singers at international conservatories and competitions. I rattled off some statistics, but he was unfazed. When I told him that most of the singers auditioning for a conservatory in Berlin were from Korea, he responded, *"Mullon Han'guk saram i norae rŭl choa haeyo"* (Of course, Koreans like to sing). And when I told him about how Korean singers were sweeping international competitions, he laughed and responded enthusiastically, *"Kŭrigo Han'guk saram i norae chal haeyo!"* (And Koreans sing well!) But when I told him that the vast majority of these singers were Presbyterian Christians, he was silent.

When he did begin to speak again, he had changed the subject. He wanted to talk about his own voice. He told me he was a fan of rock ballads but had trouble hitting the high notes. He wanted to know how opera singers learned to sing the high notes. Would he have to quit smoking to do so? How did opera singers sing so loudly? He said he also wanted to learn to sing loudly. When I asked him why, he responded that all Koreans like to sing loudly. I asked him which kinds of ballads he liked to sing. He told me his favorites were sad songs and added that most Korean men liked to sing sad songs so that they can sing with "passion" (he used the English word *passion* after using the Korean word *yŏlchŏng*). One of his favorite pastimes was to go with his friends to a *noraebang* (literally, "song room"), drink *soju* (Korean liquor), and sing sad ballads.

Abruptly, he told me that Koreans' voices had changed. Their voices used to sound passionate and sad, but now they don't. Even when they sang happy, cheerful songs, there used to be sadness in the voice. But there is no longer sadness or pain in the younger singers' voices, he told me. He used the vocal genre of *p'ansori* to illustrate this difference. The *p'ansori* voice, he said, is "husky" *(hŏsŭk'i)* and "strong." It has "power" *(him)*. Everyone used to have a voice like that. Now Koreans sing more gently, he said.

He expanded: Koreans not only sing differently now, but they speak differently as well. He told me that many young people, when they hear older people talking, think the older people are fighting. Foreigners, he said, think old people are angry all the time. But they are not fighting, he assured me. They are just talking to one another. Even if a young person thinks, "Ah, older men are too noisy," because their voices sound harsh, loud, abrasive, or agitated, these older people do not necessarily feel angry. And he went on to explain this difference through a narrative about the shift in Koreans' emotions and broader social changes in the country.

He began this narrative with the term *han*. *Han* usually describes an emotional state of unavenged injustice, of constant suffering, of inexpressible inner torment. This term and the emotional state it describes have been appropriated by various political and intellectual interests throughout the twentieth century to account for a purportedly essential attribute of the ethnonational character of Koreans.[3] But the cab driver was not constructing a genealogy of affect. Nor was he drawing my attention to the difference between ideology and history. For him, *han* was a very real thing that explained or at least described the emotional experiences that he attributed to his older compatriots.

He told me that what younger people hear in the voices of the older generation is not anger but *han*. The older generation has *han* because of Japanese colonialism, because of the civil war, because Korean farmers never had enough to eat, because the cities grew too quickly, and because everyone in the country had to work so hard.[4] But, according to him, in the last couple of decades, *han* has mostly disappeared from Korean society, especially from Seoul. And alongside the disappearance of *han* was also the disappearance of *chŏng*. The term *chŏng* has been described as a feeling of communion with others, an inclination toward generosity in times of scarcity, and a relationship-building disposition of trust and care.[5] The cab driver illustrated the connection between *han* and *chŏng* with an example. Fifty years ago, he said, nearly everyone in Korea was hungry. Food was scarce, and most people suffered. There was *han*. But when someone had a watermelon, he or she cut it up and shared it with others, so that the group could ease the hunger and suffering together. And that was *chŏng*. Like sharing a watermelon in times of scarcity, when people who suffered together also sang together, whether it was a happy or a sad song, they had both *han* and *chŏng*.[6]

It is important to see here that this person was not just throwing around hackneyed Korean expressions but rather was accounting for what he saw as a dramatic shift in sociality, in the very nature of social relations in Korea, and, especially, their mediation by things like eating and singing (both oral activities). In song, the phatic function of the voice in generating a certain kind of social contact is foregrounded.

The taxi driver told me that dramatic changes in the everyday lives of Koreans could be heard in their voices. He told me that the voices—and the voicers—of *han* and *chŏng* were disappearing, and those that remained were often misunderstood. When I asked him why, he answered with a number of related terms that all point to the themes of Korea's "development," "advancement," and "progress," which have become commonplace structuring have become commonplace structuring principles in narratives about postwar Korea.

As we drove away from Seoul, toward Incheon, where the western coast is dotted with small islands, where one can, if only momentarily, imagine the landscape untouched by one of East Asia's largest cities, the taxi driver expressed nostalgia. Expressions of nostalgia are unsurprising in Korea, where the rate of social, cultural, material, political, and economic change has been rapid and the reach broad.[7] After all, in just a few decades, South Korea went from being one of the poorest countries in the world to being one of the richest, from an almost totally rural population to an almost totally urban one, from a military dictatorship to a democracy. But the voices—the qualities of the voice—that he was thinking of were the voices of a fading Korean past. What one heard more and more was a so-called clean voice *(kkaekkŭthan moksori)*.

As I mentioned in the introduction and will describe in more detail in chapter 4, a clean voice generally is free of two things: wobbly vibrato and a raspy or fuzzy sound. The wobbly vibrato is related to the habituated use and manipulation of the vocal cords; the raspy or fuzzy or "husky" sound is related to scars or abrasions on the surface of the vocal cords themselves (resulting from specific forms of use). Both are caused by tension in or stress to the vocal cords, and both are related to a particular way of treating the body in relation to the aesthetics of sound.

So the voices I had been studying in churches and schools of music were not merely the product of a straightforward Westernization as an effect of the globalization of the performing arts industry or the aspiration to all things Euro-American. In fact, the voices of *han* and *chŏng* that the taxi driver described—voices like that of the taxi driver himself, actually—have played an important and productive role in defining and shaping the *sŏngak* voice in Korea specifically. The *sŏngak* voice as a voice of praise, as a voice of the present, is organized around, exists through, and is perceived and evaluated in terms of its differentiation from the voices of the past—of the *suffering* past.

In this manner, the shift in the perceptible qualities of voice in Korean speech and song are linked up with a much larger narrative of change. From the perspective of the vast majority of my Christian informants, most of whom attended the fanciest churches in town, the voices of *han,* and by extension *chŏng,* were the voices of a troubled Korean history that Christians like themselves have largely moved beyond—or, at least they felt that they should have moved beyond. A working-class Korean like the taxi driver expressed nostalgia for a lost Korean voice, but the wealthier Presbyterian Christians that form the center of my ethnography were engaged in the idealistic cultivation of—the celebration of—a new kind of voice within a Christian aesthetic of progress and aspiration. And this vision of progress has real consequences for the conceptualization and treatment of both sound and body as they relate to the voice, for the way the voice is used as a mediator of social relations (via speech and song), and for the way it can position people in differential relations to one another in the higher-order time-space of the nation.

LAMENTING THE LAMENT

A real and true embodiment of this new kind of voice and all of its indexically linked social values can be found in the person of Kim Yŏng-mi. Kim is a soprano and a professor of voice at the Korea National University of Arts (Han'guk Yesul Chonghap Hakkyo). She is generally considered to be one of the best sopranos in Korea and was the first Korean opera singer to have a truly international career. She attended the Conservatorio Santa Cecilia, in Rome, in the late 1970s and then went on to win numerous competitions in Europe and the United States, including the Maria Callas Competition in Milan and the Luciano Pavarotti Competition in Philadelphia. By the early 1980s, she was sharing the stage with Pavarotti himself. She almost surely would have gained international fame had she not decided to move back to Seoul in the early 1990s when she discovered that she was pregnant. She is a soprano soloist at Onnuri Church and gives numerous concerts there and at other churches, Christian-oriented concerts elsewhere in Seoul, and missionary concerts throughout the world.

In the summer of 2006, I managed to secure my second interview with Kim Yŏng-mi. Kim suggested we meet at the Seoul Grand Hyatt. The Hyatt is located on Namsan (South Mountain), which is visible in Seoul by the communication tower that stands at its peak. Kim arrived with her teenage daughter. They both ordered ice cream, and I had a cup of coffee. At the time of our interview, I was almost solely, somewhat blindly, interested in the question of vocal technique in Seoul. I began straightaway by asking her opinion on various technicalities of vocal sound production. She was resistant to my line of questioning and insisted that we "just speak naturally for a while" before getting into the details of singing. My immediate impression was that she had taken control of the conversation by quickly inhabiting the role as opera diva—a star who graces others with her presence and sets the terms for her interactions with them (not uncommon in academia either). So I followed, and we started by talking generally about my work in Korea, my life back in Chicago, her life in Seoul, and the state of the music industry in Korea (she was bothered in particular by the growing popularity of musical theater). We were getting to know one another. Our conversation became more cordial, and soon we were both laughing about her many experiences as an international opera star in the 1970s and 1980s. One highlight was her recounting of her experience of first meeting Luciano Pavarotti at his opera competition in Philadelphia (which she won). When he saw her diminutive size, he said to her, "Come here, baby. What are you going to sing for me?" Although I did not gather all of the things I was looking for from the interview—indeed, what I was looking for was not exactly there in the way I thought it was—it was nonetheless a delightful and informative hour of conversation.

As we left the lobby of the hotel, she quickly and politely offered me a ride to the It'aewŏn subway station at the foot of the mountain. I gladly accepted. We climbed into her champagne-colored Lexus SUV and began to descend the mountain. I sat in the passenger seat, and her daughter sat in the back. Kim asked me what I had planned for my remaining days in Seoul. I told her that I was planning to go to Chindo Island, where I would meet black-rice farmers and listen to their work songs. She smiled, slapped her palm against the steering wheel, and warmly ordered me to eat lots of food in South Chŏlla Province (the southwesternmost province of the Korean peninsula, where Chindo is located). She explained that the area is famous for its rich and tasty cuisine. She also mentioned the local emphasis on the arts and the expressive culture of the people there. And then she asked me if I knew the Chindo arirang.

The term *arirang* refers to a collection of Korea folk songs *(minyo)* that vary in melody, lyrics, and structure and correspond to different geographical areas of Korea. The Chindo and Ponjo arirang, which is also known as the "standard" or "new" *(sin)* arirang, from Seoul and surrounding Kyŏnggi Province, arguably are the most famous versions.[8]

All of the variations use the term *arirang,* which lacks any modern usage beyond the song. The narrator in the various forms of the song calls out to a distant lover, sometimes simply and innocently, sometimes in desperation, sometimes cursing the lover who will not return. The arirang variations are arguably the most famous pieces of folk music in Korea and have become a national emblem of traditional Korean song. Furthermore, the various arirang versions are available to all Koreans for singing and enjoyment, unlike *p'ansori,* which is seen as a specialized art form.[9]

The Chindo arirang, from the rural southwest, is often considered to be one of the most difficult to sing. While the Seoul Ponjo arirang is slow and lyrical and can easily be sung (and often is sung) in a style that approximates European-style *sŏngak,* the Chindo arirang has a faster tempo, abrupt intervals, and requires a complicated manipulation of vocal timbre. The refrain is formed out of the denotationally opaque words *arirang* and *ssŭrirang.* In particular, at the end of the third line of the refrain (see below), there is a difficult intervallic shift, which can serve as a challenge to singers.[10]

When Kim Yŏng-mi asked me if I knew this version of arirang, I replied enthusiastically that I did. That summer, I had been learning to play the *kayagŭm* (a Korean zither) and had heard my teacher play and sing the song after we learned the somewhat simpler Ponjo arirang in class. As we drove down the mountain that day, Kim Yŏng-mi began to sing the Chindo arirang, rhythmically lifting her shoulders in the manner common to people singing folk songs in Korea. She sang the first line:

Ari arirang

And I joined in for the second and third lines:

Ssŭri ssŭrirang
Arari ka nanne

As Kim Yŏng-mi and I reached the end of the third line—directly at the place that is considered to be challenging for singers—she suddenly stopped singing and grabbed her throat with her right hand. Then she shook her head and said, "I'm sorry, I cannot."

Just as she said this, we began to enter the district of It'aewŏn. Frequented by foreign tourists and the tens of thousands of U.S. military troops stationed in Korea, It'aewŏn is home to numerous stores and restaurants, dance clubs, massage parlors, and "love motels," where English is spoken. As we continued to descend the mountain, the bilingual signs in Korean and English began to give way to signs completely in English. And what had been a brief invocation and celebration of traditional Korea quickly turned into a lament. Kim Yŏng-mi told me abruptly that Korea was losing its culture. She lamented young people's loss of interest in traditional customs. She motioned to the back seat, where her daughter sat listening to music quietly through a pair of headphones, and said that young Koreans don't know who they are. And when she finally let me out of the car at the subway stop, she asked me to please study Korean traditional music as well as the *sŏngak* singing styles in which I had expressed interest.

This was a classic ethnographic moment—the kind anthropologists cherish. A somewhat technical way of describing its importance is in terms of tropic figuration, which refers to the alignment of the multiple structural layers of the event, in which one layer, our literal descent down the hill, figurated (diagrammed) another layer, the transition from celebration to lament, and vice versa. One layer became a trope of the other, depending on which layer one was looking at. The physical change from the classy Hyatt to a cityscape of massage parlors and love motels, as well as the topical change from opera and Christianity to folksongs and farmers, both became internally and mutually divided one from another through our actual singing of a folk song.

The singing of a famous Korean folk song presented the opera singer Kim Yŏng-mi with a vocal obstacle that cued up a higher-order narrative tension. Faced with this obstacle while singing a Korean folk song with a foreigner who had come to learn about her experience of operatic singing, she was forced to ask: What is the Korean story? Did her own biography belong to the Korean story, or was it something else? Who is a Korean person? What is the Korean voice? The voice itself became a site of radical dysfluency and thus linked her phonosonic voice to a higher-order voicing of her cosmopolitan perspective in contrast to the more local and provincial one invoked by the song and its sung expression.[11] The dysfluency of the phonosonic voice served in the dysfluency of tropic voicing as both the literal qualities of the folk as well as the perspective of the folk were effectively cut off from her. She was unable to quote the voice that she must have heard many times.

In Korea, Kim Yŏng-mi is the paragon of advancement in the Evangelical Christian idiom: cosmopolitan, financially successful, multilingual, and devout. And her voice—a voice to which thousands of young Korean voice students orient as an example of perfect singing—embodies and expresses all of these attributes.[12] Among Evangelical Korean Christians' voices, Kim's is an exemplary one, emanating from the authorizing ritual center of the church. Kim Yŏng-mi's voice is the voice of an advanced Christian Korea. It is a clean voice. But because of this voice, this singer could not sing a Korean folk song. Kim Yŏng-mi grabbed her throat at exactly the point when I too felt discomfort in my throat. There was too much tension in the larynx, perhaps. As I sang, I recalled how, during *kayagŭm* lessons that summer, I had tried to sing as my instructor demanded of me; like Kim Yŏng-mi, I could not complete the phrase because of extreme discomfort in my throat. I reflected on my corporeal discomfort through the notion that I was "damaging" or even "ruining" my voice. I remember feeling that I would be turning back the clock, perhaps permanently, on the progress I had made in my own study of *sŏngak* vocal technique. And my *kayagŭm* teacher mocked me, albeit gently, for my insistence on singing Korean folk songs as if I had been singing German *Lieder*. And in this instance Kim Yŏng-mi's own highly developed vocal disposition toward, that is, her bodily hexis consisting of, a certain ensemble of proprioceptive and auditory sensations established through years of practice and performance had also prevented her from voicing the attributes of Koreanness invoked by a folk song—a Koreanness that she nonetheless valued and wished nostalgically would live on.

But she was not used to singing Korean folk songs. She was used to singing Korean hymns in church. She was used to singing lyric songs, some composed specifically for her, such as one titled "Hananim ŭi ŭnhye" (God's Grace):

> *Na rŭl chiŭsin i ka Hananim, na rŭl purŭsin i ka Hananim,*
> *Na rŭl ponaesin i to Hananim, na ŭi na toen kŏt ŭn Hananim ŭnhye ra.*
> *Na ŭi tallyŏ kal kil ta kadorok, na ŭi majimak hohŭp ta hadorok,*
> *Na ro kŭ sipchaga p'umke hasini, na ŭi na toen kŏt ŭn ta Hananim ŭnhye ra.*
> *Hallyang ŏmnŭn ŭnhye, kap'ŭl kil ŏmnŭn ŭnhye, nae sam ŭl ewŏssanŭn Hananim ŭnhye,*
> *Na chujŏ ham ŏpsi i ttang palbŭm to na rŭl puttŭsinŭn Hananim ŭnhye.*

> God who created me, God who called me,
> God who sent me, by the grace of God I am what I am.
> Until I finish running, until my last breath,
> He makes me bear the cross, by the grace of God I am what I am.
> Endless Grace, unrepayable Grace, embracing my life, God's grace,
> With no more hesitation, I step on this land, holding me tight, God's grace.

And indeed, the major social transformation marked by this new kind of voice is, for Kim Yŏng-mi and other Christians like her, the transition from suffering to grace. Within this narrative, the sadness, the pain, and the struggle of the twentieth century were to give way to the joy, the comfort, and the tranquility of the twenty-first.

I suspect that Kim Yŏng-mi could hear the Korean voice she wanted to produce, but she could not produce it herself—at least not the way she heard it. It was close enough to be recognized but distant enough from her realm of acceptable bodily feeling to be unattainable. The sonic ideal did not come to successful entailment because of a competing phonic habituation that was manifest corporeally in her throat.

And our movement between two very different environments probably reinforced the sensation of displacement—in both the literal corporeal sense of an uncomfortable laryngeal position and the immaterial feeling of being out of time and place. We had been sipping coffee and eating ice cream in an upscale international hotel chain perched high up on a mountain in the center of the city, which quietly erases the folk and the traditional in favor of high-class cosmopolitanism. We descended into a loud, abrasive, urban neighborhood that advertises for many Koreans the discomfort and feeling of disjointedness that stem from more than a century of foreign military presence on Korean territory. Fittingly, as we passed between these two environments and the distinction between them was made vocal by her own inability to access a tradition she considered her own, she encouraged the foreign anthropologist to help pursue and perhaps recover a voice that she herself had replaced with another.

There are two important points to see here. First, the sound that Kim Yŏng-mi wished to express could not be expressed because of the conditioning of her body. The phonic habituation that comes with being an opera singer—a profession that conditions a body to respond differently to "right" and "wrong," or "healthy" and "unhealthy," "natural" and "unnatural" sensations in the throat and elsewhere—stifled her sonic aspirations (no pun intended). I do not claim that she absolutely could not make the sounds. She probably could have. But, like other singers, she likely "read" her body through the kinaesthetics of sound production and immediately felt that the manner of production required for the Chindo arirang was fundamentally wrong. Indeed, this kind of singing went against all of her years of training and might actually have been detrimental to the voice that she had cultivated. It transgressed the proprioceptive normativities that she had worked so hard to establish; the required method would have induced her to suffer corporeal discomfort, perhaps to feel pain. And as with the implicit prohibition on the traditional sounding voice in the church and the preference for a clean, pain-free sound, such discomfort in song only serves to invoke the suffering and pain of Korea's recent past rather than to reinforce the image of Korea's idealized future that the church and the sŏngak voice are supposed to project.

Second, Kim Yŏng-mi's vocal conflict triggered a poetic transition from celebration to lament. Kim Yŏng-mi is a model of achievement in the "Western" arts. She has gained more success and respect in this field than most in Korea—or in the world—will ever gain. But in that moment she was faced with her own body's conditioning, which was in direct conflict with her idea of the traditional. In this kinaesthetic confrontation, traditional culture might have seemed out of reach for her. Our descent into It'aewŏn likely strengthened this feeling by reorienting her sense of place.[13]

In a way, though, Kim Yŏng-mi actually was able to recover and perform some of the aesthetic attributes of the Chindo arirang, if not of traditional songs more generally. *P'ansori* and other forms of Korean singing have been said to belong to a "lamenting tradition." Although Kim Yŏng-mi could not lament through the song itself—her voice, conditioned and cultivated carefully and laboriously over three decades, would no longer allow it—denotationally she was able to do so. Her final words to me, which bemoaned the disappearance of Korean tradition, customs, and even identity, had become a lament—of a lament.

WHERE ARE THE TEARS?

To say that, for these Korean Christians, the pain and suffering of the past have (or should have) given way to the joy and comfort of the present is not to say that no one cries. Crying is fairly common in Korea, whether during prayer, on television dramas, or wherever there is heavy drinking. In this final section, I discuss the way crying is shaped and controlled within this narrative of advancement.

In the course of my fieldwork, I had long conversations about singing, performance, feeling, and emotion with Chang-wŏn, a fourth-year baritone from Seoul National University. In one of his e-mails to me, Chang-wŏn used a form of reduplicative word-play for his e-mail alias: "Elfeel-Elfill." When I asked Chang-wŏn what the alias meant, he told me "El" stood for "Elohim," a Hebrew word for divinity found throughout the Old Testament. The student explained to me that his e-mail alias meant that God "gives him feelings" and "fills" him up.

Chang-wŏn was considered by many of his peers and superiors to be an excellent singer and a great performer. In addition, he was known to be a very good person, a devout Christian, and, compared to most of his peers, poor. During one particularly interesting conversation, Chang-wŏn raised the problem of feeling "too much" during a performance and, à la Diderot's classic paradox—that in order to move the audience the actor must him- or herself remain unmoved—explained the importance of both experiencing and controlling emotions while singing:

EXCERPT 1.1

Purŭl ttae nŭn mani nŭkkiji mothaeyo. Purŭl ttae nŭn kŭrŏnikka sŭlp'ŭn norae rŭl purŭmyŏn chŏ honja issŭl ttae nŭn sŭlp'ŭn norae rŭl purŭmyŏnsŏ chŏ honja issŭl ttae ul su issŏyo. Ul ttae issŏyo. Mwŏ, "None but the Lonely Heart," mwŏ irŏk'e hamyŏn urŏyo. Honjasŏ purŭmyŏn. Pŏt [but] k'onsŏt'ŭ esŏnŭn hamyŏnsŏ ulmyŏn norae mothaeyo.

When you sing, you can't feel a lot. When singing, in other words, if I sing a sad song, if I sing a sad song by myself, when I sing a sad song alone, I can cry. There are times when I cry. Um, "None but the Lonely Heart,"[14] um, doing it this way, I cry. If I sing alone. But when I sing in a concert, if I cry while performing, I can't sing.

And he explained further:

EXCERPT 1.2

Mwŏ, Turando, nessun dorma, irŏn'gŏ hamyŏn, a, mak p'illing mak nŭkkyŏyo. Chŏsŭt'ŭ lisŭning. Kŭnde ne ka purŭl ttae ulmyŏn palsŏng i andwaeyo. Kŭraesŏ kŭttae nŭn ment'al esŏ "I'm sad, I'm sad, I'm sad" mwŏ irŏk'e hamyŏnsŏ pullŏyo. Maŭm to chintcha ulji anayo. Maŭm ŭn unŭn kŏt kach'iman nŭkkyŏyo.

Um, if I do something like Turandot, "Nessun dorma," ah, I feel a powerful feeling. While just listening. But if I cry while singing, I can't use vocal technique. Therefore, at that time, in my mind, "I'm sad, I'm sad, I'm sad," um, while doing it like this, I sing. The heart-mind actually does not also cry. It only feels as if the heart-mind cried.

On this topic of feelings, Chang-wŏn described an affective process in *sŏngak* that was quite different from the one he and his peers understood to be taking place in traditional Korean singing. In this sense, they agreed with the taxi driver I described earlier. They agreed that the expressions of sadness coming from the voices of the older generation, from traditional singing, did stem from actual experiences of suffering and sorrow. Although they reported being able to imagine the suffering of their elders, these younger singers insisted that contemporary singers do not, or should not, have actual sorrow, or *han,* in their hearts.

In musical instances that code extreme sadness, singers should be able to express these feelings and produce these feelings in others without actually experiencing the feelings themselves. For if one experienced such feelings, if the *maŭm,* or heart-mind, really did cry, as Chang-wŏn put it, then one could not actually sing. And if one can't sing, then one can't carry out the evangelical mission of bringing an audience into affective and spiritual alignment with fellow Christians. This understanding of the role of emotions in vocal performance has consequences for the effectiveness of performances of both secular and Christian music.

Practically every vocal recital in Korea ends with an encore of an explicitly Christian song performed in Korean (see chapter 6). The Christian content of encore performances operates as a metapragmatic commentary on the recital as a whole, characterizing the event as one in the service of the Christian God, addressing the audience as members of a community of believers, and coding the *sŏngak* voice as a Christian voice. That is, the voice becomes the channel through which Christian social relations are established; the channel itself should reflect the ideal qualities of the social relation that it mediates.

Singers describe this encore as a kind of emotional release, following a program of academic music for audience members listening either in judgment (peers or professors) or in obligatory patience (family members and friends). I observed a number of instances when the final Christian encore served as a space of emotional release for the singer—a point often made clearly when the singer broke into tears.

For example, in September 2008, I attended a concert of British and American art songs sung by a professor, a soprano, from one of the local colleges of music.[15] A conductor from one of Somang's church choirs had purchased tickets and invited members of the choir to attend. Four of us joined. The soprano's program consisted of standard selections from the English repertoire: John Dowland, Henry Purcell, Richard Hundley, George Gershwin, and others. My companions commented that the singer's voice was neither very loud nor very pretty. But they did report being impressed by her ability to have memorized so much English. They were careful not to be too critical, for she held a professorship in a respected music department in the city and had been an instructor of the choir conductor's. They also said that because they themselves were neither trained singers nor great connoisseurs of art songs, they did not feel themselves to be in a position to judge whether she had performed well or poorly. But they did have ample commentary on her Christian encore.

The soprano had chosen a popular Christian lyric song, "Ch'am chouŭsin Chunim" (Truly Good Lord), as her encore. The lyrics of the song are a tribute to the Christian God, who has stood beside and helped the narrator by always being near, making him or her sturdy *(kanggŏnk'e hada).* Yet shortly after the accompanist began to play, the soprano began to cry. She attempted to sing the first line, but she could not complete it. The accompanist continued to play, and the soprano entered when she could muster enough control to sustain a note, but almost immediately her voice again began to tremble and wobble, and she turned away from the audience, leaned a hand on the piano, and sobbed. She went on this way—starting to sing and then stopping to cry—until she finally reached the end of the song.

My choir companions were conflicted about this. The problem was not so much the effect the particular song had had on themselves personally—which was very little—but rather the effect the event as a whole had seemed to have on the singer herself. The choir conductor told us that preparation for this recital had indeed been very difficult for the singer and that she must have been grateful by the end to have made it through without any major disasters. Others added that she seemed humbled *(kyŏmson hada)* by the endeavor and was probably just too grateful for receiving God's help to sing.

One of choristers, Chong-ho, had a different opinion. Chong-ho said that the singer should have sung all Christian music. That way, she could have brought the audience closer to God, he said. Furthermore, he admitted that it was a good thing that she felt closer to God by the end of the performance, but it would have been better, he said, if she had done the same for the audience. What he experienced, he said, was watching her feel close to God; what he expected was that she would make him feel close to God as well.[16]

The vocal recital in Seoul is basically a self-centered ritual. Most of those who attend are not all that interested in secular art songs. The audience attends mostly out of some sort of obligation to the performer, and the Christian encore at the end is a kind of reciprocal act that at once thanks the audience for having attended, thanks God for having made it possible, and characterizes the event as a whole as a Christian event. It is through the encore that an audience formed of disparate institutional relations feels communion or fellowship; they come to groupness based on collaboratively achieved meaning. For Chong-ho, the soprano's performance on that September day appeared to be self-centered in terms of the performance of secular content as well as—and this was the problem—its Christian encore. Although the singer herself appeared to be moved by the event, according to Chong-ho, it was the singer's primary job to move the audience's emotions also, especially during the encore. He said that she should have used the praise music in the encore to give the audience "a *maŭm* that yearns for worship" *(yebae rŭl samo hanŭn maŭm).* According to Chong-ho, if she had really meant what the lyrics of the song had said, namely, that "a world in the wilderness must lean upon God" *(kwangya kat'ŭn sesang Chuman ŭiji hamyŏ),* she should have brought God to the world, through her voice, rather than having cried alone onstage. To this man, it was a missed opportunity for the display of the evangelical enthusiasm that Korean churches are known for.

Seen from this perspective, this concert stands in stark contrast to a concert given by Kim Yŏng-mi earlier that year. The concert, titled "Kim Yŏng-mi: Thirty Years of Opera, Thirty Years of Bel Canto," took place on March 8, 2008, in the concert hall of the Seoul Arts Center. The concert featured the greatest operatic hits from the Italian and French repertoire. Kim was joined for duets onstage by the local baritone Ko Sŏng-hyŏn and the tenor Kim Nam-du. Students from the Korean National University of Arts joined the three soloists on stage as the chorus for the final piece, "Libiamo ne' lieti calici" from Verdi's *La traviata.*

The arias and duets evoked a range of emotions: joy, sadness, love, longing, pain, and so on. However, the structure of the performance, similar to that of other recitals, revealed that the point of the concert was not primarily the performance of European operatic music but rather the glorification of the Christian God. As with other recitals, this was revealed by the final encore.

For her third encore, Kim Yŏng-mi announced that her final song for the evening would be "The Lord's Prayer" *(Chu ŭi kido).* Although Kim did not mention the composer, Albert Hay Malotte, I suspect everyone in the audience knew which setting of the text she meant. Kim sang the first phrase in Korean, *"Hanŭl ŭi kyesin abŏji irŭm kŏruk hasa"* (Our Father, which art in heaven, hallowed be thy name), as her students stood behind her and harmonized on an [a] vowel. Then I noticed that the young woman sitting to my left had bowed her head and interlocked her fingers in a position of prayer. I looked out into the crowd, and I could spot many others in the audience doing the same, some of them whispering silently to themselves. Here, the concert, ostensibly about a professional career in bel canto singing and opera, in its final minutes had come to resemble an offertory song from a Sunday service, where Malotte's setting of "The Lord's Prayer" is a sacred hit. [17] Unlike the soprano who cried during her Christian encore, Kim Yŏng-mi stood firmly on stage and authoritatively commanded the *maŭm* of her listeners.

FIGURE 1. Kim Yŏng-mi, poster for the concert "30 Years of Opera, 30 Years of Bel Canto" (image courtesy of Kim Yŏng-mi).

Many of the posters and advertisements for the concert featured a quote by Kim Yŏng-mi regarding the attributes of her artistic development. In this quote, Kim focused not on her technique or comfort with her voice but rather on the way in which she could control emotions—both hers and those of her audience—while singing (see the passage circled in figure 1): "Now is the point in time when I am most accomplished as a singer of *sŏngak*. I have arrived at the culmination of being able to express composure and emotion freely and with complete control when making music."[18]

Indeed, Kim Yŏng-mi marketed the event by claiming precisely the thing that, within the narrative of Christian advancement, was supposed to separate her from the suffering singers of the past: she could express composure and emotion freely and with complete control, without feeling the sadness that she was supposed to express through song. This skill contributed to the effectiveness of her encore: the prayerful poses that many audience members assumed were evidence that she had made their hearts yearn for praise. And as Kim Yŏng-mi explained to me in an interview in 2006, she knew that she had been "chosen by

God" to sing—that it was her calling, her *berufung*—when she felt happy in her heart while her audience was brought to tears by her voice. While Koreans were familiar with sadness, she said, and could draw on that for their singing, it was the profound feeling of happiness that served as a personal sign of God's grace.

Kim Yŏng-mi is a seasoned professional who stands as a sort of ideal model of the Christian singer in Korea. Her voice is constantly described as one of the cleanest in Korea, and her vocal ability has taken on an almost legendary character because of her ability to maintain its cleanliness despite having lived and performed in Korea for the past two decades. (As I discuss in chapter 6, singers report that their voices often start to deteriorate soon after returning to Korea.) Her celebratory performance pointed to a higher-order transformation of coded emotionality and its affective communication in Korea. We saw this in the taxi driver's narrative from earlier: the disappearance of *han* among younger generations is related to changes in Koreans' voices. And *sŏngak* singers at all different stages connect the increasingly clean voices of Koreans to a shift away from the suffering and sorrow conjured up by the rough, husky, unclean voices of the past. In Kim Yŏng-mi's concert, the thirty-year career of a professional is cast in terms of an achievement of emotional control over the voice and its expressive uses. Emblematized in her voice, Kim Yŏng-mi's individual career becomes a kind of model for the shift in the expressive emotionality of Koreans—specifically Korean Christians—as a whole. Her voice, for her listeners, stood for the realized aspirations of the not-so-distant Korean past.

CONCLUSION

In these examples, I have treated the voice as a nexus of the phonic and the sonic—the intersection of the production and organization of sound, on the one hand, and the uptake and categorization of sound in the world, on the other. The phonosonic nexus is inherently social; indeed, it is used as the stuff of sociality. And as such, it is encountered through social acts, through meaningful social behavior, in speech, song, and those other genres of vocalization that we have a hard time classifying (e.g., shrieking or wailing). And just as the voice involves the ongoing orientation to and alignment with certain sonic values—vowels, pitches, qualities, intonational contours—the voice as phatic mediator plays a role in a person's ongoing orientation to and alignment with certain social values. In this sense, the phonosonic voice forms a real-time, small-scale diagram of tropic "voicing" as the sociosemiotic alignment to perspective within a cultural framework of meaning.

These examples point out that the contemporary relationship between voice and emotion in *sŏngak* for these relatively wealthy, educated, Protestant Christians in Korea is—or, within the ideology of advancement, *should be*—fundamentally different from the relationship between the two in other musical forms. In this transformation of voice, there is also a transformation of sociality around a transformation of meaning. Contemporary Christian relations mediated by a clean voice are seen by my informants as different from those mediated by a rough or husky voice. Whereas the emotional and physical toil of pre-Christian life is understood to result in a kind of embodied technique of sadness and frustration expressed in the sound of the "traditional voice," for contemporary Christian *sŏngak* singers, the voice, like the *маŭm,* should remain stable, joyful, and in control, even as the affective dimension of the expressive event might move an audience to tears—and, they hope, to prayer.

CHAPTER 2

Voicing an Advanced Korea

As prayers begin at Somang Presbyterian Church on a Sunday morning in Seoul in the early twenty-first century, it is hard to imagine the chaos and tragedy that marked the recently concluded twentieth century in this country. For that matter, it is hard to imagine the recent history of this city, which changed military hands numerous times during the Korean War and now lies only about thirty miles from the demilitarized zone. While South Korea has undergone a number of radical transformations—political, economic, and social—the picture of a calm, serene, blessed, and stable Korea that is painted by the average Sunday service at Somang seems to exceed even the dramatic and extreme changes documented in South Korean life. It seems to outline not merely an image of a country that has arrived at peace and prosperity but also an aspiration for a people as they should be: an idealized nation of Christians, calmly but boldly and enthusiastically influencing the world from this small peninsula.

This chapter begins to contextualize the ideologies and practices of voice discussed in the previous chapter by examining this aspirational image of Korea as an advanced Christian nation and global spiritual center. I situate *sŏngak* and other attendant dimensions of voice within a particular Christian narrative of social change in Korea. Focusing on Somang Church, an epicenter of political and cultural influence, I show how positive change—social, political, economic, material, and so forth—is triumphantly cast as the natural product of the activity of the

Christian church. The Christian story of Korean progress laminates a narrative of spiritual enlightenment onto a more general ethnonational narrative of advancement, in which Korea moves from the periphery to the center. Then I turn to two examples in 2008 that represent competing historical perspectives of Korean progress, each presenting alternative theories of positive historical agency. The first example concerns the inauguration of Lee Myung-bak as president in February 2008. The second, contrasting example concerns the period of large-scale protest against Lee and his administration during the late spring and summer of 2008. The first views progress in Korea as the result of Christian institutions and their leaders. The second views it in terms of an ongoing struggle between the masses and the elites. Central to these contrasting views are differentiated claims regarding the legitimate voice of the country.

To return to the voice and the ethnographic and theoretical issues at stake in the rest of the book, I conclude the chapter by presenting an example of how voice manipulation in a single stretch of speech by a single person can invoke a Christian model of ideal social behavior and historical change. I return here to the voice of Somang head pastor Kim Chi-ch'ŏl to show, in the context of a narrative of progress, how a "synchronic" variation in the voice quality of his sermonic speech actually models a larger-scale, ideologically loaded "diachronic" shift in the aesthetics of voice and the ethics of behavior. This example of semiotic enregisterment shows how phonosonic differentiation "in time" can model social differentiation "over time" in relation to a particular Korean narrative of progress—an act that projects qualitative attributes of voice onto swatches of the population and whole periods of Korean history. As I explain, the differentiation is organized by what is perceived as a difference between a Christian moral position and an un-Christian moral position. These two voicings are realized via the phonosonic qualities of voice. Through this act, an immanent narrative of Christian progress can be heard in the voice itself.

The *sŏngak* voice and the perspective that it voices are especially compatible in this form of pragmatic labor: just as the *sŏngak* voice is meant to erase any sign of struggle, fatigue, hardship, and suffering, so too does Somang's worship service and the model of contemporary South Korea that it projects. Yet, as I will show, the Christian narrative of ethnonational development through spiritual enlightenment is highly contested and polemical, even in its most subtle manifestations.

THE SOUNDS AND SCALE OF *SŎNGAK*

Every Sunday in Seoul, millions of Christians participate in concerts of European-style classical singing at their respective churches. At 7:30 A.M. on Sunday mornings, Somang Presbyterian Church holds its first service of the day. The glass doors of the boxy white structure open before the service begins. People arrive early to sit near the altar and pray quietly. A woman appears from behind the pulpit, walks to the pipe organ, and begins to play hymns softly. With the gentle glow of the stained glass on the western wall of the main sanctuary, which depicts a map of the Korean peninsula, enlarged in relation to the rest of the world, the sounds of whispered prayers and sustained chords fill the chapel. By the start of the service, thousands of people are seated in Somang's main chapel, and another thousand or more latecomers have found seats in one of the auxiliary chapels or prayer rooms located throughout the church complex. There, the overflowing congregation can participate in the service via video link. The buildings of the church complex consume more than a city block and are connected by underground tunnels.

After a prayer leader reads a call to worship, a choir of more than a hundred persons sings a Gloria. Then the congregation sings a hymn together and offers a scripted prayer of repentance. The prayer leader adds an apologetic, the congregation collectively recites the Apostle's Creed, and the prayer leader and the congregation alternate in the reading of a psalm. The congregation sings another hymn, a few members of the congregation stand to offer a special prayer, and then the pastor a reads the scriptural passage that will be the focus of his sermon. Despite the amplified sounds of the prayer leader and pastor and the enormous sound produced by the voices of the congregation, the atmosphere throughout the service maintains the same calmness that was established with the first soft organ notes and whispered prayers that anticipated the start of the service.

Just before Head Pastor Kim Chi-ch'ŏl gives his sermon, the choir stands and sings an anthem. On July 6, 2008, for example (the specific importance of this date will become clearer later in the chapter), during the first service of the day, the choir performed "Manmin a ora," a Korean translation of "Come, All Ye People"—a piece written by Carrie B. Adams, a prolific American Presbyterian composer from the turn of the twentieth century. After Pastor Kim delivered his sermon, more prayers and hymns followed. During the offertory, a group of senior men from the choir gathered before the pulpit to sing an arrangement of "Amazing Grace" in Korean ("Nollaun ŭnch'ong"). While mostly untrained, their voices, like those in the choir, had a distinctly classical-sounding vibrato. They were clearly trying to sound like *sŏngak* singers. There was another prayer, and the choir ended the service with an *Amen*. The service was repeated four more times that day, with the individual prayers, the choirs' anthems, and the soloists' offertory songs being different.

Each of the five Sunday services has its own choir with more than a hundred members, and each choir is named with a biblical reference: Bethany, Hosanna, Zion, Hallelujah, and Gloria. Even the afternoon English service, which is held in the wedding chapel, has its own, smaller forty-voice choir (named "Immanuel").[1] And each choir has soloists on each voice part who rotate in delivering the offertory song. At the 9:30 service on July 6, a quartet of trained opera singers sang a setting of Psalm 23, "The Lord is my shepherd," by the Korean composer Ch'oe Tŏk-sin. At 11:30, a soprano sang the Korean translation of "I Come to the Garden Alone," by C. Austin Miles. At 1:30, a soloist sang "Ch'am choŭsin Chunim" (Truly Good Lord), a famous Korean lyrical song of praise by Kim Ki-yŏng. By the end of the day, with the choir, solo performances, and group hymn singing, tens of thousands of people at Somang Church had heard and sung songs of Christian praise in a *sŏngak* style.

Somang Church was founded in 1977 as a prayer group led by the Reverend Kwak Sŏn-hŭi in the Hyundai (Hyŏndae) apartments of the upper-class neighborhood of Apkujŏng. Like other large Presbyterian megachurches that minister to the educated middle and upper classes in Seoul, Somang Church achieved exponential growth during the 1980s and early 1990s.[2] Construction for the church building was completed in 1982 but the building had to be expanded in 1987 to accommodate the rapid growth of the congregation, which grew to approximately forty-five thousand registered members in two decades.[3] The Reverend Kim Chi-ch'ŏl was made joint head pastor in 2002 and became head pastor in 2003, when Reverend Kwak retired. According to a promotional video for the church, titled *The Story of Somang Church,* membership was about sixty thousand persons in 2006, but in the news coverage regarding the church in 2008, membership was usually estimated at seventy thousand.[4] While I conducted fieldwork, the church was managed by more than twenty pastors, and there were eleven senior elders *(wŏllo changno),* forty-one retired elders *(ŭnt'oe changno),* eighty-one business-affairs elders *(samu changno)*, and two inactive elders *(hyumu changno)*.

Somang Church is well known throughout Korea, in part because one of its elders, Lee Myung-bak (Yi Myŏng-bak), was president of the country from 2008 until early 2013. In general, members of Somang Church, like President Lee, have a reputation for being successful, wealthy, powerful, and conservative. Known in Seoul as the "intellectual" church, Somang is attended by many academics, celebrities, politicians, and other public figures. In 2007, the left-leaning newspaper *Han'gyŏre* reported that Somang was attended by approximately 60 former and incumbent government ministers, 10 university presidents, and 150 popular entertainers.[5] Many of my informants outside the church charged that Somang Church, as well as others like it, was merely a place for wealthy people to congregate and reinforce their power over the country. And many of my informants within the church suspected others of joining their church with explicit designs to network with rich and powerful people and thereby become like them.

The church is located in Apkujŏng, a wealthy shopping area south of the Han River (Kangnam). Near Somang Church are expensive boutiques, gourmet restaurants, and luxury car dealerships (e.g., Ferrari). Apkujŏng is also known for having a higher density of cosmetic surgery clinics than any other district in Seoul.[6]

The site of the church consists of a main building with a sanctuary, plus a prayer room and an underground labyrinth of smaller chapels and rooms. There are two large church-owned parking lots in front of the church. The main building is connected to the Mission Building *(sŏn'gyogwan)* by an underground tunnel. The Mission Building contains the wedding chapel, a number of prayer and meeting rooms, the children's center and library, and a cafeteria. The cafeteria is officially called the "fellowship room" *(ch'in'gyosil)* but most congregants simply know it as the cafeteria or restaurant *(siktang)*. There are also two other newer buildings in the complex, called the First Education Building and the Second Education Building. Somang Church also has facilities outside Seoul, including another satellite church in Pundang (a suburb south of Seoul), the Somang Academy in Suwŏn (a city south of Seoul, which has a large military presence), and a retreat center *(suyanggwan)* in Kyŏnggi Province, just outside Seoul. Each Sunday, the small streets surrounding the church grounds are filled with people pouring in and out of the church buildings. Church volunteers stand at strategic points throughout the neighborhood to help guide the flood of luxury cars and pedestrians dressed in their Sunday best.

In addition to the five regular Korean services and the English service, there also is a "praise worship" service *(ch'anyang yebae)* on Sunday afternoon. With its Christian rock music and more casual style, the *ch'anyang yebae* is viewed as a supplemental service for young unmarried people to mingle, not a replacement for the regular Korean services. On Wednesday evenings the "third day prayer service" *(samil kidohoe)* is held. And every morning at 5:30 A.M., Monday through Saturday, there is the early dawn prayer meeting *(saebyŏk kido)*—a standard form of worship in Korean Protestant churches. Also numerous events and trainings are targeted at various demographic slices and special interests of the congregation, such as children's Sunday school, men's prayer groups, women's prayer groups, new-member services, and various mission groups organized around and aimed at particular professions (e.g., police, military, finance, academia, the construction industry, etc.).

At the pulpit, Head Pastor Kim Chi-ch'ŏl, a professor of theology, appears focused, intellectual, and polished, and his speech is generally quiet and calm. Members describe Somang's liturgical style as "holy" *(sŏng sŭrŏun, sinsŏng han, kŏruk han)* and "solemn" *(changŏm han, changjung han)*.[7] They cite the peaceful worship, the classical singing, and Reverend Kim's quiet sermonic style among their reasons for attending Somang Church in particular. While Somang Church is perhaps the most striking example of *sŏngak* singing in the liturgical styles of Korean Christianity, many congregations of comparable size throughout the country, such as Yŏngnak, Onnuri, and Myŏngsŏng, also emphasize a "classical" sound in much of their sung praise and, like Somang, sometimes feature full symphony orchestras in their services. Thus, on any given Sunday in Korea, hundreds of thousands, if not millions, of the country's Christians receive what they believe to be the authoritative word of God *(Hananim ŭi malssŭm)* in and in association with the *sŏngak* voice.

Despite internal factions that have arisen from the complications of rapid growth and pastoral succession (more on this below), Somang Church service is designed to incorporate congregants into a stable, ordered, peaceful community, the members of which are bound harmoniously to one another and to their god in their wealth, health, and success. And wealth is important: Somang is a rich church serving a rich congregation. This ritualized stability stands out not only against the recent memory of the noise, grit, and chaos of the metropolis's crowded streets but also against the collapse of nearly a half-millennium of neo-Confucian dynastic rule (1392–1910), Japanese annexation and colonization (1910–45), U.S. military presence (1945–present), the Korean War (1950–53), national division (1945–present), and a military dictatorship that ended only with direct presidential elections in 1987.

Just as Somang Church's solemn, refined, consciously upper-class style presents a stark contrast to the ecstatic Pentecostal worship services of places like the Yoido Full Gospel Church, which historically ministered to the working class, for someone familiar with recent Korean history, it might also appear as if the church's style has been formed out of a more general and explicit opposition to, or refuge from, the turmoil of Korea's twentieth century. The kind of sociality that is achieved in this ritual space is so fundamentally different from the most striking images of twentieth-century Korea—casualties from the war, shantytowns in and around Seoul, activists in the streets protesting an autocratic regime—that we are compelled to ask: What model of society is being projected from this church? What sociocultural idea of Korea is being cultivated here? And what is the role of the voice in this cultivation?

SOCIAL CHANGE THROUGH SPIRITUAL ENLIGHTENMENT

Christian churches in Korea take a lot of credit for the social, political, and material development of the country. The history of Korean Christianity has, from the beginning, been one of self-evangelism. In 1777 Korean Confucian scholars began studying Jesuit tracks, and in 1784, one of these scholars received a Catholic baptism in Beijing and returned to Korea to evangelize; followers smuggled a Chinese Catholic priest into Korea only in 1794.[8] However, the Protestants I spoke with usually began their narrative with the first Presbyterian and Methodist missionaries of the 1880s and 1890s. In particular, they rooted their narratives in a story of how Protestant missionaries brought Western medicine to Korea, taught the masses to read, liberated women, contributed to the nationalist movement against Japanese colonialism, and initiated a process of social and spiritual enlightenment.[9]

These sentiments continue to echo in the sermons of Protestant pastors like Kim Chi-ch'ŏl. For example, in a sermon given on August 3, 2008, titled "Why Do You Labor?" (Ŏtchi hayŏ sugo hanŭnya?), Pastor

Kim made clear that Christianity—with its institutions and their leaders—was at the helm of social change and progress in Korea.[10]

EXCERPT 2.1

Uri nara nŭn kwagŏ e irŏn tongnyŏk ŭl irŭk'ilmanhan chŏngsinjŏk igo yŏngchŏk in chiju ka ch'wiyak haessŭmnida. Sumanŭn usang sungbae ŭi nara yossŭmnida. Kwisin ŭl sŏmginŭn syamŏnijŭm ŭi nara yŏssŭmnida. Ŏryŏpko himdŭn il man saenggimyŏn chŏmchip ŭl tŭnadŭrŏttŏn saramdŭl i suŏpsi manassŭmnida. Kŭrŏnde Yesu Kŭrisŭdo ŭi pogŭm i uri paeksŏng ŭi kasŭm sok e p'agodŭrŏssŭmnida. Kŭ sok e yŏngchŏk in mongmarŭm i issŏssŭmnida. Kidokkyo in'gu ka pae ka toeŏ kyohoe ka sŏngjang haessŭmnida. Sahoejok in pyŏnhwa ŭi kach'i rŭl chudo hanŭn kyohoe ka toeŏttŏn kŏt i 20-segi ŭi il il iossŭmnida.

In the past in our country, the mental and spiritual leadership was too weak to generate this motivational power. It was a country of a lot of idol worship. It was a country of ghost-worshiping shamanism. There were countless people who frequented fortune-tellers whenever hardships and difficulties arose. But the Gospel of Jesus Christ penetrated the hearts *[kasŭm]* of our people. Inside them was a spiritual thirst. The Protestant population doubled and the church grew. The churches developed to lead in the promotion of the values of social change in the twentieth century.

By characterizing shamanic popular religion as a kind of superstition, the excerpt clearly displays the elements of a rupture from an irrational past of spiritual darkness that Christian missionaries throughout the world have put forth as central to their own narratives.[11]

The story of Korea's rupture from its pagan past is condensed in particular individuals' conversions to Christianity. A recurring theme in Korean Christian sermons is the relationship between individual conversion and broader sociocultural transformation. Along these lines, Kim gave a sermon earlier that year, on February 24, 2008, titled "Ŭi rŭl wihayŏ pakhae rŭl pannŭn cha ŭi pok" (Blessed Are Those Who Are Persecuted for Righteousness).[12] In the sermon, Kim assumes the perspective of a missionary, attempting to align inner belief with outer behavior and viewing the process of conversion as a theory of social change.[13] Focusing in particular on the role of confession, Kim told his congregation that Christianity was not just "a private revolution of an individual person" *(in'gan ŭi kaeinjŏk in hyŏngmyŏng)* but also is and was "a social revolution" *(sahoe hyŏngmyŏng)*, emphasizing his view that the individual spiritual dimension and the practical social dimension are linked.

This can be seen more clearly in Kim's discussion of the March First movement (Samil Undong), the eightieth anniversary of which would follow only a few days later. The March First movement took place in 1919, when thirty-three nationalists signed a declaration of Korean independence and read it aloud in Seoul's T'apkol Park. Of these signatories, nearly half were Protestant church leaders.[14] The event sparked mass protests throughout the country, during which Koreans shouted *"Tongnip manse!"* ("Long live [Korean] independence!").[15] Pastor Kim characterized the March First movement as one of Christianity's key moments in the history of Korean independence:

EXCERPT 2.2

Orhae uri nara nŭn Samil Undong 80-chunyŏn ŭl massŭmnida. Ilbon chegukchuŭi rŭl taehang haettŏn uri chosangdŭl ŭi tongnip ŭl hyanghan yŏlchŏng kwa hŏnsin e konan ŭi yŏksa ka tongban toeŏssŭmnida. Samil Undong ŭn kungmindŭl ŭi chayu wa chilli wa saengmyŏng e taehan kalgŭp ham i ch'ongch'ejok ŭro irŏnan sakŏnŭro konan ŭi yŏksa ka tongban toeŏ issŭmnida. 1919-yŏn Samil Undong i irŏnan chi 4-kaewŏl hu K'aenada Changnogyo sŏn'gyosadŭl i moyŏssŭmnida. Samil Undong manse sakŏn e kadam han Chosŏn saramdŭl i Ilbon'gun e ŭihaesŏ ŏlmana manhaeng ŭl tanghaennŭnji nonŭi hamyŏnsŏ 1919-yŏn 7-wŏl 10-ilcha ro tangsi Chosŏn ch'ongdok Hasegawa ege taŭm kwa kat'ŭn hangŭisŏ rŭl ponaessŭmnida.

This year our country celebrates the eightieth anniversary of the March First movement. It is accompanied by a history of hardship endured by our ancestors, who opposed Japanese imperialism out of passion for and devotion to independence. The March First movement was a historical event that arose extensively from the hunger of the Korean people for freedom, truth, and life, and the movement was accompanied by hardship. Four months after the March First movement in 1919, Canadian Presbyterian missionaries gathered. The missionaries discussed how many atrocities the Japanese military committed against the people of Chosŏn who participated in the March First movement, and on July 10, 1919, they sent a written protest to Hasegawa, the Japanese governor-general in Chosŏn at the time, saying the following.

Kim then recited the letter, which called for the Japanese colonial government to stop suppressing the movement, to refrain from violence against the people, to allow peaceful demonstrations, and to cease discrimination against Christians. It numbered all of the different atrocities enacted against "the people of Chosŏn."[16] Kim concluded that this written document "testified" *(chŭngŏn hada)* that Christian missionaries had been leaders in the early calls for independence. He said it was important for the congregation to understand this historical fact *(sasil)*, because the history of modern Korea—the story of democratization, advancement, development, growth, and maturation—was intrinsically connected to the church:

EXCERPT 2.3

Samil Undong ttae Kidokkyo nŭn ŏnŭ chonggyo poda minjok chonggyo rosŏ k'ŭn yŏkhal ŭl kamdang haessŭmnida. Igŏt ŭn pogŭm undong i kot minjok undong, tongnip undong kwa manmullyŏ issŭmŭl al su issŭmnida. Isŭrael paeksŏngdŭl i aegupttang esŏ haebang toeŏ chayu rŭl hyanghan Ch'uraegup Undong i kot Taehan Min'guk ŭi tongnip chayu undong im ŭl Kidokkyo chidojadŭl ŭn kip'i insik hago minjok undong e tongch'am haessŭmnida.

At the time of the March First movement, Protestant Christianity played a more significant role as a national religion than any other religion. It indicates that the movement of the Gospel was interrelated with the nationalist movement and the independence movement. The Christian leaders took part in the nationalist movement, deeply understanding that the independence and freedom movement of the Republic of Korea was equal to the Exodus movement of the Israelites who aimed for their liberation from Egypt and the freedom of the people.

Reverend Kim uses the name "the Republic of Korea" (Taehan Min'guk) to refer to the events of 1919, when independence was declared and a provisional government was formed. Officially, the Republic of Korea was not founded until the constitution of 1948. Kim's retrojection of the contemporary state into an earlier time further emphasizes his argument that the foundations of the country lie in its Christian beginnings, not merely in its political recognition by other world powers.

This historical view is accentuated by Kim's use of the terms for "ancestor," or "predecessor" *(chosang, sŏnjo)*, in other parts of the sermon.[17] For contemporary Christians, credit is certainly owed to the foreign missionaries who sacrificed their lives for Korea but is also centrally owed to the Koreans who converted to Christianity and suffered the consequences. In the same sermon of February 2008, Kim singled out the Christian church and its members as the center of national progress and the Korean Christians of the past for suffering hardships in order to bless the later generations.

EXCERPT 2.4

Ŭi rŭl wihayŏ uri sŏnjodŭl i kot'ong ŭl padŭn kŏt imnida.

Our ancestors endured pain for their righteousness.

EXCERPT 2.5

Uri sŏnjodŭl ŭi Hananim e taehan sarang, minjok e taehan sarang, chayu wa chilli wa p'yŏnghwa e taehan sarang ttaemune padŭn konan ŭro malmiama uri ka ch'ukpok ŭl padassŭmnida.

We received blessings that arose from the hardships that our ancestors endured for their love for God, love for the Korean people, and love for freedom, truth, and peace.

In the sermon, Reverend Kim located "our ancestors" in the Christian population that opposed Japanese colonialism. By linking the early Korean Christians' passage through the beginning phases of ethnonational development to the Israelites' passage out of Egypt, and by comparing current Korean missionaries throughout the world to the earlier missionaries who came to Korea from Canada, Great Britain, and the United States, Kim effectuated an implicit shift in the referential scope of the words for "ancestor" or "predecessor." In Kim's statements, the ancestors are not the ancestors of Confucian ancestor worship practice, going back generations patrilineally.[18] During the Chosŏn dynasty, the concept of ancestry was bound to patrilineal succession within a kinship structure based on agnatic bloodlines. In her study of the Confucian transformation of Korea, Martina Deuchler writes:

> The ancestors and their descendants, Chu Hsi remarked, consist of the same mind matter (Chin. *ch'i;* Kor. *ki*). Although a man's *ki* dissipates upon his death, its substance is preserved in his descendants. If they exert their utmost sincerity and reverence, they can call back their ancestors' *ki* during the ritual (Chin. *chi-szu;* Kor. *chesa*). Therefore, people unrelated by blood to the dead cannot perform ancestral sacrifice for them. Chu Hsi likened the succession of generations to the relentless forming and breaking-up of waves; although no one wave is the same as the one that came before or will come afterward, all waves consist of the same water. Similarly, the same *ki* unites the ancestors and their descendants in the ritual process.[19]

Kim's sermon does not treat ancestors in this manner. Ancestors are not all members of past generations related by blood but rather are restricted historically (if implicitly) to the period of modernization, democratization, and spiritual enlightenment of Korea. If they are elevated, it is for their participation in the Christianization of the country, not merely for their status as patrilineal predecessors.

Furthermore, for contemporary Protestants, the lineage of faith that limits these spiritual ancestors to Christian predecessors also transforms the foreign Protestant missionaries who came to Korea in the late nineteenth century into a kind of ancestor of present-day Korean Christians.[20] By following the lineage of historical proclamations of faith and evangelical activity, contemporary Korean Christians can trace their own spiritual heritage back to earlier missionaries—and back to the Israelites. This is a perspectival shift away from Korea's oft-touted "five thousand–year history" dating back to the mythical founder of Korea, Tan'gun, and toward the Protestant Christians of Korea's recent past and a more distant biblical past within a single, unified narrative of Christian history.[21]

The shift in the extensional scope of the word *ancestor* signals a shift in the narrative of Korea outlining a chronotope of the nation.[22] Within this Christian chronotope of "Korea"—itself a culturally conceptualized and linguistically materialized intersection and institutionalization of categories of time, space, and personhood—the work of democratization and enlightenment began with the first conversion to Protestant Christianity on the peninsula and spread over time throughout the country and continues to emanate into the world via missionary activities.[23] This narrative models Korea's history on the biblical poetics of the crucifixion and resurrection, of sin and redemption, of suffering and healing, of exodus and homecoming. Macrocosmic categories of time, space, and person converge in the microcosm of church ritual, forging a markedly Christian narrative of progress.

CHRONOTOPIC CLAIMS AND THE POLITICS OF CHANGE

On December 19, 2007, Lee Myung-bak, of the conservative Grand National Party (Hannaradang), was declared the winner of the election for president of the Republic of Korea. With 48.6 percent of the vote, Lee won by a landslide in an election with extremely low voter turnout by Korean standards.[24] Chung Dong-young (Chŏng Tong-yŏng), of the United New Democratic Party (Taet'onghap Minjusindang), was a distant second with only 26.2 percent of the vote.[25] It was the fifth general election since Korea's democratization in 1987 and signaled a significant shift to the political right after ten years of center-left administrations.

In his inaugural speech on February 25, 2008, Lee praised the country for having achieved industrialization and democratization in only six decades. So rapid was the country's economic development that it became known as the "Miracle on the Han" (*Han'gang ŭi kijŏk*, referring to the Han River, which runs through Seoul).[26] Lee also declared 2008 the first year of Korea's status as an "advanced nation" *(sŏnjin'guk)*, and he asked the citizens to create a "new myth *[saeroun sinhwa]* of the Korean peninsula" through harmony, cooperation, social integration, and economic development. Drawing on his campaign theme, Lee, a former Hyundai executive and mayor of Seoul (2002–6), pledged that his administration would operate under the principle of "pragmatism" *(siryong)* rather than "ideology" *(inyŏm)*.[27] This statement was a not-so-subtle jab at the previous two administrations. During the previous decade, Lee claimed, Koreans found themselves "sometimes hesitating and frustrated."[28] Now, he announced, he would introduce pragmatism as a principle for governing the country. "If the things we are used to are irrational or do not fit with the times," he announced, "we must resolutely part with them."[29] Lee described pragmatism as "the zeitgeist that embodies a life that healthfully and beautifully unites man and nature, matter and spirit, and individual and community."[30]

Lee's characterization of the political turnover in which he was participating invoked widespread modernist narratives of ruptures from a traditional past—as the transition from irrationality to rationality, from impractical thought to practical thought.[31] At the same time, it cued up the longer temporal frame of a specifically Korean narrative describing the country's modernist advancement over the course of a century. In Lee's framing of the more recent past as irrational and impractical, we hear echoes of earlier political and intellectual leaders who attacked Korea's premodern Chosŏn dynasty, which governed from 1392 until Korea was declared a protectorate of Japan in 1905 and officially annexed in 1910. During the colonial period, the intellectual and author Yi Kwang-su attacked the Chosŏn dynasty for having "a record of worthless ideas and empty debates."[32] And in the 1960s, the former president and military dictator Park Chung-hee (Pak Chŏng-hŭi, in office 1963–79) blamed Korea's poverty on its "criminal" and "evil" Yi (Chosŏn) dynasty heritage.[33]

Like the Presbyterianism of Kim Young-sam (Kim Yŏng-sam, in office 1993–98), Korea's first democratically elected civilian president, Lee's public Christianity gave these calls for renewal a religious character.[34] Kim Young-sam had promised that, if elected, "hymns would continuously ring out from the Blue House."[35] Lee's promises of change were also grounded in an Evangelical Christian worldview, which is illuminated by the relationship of his inaugural speech to the sermon given by Pastor Kim Chi-ch'ŏl just one day prior.

Pastor Kim Chi-ch'ŏl gave the sermon on the March First movement, "The Blessings of Those Who Are Persecuted Because of Righteousness," on Sunday, February 24, 2008. In the sermon, Kim also talked generally about the last century of Korean history, during which time Koreans experienced the pain *(kot'ong)* of modernization, colonization, war, military dictatorship, and national division. The sermon began by describing the growing pains children suffer in their joints as a metaphor for a society suffering poverty and social disaster on the way to maturity. It anticipated many of the statements made by Lee the following day. Particular similarities between the sermon and the political address suggest some degree of coordination between the two. For example, take the following two narrative statements:

EXCERPT 2.6 (LEE MYUNG-BAK, FEBRUARY 25, 2008)

Toum ŭl pannŭn nara esŏ pep'unŭn nara ro olla sŏssŭmnida. Ije sŏnjin'guktŭl kwa ŏkkae rŭl naranhi hal su itke toeŏssŭmnida.

[Korea] has risen from [being] a country that accepts help to [being] a country that gives help. Now we have become able to stand shoulder-to-shoulder with advanced countries.

EXCERPT 2.7 (KIM CHI-CH'ŎL, FEBRUARY 24, 2008)

Sidae ka sŏngsuk hago nara ka palchŏn hanŭn sumanŭn kwajŏng ŭl pomyŏn kot'ong kwa siryŏn ŭl igyŏnaen yonggi rŭl kajin saramdŭl ŭi hŏnsin i issŏttŏn kŏt ŭl pol su issŭmnida. Ttaeronŭn pakhae wa p'ippak, chorong kwa myŏlsi rŭl padŭmyŏnsŏdo ch'ungsŏng haettŏn saramdŭl ro malmiama yŏksa ka palchŏn toego sŏngsuk toeŏ wassŭmnida. Sŏngsuk ŭi kwajŏng enŭn siryŏn sok esŏ yonggi rŭl naen saramdŭl i issŏssŭmnida. Uri nŭn tchalbŭn sewŏl tongan minjuhwa rŭl iruŏ wassŭmnida. Ije segye yŏlbang kwa tŏburŏ sŏnjinhwa rŭl hyanghan kwajŏng chung e issŭmnida.

You can see that the country's various processes of development and maturation over time became possible because of the devotion of the people who had the courage to overcome pain and hardship. The history of development and maturation arose from the devoted people who sometimes faced oppression and persecution, as well as ridicule and contempt. During the maturation process, there were people who mustered the courage to endure this hardship. In a very short time, we have come to achieve democratization. Now we are in the process of advancement together with the nations of the world.

The surrounding political importance, the calendric proximity of the two days, the close personal and institutional connections between the two men, the parallel narrative structures, and the particular phrasal similarities (e.g., "shoulder-to-shoulder with advanced countries"; "together with the nations of the world") suggest that some direct coordination between Reverend Kim and President Lee had taken place before their respective broadcasts.

Yet during Kim's sermon of February 24, 2008, there was no explicit mention of Lee until the final prayer, when Kim said to the congregation,

"As we pray for our country and our new president, help us open a new era as the people of the Lord."[36] In Lee's speech, there was no explicit mention of Christianity or Somang Church—even though as mayor of Seoul in 2004 he had dedicated the city to God.[37] However, for listeners familiar with Somang Church's main chapel and the soft light filtering through its western windows, the following statement from Lee's inaugural address would have conjured up a clear image:

EXCERPT 2.8

Kungmin ŭi maŭm sok e innŭn Taehan Min'guk chido rŭl segye ro nŏlp'igessŭmnida. Segye ŭi munmul i kŏch'im ŏpsi tŭrŏ wasŏ i ttang esŏ saeroun kach'i ro ch'angjo toege hagessŭmnida. Kŭrihayŏ Taehan Min'guk i segye rŭl hyanghae saeroun kach'i rŭl naebonaenŭn nara sŏnjin illyu kukka ka toege hagessŭmnida. Sŏndae ŭi kiwŏn igo, tangdae ŭi hŭimang imyŏ, hudae waŭi yaksok imnida.

We will spread the map of the Republic of Korea, which lies within the hearts [maŭm] of the Korean people, throughout the world. We will make the civilizations of the world enter unhindered, and we will create new values in this land. And so we will make the Republic of Korea become a first-class advanced nation that sends new values out into the world. It was the prayer of previous generations, it is the hope of the current generation, and it is a promise to future generations.

Certainly these statements played on a theme familiar to the broader Korean public, that is, the theme of Korea's "will to greatness," which, as Carter Eckert has put it, is a "certain psychic presumption that Korea is an inherently great country, destined to play a leading role in the history of the world."[38] However, there also appear to be "metamessages," clues that indicate a more specific audience than the "everyone" to which they claim to be addressed.[39] Lee's description of a future Korea serving as productive center of contemporary values in a global society of advanced nations was evocative of a prominent visual image displayed in the stained glass of the western wall of the main sanctuary of Somang Church (see figure 2 and figure 3):

In figure 2, the Korean peninsula—which includes North Korea—is colored in dark blue, centered, and enlarged in relation to the rest of the world. Korea sits at the "heart" of the map; the rest of the world, colored in light blue, is adjusted both in scale and orientation to the prominence of the dark blue peninsula. The three curved lines that run through the map constitute an element from the church's logo—a rainbow "express[ing] our hope in His promise and signifying the Father, Son, and the Holy Spirit."[40] The full impact of the stained-glass diagram

FIGURE 2. Somang Presbyterian Church, stained glass, interior (photo by author).

FIGURE 3. Somang Presbyterian Church, stained glass, exterior (photo by author).

can be experienced only from the interior of the church's main sanctuary, where it appears illuminated. This means that only Lee's listeners
who had attended services at Somang would have conjured up this particular image.

President Lee's and Reverend Kim's statements about Korea's
advancement and its assumption of a central place in the affairs of the
world created a kind of interdiscursive loop that was evocative of the
stained glass on Somang Church and certainly of the evangelical design
it depicts. In Korean, *somang* means, literally, "hope," "wish," or
"desire"; in a promotional video for the church titled *Lord, Send Me,*

Reverend Kim says he believes in his heart *(maŭm)* that the church is the hope *(somang)* of these times *(i sidae)*; in the stained-glass map, a church-influenced Korea is positioned at the "heart" of the image, suggesting it is the hope of the world; and in Lee's speech, the people of Korea will have in their own "hearts" the map depicting "hope of the present age" *(tangdae ŭi hŭimang)*.[41] For Lee and Kim, Korea's narrative of advancement is told through the lens of its Christianization and through the Christian influence it will exert on the rest of the world; it is a narrative not just of advancement over time but also of the spatial shift from periphery to center. And Lee's proposal for a "new myth of the Korea Peninsula" did not merely describe a turnover of political power from the political left to the political right. On an even larger scale, Lee's call for the shift from "ideology" to "pragmatism" can be read as a call to Koreans to replace a narrative of suffering with one of hope, one of resentment with one of leadership, even, perhaps, an irrational and superstitious origin story of the Korean people (i.e., the myth of Tan'gun) with a new narrative that traces the birth of the modern Korean nation to the arrival of Protestant Christianity in the nineteenth century. Such a move shifts the legitimacy of the Korean nation from the glory of a distant, mythical past, and the struggle and suffering of the more recent past, to the near and practically attainable future.

Within months of his inauguration, however, Lee Myung-bak faced a political challenge to his statement—his chronotopic claim—that Korea had joined the ranks of the advanced nations. As a form of self-authorization, Lee claimed that there is a specific chronotope of ethnonational progress (which he would now lead) and simultaneously made claims on the citizens of Korea to inhabit the models of personhood framed by this chronotope. But there was a problem. While the Lee administration described its policies as "future-oriented" *(mirae chihyangjŏk)*, a series of large-scale public protests soon emerged in opposition to his government, one key message of which was that Lee himself was in fact a relic of Korea's troubled past.

CONTESTED CHRONOTOPES AND THE AGENTS OF HISTORY

The problems began when the Lee administration announced in April 2008 that it would accept U.S. beef imports from cows older than thirty months. The South Korean market had been closed to U.S. beef since a case of mad cow disease was discovered in 2003.[42] On May 2, 2008, protesters held the first "candle-light demonstration" *(ch'otpul siwi)* against the new trade agreement. The demonstrations quickly escalated to large-scale protests in Seoul's public spaces and throughout the country.

Protesters were originally motivated by a report, which aired on April 29, 2008, on the Munhwa Broadcasting Corporation (MBC) news program *PD Such'ŏp* (PD Notebook), titled "Miguk soegogi ŏlmana anjŏn han'ga?" (How Safe Is American Beef?). The program showed footage of a "downer" cow in the United States and inaccurately reported that it carried mad cow disease (bovine spongiform encephalopathy, BSE; Kor., *kwangupyŏng*). Even though much of the report turned out to be inaccurate—which PD Such'ŏp admitted and for which its broadcasters issued an apology—the momentum of public protests did not wane.[43] Soon tens of thousands of Seoul's citizens were gathering regularly in Seoul's public spaces to stage candlelight demonstrations against the Lee Myung-bak government. Whether the program's inaccuracies were the result of intentional distortion (as the political right claimed) or accidents in translation (as the political left claimed), they sparked a major political confrontation.[44] The protests continued for months, with some estimated to have drawn a hundred thousand people.[45]

At Somang Church, people's reactions to the protests ranged from mild irritation to outright hostility. All of the church members with whom I spoke condemned the protesters, calling them "stupid" *(pabo)*, saying they couldn't think for themselves, or simply exclaiming, "I hate them" *(sirŏ)*. Given Lee Myung-bak's status as an elder in the church these people attended, their responses were unsurprising to me.

Many of my other informants and acquaintances outside the church condoned, supported, or even participated in the protests. Many of those who participated said they joined the more peaceful gatherings simply as a way to spend time with their friends and could articulate only vaguely the particular politics of the demonstrations. But even when the protests turned violent, many of my informants still insisted that such clashes were necessary for the development of Korea's democracy. They told me that if the people did not join together, participate, and act, "democracy in Korea would end" *(Han'guk ŭi minjujuŭi ka kkŭnnalgŏyeyo)*. When I asked them if they would continue to protest even if it turned out that claims about mad cow disease were proven entirely false, they told me they would. Some told me that the protests were not just about mad cow disease but also about the "people" *(minjung)*.

With this term, these informants revived a concept that had played a crucial role in shaping conceptualizations of civil society in the 1970s and 1980s. Intellectuals adopted the term *minjung* to argue that the masses, rather than the elites, are the true subjects of history.[46] Activists in the *minjung* movement positioned themselves as carrying on a historical tradition of dissent against the state that could be traced back to the Tonghak rebellion of 1894, during which peasants rose up against the *yangban*.[47] With slogans such as *"minjung, minjok, minju"* (people, nation, democracy), the *minjung* movement had become, by the late 1980s, a driving force for Korea's transition from an authoritarian military regime to a parliamentary democracy.[48]

The 2008 beef protests revived a perennial debate about whether the "people" or the "elites" are the agents of history. Whereas President Lee and Pastor Kim offered a narrative frame for the advancement of the country—a chronotope of ethnonational development and spiritual enlightenment driven by Protestant Christianity, its leaders, and its institutions—supporters of the protests constructed an oppositional narrative frame around the role of the common people in Korea's development. The former is built on the model of Christian missionization, in which individual foreign missionaries, led by God, brought the Bible and modernity to Korea. The latter chronotope framed the narrative of a people in natural opposition to a powerful state, to powerful institutions, to powerful persons, and to powerful foreign influences. On the basis of this latter model, Lee was accused of using his elite status to sell out the people to foreign interests (the United States' interests in particular) just as the *yangban,* who had controlled Korea for five centuries, were said to have eventually sold out the Korean peasants to the Japanese.

A political action group called Workers Solidarity, Unite (Nodongja Yŏndae Tahamkke) produced and released a video online titled *Candlelight Demonstrations against Mad Cow Disease—Illegal? True Democracy?* which documented the development of the first candlelight protest in 2008.[49] Similar to the way Lee presented the transition to his presidency as a microcosm of the country's large-scale transition to modernity, the group's narrative strategy utilized the chronotope of the first candlelight vigil as a kind of microcosm of the larger-scale political momentum and development of activism in Korea. In this latter version, both the relative micro- and the macroscale narratives tell a story of the popular masses as the agents of history. The masses in the 2008 protests, however, were neither the furious and hungry peasants of the Tonghak rebellions nor, as Namhee Lee put it for the *minjung*, "those who are oppressed in the sociopolitical system but who are capable of rising up against it."[50] They came mostly from the urban, relatively educated middle class of one of the richest countries in the world.[51] In the video, the sequencing of what we might call the endo-evenemential (event-internal) narrative becomes a diagram for the larger exo-evenemential (event-external) narrative of which it is a part.[52]

The endo-evenemential narrative of the 2008 candlelight protests begins with a documentary scene of lively youths walking through a narrow street. The Korean text superimposed over the images reads, benignly, "May 2, 2008, 5:30 P.M., Hoegi Station." At twenty seconds, these same sociological types, young girls and boys, are captured on film leaning over a table to sign a petition for the event that would take place later that evening. The text reads, "Street campaign for the 7:00 P.M. candlelight demonstration against mad cow disease." By thirty-four seconds, the scene has shifted to the place and time of the demonstration, with these same types of persons walking toward Ch'ŏnggye Plaza. At forty seconds, in a moment of narrative doubt, there is an image of hundreds of people preparing to cross a street. The text asks, "How many people have come?" Then the scene shifts dramatically to the growing numbers of people gathered in the plaza, whose candles light the space of protest even as the darkness of night surrounds them. Finally, at two minutes, the culminating scenes of this narrative depict thousands of people gathered together—individuals, friends, families, citizens— "each proudly joined together in a battle cry."[53] The superimposed text on the final frame reads, "Shouts continuously emerged here and there" (figure 4).[54]

The exo-evenemential narrative places the story of the 2008 candlelight demonstrations within a longer history of collective protest in Korea. It begins at four minutes and twenty seconds with images from the April 19 Revolution of 1960, when student and labor protests led to the overthrow of Syngman Rhee's (Yi Sŭng-man) government. Protests were sparked by the discovery of a student in Masan Harbor who had been killed during an earlier anti-government demonstration. This is followed by images of the Kwangju Uprising of May 18, 1980, when the citizens of Kwangju rose up against Chun Doo-hwan's military government and were crushed. The scenes continue forward in time to

FIGURE 4. Candlelight demonstration, 2008, endo-evenemential narrative.

the nationwide protests in June 1987, which forced Chun Doo-hwan to allow open elections. Images of the sometimes violent clashes between protesters and the state in the decades following the war through the 1980s give way to the more peaceful images of the candlelight demonstrations held for two junior high school girls killed by a U.S. Army tank in 2002 and similar candlelight demonstrations held to protest the impeachment of President Roh Mu-hyun (No Mu-hyŏn) in 2004.[55] (Roh committed suicide in 2009.) Finally, the sequence arrives at images of the 2008 candlelight demonstration, which filled the streets of central Seoul. Starting at four minutes and thirty-four seconds, the text superimposed over four frames reads, "We remember that we marched on the streets standing firmly on history and that every time you incriminated and threatened us, history always documented our cause justly" (figure 5).[56]

The beef protests became a channel through which an alternative story of ethnonational development, modernity, and civic participation could be told. On the one hand, the version espoused by Lee Myung-bak and Kim Chi-ch'ŏl placed the church and associated institutions at the helm of Korea's transformation. The "real" starting point was

FIGURE 5. Candlelight demonstration, 2008, exo-evenemential narrative.

traced to the arrival of Protestant missionaries in the late nineteenth century. On the other, the version told by the beef protests downplayed the role of institutions, of elite spiritual leaders, and of Christianity and instead emphasized the role of the wakening of the local masses as they came to collective consciousness of their political authority—even if institutions and affiliated personal networks (e.g., at universities) were at the heart of the movement. The "real" starting point could be traced to the peasant rebellions of the late nineteenth century.

The events that punctuate Korea's tradition of dissent and protest are construed as steps along the path of ethnonational development.[57] For example, Cumings writes of the Tonghak uprising: the "massive rebellion also cleared the way for Korea's first truly modern reforms. As commercial and industrial efforts began and semifeudal restrictions on Korea's multitude were lifted . . . it is from 1894 that we can speak of Korea's modern period."[58] And in terms of the 1987 democracy protests, Cumings writes, "Civil society began to waken again with the February 1985 National Assembly elections, and by spring 1987 an aroused, self-organized, and intersubjective citizenry took over the streets of the major cities, with late-coming but substantial middle-class participation," which forced Chun Doo-hwan, then military dictator of Korea, from power.[59] Related to the topic of civil society is of course the

Habermasian concept of the public sphere, which was highlighted in the online forums that were essential for circulating information about the issues and the candlelight protests themselves. The democratizing function of the relationship between civil society and the so-called public sphere has been of central concern in the historical study of Korea. For many activists and intellectuals, the history of protest in Korea becomes the history of the struggle for a modern, politically engaged public sphere in the face of state-orchestrated violence.

The Christian narrative of ethnonational development through spiritual enlightenment is highly contested and polemical, even in its most subtle manifestations. While millions of Christians gathered in Christian churches like Somang to pray for their president, hear the sounds of *sŏngak,* and listen to sermons that described them and their fellow believers as members of an advanced nation, others gathered in the public spaces of Seoul, chanting a battle cry against the government and demanding the president's impeachment or resignation. In 2008, each side saw the other as a stubborn relic, as unwanted residue of Korea's troubled past. In 2013, Park Geun-hye (Pak Kŭn-hye), the daughter of Park Chung-hee, succeeded Lee Myung-bak as president, and South Korea witnessed a real resurrection of the past.[60]

VOICING ADVANCEMENT THROUGH THE VOICE OF JESUS

Now that I have sketched out the Christian chronotope of Korean progress, I want to turn back to the way this narrative becomes manifest in the human voice. On July 6, 2008, at the height of the protests, on the same day that Somang Church's congregation heard "Amazing Grace," "I Come to the Garden Alone," and "Truly Good Lord" sung in a *sŏngak* style, Reverend Kim Chi-ch'ŏl gave a sermon titled "Jesus's Sigh When He Looks at These Times" *(Sidae rŭl hyanghan Yesunim ŭi t'ansik).*[61] Kim's sermon dealt with the topic of false accusations and ungrounded criticism. He characterized Jesus as "a spiritual and mental person" who did not give political speeches and, although he cared about the poor, did not try to start a workers' revolution.[62] According to Kim, the mind of Jesus was so advanced that his understanding of God's words far exceeded that of his followers: Just as "an elementary school student cannot easily understand the lecture of a university professor," we cannot understand all of the words of God as Jesus did.[63] He called on the congregation to engage in serious and sincere study and prayer to achieve spiritual "maturity" *(sŏngsuk)*. It was a lack of such maturity that led people like the Pharisees to criticize Jesus. The implicit message was that a lack of mature, developed, or advanced thinking leads people to engage in angry protest rather than in peaceful discussion and debate.

Somang Church presents itself as place of peace and peacefulness, of both righteous behavior and sensorial serenity. It is known for its classical music, its choirs, and the overall softness and solemnity of it worship service. In line with this aesthetic, Kim's own sermonic voice is generally hushed and soft, as if he were having a calm face-to-face conversation with his listener. His sermons direct the congregants to behave as Christian models for other Koreans and, on a larger scale, to use Christianity to make Korea a model for the rest of world.[64] Just as the singers and choirs provide a model for upper-class Christian vocal practice for tens of thousands of people in this particular church each week, Reverend Kim's own sermonic voice also serves as a model of Christian speech. As many congregants told me, his speech functions as an example of the way Christians should talk—softly, clearly, learnedly—as a prototype of a particular sort of Christian communicative register.

In line with his charge of modeling Christian speech for the congregation, Pastor Kim performed in hypothetical quotations the Pharisees' criticisms of Jesus and Jesus's response. Many of his words were not taken directly from the Bible but were adaptations of the quoted speech reported there, designed to illustrate the different perspectives of Jesus and his detractors.[65] As he performed these different positions, he manipulated his voice to differentiate the speakers. What might simply sound like differentiated forms of emphatic speech or affect were in fact highly structured oppositions in both the phonic and sonic dimensions. When he parodied the complaints of the Pharisees against Jesus, he departed from his own soft-spoken manner and produced a relatively tense, pressed voice quality. I call this the "ventricular" voice because of the way he constricted his pharynx, raised and tightened his larynx, and also raised and varied his pitch to a kind of slight whine. Then when he voiced Jesus's rebuttal, he produced an intense but yawnlike voice quality. I call this the "faucalized" voice, because in producing this sound, he expanded his pharynx, lowered and relaxed his larynx, and lowered the pitch to deliver stern but not overly excited admonishment.

In the transcript below, I have left Pastor Kim's sermonic voice unmarked. I have underlined the words of the critics of Jesus, which represents a more ventricular style. And I have presented the speech of Jesus in boldface, which represents a more faucalized mode of vocalization. While Kim maintains the qualitative distinctions according to the voicing distinctions of the text, aspects of the more ventricular pole of this continuum of prosodic register phenomena seem to "leak" both into his normal sermonic speech and Jesus's admonishing speech. I have marked these instances of leakage with a dotted underline.

EXCERPT 2.9

1. *Yesunim kkesŏ osyŏssŭmnida.* — Jesus arrived.

2. *Kŭ pun ŭn chanch'i rŭl pep'usyŏssŭmnida.* — He held a feast.

3. *Kŭrigo manŭn saramdŭl ŭn ch'uk'a haessŭmnida.* — And many people congratulated him.

4. *Hamkke mŏkko masyŏssŭmnida.* — They ate and drank together.

5. *Kŭttae Parisaeindŭl kwa sŏgigwandŭl ŭn Yesunim ŭl pinan haessŭmnida.* — At that time, the Pharisees and lawyers criticized Jesus.

6. *Chŏ saram mŏkko masinŭn cha ya!* — "Hey, that person is a glutton and a drinker!"

7. *Mŏngnŭn kŏt ŭl choa hanŭn cha ya!* — "Hey, that person likes to eat!"

8. *Sul e ch'wihan cha ya!* — "Hey, he is a drunkard for wine!"

9. *Chŏ saram ŭn choeindŭl kwa seridŭl ŭi ch'in'gu ya!* — "Hey, that person is a friend of criminals and tax collectors!"

10. *Chŏdŭl kwa hant'ongsok iya!* — "Hey, he is in with them!"

11. *Hamyŏnsŏ Yesunim ŭi mosŭp ŭl pinan hago pip'an haettŏn kŭ sasil i sŏnggyŏng sok e kirok i toeŏ issŭmnida.* — And it is recorded as fact in the Bible that they criticized and passed judgment on the figure of Jesus.

12. *Yesunim ŭn idŭl ŭl pomyŏnsŏ kkok kŭrŏk'e pan hasimnida:* — As Jesus looked at them he certainly contradicted them in this way:

13. **Nŏhŭidŭl i tŭnnŭn kwi ka ŏpkuna.** — "Ah, but you don't have ears that listen."

14. **Nŏhŭidŭl i ponŭn nun i ŏpkuna.** — "Ah, but you don't have eyes that see."

15. *Nŏhŭidŭl i kkaedannŭn*
maŭm i ŏpkuna.

"Ah, but you don't have hearts
[maŭm] that are awakening."

16. *Nŏhŭidŭl i Hananim ap esŏ*
chagi chujang man hago
Hananim ŭi malssŭm ŭi
kip'i sok e tŭrŏ itchi ank'o
itkuna hamyŏnsŏ t'ansik
hago issŭmnida.

"Ah, but you <u>only assert yourself</u>
<u>before God and do not take in</u>
<u>deeply the Word of God</u>," he said
as he sighed.

17. *Chagi chujang man toep'uri*
hago innŭn saramdŭl, nam ŭi
mal e kwi rŭl kiuriji annŭn
saramdŭl, chagi ŭi kojŏng
kwannyŏm ŭro nam ŭl
chŏngji hago pinan hanŭn i
Parisaeindŭl kwa sŏgigwandŭl
ŭi mosŭp ŭl hayŏsŏ Yesunim
kkesŏ t'ansik hago kyesin kŏt
imnida.

Jesus was sighing at the people who
only repeated their own argument
and the people who could not lend
their ears to the words of another
person, because they were similar to
the <u>Pharisees and the experts in the</u>
<u>law who criticized</u> and silenced
others with their own fixed
concepts.

The result was an indexical linking of the perceived sensuous qualities of sound with different moral positions, different moral positions
with different types of people, and different types of people situated
within a Christian narrative.[66] The structure of differentiation that Kim
sets up—his own narration and the reported speech of others—displays
a kind of prosodic contrast between Jesus and the Pharisees. The acoustic difference between these two forms is quite clearly visible in spectrographic analysis of phrases at the most extreme binary poles of the two
phonosonic styles. Figure 6 is a spectrogram of the Pharisees' phrase,
"choeindŭl kwa seridŭl" (criminals and tax collectors), in line 9. The
analysis shows a variable pitch line with acoustic energy spread out in
the higher frequencies. This corresponds to the narrowing of the vocal
chamber and the brightness and shrillness of Kim's high-pitched speech
during this stretch of the recording.

Figure 7 is a spectrogram of Jesus's phrase, *"Nŏhŭidŭl i ponŭn nun*
i ŏpkuna" (Ah, but you don't have eyes that see), in line 14. Notice the
consistent density of acoustic energy in the lower frequencies. The location of these dark patches corresponds to an expanded vocal cavity and
the warmer, more resonant sound of Kim's lower-pitched speech during
this stretch of the recording.

Kim favors Jesus's speech over the Pharisees' speech. Yet the qualitative setting—his *qualic tuning* (see chapter 5)—of the less-favored form,
the ventricular voice, occasionally breaks through into both his own

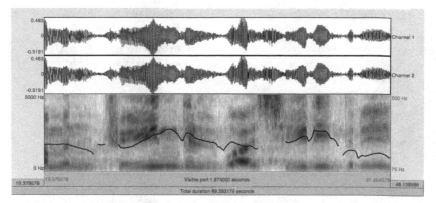

FIGURE 6. A spectrogram of the voice of the Pharisees.

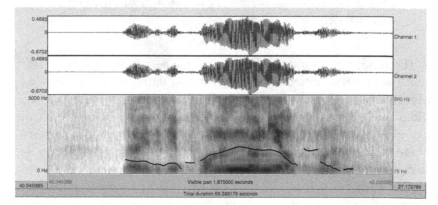

FIGURE 7. A spectrogram of the voice of Jesus.

narration and into his performance of Jesus's speech. By looking closely at when the qualia of the Pharisees' speech leak prosodically into Kim's and Jesus's speech, we can see that this register leakage is not completely arbitrary. Each time speech qualia associated with the Pharisees occur outside Pharisee speech, it is on a passage that in some way invokes the position or stance of the Pharisees. In line 4, "They ate and drank together," Kim is describing the events that the Pharisees saw, causing them to accuse Jesus of being a drinker and a glutton. In that moment, Kim the sermonizer seems to speak as a Pharisee—as if viewing Jesus from a Pharisee's perspective. And in line 17, describing the discursive actions of the Pharisees, Kim himself uses the verb *to criticize (pinan hada)*. Here, the speech being described becomes the metapragmatics of description: by critically describing the Pharisees' criticisms, Kim himself becomes a criticizer (i.e., momentarily "like" a Pharisee). And in line 16, when Kim performs Jesus's voice, saying, "but you only assert yourself before God and do not take in deeply the Word of God," it is again in the description of speech, "to assert" *(chujang hada)*, that the associated ventricular qualia of the act of assertion permeate the event of its description. In this manner, the vocal qualia of the Pharisees' assertions leak into Jesus's description of them (as performed by Pastor Kim). Kim's sermon illustrates the difference between harsh criticisms made by the unenlightened and the responsive "sighs" of the enlightened; the contrastive registers and their occasional leakage across roles invoke a higher indexical order of social positions and their associated values.[67]

Although we cannot make any claims about Kim's intention or awareness regarding the specific forms of qualic tuning he employed, nor can we assume that these qualic forms are always superimposed onto the types of speech reported above (they are not), it is quite clear that Kim subjects his own narrative voice to the internal configuration of oppositional voices that he himself has established in this allegorical passage of the sermon. Two important things emerge from these two qualically differentiated, narrative-internal registers. First, Kim aligns his own speech with that of Jesus both in the way his speech and Jesus's speech condemn the Pharisees and those who behave like them and in the way his speech and Jesus's speech are qualitatively differentiated from the Pharisees' speech. Second, the vocal qualia of the Pharisees as performed by Kim stubbornly break through into speech that condemns the Pharisees—that is, into the speech of Kim as sermonizer and the speech of Kim as Jesus. Both the preacher's speech and Jesus's speech are permeated in the same way (via qualic leakage from the described/ reported to the describing/reporting). They are in a sense saying the same thing in the same way and are thereby affected in the same way by the force of the qualitatively marked moral opposition.

This becomes a problem of voicing when these quotations illustrate the different positions of Jesus and his detractors and are revealed as different moral positions in relation to a spoken denotational text. As I explained in the introduction, voicing pertains to the inherent relationality of utterances and semiotic forms in discourse, in terms of which the animator of some discursive form can assume or invoke a culturally recognizable perspective—whether relatively individual and particularized or social and generalized. By reproducing and rearranging preexistent discursive forms during communicative events, people align with and distance themselves from such forms and the identities and values that they invoke. One voices oneself in relation to these circulating forms and thereby assumes a moral stance or perspective, invokes an interest or claim, points toward authority or history. In the case of Pastor Kim, the semiotic elements of the different voicings both index and give an attributional contour to differences in personhood, which Kim casts as a difference between Christian and non-Christian. What this particular voicing structure reveals, via the phonosonics of vocalization, is the perceived persistence of purportedly un-Christian, unenlightened, immature perspectives in a Christian, enlightened, and mature generation or period of time *(sidae)*. Like Jesus in his time, present-day Christian leaders (e.g., Lee Myung-bak and Kim Chi-ch'ŏl) face criticism from the unenlightened and also must control their responses (and produce a sigh rather than a yell) so as not to reproduce aspects of this critical voice.

The perception of the stubborn persistence of the unenlightened past and its violent manifestations also has a deeply personal dimension for Reverend Kim, who has been the object of resentment and even attacks by other church leaders as he has attempted to make changes to Somang Church. On Sunday, January 2, 2011, just after the first service of the day had ended, while Kim was eating breakfast, some assistant pastors assaulted him in his office. Kim had to have surgery for the broken bones in his face. According to my informants, Kim had relieved these persons of their pastoral duties. They had come to protest, and the argument turned violent. Though factions had emerged among the elders and pastors after the retirement of the founding pastor, Kwak, and the transition of leadership to Pastor Kim, there were rumors that the assisting pastors had been relieved for misconduct, although no one could (or would) say of what sort. People chalked the conflict up to common struggles over institutional power and Pastor Kim's necessary attempts to clean up the church by purging it of whatever residue of corruption might remain.[68] Although the altercation took place after I left the field, there had been some foreshadowing during my time in the church. When I commented, in 2008, on how healthy, awake, and sharply dressed one of Somang's pastors appeared, despite the long working hours and purported ascetic principles of pastoral work, an informant said, simply, "They eat well." Such lighthearted comments point to the awareness among church members that representatives of the church do not always practice what they preach.

The voicing structure represented above, then, serves as a metaphor, an icon, as well as a metonym, an index, of the larger problem it is supposed to describe: the apparently irrational, uninformed, and even corrupt attacks on a legitimate leader. Through the performance of these voicings within the sermon, Kim models the allegorical story that he tells about the social events surrounding his sermon. Political protestors, like Jesus's detractors, launch a battle cry against Korean Christianity and its chosen leaders. The protests, like the vocal qualia of the Pharisees, like the violent infighting in the church, were branded by these Christians as relics of an irrational, immature, pre-Christian, superstitious past that stubbornly live on as residue in the contemporary period. Just as the ventricular voicings of irrational criticism break into the more faucalized utterances and sighs of the enlightened, the protests on the streets stubbornly persist even in an advanced, democratic society.

CONCLUSION

The voicing structure in Pastor Kim's sermon alerts us to the way a Christian narrative of progress relates to the voice generally and to *sŏngak* singing in particular. First, recalling the introduction, we should note that two related kinds of voice are at play in Kim's sermon. One kind is the literal phonosonic voice—the "voice voice"—that emerges from vibrations and resonance in the vocal tract. It is the site in which the phonic production and organization of sound intersect with the sonic uptake and categorization of sound in the world. It contributes to the meaningful segments of speech and song, as well to broader soundscapes and institutionally anchored acoustemologies.[69] The other kind of voice is a tropic extension of voice. It describes an alignment to, or a taking up of, a kind of perspective or moral stance in respect of semiotic text. It is the expression of an interest in relation to, or explicitly against, other interests in the social world. It contributes to the polyphony of social voices in the world. Pastor Kim, using manipulations of the first kind of voice, expresses and differentiates between two perspectives, from which he selects one to align with and in terms of which he can voice himself in the second sense of the word.

The chronotope of Christian progress mediates between voice in the first sense and voice in the second sense. It is by invoking this chronotope that the literal phonosonic voice can be used to tropically voice a moral perspective. The voices of exemplary others are taken up here to frame the progression toward a Christian present and future and away from a pagan past; they are identified in Kim's sermon not only by what they say but also by how they say it. Speaking to Christians whose biographical lives are supposed to be organized in terms of a steady progression toward spiritual maturity, Kim presents the ventricular style of the Pharisees as the voice of the past and the faucalized style of Jesus as a future point of aspiration. This synchronic variation in discursive time models a diachronic story of vocal change over ethnonational time. And Kim's sermonic style is a basis for the overall acoustemology of the church within a liturgical aesthetics of peace and repose—a soundscape that is ideologically loaded with a particular, moralizing account of Korean progress.[70] To join the community of believers in Somang Church and emphasize the abstract principles of church liturgy is to ritually perform a specific view of ethnonational advancement through a specific view of spiritual enlightenment.

As I will show throughout this book, this kind of qualic differentiation, captured above in a single stretch of speech, is writ large as a cultural model of differentiation of voice from the point of view of churches like Somang, with its clear manifestation in the explicitness of singing style as a semiotic register. In this specific instance, Kim's vocally mediated prosodic differentiation of social voices extends both qualically and temporally to the same differentiation that singers and many Koreans more generally—not just Christians—see between *sŏngak* and more traditional forms of expressive vocalization and song. That is, the ventricular style, the sounds produced by narrowing and tensing the vocal cavity, with its most extreme manifestation in a kind of roughness or coarseness of voice, is readily associated with traditional Korean singing. The faucalized style, the sounds produced by expanding and relaxing the vocal cavity, if still stern in Kim's performance, is associated with European-style classical singing, that is, the *sŏngak* that Christians at Somang Church and elsewhere hear and try to emulate every Sunday.[71]

The clear distinction between these two styles in Korea is made clear in Keith Howard's account of vocal style and aesthetics in the southern regions:

> Vocal technique characterized the Namdo style. Singers uniformly made great use of glottal stops and vocal production that was, with the exception of similar diaphragm pressure to support the breath, the opposite of *bel canto* in the West: where Lotte Lehmann felt singers should open their throats so that it felt as if a boiled egg was trapped there (see Manen 1973),

Namdo singers emphasized restriction in the throat; where a student of *bel canto* might feel sick because of openness, a Namdo singer might feel the same because of tenseness.[72]

As I explain in more detail in the following chapters, it is precisely this older, tenser style of singing that serves as the voice of an exemplary other for singers of *sŏngak*. Their aim is to move vocally as far away from this method of sound production as possible. Both vocal styles are intimately linked to the semiotic voicings at play in Kim's sermon, which projects a chronotope of Christian progress from the prosodic differentiation of speech (voice in the first sense) onto a sociosemiotic space of differentiated moral perspectives (voicing in the second sense). Vocal manipulation and the broader aesthetics of church liturgy situate these different perspectives within this narrative. And yet, like the protesters and the Pharisees, these older vocal sounds, their associated bodily dispositions, their moral perspectives, and their political motives seem to persist and threaten the Christianizing present—and the fully Christianized future—as a kind of residual embodied history of expressivity.[73]

CHAPTER 3

Cultivating the Christian Voice

In September 2008, I received an e-mail from a church soloist, a tenor, who was studying for his master's degree in voice in Seoul. When I had received e-mails from him before, they had been generated from an e-mail alias that combined the name of the prestigious university he attended, the English word *vocal,* and his birth date. This time, the e-mail was from a different account. The new e-mail address contained the English word *praise,* followed by his birth date. And the outgoing e-mail alias that appeared in place of his e-mail address was written in Han'gŭl as follows: 주님사랑성악사랑. Translated directly into English, *Chunim sarang sŏngak sarang* would be "Lord-love-*sŏngak*-love."

The phrase was likely a play on the common phrase for Korean linguistic nationalism, *kugŏ sarang nara sarang,* or "Korean language-love-country-love": to love the Korean language is to love Korea—to be a linguistic patriot.[1] But the e-mail alias also conjured up for me the partial reduplication that appears so often in Korean's extensive lexicon of denotationally iconic words (aka "sound symbolism"), such as *singgŭl pŏnggŭl* (smilingly) or *ult'ung pult'ung* (bumpy, uneven). It also quite clearly illustrated the pervasive public self-presentation of *sŏngak* singers as Christian. When I asked this singer why he had chosen this particular alias, he explained to me simply that he loved God and he loved *sŏngak.* He was also careful to make it clear that his love for God came before his love for *sŏngak,* that is, that he loved *sŏngak* because he loved God. The playful poetics of this e-mail alias suggested more than mere religious affiliation and aesthetic taste. The phrase summed up a basic argument of this book regarding the sociality of voice: namely, that in orienting to and cultivating particular shared qualities of voice, these Christians orient to and cultivate their individual and collective relationships with their deity and with one another. And the phaticity of voice— the emphasis on the mediating channel, on the sociality, on the sense of contact—is achieved through qualitative differentiation.

This kind of personal advertisement of a singer's deep Christian commitment is not uncommon in Korea, where an "evangelical ethos" pervades most of Protestant Christianity.[2] Typically, to be a *sŏngak* singer in Korea is to be a Christian singer. And to be a Korean Christian is to be an Evangelical Christian. While there are Catholic singers, as well as the occasional Buddhist or irreligious singer, the population of people engaged in *sŏngak* study and performance are overwhelmingly self-identified as Evangelical Protestant Christians. And for this particular singer, the very act of communication was inflected by this ethos both in his presentation of self by e-mail and through the type of singing he had chosen to pursue and the voice qualities he had chosen to cultivate. As I will explain, to sing in a *sŏngak* style in Korea is, for most singers, to sing in a Christian style (whereas to simply play Western classical in Korea music is not).

In this chapter, I explore the emergence of *sŏngak* as a semiotic register of communication and its connection to Evangelicalism within the Korean Christian church. I do so in three parts. First, I locate the role of singing broadly, for Korean Christians as a privileged form of social action. I show how *sŏngak* sits at the intersection of singing and evangelism, serving the parallel claims of Koreans' supposed in-born capacity for song and for spirituality.

Second, I explore how the systematic differentiation of voice qualities relies on and produces higher-order social categories that belong to the Christian narrative of progress described in chapter 2. In this way, I explore more fully the cultural meaning of this semiotic register at the level of the voice itself and of the voicings that it enables according to the aesthetic dimensions of this narrative. In so doing, I detail the ideological positions that govern the valorization of particular vocal sounds and their enregisterment among Christians in Seoul by exploring the way *sŏngak* singers distinguish their style of singing from what they perceive to be a traditional style. In light of the history of *sŏngak* within and beyond the church, even simple descriptions of the manner of sound production and preferences for different singing styles index a powerful aesthetic and ethical framework regarding appropriate and effective forms of communicative action. Nomic assertions like "we don't sing like that" or normative statements like "one shouldn't sing like that" invoke a whole evaluative framework of hearing and participating in the phonosonic life of an institution.[3]

Finally, I look at aspects of variation and change in vocal aesthetics that connect the relatively more "expressive" dimensions of voice to the relatively more "embodied" dimensions of voice in the contexts of its Christian enregisterment. As sonic forms are coded as more or less Christian in ritual centers of semiosis (like churches), the phonic processes of vocalization are identified and regimented in the form of bodily habituation, with accompanying local theories of naturalness and corporeal comfort. Via the explicit aesthetics of vocal sound production, sound and body are calibrated to each other and oriented to the normative standards of the church, where, in the manner of Reverend Kim Chi-ch'ŏl, discussed in chapter 2, typifiable personae are established through performance. In the singing culture of churches throughout Seoul, this can be seen as variation in both sound and bodily activity across contemporaneous practices (i.e., synchronically) and as change in practices over time (i.e., diachronically). I arrive at how the voice becomes an emblem of progress for these Christians, a communicative medium spanning bodily manipulation and sonic entailment to exhibit the idealized qualities of larger-scale social change in Korea.

NATURAL SINGERS, NATURAL EVANGELISTS

Interest in European-style classical music, its instruments, and techniques of sound production has been closely connected to the establishment of Christian congregations in Korea.[4] While first introduced into Korea via military bands, European-style classical music, and vocal music in particular, became a liturgical centerpiece in the early Protestant Christian churches. In general, hymns sung in Korean churches resemble the hymns sung in England and the United States.[5]

Both the Protestant Bible and hymnal were printed using the Korean native script, Han'gŭl, rather than the Sino-Korean Hancha favored by the *yangban*. This choice of script played an important role in making the gospels available to a wider segment of Korean society.[6] By the end of the Chosŏn dynasty, women were excluded from participating in ancestral rites and prevented from learning to read or write, and particularly women of the upper classes were forbidden to leave the inner chamber *(anpang)* of the house without being covered completely by a burkalike *changot* or *ssŭgae ch'ima*.[7] Alongside establishing modern hospitals and educational institutions, the Presbyterian and Methodist missionaries provided a space for the wider socialization of women and also the means for them to learn to read and write.[8] According to missionaries, church historians, and scholars of religion, the emancipatory promise of Christian institutions in the specific Korean context led to a great many conversions from the early Protestant mission period from the late nineteenth century through the early twentieth century.[9] During my field research, a number of people—including non-Christians—told me stories about how their grandmothers and great-grandmothers, once discouraged from reading, or writing, or leaving the house, began to attend church in their old age to learn to read and to have a chance to sing songs in public.

To this day, Korean Christians emphasize the role of hymns in the Protestant evangelization of Korea a century ago, as well as in the contemporary evangelical activities undertaken by Koreans at home and abroad. In the preface to *Come, Let Us Worship: The Korean-English Presbyterian Hymnal and Service Book,*[10] the anonymous editors make this point explicitly: "Korean Christians are a singing people. Since the beginning of the Christian movement in Korea, hymn singing has been a vital component of the worship life of the community. Hymn singing not only prepared the soil of the people's hearts for fruitful planting of the Word of God, but it also served as the primary instrument by which Christian teaching was transmitted until the whole Bible was translated into Korean in 1910."[11]

Group singing, group Bible study, and group prayer proved to be effective ways of drawing in potential converts. Not only did singing provide a culturally accessible way to institutionalize Christian practice in nineteenth- and early twentieth-century Korea; it also provided a way for would-be believers to read the gospels. As elsewhere, hymn singing and Bible study are deeply entwined in Korean Christian worship practices. This fact is emphasized in Korea to the extent that many of my informants claimed that Bibles in Korea are unique, because Korea has been the only country where the hymnal is always included in the back of the Bible. Although I have been unable to verify the validity of this claim, it is notable that Korean Christians themselves consider this a distinguishing factor of their religious practice. In any case, singing has been an indispensible way for evangelists to bring Christianity to Korean culture and vice versa.

Mention of singing in Korea at the level of "national character" dates back at least to the Chinese historian Chen Shou (233–97 C.E.), who wrote in *The Records of the Three Kingdoms* (Sanguozhi) that the inhabitants of what is now the Korea Peninsula and Manchuria loved to sing and dance in groups:

> On New Year's Day, according to the Yin version of the lunar calendar, the people in the kingdom of Puyŏ hold a festival in honor of the heavens. At this festival, which is called "The Festival of Welcoming Drums" [Yŏnggo], they drink, dance, and sing endlessly. People of all ages fill the streets of the village day and night, singing and making merry for days on end.
>
> In the kingdom of Mahan, the people hold a festival in honor of the gods after finishing the spring planting in May. They drink and sing for days on end at this festival. They dance in large groups, moving back and forth and repeatedly bending their bodies toward the ground and rising up again. They move their hands and feet to the rhythm of their bodies.
>
> The people of Koguryŏ like to sing and dance. Men and women in the villages throughout the country gather every night to sing and dance.
>
> In Chinhan, people like to dance and sing while drinking and playing the zither *[kŏmun'go]*.[12]

More recent reports contain numerous accounts of the role music and singing played in facilitating communal work and social relations in Korean social life.[13] In *The Passing of Korea,* a study of the country on the eve of its loss of independence to Japan, the missionary Homer Bezaleel Hulbert noted the way children gathered together on summer evenings, singing in unison, "each one shout[ing] at the top of his or her voice, and at a little distance the effect is not disagreeable." Hulbert continues his description by mentioning as well the labor songs, "which form, to the Western ear, the most charming portion of Korean music."[14] After offering his theory that this mode of social singing is related to the immersion of the self within a social whole, Hulbert goes on, somewhat reductively, to offer a kind of "yo-heave-ho" theory of Korean musical sociality:

> The unit of society is not the individual nor even the family, but it is the clan, the company, the crowd. Thus in their work they band together and accomplish tasks by the multiplication of muscle. This necessitates a rhythmic motion, in order that force may be applied at the same instant by every arm. Each band of ten or twelve has its leader, whose only duty is to conduct the chorus. He stands at one side and chants a strain of four syllables, and immediately the men take it up and repeat after him. No work is done while he is singing, but as the men take up the chant they all heave together. It seems a great waste of time, but it would be very difficult to get Koreans to do certain forms of work in any other way.[15]

Alongside Bible study, singing also served the expansion of the church by structuring the organization and participation of labor for church purposes. The missionary Daniel Lyman Gifford described in his memoirs, *Every-Day Life in Korea,* the way the newly baptized men—some of whom were *yangban* and therefore unused to manual labor—erected a church with their bare hands by "turn[ing] this work into a frolic, by heaving the stone in time to the chanting of a chorus that is responsive to the solo singing, usually improvised, of one of their number."[16]

At the beginning of the twentieth century, the Protestant church was unique in being a religious place that featured communal singing.[17] And insofar as Koreans' membership activities in the church included not only praise and Bible study but also work—manual labor, the selling of Bibles, evangelical activities, cooking, and so forth—one can imagine how the combination of a soloist as vocal leader and a chorus of vocalizing laborers would shape the social structures of church life. Consider as well the specific social value placed on the singing voice in Korea: in 2006 the head of a black-rice farming village called Sop'ori, on Chindo Island, in South Chŏlla Province, told me that a man who cannot sing is not powerful.[18] This cultural disposition toward song and the social expectation that all members will sing might help explain why Stuart Ling, Korean War soldier-turned-music teacher, wrote an article titled "Singing in Korea," in which he extolled the vocal skills of Koreans and marveled at the ubiquity of professional-quality singers during the Korean War.[19] Having observed some choir performances and rehearsals organized by a local chaplain, Ling pointed to a culturally grounded passion and lack of inhibition as the reasons why "they are not afraid of their own voices."[20]

More than fifty years after Ling published his observations, people involved in classical singing around the world also have taken note of Koreans' seemingly "natural" or "in-born" *(t'agonan)* capacity for singing. This often takes the form of essentializing ethnotheories that attribute the success of Korean singers to a variety of racial, ethnic, and linguistic factors. Such conceptions include the physiognomy of Korean faces, a fiery passion stemming from traditional Korean forms of coded emotionality, a perceived similarity between the Italian and Korean languages ("pure" vowels), similarities between Italian and Korean climates (hot summers) and geographies (hilly and peninsular). A well-known Korean soprano joked that the success of Korean singers on international stages must have something to do with *kimch'i,* the pickled vegetables that accompany nearly every meal. A professor of voice at a German conservatory referred to Korean singers as the "Sicilian Asians" because of the power and intensity of their voices. A Japanese acquaintance of mine even told me that successful singers in Japan are rumored to be ethnic Koreans who changed their names during the Japanese colonial period. She explained that it was the only way the Japanese public could account for the success of these people. The Japanese, she said, simply do not sing that well. And as one international Korean opera star told me, "In Korea we sing without shame."[21]

In general, there is a widespread belief in the superiority of Korean voices, whether as a product of "Koreanness" as culture and socialization or as a kind of natural genetic trait of "Koreans." In a similar way, there also has been a tendency to describe Koreans as naturally disposed toward Christianity. "A highly spiritual people" who are "natural evangelists," Koreans, it seems to some, needed only to receive the Gospel in order for their spiritual energies to be directed away from shamanism or Buddhism or even Confucianism and channeled toward Christianity.[22]

By the late nineteenth century, Pyongyang had such a pronounced Christian presence that missionaries referred to it as "the Jerusalem of the East."[23] During the country's colonial occupation by Japan, the activities of Korean churches and missionaries were increasingly restricted, and following the Second World War and Korea's division at the 38th parallel, thousands of Christian refugees fled to the South from Pyongyang and the northern provinces. In 1960, Protestant Christians accounted for only around 5 percent of South Korea's population, but by the late 1990s, approximately 20 percent of the population reported themselves to be Protestants.[24] Most commonly, scholars attribute the growth of Protestant Christianity to the missionary establishment of the first Western medical and educational institutions; to Korean nationalism during Japanese colonial rule; to the needs of populations "thrust into modernity" through economic transformation, industrialization, and urbanization; to specific missionary models; to Korea's own domestic evangelical campaigns; and to loyal congregationalism as reflecting a more general culture of neotribalism.[25]

To authorize and explain contemporary Koreans' evangelical zeal (as instantiated by the vast number of missionaries abroad), Christians often simply point to the sacrifices of foreign Protestant missionaries who translated the Bible into Korean and established medical and educational institutions.[26] This narrative of sacrifice sets up a specifically Christian arrangement of reciprocity, with a nation that "received help" from missionaries in the past emerging as a nation that "gives help" via missionaries in the present and future (see chapter 2). Singing is central to this equation.

Somang Church in particular is known among Christians in Seoul for the value it places on its choirs and choir members.[27] An Italian scholar who was visiting Seoul and had familiarity with Korean Presbyterian churches claimed that "everyone knows" that wealthy Korean Christian men look for potential wives among the women who sing in Somang's choirs. Many of the women, he said, will have studied voice at university, which serves as an index both of their class status and of their commitment to the church. Just before I left Chicago for long-term fieldwork, a Korean scholar visiting there told me that singing was the "golden ticket" for entering and learning about the life of churches like Somang. And when a Christian graduate student in Seoul found out that I was singing with a choir at Somang and would be performing with the choir at one of the congregants' weddings, she expressed her envy by telling me that it would be a "great honor" to have members of a Somang Church choir sing at her own wedding. Alas, she said, she had just a couple of music students recommended to her by a friend.

The choir and the singing voice are essential elements of Somang's practices of converting and cultivating Christians. For Somang ritual, *sŏngak* style singing has a purifying effect that helps create the ritual space in which the "true Word of God" can be passed on to the congregants. Choirs are typically formed of music students or recent graduates (who are often soloists at other churches as well), titled members of the church (e.g., elders and deacons), and members of the general congregation (some of whom may have studied voice in college). To audition successfully and sing in the choir is to send a signal to the congregation that one is of a certain caliber, not only of musicianship, but also of Christian personhood. Within the choirs themselves, the soloists—both their voices and their conduct—are held up as examples to which the rest of the choir must orient. This means that they are often held to a higher all-around standard of public behavior than other choir members. In my observation, the only member who was ever asked to leave the choir was asked to do so for missing rehearsals, declining to lead the choir in prayer, and failing to display sufficient enthusiasm, rather than for exhibiting any particular vocal shortcoming (he was a voice student).[28] However, if a person's singing is not sufficiently persuasive (for reasons of voice quality, musicality, pitch, or even emotionality), soloists might also be subtly encouraged by the conductor to seek additional training.

The evangelical function of *sŏngak* singers manifests outside the church in the form of Christian singing groups that engage in missionary activities abroad that are based primarily on the performance of *sŏngak*. For example, Christian students (from a number of different churches) in the voice department of Seoul National University created the SNU Praise Missionary Chorus (Sŏul Taehakkyo Ch'anyang Sŏn'gyodan). The chorus raises money through its concerts in Korea to fund mission trips throughout the world to evangelize through song. The chorus combines classical art music with explicitly Christian music to bring both "high culture" and the gospel to the unbaptized peoples of the world.[29]

Although they considered school to be extremely important for education, socialization, and certification, students in the SNU Praise Missionary Chorus and beyond generally described the main purpose of their vocal training as the fulfillment of their evangelical aspirations. Even as some of these singers moved abroad to attend a foreign conservatory or embarked on international professional careers as opera singers, they still were grounded in Christianity and the church as the foundation of their singing activities. For example, six years after winning first prize at the Placido Domingo International Voice Competition 2001, the young Korean tenor Kim Woo-kyung (Kim U-gyŏng) made his Metropolitan Opera debut opposite the now-famous Korean soprano Hong Hei-kyung (Hong Hye-gyŏng) in a 2007 production of Verdi's *La traviata*. Both leads have presented Christianity as a part of their professional identities. Hong speaks publicly about her "deep Christian faith" within Korean Presbyterianism.[30] Kim's professional website at that time was copyrighted by Gongdeok (Kongdŏk) Presbyterian Church.

Sŏngak as a semiotic register in Korea can be powerfully linked to a person's self-identification as a Christian. An interview with a baritone named Yŏng-gwang (lit., "Glory") provides evidence for this. Yŏng-gwang is the son of one of the top pastors at one of the largest Presbyterian churches in the world. In one of our discussions about singing, Yŏng-gwang compared the development of a singer's vocal technique with the development of personal faith. For this singer, they were parallel processes following similar paths, which, as he traced them in the air, mirrored each other. Yŏng-gwang explained that in the cultivation of both *sŏngak* singing and faith, a Christian faces periods of progress and setbacks as he or she seeks to overcome the habits in feeling and thought that one acquires by living in the world. Much like the singer whose e-mail alias announced to the world that he loved Jesus and *sŏngak,* Yŏng-gwang saw personal progress as the cultivation of a deeper and more complete understanding of the self as an expression of God, which can be manifested in the world through evangelism and song.

For some, like the members of the SNU Praise Missionary Chorus, an explicit mention of faith is always present in their self-descriptions as singers (even for those whom others consider to be less than ideal Christians). For others, a feeling of indebtedness to God for the health, stability, or beauty of the voice comes later in their career. Shin Youngok (Sin Yŏng-ok), a well-known professional soprano who graduated from Sŏnhwa Arts High School and SNU, wrote a book about the relationship between her faith and her career, titled *Sin Yŏng-ok ŭi ch'ansong: Hananim i sarang hasinŭn segye ŭi p'ŭrimadonna* (The Praise of Shin Youngok: The Prima Donna of the World Whom God Loves). The small book is divided into four parts and narrates her professional autobiography in terms of her relationship to God. In the final section, "Becoming the Messenger Who Communicates God's Love,"[31] Shin describes how a fellow Korean Christian finally convinced her (later in her life) that she should treat her voice as a vehicle for praising God. Whether or not the link is made explicit, for the Korean singer of *sŏngak,* the voice as an object of cultivation is intrinsically linked to a broader evangelical mode of sociality that is being forged in the church.

BLENDED REGISTERS AND CHRISTIAN ENREGISTERMENT

Korean Christians still celebrate—or recognize, at a minimum—two traditional holidays, both of which follow the lunar calendar, even though they are not technically Christian holidays: Lunar New Year's Day (Sŏllal), in late winter, and the Harvest Moon Festival (Ch'usŏk), in early autumn. Historically they were days on which Koreans would carry out elaborate forms of ancestor worship. Among non-Christians, this practice is still alive. And even though ancestor worship has largely been erased from Christian practice, Korean Christians still use these holidays to visit family outside Seoul, present gifts to the elderly, and eat together.[32] Stress can build as these holidays approach, when the wives of eldest sons prepare food for consumption (and judgment) by the patrilineal network, and members of the extended family dread the clogged highways they will have to travel, which turn what normally might be a quick drive into an all-day affair.

During these holidays, Christian churches occasionally allow the less-threatening elements of Korea's non-Christian past into worship services. For example, a pastor might wear the traditional *hanbok* as he preaches, or a church group might organize a game of *yut* for the Sunday school children. It is not uncommon to hear traditional Korean instruments in the service, such as the *taegŭm* (a flute) or *kayagŭm* (a zither).[33] The extent to which this is the case depends in large part on the denomination and the policies of the individual church.

In 2008, Ch'usŏk fell on September 14, a Sunday. At Somang Church, Reverend Kim did not wear a *hanbok*, instead donning his normal suit and tie. He gave a sermon titled *"Hamkke chŭlgŏwŏhara"* (Let's Enjoy Together), based on Deuteronomy 16:13–17, which gives instruction for the celebration of the Feast of Tabernacles. Pastor Kim instructed his congregation to be joyful with their neighbors and to form a community of believers that is happy in God. Making no mention of the ancestors, he told the congregation that Christians should celebrate and be thankful for God's gift of abundance (a fitting sentiment in the wealthy Somang Church). He lamented the increasing number of suicides in South Korea and encouraged the congregation not merely to drive forward without ceasing, as they had done throughout the twentieth century, but also to find happiness in the joys of their present lives.[34] He also encouraged them to join in the world that God created and enjoy human relationships.[35] In this joy of community, explained Kim, believers can renew the law of God and start again, with the challenge of rebirth overcoming the challenges of the past. Kim's sermon invoked the same chronotope that he had made explicit at several points before, namely, that Korea had arrived in the present as an advanced nation and emanating spiritual center, and its people no longer had to suffer through the process of national maturation and relentless striving that had been so painful for their Christian predecessors.

The music performed at the church services that day was like that of other days, Christian songs sung in a *sŏngak* style, with the exception of one piece. During the fifth service, a member of the chorus played the offertory song *(hŏn'gŭmsong)* as a solo instrumental version of "You Raise Me Up," an inspirational pop song that has become a part of the standard Christian church repertoire in Korea. She played it not on the violin or cello (which would have been normal for the service) but rather on a two-stringed bowed traditional instrument called the *haegŭm,* accompanied by a piano.

As I listened to the buzzing, almost nasal sound of the instrument, I was struck by how out of place it sounded in relation to the music one normally hears at Somang Church. I realized suddenly that although various aspects of pre-Christian Korea appeared occasionally in church services, I had never once heard a remotely traditional-sounding *voice* singing in the church. Whatever traditional instruments might have appeared from time to time, church choirs at Somang Church always maintained a vocal style modeled on European-style classical music, even when they sang music with traditional elements (e.g., composed from a pentatonic scale), performed wearing a *hanbok* instead of choir robes *(sŏnggadae ŭibok)*, or were accompanied by the *changgu* (an hourglass-shaped Korean drum). That is, even when explicitly marked aspects of pre-Christian Korea were celebrated—or tolerated—traditional-sounding voices were silenced entirely.

When I asked people at Somang Church whether any specifically Korean vocal styles could be used in church services, they consistently told me that traditional *(chŏnt'ongjŏk in)* styles of singing were not appropriate for church. "We don't sing like that here." This ban extended to the singing styles of Confucian court music *(aak)*, "folk" music such as work songs *(nodongga)* or folk songs *(minyo)*, the sung narratives of *p'ansori*, and older styles of "popular" music, such as *t'ŭrot'ŭ* ("trot").[36] In general, and with the exception of the Christian pop songs that one heard at the youth service on Sunday afternoons, anything that did not sound like *sŏngak*—even coming from untrained singers—was deemed inappropriate for church.

In trying to figure out why traditional vocal styles should be off limits at church, I phrased my questions in a number of different ways. Everyone I asked, without exception, told me that traditional styles—though they might be artistic, technically demanding, and valuable as cultural "heritage" *(munhwa yusan)*—were nonetheless "opposite" *(pandae)* to or "totally different" *(chŏnhyŏ tarŭda)* from the singing technique *(palsŏng)* or method *(pangbŏp)* that should be used in church. I was told that traditional vocal sounds were emotional but not always beautiful. They could reflect sadness but could not glorify God or reflect his grace. I was told that the sounds were not holy or were unnatural. They were not styles for praising God, because they sounded too sad and conjured up too much of the suffering of the past. Even informants who lacked a technical vocabulary for describing such things concurred that there was no place for traditional vocal qualities in the worship services of Somang Church. Some people even corrected my approach to the question: to their Christian ears, the sounds of classical-style singing in church were as thoroughly Korean as any traditional sounds one might encounter. It was the traditional vocal styles that sounded foreign to them.

In these simple descriptions, nomic assertions, and normative statements, I encountered a specific, ethically charged, ideologically loaded articulation of an overarching aesthetic framework, situated historically in a broader story about singing in Korean churches. Vocal sounds were evaluated and differentiated according to their appropriateness and effectiveness for certain practices deemed essential to the viability and perpetuation of the institution. Within the institutional ideology of the church, older vocal styles were not deemed suitable for praise and thus had no place in a worship service. While there might be a place for traditional sounds of other sorts in and beyond the church, the Christian *voice* had to be purified and purged of these sounds. For the sung voice, only *sŏngak* sounds were deemed worthy to represent the values of the church.

At the level of the vocal apparatus itself, an important technical distinction between traditional singing styles and *sŏngak* stems from the different uses of what singers call "head voice" and "chest voice." These different voices are also sometimes referred to as vocal registers, extending metaphorically the notion of pipe organ registration, which combines different stops to create particular kinds of timbre that can be used to "play the same thing."[37]

The notion of the "head" and "chest" as descriptors for vocal registers pertains to the manner of vocal-cord vibration, the proprioceptively felt place of these vibrations in the singer, and the qualia of the sound that a listener perceives. Such perceptions are often dependent on metaphor for their verbal description. Chest voice seems to emerge from the throat and chest, with a "denser," "heavier" sound. Head voice has a "lighter," "thinner" sound and seems to resonate in the face or head.[38] In traditional Korean singing (as in most singing styles, actually) and most notably in *p'ansori,* there is an audible and distinctive "break" between registers, with a highly developed and nuanced chest register and a contrasting, marked head register, sometimes followed by an even higher "falsetto" produced by the edges of the vocal cords.[39] In *sŏngak,* there is a mixing, blending, or unifying of the different registers so that the voice sounds "even" from the very bottom to the very top of the range, neither hollow or breathy on the low notes nor strained or squeezed on the high notes. In order to achieve this blending, a singer must develop and strengthen the head voice, so that it can be "carried down" the scale, rather than "pushing" the chest voice "up." So important is a reinforced head voice for distinguishing sŏngak and its attributes in Korea that many of my nonspecialist informants emphasized the chest voice when emulating traditional singing and emphasized the head voice when emulating sŏngak singing.

In fact, sŏngak singers often begin their biographical narratives of singing by talking about the first time they were able to leave the chest voice and produce sounds in the head voice. Technically, the word for chest voice in Korean is hyungsŏng, and the head voice is tusŏng. While tusŏng is widely used for head voice, chest voice is often referred to as chinsŏng ("true" voice, in contrast to kasŏng, or "false," voice, i.e., falsetto) or as saengsori ("raw" or "unconditioned" sound). Often it is simply described with the loan-word compound pelt'ing saundŭ (belting sound). For many singers, this practical realization of the difference between the two kinds of voices generally takes place in a school or a church choir, where an attentive choir conductor takes an interest in a younger singer and encourages the development of this new kind of vocal register.

Take, for example, Yun-gyŏng, who was a student at one of Seoul's top voice programs when I got to know her in 2008. In one of our discussions of her development as a singer, she began immediately with a distinction between the way most children sing and the way she had begun to sing in order to audition for a junior high school for the arts. She demonstrated this distinction by producing a glissando on a faucalized yet focused head voice articulated on a highly rounded [u] vowel (represented by an arced arrow), followed by three separated, nasal-sounding, ventriculated chest voice sounds on a widely articulated [a] vowel (represented by three consecutive horizontal arrows). The first [a] vowel was initiated with a nasal [n], and the following sounds were each initiated with a marked glottal onset. And unlike the glissando [u], she produced the three [a]s pitched as three separate notes (the first and the third being the same pitch) to contrast not only the qualia of the voice but also the un-legato (i.e., unconnected) and abrupt sound of the child's chest voice. In this example, the vocalic change, emphasized by the labial rounding versus spreading, gentle versus abrupt onsets, and smooth versus rough tonal transitions (indicated with arrows), structured Yun-gyŏng's example of the difference.

EXCERPT 3.1

Y: Ch'odŭng hakko i hangnyŏn ttae, tongyo, aegidŭl purŭnŭn kŏ. Irŏhan sŏngakchŏk in

/u: ~ /

irŏn palsŏng i anira irŏk'e

/ na: → ʔa: →ʰ ʔa: → /

irŏn norae rŭl hadaga, ch'odŭng hakkyo [inaudible] toemyŏnsŏ yewŏn, kŭ, Yewŏn, Yewŏn Hakkyo, yesul chunghakkyo e kagi wihaesŏ [. . .] Sŏul Yesul Kodŭng Hakkyo kagi chŏn e Yewŏn Chunghakkyo. Yewŏn Chunghakkyo kagi wihaesŏ ije, kŭttae put'ŏ, ije

/u: ~ /

irŏn palsŏng ŭl yŏnsŭp haessŏyo.

N: Ŏttŏk'e i tusŏng ŭl paewŏssŏyo? Ije tarŭn aedŭl i
/ʔa:/

Y: Ch'ŏŭm enŭn kasŏng, ttŭiwŏsŏ, kŭge irŏk'e, ŏ,

/u: ~ /

irŏn sori rŭl sŏnsaengnim i, ŏ, kŭrŏn sori rŭl naeya handa. Kŭrŏn sori rŭl naemyŏnsŏ [inaudible], mwŏrago, [inaudible] t'imbŭl?

N: /tæmbɤ/

Y: /tæmbɤ/. Ije ch'ŏŭm enŭn

/uʰ:/

irŏn sori yŏttaga chŏmjŏm [inaudible] sal ŭl puch'igo sal ŭl puch'yŏsŏ yakkan chogŭm chogŭmsik pantchak pantchak hage. Ta kŭrok'e norae rŭl haetchyo.

Y: In the second year of elementary school, children's songs, what all children, kids sing. Not this kind of sŏngak-style

/u: ~ /

not that vocal technique, but this way

/na: → ʔa: →ʰ ʔa: → /

I sang this way, then after entering elementary school [inaudible], in order to go to Yewŏn, um Yewŏn, Yewŏn School, a junior high school for the arts [. . .] Before I went to Seoul Arts High School, [I went to] Yewŏn Junior High School. In order to go to Yewŏn Junior High School, from then on, from that time, from then on I practiced

/u: ~ /

this vocal technique.

N: How did you learn this head voice? At that time other kids [were doing]   /ʔa:/

Y: At first, falsetto, floating, that is, um,

/u: ~ /

this kind of sound. The teacher, um, said I needed to make that kind of sound. Making that kind of sound, [inaudible] how do you say, [inaudible] timbre [t'imbŭl]?

N: Timbre.

Y: Timbre. At that time, at first it was a sound like

/uʰ:/

and then [inaudible] little by little I added weight, and by adding weight, slightly, bit by bit it began to sparkle. I sang everything like that, you know.

As she explained the development of her head voice in this last turn, she produced a very breathy falsetto on [uʰ] as a kind of pure head voice with no depth or color (the superscript *h* denotes breathiness). But little by little, she explained, she was able to "add weight" and gradually the voice began to "sparkle," as her earlier examples of [u] had done. This adding of weight and sparkling is the function of blending the head voice with the chest voice, so that a reinforced head voice has both "depth" and "ring" to it, while not sounding tight or forced as a pure chest voice. This mixing of phonosonic qualia is often referred to by yet another metaphor, the Italian dvandva compound *chiaroscuro* (light-dark).

When I asked Yun-gyŏng why she decided to become a singer, she explained that she had originally wanted to become a dancer, but because of her small stature she had a "handicap" *(haendik'aep)*. So she transitioned to voice with the encouragement of her Presbyterian church choir conductor and her parents.[40] She then told me that at that time she had attended the Saemunan Church and added proudly that it was the first church in Korea, founded in 1887 by the Presbyterian missionary Horace G. Underwood. It was in this church where she first was encouraged to continue singing, and it was with this institutionalized support that her voice developed into something she could call *sŏngak:*

EXCERPT 3.2

Kŭ kyohoe e tanidaga chigŭm ŭn tarŭn kyohoe ro omgigin hannŭnde, kŭ kyohoe e tanimyŏnsŏ norae rŭl mani chŏphaetchyo. Kŭrigo sŏnggadae e issŏssŭl ttae, sollo rŭl chihwija sŏnsaengnim i chayŏn sŭrŏpke sik'yŏ chugo, kŭrŏk'e hamyŏnsŏ chuwi esŏ "chal handa, sori yeppŭda." Irŏk'e chŏmjŏmjŏm kŭrŏk'e hadaga, sŏngak ŭl hage toen kŏt kat'ayo.

I used to attend that church, but now I have moved to another church. When I attended that church I learned many songs. And when I was in the choir, the conductor naturally gave me solos, and in so doing, [people] around me [said,] "Good job, pretty voice." It seems in that way, gradually I proceeded and got into *sŏngak.* [laughing]

My discussion with Yun-gyŏng moved from solos in church to her training at school, to her current teacher, to her desire to go to Vienna for further study, to the loudness of her voice, and finally to the details of her technique, such as singing high notes and breathing. Our conversation about singing loudly led me to ask her opinion of Korean traditional singing styles, to which she responded:

EXCERPT 3.3

Y: *Nŏmu uri rang chŏngbandae. Norae inde kat'ŭn norae chiman chŏngbandae.Uri nŭn mok i tach'imyŏn andoenikka irŏk'e hangsang pudŭrŏpke sori rŭl naenŭn pangbŏp ŭl yŏn'gu hago, muri ka kaji ank'e orae yŏnsŭp hanŭn pangbŏp ŭl yŏn'gu hago, kyaene nŭn p'okp'osu mit esŏ hanbŏn mok i t'ŏjyŏya toejanayo. P'i rŭl t'ohaeyajiman kyŏngji e irŭrŏtta. Kŭraesŏ, mak kwansim i itkŏna kŭrŏch'i ank'o, na rang tarŭn norae sujun. Irŏn kŏt kat'ayo.*

Y: It's too much the complete opposite of us. Although it's singing, even if it's also a type of singing, it's the complete opposite. Because we should not injure our throats, we study this method of producing sound softly all the time, and study a method of practicing for a long time without excess, whereas they have their throat burst one time, standing underneath a waterfall, you know. Only after they throw up blood do they attain mastery. Therefore, I am not very interested. I regard it as a different standard of singing. It's like this.

N: *Mani tŭrŏ pwassŏyo?*

N: Have you heard much of it?

Y: *Mani tŭro pojinŭn anassŏyo.*

Y: I have not heard much of it.

N: *Choa haeyo?*

N: Do you like it?

Y: *Ani, pyŏllo.*

Y: No, not really.

N: *Kŭrŏnde i pilding esŏ manŭn p'ansori rŭl kongbu hanŭn saramdŭl i innŭnde i saram irang kwan'gye issŏyo? I saram hant'e mani mal haeyo?*

N: But in this building there are a lot of people who study *p'ansori*. Do you have relationships with these people? Do you speak to these people much?

Y: *Aniyo. Pyŏllo. Sŏro e taehaesŏ ch'amgyŏn hagŏna kŭrŏn kŏn ŏpsŏyo. Ŏttŏk'e pomyŏn toege tarŭnikka.*

Y: No. Not really. We don't interfere with each other or anything like that. It is because [we] are extremely different.

Just like others I met at various churches and music schools throughout Seoul, Yun-gyŏng explained that traditional singing was the "complete opposite" of *sŏngak*. She sought to protect her voice and treat it softly and contrasted this practice with the way *p'ansori* singers are mythically expected to bleed from the throat in order to achieve greatness. And although she shared the practice rooms, indeed the entire music building, with singers of traditional music, she had heard little of it and had hardly any contact with the other students. However you look at it, she said, even if they are singing the same song, *sŏngak* singers and traditional singers are "extremely different." One of the reasons for this difference—and for the restricted social relations that such a difference engenders—is the difference in vocal qualia and their ideological loading.

One of the key differences between traditional singing and the *sŏngak* style adopted in Yun-gyŏng's church and elsewhere is in the treatment and conditioning of the vocal apparatus itself, that is, the bodily action and its attendant sensations involved in singing. As I discussed in chapter 1, *sŏngak* singing relies on formant resonance (peaks of acoustic energy created by positioning and shaping resonators in the pharyngeal, oral, and nasal cavities) instead of glottal friction (produced by tension of the vocal folds) for amplification. Forms of Korean vocalization normally classified as traditional, on the other hand, while also not originally intended to rely on prosthetic amplification from microphones, have a very different method of sound production and system of aesthetic evaluation. As Byungwon Lee writes in *Styles and Esthetics in Korean Traditional Music*, a "raspy, buzzing sound is the preferred timbre in the Korean voice."[41] This sonic ideal and its phonic design are often related to *p'ansori* singing as a kind of baseline standard for the traditional sound. While *p'ansori*'s cultural value usually is exalted as Korea's version of European opera, its aesthetic of sound and method of production concerning the body are generally contrasted with Western music. A publication on *p'ansori* issued by the National Center for Korean Traditional Performing Arts (NCKTPA) does just this:

> Traditional musics of different countries use a large variety of vocal production methods. As the bel canto style is used in Western classical music, *p'ansori* also has a unique method of producing vocal tones. In bel canto, vocal tones are produced by using abdominal breathing to draw air through an open larynx while focusing resonation in the facial "mask." *P'ansori* also uses abdominal breathing. However, tones are produced as the air is forcefully thrust through taut vocal cords and larynx, thereby creating a harsh or rough tone quality, as compared to the clear sound of bel canto singing.[42]

This contrast applies to the binary between the sonic aesthetics of traditional and more modern forms and also to the competing ideologies of the use of the body in the phonic production of vocal sound.[43] For instance, Johan Sundberg, the leading expert on the phonetics of European-style classical singing, and two of his colleagues wrote an article on what they termed the "throaty voice" for the *Journal of Voice*. Note the ideological distinction between "healthy" and "unhealthy" manners of vocalization invoked in their reported findings below:

> Our results strongly suggest that throaty voice quality is associated with a narrowing of the pharynx. It is tempting to speculate that this narrowing is

caused by a contraction of the middle constrictor muscle, which also tends to raise the larynx. A raised larynx is often associated with a more *hyperfunctional* type of phonation. Thus, a narrowing of the pharynx would easily (if not necessarily) lead to a firmer glottal adduction. This result, in turn, may explain why throaty/guttural quality has been regarded even as *harmful to the voice. Hyperadduction* increases *collision force* of the vocal folds during phonation, which means higher *mechanical loading* on the vocal fold tissue and, hence, a higher risk for *tissue damage.* (italics mine)[44]

It is important to note here that the phenomena of "tissue damage" and "harm" are observed from the perspective of European classical music training, which associates the "functional" with the "beautiful." The phonic combination of a higher larynx, restricted pharynx, and higher subglottic pressure delivers a sound (e.g., raspy, harsh, rough) and a bodily experience (tense, squeezed, painful) that is understood to opposite to the values of Western classical singing. Traditional musicians do not necessarily see traditional Korean styles of vocalization as harmful or damaging. The 2004 publication of the NCKTPA claims that singers develop "special calluses" and "end up having different vocal cords from those of other people."[45]

A Korean television documentary on *p'ansori* singing explores the differences between *p'ansori* singers and *sŏngak,* or Western *(sŏyang),* singers. *Sori rŭl ŏtta, tŭgŭm* (Receiving the Sound, *Tŭgŭm*) features Professor Hong Ki-hwan, of Chŏnbuk National University Hospital, who explains that the vocal cords of a *sŏngak* singer are normal *(chŏngsang ida),* perfect *(wanbyŏk hada),* and clean *(kkaekkŭthada)*—without flaws or scars *(hŭm i ŏpta).*[46] In contrast, he explains that the vocal cords of a *p'ansori* singer are rough and uneven, allowing streams of air to pass through the vibrating vocal cords, thereby creating a *"shwin sori"*—a sound that is "hoarse." The film presents video stills of the anatomical differences of the vocal cords of the two kinds of singers (figures 8 and 9).

Students and professionals of Korean traditional music often mentioned this embodied distinction to me. One young *p'ansori* singer told me that the vocal cords in singing are just like the fingers in playing the guitar or the violin: a singer needs to build up calluses. A singer will get blisters and she will bleed, but if she keeps practicing, at some point she will finally be able to sing.[47] One of the ways in which this training takes place is by sequestering oneself in a forest and attempting to sing "over" the sound of a waterfall, as Yun-gyŏng described above. This legend is widespread in Korea, and many traditional musicians as well as nonexperts recounted versions of this method for me. The 2004 NCKTPA

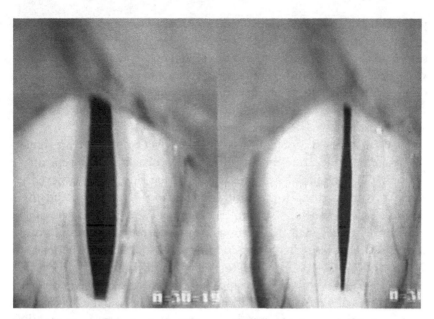

FIGURE 8. Vocal cords of a singer of Western classical music (courtesy of Professor Hong Ki-hwan).

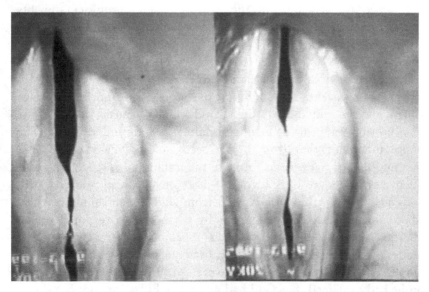

FIGURE 9. Vocal cords of a singer of *p'ansori* (courtesy of Professor Hong Ki-hwan).

publication on *p'ansori* states, "*[P'ansori]* singers work diligently to master the distinct vocal timbres required by the genre. . . . *p'ansori* singers in the past often went into the mountains in order to train their voices; there they would practice against the sounds of waterfalls and other sounds of nature. Formerly, it was believed that only when a singer developed a voice that could eclipse the sound of even a mighty waterfall had s/he mastered the desired vocal quality."[48]

Such instances of bleeding and singing over waterfalls are cited throughout the literature on *p'ansori*.[49] Legend has it that once a singer's sound can be heard over the waterfall, the singer has achieved a stage of vocal perfection or maturation, *tŭgŭm ŭi kyŏngji*. And this *tŭgŭm*, or achievement of sound, is generally thought to be possible only through a regimen that combines often corporeally painful vocal practice with suffering and hardship in one's broader life experiences. The 2004 NCKTPA publication states that *p'ansori* singers "often have to endure extreme physical hardships in order to develop the necessary vocal timbres of *p'ansori*."[50] Many of my informants told me that teachers still take their students into the forest to practice next to waterfalls but that the event is usually organized around seeing how "it used to be," rather than employed as a contemporary practice. This ideology of self-induced physical hardship and the resulting phonosonic entailments of roughness and harshness are much of what students and professionals of *sŏngak* in Korea find so antithetical to their own aesthetics and singing style.

For a group that sees itself as advanced, spiritually enlightened, blessed with peace from the suffering of the ancestors, indebted to Jesus Christ, and committed to glorifying God with holy music, the life of the *p'ansori* singer appears to be one of pointless labor and suffering. The important point is that, from the perspective of my Presbyterian Christian informants, the various forms of the traditional voice and its productive practices are backward, self-destructive, forced, undeveloped, and unclean. That the voice is a gift from God, which should be cherished and protected, is made clear by Chang-wŏn's response to my question as to whether the voice varies among different genres and modes of vocalization, for example, between speech and song or even among different emotional states expressed through the voice. Earlier on he had explained that God had given him his voice and that therefore he should take great care of the gift. He insisted that natural singing is singing in the manner intended by God, and *sŏngak* technique is the technique best designed to cultivate an evangelist-singer by revealing the natural, God-given voice. Here he explains how a Christian might think about caring for and cultivating the voice in this way.

EXCERPT 3.4

Norae rŭl chal, choŭn sori ro norae rŭl haryŏmyŏn, ŭm, igŏl ŏttŏk'e pomyŏn Kidokkyojok in saenggak il su innŭnde Hananim i na hant'e chun kŏllo [k'ŏt ŭro] kajang choŭn sangt'ae ro kajang p'yŏnan hage norae rŭl haeya. Inwijŏk in him i tŭrŏ kaji anaya. Kajang chayŏn sŭrŏun moksori ka naondago mal hagŏdŭnyo. Inwijŏk in, mwŏ,

[ʔʌ] [ʔʌ]

irŏk'e hamyŏn pyŏllo choŭn moksori ka naoji annŭnda. Kŭraesŏ

[a], [a]

irŏk'e haessŭl ttae choŭn moksori ka.

Singing well, if you want to sing a song with a really good sound, um, I suppose this could be a Christian way of thinking about it. Using what God has given me, I have to sing in the best condition and most peacefully. Artificial [lit. "man-made"] power shouldn't enter into it, so that the most natural voice comes out, they always say. If you make an artificial sound like

[ʔʌ] [ʔʌ]

then the sound that comes out won't be particularly good. Therefore if you do it like

[a], [a]

it's a good voice.

In a manner similar to Yun-gyŏng's description of developing the head voice, Chang-wŏn used vowel differentiation and an exaggerated glottal onset to demonstrate the difference between natural and artificial vocal sounds. He then later explained that whether one is feeling upset or joyful or holy or solemn, the tone or character of the voice might change, but the God-given voice itself should not change. In this manner, the voice is like faith: cultivating vocal or spiritual maturity means revealing and focusing on God's gift or will.

According to these singers, the singing styles of the past, while valuable as relics of history, are products of an inferior worldview; such methods of training are the attempts of people who lack proper teachers to learn how to sing—just as, within this ideology, shamanism and Buddhism in Korea are viewed as the attempts to reach God by people without the Gospels. Singers of *sŏngak* do admit that traditional singing styles can display a certain technical virtuosity, require musical mastery and talent, and have some qualities of beauty. But for many of them, these styles, like the voices of students who have not yet learned how to sing "properly" or whose throats are not "ready," are stunted, held back, forced, and artificially manipulated. For these singers, the traditional styles are, in short, "unnatural," "unhealthy," and "unfree."

For these singers, the basis for Korean vocal aesthetics and affective relation to sound no longer should be the suffering of the past or the struggle for independence, development, or democracy, but rather the beauty and grace of Jesus Christ who has blessed their country with advancement and abundance. The narrative cued up by the vocal ideal of *sŏngak* fits with that of the church overall. It relegates suffering and hardship to the past and treats the contemporary period as an emergent time of peace, beauty, and enlightenment. The strained vocal cords and their calluses, set to vibration by air through a tensed throat, become the expression and the embodiment of the generalized qualities of a troubled, pre-Christian, Korean history. *P'ansori*'s practical and aesthetic opposite, *sŏngak*, with a focus on preventing vocal fatigue and wear, and a method for producing a sound that is clear and clean, rather than raspy and rough, becomes the emblem of a beautiful, advanced, Christian present—and of the people who inhabit it.

PHONOSONIC VARIATION AND CHANGE

In an article titled "Mission to Korea," published in 1949 in the *Music Educators Journal,* shortly before the start of the Korean War, Max Noah described what he perceived to be the state of music education in Korea. The author had come to Korea under the auspices of the U.S. military government there to train teachers in the "methods, techniques, and procedures . . . essential to education in a democratic society." Describing what he called a people "in a stage of transition from a feudal to a modern society," Noah began by listing some of the aspects of this transition. Early in the article, he observed that while certain infrastructural pieces of a modern society were visible, there was at the same time a lack of modern behavior. Focusing on music education and training, which he described as basically a Japanese system established through the colonial period, Noah stated, "Korea has always been a musical nation. . . . Music in Korea has changed as the country's people have changed," and linked changes in the genres of musical expression to sociocultural transitions. He followed with a brief discussion of music in Korea, from the "primitive" time when "music was used only to frighten away evil," to the Chosŏn dynasty and Korean court music, to Japanese annexation, when native Korean cultural elements were suppressed, and then to the contemporary status of Western music.[51]

Noah explained that he was impressed by the widespread teaching of Western music in the schools but was disappointed in the way that it was being transmitted. His main concern was that the militaristic uses of music and its emphasis on powerful singing were preventing Koreans from understanding and enjoying the beauty of the art form and cultivating the aesthetic sensibilities necessary for a developed nation.

> [Under Japanese rule] Patriotric and martial rhythms in both vocal and instrumental music produced loud singing and playing, feelings of heroism and fighting spirit. There was small consideration for the correct use of the child's voice or the child's attitude toward the appreciation of the beautiful tones of color which are intricate ingredients of voice blending. . . . The standards of the high school performances are comparable to those found in the elementary schools, technically good but tonally very bad. . . . Most chorus directors use selections from the operas and oratorios which, in most instances, result in forced singing and shouting tones.[52]

I have extracted an image from Max Noah's 1949 article (figure 10). The image, under which Noah wrote the caption, "Fifth-grade girls, Chong Ge Elementary School, vocalizing," presents a clear example of the embodied, corporeally habituated phonic method that produced the sonic entailments to which Noah was reacting. In this case, it is not merely the treatment of the vocal cords, hidden from the eyes of the listener, as in figures 8 and 9 above, but also the visible facial kinesics of the singer that are linked to the vocal style and its sonic entailments. This can be seen in the mouth shape of the young girl just to the right of center in the front row of figure 10. Vocalizing on what is probably an [a] vowel, the aperture of the mouth is wide and the buccal cavity is shallow, with the tongue presumably flattened at the bottom of the mouth, the larynx raised, and the resonant space restricted to the front of the mouth. Instead of supplying my own ideologically loaded descriptors for the qualia I imagine I would experience when hearing such a voice, I will simply say that this mouth shape and phonic production method will generally result in the kinds of sounds that Yun-gyŏng described above regarding the ventriculated voices of children and the sounds of children singing that Homer Hulbert, in his 1909 memoirs of Korea, described as "each one shout[ing] at the top of his or her voice," that is, the "belting sound" that children make before they learn to use the so-called head voice.[53]

This mouth shape can be observed in the singing practices of older people as well. For example, on a trip to Kŭmgangsan (Diamond

FIGURE 10. Children vocalizing in Seoul, ca. 1949 (photo by Max Noah).

Mountain), in North Korea, I shared a bus with a group of rowdy, fun-loving men and women in their fifties, sixties, and seventies. Most of them had come as a group from Pongch'ŏn, a working-class area in the south of Seoul. These people were generous with their food, endearingly teased our young, inept tour guide, and, despite the sometimes-frightening scenes and grim landscape outside our bus, joked and laughed constantly. On the afternoon of the second day, we had just finished a hike and were waiting in a dirt parking lot near the trailhead. Behind the buses was a row of outhouses, beyond which were a dozen or so soldiers with guns who watched over a dozen or so peasants engaged in something that resembled digging (although I could never quite make out what kind of work was actually being done). My older traveling companions sat down beside the outhouses, opened bottles of soju, and began drinking the liquor out of paper cups. When the tour guides asked them to return to the bus (presumably for their safety), some of them became agitated—and grew even more so when we were forced to wait on the bus without moving. To break the sour mood, one man decided to stand and sing "at the top of his voice" in a manner that songak singers later described, when I played the recording for them, as rough, unhealthy, and—with a descriptor that I discuss in detail in chapter 4—unclean.

As the man sang the line, *"A tto tasi ch'ajaoma Pusan hanggu ya!"* (Ah, I'll come back again, Pusan Harbor!) from the popular song, "Chal ikkŏra Pusanhang" (Farewell, Pusan Harbor), the shape of his wide mouth resembled that of the young girl pictured above. So wide was his mouth that one could see the flatness of his tongue. And so tense were the muscles of his throat that they bulged through the skin. While this song was simply a popular tune of this man's generation—by no means *p'ansori,* which is considered a form of high art that takes a lifetime of dedication to master and which few dare to undertake—his way of singing it nonetheless bore a striking resemblance to many of the mouth shapes and facial gestures that one can observe among *p'ansori* singers onstage. Similar phonic combinations of articulation and muscular tension produce similar sonic entailments, such that the voices of the young girl in the middle of the twentieth century and the grown man at the start of the twenty-first century approximate, within a cultural system of vocalic differentiation, the sound of *p'ansori* singers as compared to that of *sŏngak* singers. Hence it was no surprise that my informants, in structured exercises as well as in informal conversation, referred to all of these kinds of voices as unhealthy and unclean.

In contrast, consider a singer like the soprano Kim Yŏng-mi, a particularly powerful example of the personification of what many Christians in Korea view as the emblematic voice of holy Christian personhood. When she sings—whether it is gospel music or opera—her lips are extended and rounded, and her jaw is low rather than wide, creating more vertical space in the vocal chamber. Kim Yŏng-mi stands as an exemplary singer and as an exemplary Christian in Seoul, and her vocal style, the sound she produces, and the manner of its production together serve as a phonosonic prototype for the stereotyped reproduction of vocalization for other Christians in Seoul. She is authorized by wealthy churches in Seoul, which, as we saw in chapter 2, project a chronotope of Christian progress onto Korean society and thereby divide members of its population into the categories of an enlightened, Christian present and an unenlightened, un-Christian past. Kim's voice becomes a semiotic expression of institutional—ecclesiastical—interests by anchoring these dimensions of sociocultural progress to the enregisterment of *sŏngak* as an expression and embodiment of Christian personhood.

The bodily dimensions of phonosonic enregisterment were visible in the mouth shapes of the members of the Somang Church choir with whom I sang during my fieldwork. These singers' mouths made a similar shape, far more vertical than the horizontal shapes we saw in figure 10 above. The vertical rounding and aperture of the mouth during song can even serve as a sign to nonspecialists of proficiency in *sŏngak*: one of my non-Christian friends, who was neither a singer nor a connoisseur of *sŏngak*, immediately and correctly identified one of the soloists of the choir in a video recording simply on the basis of the shape of the singer's mouth.

In this choir, the topic of "voice blending," mentioned in the quote by Max Noah above, was prominent in the choir conductor's directives for the singers. In trying to train members of the choir to sing so that individual voices did not stick out, the conductor often mobilized various types of personhood as stereotypical figures of alterity; singers were instructed not to sing like these people. These models often took the form of typifiable personae as a kind of residue of Korea's past and also, but more implicitly, as examples of the lower classes. For example, when men in the choir would sing too forcefully, with too much sub-glottic pressure and with so much tension at the glottis that the fundamental pitch was weakened (i.e., their pitch was "flat"), she would ask them not to sing like such *ajŏssi*. The term literally means "uncle" but was understood in this context refer to older men with a reputation for disregarding contemporary, refined social decorum.[54] I often heard male singers in the choir reprimanded, albeit in a lighthearted way, for singing with an *ajŏssi* voice, as if the singer had been among friends with a microphone in a song room, or *noraebang* (or on a tour bus in North Korea). In such cases, the conductor would ask them to sing more softly, with more "elegance," using the loan word *ellegangsŭ*.

Likewise, when women in the choir would sing with too much vibrato or would sing so loudly that they appeared to be singing for themselves rather than for the congregation, the conductor would remind them that church service was not a *kuyŏk yebae*. Korean churches are often so large that they must be organized into regional groups to maintain social and ecclesiastical cohesion. The *kuyŏk yebae* (district worship) is a local prayer gathering of a regional group at a small scale, usually populated by middle-aged, married women, often, somewhat pejoratively these days, referred to as *ajumma* (literally, "auntie"). Participants in a *kuyŏk yebae* are thought to sing loudly and shrilly together, without regard for an audience. In contrast to *samo* (literally, "wife of a teacher," usually combined with the honorific suffix *-nim*), which is the respectful term used for women who are seen to have "money and taste," *ajumma* has come to mean women who are not young, not sophisticated, and not rich.[55] At the *kuyŏk yebae*, one's enthusiasm and sincerity of purpose (whether that purpose is to sing to God or to demonstrate one's devotion in public) are thought to override the aesthetic standards and evangelical purpose of choral performance; the *ajumma* voice is thus identified with the hymns that are sung in this manner.

From the perspective of the advanced singer of *sŏngak*, the residue of Korea's past is still present even in the voices of contemporary Christians. Both categories of person, *ajŏssi* and *ajumma*, are known for disruptive behavior: whereas the *ajŏssi* is known for his space-consuming wide stance on subways, his abrasive speaking voice on cell phones, and the noise he makes while eating, the *ajumma* is known for aggressive behavior at markets, assertiveness in interaction, and general pushiness regarding matters having to do with her family. For this upper-class, educated, relatively wealthy choir, the roughness and abrasiveness of the *ajŏssi* voice become a reminder of the hypermasculine men of Korea's militarized past and the machismo of older and lower-class males; the shrillness and exaggerated vibrato of the *ajumma* voice become a reminder of "a generation of aggressive modern wives, the backstage managers of rapid industrialization," as well as those who are still striving for social mobility within the church.[56] In the conductor's directives, the indexical linkage between a style of vocalization and a type of person is made iconic, so that the qualities of the style are presented rhematically as the qualities of the person. Furthermore, in both cases the conductor used these categories of person to remind the choir that they were not singing for themselves or their friends; they were singing for God and the congregation. She wanted to make sure they knew that there would be an audience.

If the *ajŏssi* and *ajumma* are the characterological types, the typifiable personae, in contrast to which one is supposed to sing, the prototype that one is supposed to emulate is made clearer in figure 11, a photograph taken just outside Somang Presbyterian Church's main sanctuary.

These two figures are child-angels. Their hands are clasped together in prayer. There is not a hint of suffering in their faces, of tension or tissue damage in their throats. There is only the earnest, if innocent, expression of the desire to praise and glorify their God in a voice that sounds pure and clean. And their singing mouths, like Kim Yŏng-mi's, look like the rounded bells of trumpets stretched vertically. The particular rounding of the mouth—from horizontal to vertical—becomes an index of the transition from older styles to the *sŏngak* style, just as Yun-gyŏng's account of her transition from pure chest voice to a blending of

FIGURE 11. Statues of child-angels singing, Somang Presbyterian Church (photo by author).

chest and head voice was demonstrated by moving from a widely articulated, ventricular [a] to a more rounded, faucalized [u].[57]

These child-angles are featured not only in statue form but also on
the church's website, where anyone can watch streaming video of the
church's various choirs and soloists perform for the congregation dur-

ing the multiple services each week. Embedded in the image are the words "Praise | Speak to the entire assembly of Israel and say to them: 'Be holy because I, the LORD your God, am holy'" (from Leviticus 19:2).[58] It is noteworthy that this passage should come from a Bible chapter that is concerned centrally with cleanliness and holiness—themes I explore in detail in chapter 4.

These statues are models of a phonosonic event that ties the broad and diverse dimensions of embodied and expressive qualia of Evangelical Presbyterianism in Korea to an institutionalized ritual of communicative interaction. Singers like Kim Yŏng-mi are the specialists, the authorized performers, of these rituals and are personified points of vocal orientation for Christians throughout Korea. Yet in their own performances, Kim and her peers are also orienting to something—to standard, normative, ideal, or familiar sensations of some sort. The intersection of Korean Christian framing narratives—ethnonational development and spiritual enlightenment—provides the chronotope through which the aesthetics of progress can be not only imagined but also heard and felt as such.

These examples do not merely point to sociological variation and correlation of the vocal qualities and stated religious affiliation of persons residing in Korea. Nor do they suggest the rigid class-based habitus of social position. Nor are they limited to a generalized ethical receptivity and responsiveness through conventionalized or specialized practices of listening.[59] Rather, the multiple dimensions of embodied and expressive lived experiences in singing are oriented to these churches as specific ritual centers of semiosis—sites from which authorized examples of the beauty of the voice, the enlightenment of the heart, and the advancement of a people emanate. A simple statement like "We don't sing like that here" or "*sŏngak* singing sounds more holy" are ideologically loaded and prototype-oriented statements of evaluation invoking an elaborate Christian framework of proprioceptive and communicative normativities that shape sociocultural life in Korea via the enregisterment of the human voice.

CONCLUSION

In late 2008, I had a conversation with a soprano named Ye-ryŏng. At that time, Ye-ryŏng was a master's student in voice and also a soloist at Somang Church. I mentioned to her that much of the dissertation I was writing at the time would deal with the role of the church and

Christianity in Seoul's vocal culture. She asked me why I thought Americans would find the relationship between *sŏngak* and churches interesting. I told her that in my experience, many of the trained singers in the United States and Europe who sang in churches as paid professionals were not *necessarily* religious. Then I continued, *"Han'guk esŏnŭn—"* (But in Korea), and the young woman interrupted and completed my sentence for me, excitedly: *"kyohoe e taninikka sŏngak ŭl haeyo!"* ([We] sing classical music because [we] attend church!). While Ye-ryŏng's response could be taken as a straightforward causal account of the Westernization of Korean music through the introduction of Christianity to Korean society, her own biographical relationship with *sŏngak* in the context of Korean Christianity and her socialization into a particular church suggests that a more specific and nuanced interpretation of this statement is required.

Just before I left Seoul in early 2009, I suddenly and unexpectedly lost my voice. I was supposed to sing the offertory song for a service at Somang, but I could not. So Ye-ryŏng took over, happily, without complaint. After the church service, the choir gathered at a coffee shop to wish me farewell. I sat next to Ye-ryŏng, and we talked about the problem of losing one's voice. Ye-ryŏng's boyfriend also joined us that day. A tenor, he had studied voice with a very senior professor, but he could no longer sing. Many whispered that he had lost his voice because of bad instruction. But as a loyal and deferential disciple, he never publicly blamed his voice loss on his teacher but instead blamed himself for his shortcomings. With the help of his peers' collaborative silence on the topic, he quietly switched to piano accompaniment as a way to remain in the *sŏngak*—and church—scene.

As we discussed my immediate vocal problems and his more chronic ones, Ye-ryŏng volunteered a bit of her own history. When she first arrived at SNU and began singing regularly in both school and church, she lost her voice regularly. It hurt to speak and sing, and her condition stubbornly would not improve. At one point she had to stop using her voice for the evangelical work that she felt was her calling, and it deeply saddened her. But then, over the course of a few years, her condition improved. She did not lose her voice anymore, nor did she suffer regularly from vocal fatigue. I asked her what had changed, and she answered, simply, "prayer" *(kido)*. I asked if she had prayed for a better vocal condition. She said she had indeed prayed for help from God but also explained that she had begun to pray differently. She used to pray very harshly, very loudly, very emotionally, for hours on end.[60] At her home church in a small city south of Seoul, she had grown up praying loudly and fervently with the rest of her church congregation. When she moved into the dormitories near SNU, she continued that practice, besides working all week for various churches as a soloist and as a conductor of a children's choir. But since joining Somang Church, where people prayed quietly and Pastor Kim delivered sermons more softly than her home-church pastor, she had changed her style of prayer. Now she still prayed for as long and as often but more softly, more gently, almost with a whisper. Before, she explained, she had "squeezed" *(tchada)* her throat in prayer, but these days she tried to relax and "open" *(yŏllida)* her throat. This change, she said, was allowing her voice to remain fresh and strong.

In adjusting the style of her prayer to match the style of Somang Church, Ye-ryŏng believed she had improved her singing voice. Although she missed the more fervent prayer style of her youth, she saw the healing and repair of her voice as proof that Somang Church's style of vocalization—in prayer, preaching, and song—was the right way to allow the natural, God-given voice to emerge. It was not that she simply prayed for a better voice but that she changed her whole style of prayer to more thoroughly align with the enregistered semiotics of a place like Somang. In changing the way she prayed, she made her prayers more effective. Thus, it was not merely Christianity, not merely her attendance at church, that helped her advance in her vocalization. Rather, it also was the aesthetics of Somang's brand of Christianity that affected not only what she sang but also how she sang, not only what she prayed for but also how she prayed. A particular Christian aesthetic of progress, institutionalized on a massive scale at Somang Church, was realized in her own progress as a singer of *sŏngak*. Her prayers were answered, literally, by a new enregisterment of voice.

CHAPTER 4

The Clean Voice

In November 2008, the South Korean tenor Kim Woo-kyung gave his first concert in Seoul after studying and performing abroad for nearly ten years. Unlike singers who return to Seoul from study and work abroad to begin professional careers at home, Kim was in Seoul for only a short time before returning to his international career. For this reason, the concert was billed not as a "homecoming recital" *(kwiguk tokch'anghoe)* but as a "first recital" *(ch'ŏt naehan risait'ŭl)* in Korea.

The performance took place in the concert hall of the Sejong Center for the Performing Arts, in downtown Seoul. Predictably, the audience comprised voice students, church relations, and *sŏnbae* and *hubae* (relative seniors and juniors) from Hanyang University, where Kim had studied before moving to Munich in 2000. The first half of the concert featured Robert Schumann's song cycle *Dichterliebe,* and the second half featured well-known opera arias in German, Italian, French, and Russian. The multiple encores were also predictable: he sang more opera aria "hits" for tenor, as well as the Korean-language version of Albert Hay Malotte's "The Lord's Prayer" (Chu ŭi kido). As I had seen in other performances of this sort, members of the audience ceased their shouts of "Bravo!" and "Encore!" during the Christian song and instead bowed their heads and clasped their hands in prayer. In this act of both professional accomplishment and unflinching public evangelism, the event and its participants were positioned explicitly as Christian. However, in a moment of exception, after the solemnity of "The Lord's

Prayer," the applause and shouts resumed, and Kim was forced to sing two more encores: first, Lehar's operetta aria "Dein ist mein ganzes Herz," and then the second verse to Verdi's "La Donna è Mobile," which ends on a high B natural.

As I left the concert hall, I ran into Sang-u, a voice student, and his girlfriend, a piano student. I asked the two of them what they thought about the performance. Sang-u replied enthusiastically, "It was so good! His voice is completely clean" *(wanjŏnhi kkaekkŭthaeyo)*. I didn't take much notice of this characterization at the time, since singers of classical music throughout the world sometimes use "cleanliness" as a descriptor for voice quality or the execution of a performance (e.g., free of mistakes). However, a few days later when I arrived at Somang Presbyterian Church for choir rehearsal I spoke with Ye-ryŏng, one of the soloists there. This soprano, a master's student in voice, had also attended Kim's concert. She told me that she had immediately begun to cry when he began to sing the first lines of *Dichterliebe*.[1] I asked why, and she responded that she couldn't believe how clean his voice was. She said she had never heard a Korean tenor with a voice so clean.

After speaking with a number of voice students who had attended the concert, it became clear to me how ethnographically important were their characterizations of the voice as clean. Following this concert, singers and nonsingers repeatedly cited Kim Woo-kyung's voice as an example of vocal cleanliness and stressed that such cleanliness was a rare quality in Korean voices. According to these informants, the beauty of this singer's voice and his ability to move his audience's emotions were related to the status of his voice as one of the cleanest anyone had ever heard. What they were hearing (i.e., the sonic attributes of the voice) was the result of cultivated phonic activity according to the principles of European-style classical singing. But even the most proficient of vocal technicians, teachers or students, did not comment in detail on these aspects of Kim's technique. They commented on the clean sound of the voice.

In the present chapter, I focus on this idealized quality of the voice—"cleanliness"—to show how the production and experience of this quality as such is connected to its temporal positioning within the Christian narrative of Korea. Similar to the way in which Nancy Munn described an "intersubjective spacetime" organized in terms of the experience of particular qualities as conventional qualisigns (i.e., types of qualia that are widespread, recognizable, and socially effective) emer-

gent in the context of particular activities, I describe how the phonosonic normativities of the increasingly clean Korean voice serve to
anchor a particular community—and its culture of sociality—in time
and space.[2] In this case, upper-class, Presbyterian Christian notions of
time and space contribute to a chronotope of ethnonational progress;
this chronotope serves as the framework through which a quality like
vocal cleanliness can be heard as such. Throughout, I ask why this particular vocal style should be the emblematic voice for this group beyond
the basic story of modernization or cultural globalization in the form of
Westernization. That is, what is particularly Christian about this singing style, about the vocal attributes, for these Korean singers and others? How does one hear—or apperceive—Korean Christianity in a
sound?

To answer these questions, I trace conceptualizations of cleanliness
and related notions of sanitation, hygiene, and health through a number of different dimensions of social life in Korea to show how this
particular idealized quality of the voice, as inferred through the phonosonic qualia of vocalization, is related to the role of the voice in the
expression and embodiment of ethnonational development and Christian enlightenment. First I discuss the phonosonic attributes of what
informants described as a "clean" or "unclean" voice. I show how
these qualitative attributes are related and polarized according to a
chronotope of development that positions the unclean, murky,
unhealthy voice at an undeveloped stage and the clean, clear, healthy
voice as more advanced. Then I discuss the broader relationship among
tropes of cleanliness and development as they concern perceptions of
bodily experience and expressive forms. Finally, I turn to ideologies of
bodily and spiritual cleanliness in Korean Christianity, focusing especially on the relationship between the *маŭm* and the voice. The clean
voice, as a reflection of a clean *маŭm,* emblematizes the overlapping
narratives of spiritual enlightenment and ethnonational development
in the social space of upper-class Korean Presbyterian churches and
beyond.

Let me be clear. This chapter is not intended to reproduce established
arguments about the relationship between ideologies of cleanliness and
modernity (or, for that matter, purity and sacred spaces). Cultural
notions of sanitation, hygiene, and cleanliness and the application of
these terms to certain segments of society obviously play a significant
role in narratives of European social development, as well as in Asia
and elsewhere.[3] And it is not surprising that a narrative of moderniza-

tion and a narrative of sanitation intersect in the history of the Christian church in Korea. Indeed physical and spiritual cleanliness and medicalized health have often been emphasized in colonial mission encounters.[4] Even with its own preexistent pollution prohibitions and rituals of purification, Korea was no exception, and underwent "cleansing" both by Protestant missionaries and the Japanese colonial regime in the late nineteenth and early twentieth centuries.[5]

My aim here is to explain ethnographically what a clean voice *means* within the context of Christian South Korea. And, furthermore, I show how cleanliness traces a pathway of qualitative linkages—what I have elsewhere called qualic transitivity—from the voice, to the bearers of voice, to the relations mediated by the voice in the phatic production of Christian sociality.[6]

I conclude by arguing that tropes of cleanliness are more than just aesthetic standards for Christian voices in Korea—or, rather, that aesthetic standards are much more than the simple expression of preference, taste, or judgment. Rather, the continuum of cleanliness as a qualitative framework figures into the higher-order chronotope of progress that is ritually invoked in the large Presbyterian churches of Seoul and their linked institutions, namely, *sŏngak* voice programs at universities and the nominally public and secular performances of *sŏngak* throughout the city. These narratives and their comprehensive chronotopic framing align body and sound with specifically Christian perspectives within the Korean cultural context. What we call "embodied" or "expressive" qualities of the voice are hooked to, indeed, are dimensions of, the ritual institutionalization of normativities of sound production as communicative interaction.

POLARITIES AND TELEOLOGIES

After realizing—somewhat suddenly and late in my fieldwork—that my informants constantly used the notion of cleanliness in their descriptions of voices, I asked some of them to describe this vocal quality. They described the clean voice mainly in terms of the suppression and removal of two types of unwanted vibration: firstly, the "fuzz" sound caused by pressed vocal cords, abrasions on the vocal cords, or other forms of obstruence along the vocal tract; and secondly, the "wobble" sound created by unstable vocal adduction and habituated muscle tension. For example, here are some of their descriptions of the clean voice:[7]

EXCERPT 4.1

1. *Kkaekkŭthan moksori rago hamyŏn paibŭreisyŏn i chayŏn sŭrŏpko nŏmu nŭrigŏna pparŭgŏna haji anaya hanŭn kŏt katkoyo. Kŭrigo him ŭl chuji ank'o chayŏn sŭrŏpke sori ka ullyŏjil su ittorok sori ka aptchok ŭro naenwajyŏ issŏya hago p'ŭreijŭ sijak kwa kkŭt i chal yuji toenŭn hohŭp wie sori ka noajyŏya toenŭn kŏt kat'ayo.*

I think if a voice is clean, the vibrations are natural and not too slow or too fast. And one should not strain but should make a sound that comes forward so that it can resonate naturally. I think the sound should come out with the support of well-maintained breath at the beginning and end of a phrase.

2. *Saram moksori ka "kkaekkŭthada" nŭn kŏt ŭn hŭndŭllim i ŏpko, kŏch'in sori ka ŏpsŭmyŏ, anjŏngjŏk idaranŭn ttŭt kwa pisŭthage ssŭinŭn kŏt kat'ayo.*

I think when we say a person's voice is "clean," it is close to the meaning that there is no shaking and there are no rough sounds and that the sound is stable.

3. *"Kkaekkŭthada" sori ka malko ch'ŏngahada. Chijŏbunhan ttŏllim ŏpsi anjŏng toen hohŭp wie nanŭn malko ch'ŏngahan sori rŭl mal handa.*

A "clean" sound is clear and elegant. It is a clear and elegant sound based on stable breathing without messy trembling, it is said.

4. *Norae esŏ kkaekkŭthadanŭn mal ŭn tarŭn nappŭn pŏrŭt ŏpsi kkalkkŭmhage purŭndaranŭn ttŭt in kŏt kat'ayo. Tto kkaekkŭthan moksori nŭn mok sangt'ae ka kŏn'gang hago mok sangt'ae ka kkaekkŭthaeya kkaekkŭthan sori ka naonŭn kŏt kat'ayo. Mok e karae ka kkiŏttadŭnji hudu na sŏngdae e sangch'ŏ ka issŭmyŏn kkaekkŭthan sori ka annawayo. Kŭraesŏ kkaekkŭthan moksori rŭl naeryŏmyŏn kŏn'ganghan mok sangt'ae rŭl kajigo issŏya toendago saenggak haeyo.*

I think the word *clean* in describing singing means neat and efficient singing not disturbed by bad habits. Also, I think a clean voice can be produced when the condition of the throat is healthy and clean; in order for a clean sound to come out, the condition of the throat must be clean. If there is phlegm caught in the throat or if there are injuries to the larynx or the vocal cords, a clean sound doesn't come out. Therefore if you want a clean voice, I think you have to have a healthy throat condition.

5. *Kkaekkŭthada: Malgŭn sori.*
Chabŭm i ŏpko,
sŏnmyŏnghan sori.
Kŏn'ganghan sŏngdae esŏ
naonŭn sori. Sangdaejŏk in
p'yohyŏn ŭronŭn "hŏsŭk'i"
hada. Ex: Sonyŏn, sonyŏ
hapch'angdan ŭi
kkaekkŭthan moksori.
"Chime bell" kkaekkŭthan
sori (kyunyŏl i ŏpko, tukke
ka ilchŏnghae sori ka
kkaekkŭthage nanŭn kŏt).

Clean: clear sound. Lucid sound without static. The sound that comes from healthy vocal cords. An opposite expression is to be "husky." For example, boys, the clean voice of a boys and girls chorus. The clean sound of a "chime bell" (without cracks, the sound that comes out cleanly and with uniform thickness).

In order to see how my informants would categorize vocal sound more generally, I posted some excerpts of singing online and asked both voice students and professional singers to comment on them. I asked them to describe both the qualities of sound and the manner of sound production, but also told them that they were free to respond in any way they liked, at any length or detail, in general or specific terms, and so forth. I mixed genres of singing, including opera, popular music, Korean *p'ansori*, Argentine gaucho singing, and North American country and western, among others. In selecting examples of European-style classical singing, I tried to choose voices I thought they would not immediately recognize, with the exception of one (Maria Callas).

In general, the voices that were described as cleaner or healthier were produced using minimal glottal friction and maximal formant manipulation and resonance. This approach requires low subglottic pressure and an expanded pharynx. It requires reduced muscle tension and maximal agility. The voices deemed unclean or unhealthy were almost always produced using more forceful laryngeal adduction, glottal friction, subglottic pressure, and tension throughout the articulatory chambers of the throat and mouth. Furthermore, inferences about a lack of cleanliness or of health of a voice were based not only on the perceived mode of production (e.g., a "tense" sound, "forced" tone, or "held" voice), but also of the signs of "damage": the vocal "wobble" stemming from habituated vocal adduction; the "fuzz" or "hiss" of high frequency static above the fundamental tone caused by the air friction that emerges from abrasions on the vocal cords.

Important to note is that respondents' judgments were also situated within, and influenced by, a more complex cultural system of interpretation and evaluation in which the qualia of the voices and their recordings were associated with the location of the singers within a chronotope of both biographical and cultural development. The only voices they chose to describe as clean were featured in two recent recordings of early European music.[8] Even though the two singers mentioned below are relatively unknown performers and even display traces of "early music" technique that mark their voices as unable to fill concert halls with sound (i.e., not the "big" sound of later operatic singing), their voices were described as clean and healthy.[9]

EXCERPT 4.2

1. *Maekkŭrŏpko, kkaekkŭthadanŭn p'yohyŏn iya. Sori myŏn esŏ yaegi handamyŏn almaengi ka tŭrŏ innŭn soriralkka? (sori an e mwŏn ka "Kern" kat'ŭn ke ittanŭn ttŭt). Choŭn kŏya . . . hŏhaji ank'o . . . ŭmakchŏk t'ek'ŭnik ŭro pomyŏn sori rŭl milji annŭn palsŏng i choŭn kŏt kat'a.*

    Smooth and clean expression. If I just talk about the sound, it could mean a sound with an essence? (I mean that there is something like a core inside the sound). It is something good . . . not hollow. . . . With regard to musical technique, I think a vocal technique that doesn't push the sound is good.

2. *Koŭmak katko yojŭm saramdŭl ege inki innŭn ŭmak iya. Ch'a kat'ŭn ŭmak iralkka? Kkaekkŭthago ch'ŏngmyŏnghan sori. P'yŏngmyŏnchŏk igo saekkal ro p'yohyŏn hamyŏn . . . hŭinbaeksaek.*

    It is like early music and music that is popular among people these days. Can I say the music seems like tea? A clean and clear sound. It is even, and if I describe it in terms of color . . . white.

Flamenco singing presented listeners with a kind of qualitative opposite. My informants described the throat and the sound of El Camerón de la Isla as rough, raspy, rotten, old, and unclean.

EXCERPT 4.3

1. *Kŭ nŭn imi chasin ŭi palsŏng ŭl t'onghae t'akhan sori rŭl naenŭnde iksukhaejyŏ itta. Konggan ŭi sayong kwa hohŭp podanŭn sŏngdae sayong e ŭijon hanŭn moksori ch'ŏrŏm tŭllinda. Kkaekkŭthaji ant'a.*

    He has already become used to his own technique of producing a raspy sound. It sounds like a voice that relies on the vocal cords more than using space and air. Not clean.

2. *Sori—chiksŏnjŏk. Pangbŏp—mok e him ŭl kŏŭi chuji annŭnda, hajiman nŏmu saeng moksori. Myosa—kŏch'ilda.*

    Sound—straightforward. Method—puts little strain on the throat, but the voice is too raw. Description—rough.

3. *Sori ka kanghada. Sŏngdae rŭl tairekt' ŭro sayong hana kasŏng to sŏkkŏsŏ sayong. Sori ka chogŭm nŭlgŏtta.*

The sound is strong. He uses the vocal cords directly but with the falsetto combined. The sound is a bit old.

4. *Kŏch'iljiman chayuropko ridŭmgam i issŏ. Him to itko sŏngdae rŭl mani ssŭnŭn palsŏng igo minsok ŭmak nŭkkim iji, mwŏ, uri nara nŭn ch'ang igo kŭtchok ŭn.*

Although it is rough, it is natural and has a sense of rhythm. It is a vocal technique that is powerful, that uses the vocal cords a lot. It feels like folk music, well, their counterpart to the *ch'ang* of our country.

In the final response above, the listener compares the flamenco singing to *ch'ang*, another term for *p'ansori*. Although there are of course many types of traditional Korean music, *p'ansori*, now considered a "high art" despite having been sung in the past by members of the lower classes, stands out as an oft-cited epitome of the Korean aesthetic of *han*. And so it is no great surprise that similar descriptions would be used for a recording of someone like Pak Tong-jin singing an excerpt from a *p'ansori* composition, *Ch'unhyangga*. There was a fairly unified response in the descriptions of Pak's voice, his vocal method, and the sonic entailments of his phonic approaches to singing. As with the recording of flamenco above, listeners described this *p'ansori* singer's voice as "not clean." Furthermore, the affective dimension of the sound was also emphasized, particularly in terms of the sorrow or sadness the voice conjured up for listeners. Below are some of the responses that connect the phonic method of sound production to the affective dimension of its sonic entailments.

EXCERPT 4.4

1. *Sori—kŏch'im & "husky voice." Pangbŏp—mok ŭl mani sayong, kongmyŏng podanŭn chiksŏnjŏk ŭro. Myosa—kŏch'in & kusŭlp'ŭn.*

Sound—rough & husky voice. Method—uses the throat a lot, it is straight, rather than resonant. Description—rough & sorrowful.

2. *T'ansik . . . pijanghan sori. Palsŏngpŏp ŭn chal morŭjiman chillŏnaenŭn sori, ttŏnŭn sori, kkŏngnŭn sori ka p'oham toeŏ issŏ.*

Groaning, sighing . . . a tragic sound. Regarding the vocal method, I am not sure, but it includes shouting sounds, shaking sounds, breaking sounds.

3. *Han'guk ŭi p'ansori. P'ansori ch'angpŏp ŭn ilburŏ mok ŭl sanghage hayŏ sŏngdae e manŭn sangch'ŏ ka nago amunŭn kwajŏng sok esŏ irŏn sori ŭi kyŏlgwamul ŭl mandŭrŏ naenda. Kip'ŭn kamsŏng ŭl p'yohyŏn hanŭn tee aju hyogwajŏk ida.*

P'ansori of Korea. The *p'ansori* singing method results in this sound from the process of hurting the throat on purpose to produce many wounds on the vocal cords. It is very effective for the expression of deep sensitivity.

4. *Chwiŏtchanŭn tŭthan inwijŏk in paibŭreisyŏn ŭl mandŭnŭn kŏt ŭl al su itta. Chayŏn sŭrŏun paibŭreisyŏn i anira mach'i t'ŭril hanŭn tŭthan sŏyang ŭmak ŭi kijun ŭro pomyŏn olch'i anŭn palsŏng ina Han'guk ŭi sidaejŏk chŏngsŏ [in] "han" iranŭn chŏngsŏ chal mudŏnanŭn t'ek'ŭnik.*

I notice that he makes artificial vibrations that seem to be grabbing and squeezing. Not natural vibrations, but something like trills, which seems to be an incorrect vocal technique when viewed from the standards of Western music. However, it is a technique that reflects well the Korean sentiment of the times, the sentiment of "han."

Notice here how the roughness of the vocal cords, the corporeally experienced pain of the method of vocal production, the embodiment and expression of sadness, and the wounding of the body are all tied together in these listeners' experiences of *p'ansori* as a sorrowful type of singing. All of these responses fit into a fairly common repertoire of descriptors for traditional Korean singing and coded emotionality: sound, body, and affect all fit into a model of a material and cultural past.[10]

Yet none of these responses characterized a voice explicitly as "dirty" *(tŏrŏpta)*. What at first appears as qualitative polarity between a clean, clear, healthy voice and an unclean, murky, unhealthy voice might be better characterized in the first place as an orientation toward vocal cleanliness as an aspirational quality. The polarity emerges when cleanliness and its absence are linked indexically to stereotypic and culturally significant personae that are seen as sociohistorically opposed. Furthermore, the earlier description of the rough voice as an "old voice" and of the *p'ansori* voice as reflecting the "sentiment of the times," namely, *han,* alerts us to the way the vocal technique, its sonic entailments, and its affective charge all are situated in a kind of narrative of change in Korea over time.

It should not be surprising that the categories of modernity and tradition in this framework should be differentiated from, and valuated in opposition to, each other. It is interesting, though, that this chronotope of emotional and vocal transformation over ethnonational time is so powerful that it pervades even the descriptions of European-style classically trained voices that were recorded in during the middle of the twentieth century. Older recordings of classical singers—recognizable because of the suppression of certain frequencies in early recording technologies—while not considered as rough or unclean as those of *p'ansori* or flamenco singers, were nonetheless often described using these terms. This included both a singer who was praised for her artistry but criticized for her technical shortcomings (Maria Callas) and one who still serves as a paragon of vocal stability, despite instability in other areas of his life (Jussi Björling).[11] In particular, respondents commented on these singers as if they were still in the early stages of vocal development; that is, they said things about these singers they would have heard others say about themselves. And in these descriptions, the qualities they described effectively situated the voices somewhere in the middle of a continuum of technical development.

EXCERPT 4.5 (MARIA CALLAS)

1. *Sori nŭn kŏch'iljiman hohŭp ŭi konggŭp i ch'ungbunhaesŏ p'yŏnan haeyo.*

The sound is rough, but because of the abundant breath support the sound makes one comfortable.

2. *Ullim ŭi konggan i maeu chot'a. P'oint'ŭ ka aptchok e itta. Sori nŭn kanghago lirik hana pudŭrŏpchinŭn mothada.*

The resonance space is very good. The point is forward. The sound is strong and lyrical but not soft.

3. *Ŏduun, ch'ŏngsŭngmajŭn, anjŏng toen.*

Dark, pitiful/sorrowful, stable.

4. *P'yŏnanhan sori chungjŏŭm put'ŏ koŭm kkaji t'ongil toen sori hajiman sori chach'e ŭi pitkkal ŭn kkaekkŭthaji ank'o t'akhada.*

The sound is comfortable, unified from the low notes to the high notes, but the color of the sound itself is not clean and is raspy.[12]

EXCERPT 4.6 (JUSSI BJÖRLING)

1. *Mok ŭl mani ssŭgo k'o tchok e sori rŭl mani ssŭneyo.*

[He] uses the throat a lot and uses lots of sound that involves the nose.

2. *Hyŏ ka mallyŏ issŏsŏ mok i tach'yŏ itta. Konggan i ŏpsi ap ŭroman sori rŭl [nae] ryŏgo haesŏ pulp'yŏn hada.*

He curls his tongue, closing his throat. It's uncomfortable because he produces the sound only toward the front, without space.

3. *Taptaphan, sori rŭl nŏmu chamnŭn, pitkkal i kanghan.*

Stifled, too much grabbing the sound, strong in the tonal color.

4. *Mok ŭl chamnŭn nŭkkim*
t'ŭgi, i.e., parŭm ŭn nŏmu
masŭkkera rŭl sin'gyŏng ssŭn
namŏji ap ŭro chinach'ige
kkiwŏtta. Yakkan ŭn
ppyojokhan sori.

[There is] a peculiar feeling of
holding the throat, i.e., regarding
the pronunciation, he is too
concerned with the "maschera"
[Italian for *mask*] excessively
holding forward.[13] The sound is a
bit pointed.

5. *Sori—yakkan p'ŭllaethan*
t'akhan sori. Pangbŏp—
masŭk'era rŭl iyong hago itta.
But [Eng.] mok ŭl sayong
hanŭn nŭkkim (ch'ich'arŭm).
Kkaekkŭthaji ant'a. Myosa—
napchakhan.

Sound—a bit flat, raspy sound.
Method—He is using the maschera,
but there is the feeling that he is
using the throat (a sibilant sound).
It is not clean. Description—
flattened.[14]

The older singers, whose earlier recordings make them sound different from contemporary singers, are also situated along a qualitative continuum, framed by a narrative of development. They are positioned somewhere in the process of developing their technique and sound—somewhere from unclean to clean, from unhealthy to healthy.

Although the respondents sometimes described the voices of popular music as "mic voices" (suggesting that the sound was not "natural" but was highly modified through electronic amplification and adjustment), they did not comment on the possibility that the more recent singers of classical music, such as the singers of early music, also could have had their voices edited or "doctored" during the recording and production process (which was not an option for the older singers of classical music).[15] This is somewhat surprising, given that most of the respondents were quite open about how they manipulated their own audition recordings before sending them off to competitions and conservatories for screening. This elision points to the fact that a chronotope of vocal development from unclean to clean—both biographical and cultural—is a powerful frame for the evaluation of vocalization among these singers in Korea. At a more general level, the perception of phonosonic qualia seems to be structured by this narrative, leading even the local experts to conclude that these older *sŏngak* singers must be less advanced. The qualities of advancement are expressed primarily in the terms of cleanliness and clarity. For Korean singers, striving toward the clean voice is more than just a temporal progression. As I will explain, it has a spatial dimension as well.

POWER AND BEAUTY

Singers characterize study and work outside Korea as necessary not merely for certification but also for a singer's vocal advancement and transformation. Abroad is the place where singers hear and feel their voices becoming cleaner. Youn Kwangchul (Yŏn Kwang-ch'ŏl), a world-famous bass, explained to me the way his teacher in Germany had to "clean" his voice of the Slavic influences he had picked up while studying in Bulgaria, where a strong chest voice was emphasized in all situations. And Su-yŏn said the same thing about her training in Europe but focused it explicitly on the Korean influence; she had to clean her voice of the habits she had acquired from her teacher and from Korean audiences, who expect a big, piercing sound. Some singers, however, are resistant to this aesthetic framework and instead infuse more traditional phonosonic approaches into their *sŏngak* singing. Chong-p'il was one of these singers.

Chong-p'il arrived in the voice department at SNU after repeatedly losing his voice when singing popular Christian music at church. But even after four years of training with one of the most famous professors on the faculty, he still complained that his voice had grown increasingly husky.[16] As we ate lunch together on the day of a spring recital in which we would both perform, he insisted that he still intended to go abroad to continue his vocal studies, just like his peers. He had decided that his voice would fit better in Italy than anywhere else. He explained that Italians were the most passionate of all the Europeans and then mimicked the phonosonic style that he perceived to be most qualitatively Italian: he lifted his hand into the air, palm up, opened his mouth wide and produced a harsh, sibilant sound to represent the intensity of Italian singing.

The sound he produced was what I have termed the *fricative voice gesture* (FVG).[17] Fricative voice gestures generally are voiceless, high-pitched emissions of sound that are produced by air friction along the vocal tract. They are used in Korean as expressions of personally felt intensity, both as isolated reactive utterances and as a form of intensification superimposed as a prosodic feature onto speech itself. They also are often marked as old-fashioned, low-class, and outmoded by younger, wealthier Koreans (even though many of these younger, wealthier speakers actually also regularly produce these sounds). And unlike Chong-p'il, singers frequently produced isolated FVGs as qualitative icons of a particularly unclean, unhealthy, dangerous mode of vocalization.

For example, Chang-wŏn, the baritone discussed in chapters 1 and 3, talked about how one must sing classical music as if "breathing in," with a high soft palate, a low larynx, and an expanded pharynx. He told me that one should not feel as if he is "breathing out," with air friction against the glottis and vocal tract. As he demonstrated, he produced a harsh FVG as an icon of the frication caused by breathing out. According to Chang-wŏn, that sound represents the method of a less developed singer who cannot produce a clean sound.

Another singer, a young tenor named Hyŏn-ho, described the way he used to sing when he first arrived at university, before he knew anything about vocal technique. He explained that he would enter a practice room, shut the door, and simply sing as loudly and powerfully as he could for as long as he could. He told me that this practicing style led to vocal fatigue and occasional voice loss.[18] This singer described his former ways as the opposite of "natural singing." To supplement this description, he produced an FVG on an [a] vowel. In a spectrographic analysis, the FVG appeared as a peak in high-frequency acoustic energy. Such images are associated with white noise or static in acoustic environments or with the sonic "hiss" of abrasions on the vocal cords, as well as with consonantal sibilants such as [f] and [s].

And a young soprano, Ŭn-yŏng, like Yun-gyŏng in chapter 3, described the legend how singers of p'ansori supposedly induced their vocal cords to bleed while singing to build up enough scar tissue to endure the performance demands of the genre. The soprano explained that tŭgŭm, the arrival at vocal maturity in p'ansori, was achieved by grinding the vocal cords together, the sound of which she represented by producing an FVG. Ŭn-yŏng then situated this evaluative gesture within a narrative of Korean cultural transition and modernization. She told me such a singing method might have been appropriate for expressing the pain and sadness reflected in Korean traditional music—important affective modes of Korea's troubled past, of han—but was not appropriate for expressing contemporary sentiments. She explained this in terms almost exactly the same as the comments on p'ansori vocal technique reproduced above.

Ŭn-yŏng was dealing with her own vocal difficulties during my fieldwork and often did not participate in class vocalizations. At first she insisted, however, that her struggles were not the result of bad singing or instruction—an admission that would have been nearly impossible given the shame that such a revelation would have brought to her teacher. Later on, as she grew more comfortable with me, she privately complained that she learned nothing from her teacher, even though she was expected to bring gifts and money to her lessons. But our conversation about vocal cleanliness took place during our first interview, and, being cautious, she construed her vocal problems as the result of her own bad speaking habits. As we ate lunch at her university one afternoon a few weeks later, she told me that she had developed nodules on her vocal cords because she used to "talk like other Koreans," using loud and harsh sounds. She then produced an FVG to illustrate this. I asked her when she had first noticed problems with her voice, and she told me that it was when she spoke or sang and her voice didn't sound clean. She went on to say that she had changed her speaking style to a softer, quieter way of speaking and now focused on singing with a clean, beautiful voice rather than a loud, powerful voice.

The use of the FVG as a metasemiotic descriptor offers clues to a particular speaker's stance on the standards of vocalization—on sound and its production—as well as on an individual's position as a vocalist within an aesthetic hierarchy of vocal types. Whereas Hyŏn-ho, Chang-wŏn, and Ŭn-yŏng used the FVG as an icon of the qualia of poor technique or unclean singing—pain, friction, lack of control, rough sounds—Chong-p'il used the FVG to signal his positive evaluation of a vocal and expressive style. The use of the FVG indicated to me that this student had not yet come to understand what the other students understood regarding singing *sŏngak:* that extreme frication in vocal production is a hindrance to expressive development rather than an effective expressive tool. This student lauded what he considered to be the sound of Italians by using the very sound the others had used to characterize negatively what they judged to be bad singing. Although he drew the FVG from the same phonosonic repertoire used by his peers, Chong-p'il demonstrated a starkly different understanding of its use. His estimation of its utility revealed his own standing in relation to the other students of his class in terms of perceived vocal development, where his voice was heard as husky, rough, and unclean.

That same spring, Chong-p'il and some other singers performed in a student recital for their class on Korean art songs. The recital was titled "Uri ka purŭnŭn uri norae" (Our Songs That We Sing). As I waited in the lobby on the day of the concert, I met a young singer who went by the English name Paul. Paul, who told me his father was a pastor at one of the largest churches in Seoul, had transferred to Juilliard after his first year at SNU and was back in Seoul only to visit friends and family. As we sat next to each other in the concert, he told me confidently that all of the vocal students in Korea sang incorrectly, even those considered by the faculty to be the best singers. He said they all had the same faulty method of vocalization, which focused too much on power and not enough on beauty. He said, "In the U.S., we even have a word for it. We call it 'pushing.'" In Korea, this combination of subglottic pressure and tightly adducted vocal cords is usually referred to as "holding" *(chapta)*. Then he told me that he himself had not realized that he was pushing or holding his voice until he went to Juilliard. He said he had no idea that what he had been doing was wrong, because he had always been encouraged to sing that way. He told me that when he finally met his teacher at Juilliard, he learned how to let his voice "blossom." He said that at Juilliard the differences between those who push and those who don't are extremely clear. Some "get it" and some don't, he said. But in Seoul, the difference was not so clear, because everyone pushes.[19]

For the recital of Korean songs, Chong-p'il sang a song titled "Ch'ohon," a poem by Kim So-wŏl (1902–34) set to music by Ch'oe Pyŏng-ch'ŏl (1936–). The title of the song refers to an invocation of the spirit of a deceased person, and the song itself is a lament sung from the perspective of a person who is calling out for a lover who does not respond. The narrator tells the story of calling out repeatedly the name of a lost love but to no avail. The song begins low in the tenor range, on an F:

> *Sansani pusŏjin irŭm iyŏ!*
> *Hŏgong chung e haeŏjin irŭm iyŏ!*
> *Pullŏdo chuin ŏmnŭn irŭm iyŏ!*
> *Purŭdaga nae ka chugŭl irŭm iyŏ!*

> Name that is shattered into pieces!
> Name that is worn into thin air!
> Name which no one claims, even when called!
> I will die while calling the name!

Over the next few measures, the melody crescendos and rises to a high F, right in the middle of the tenor's passaggio, and then ascends to an A-flat, well into the tenor's upper register:

> *Sarang hadŏn kŭ saram iyŏ!*

> That person I loved!

As Chong-p'il's voice increased in volume and ascended in pitch, it grew rougher and his face became more distorted. He managed to sing the high F in what sounded like a yell, but as he ascended to the A-flat he could no longer maintain the intensity of glottal adduction against the increasing subglottic pressure, and his voice broke into a kind of breathy falsetto. At that point, Paul turned and looked at me with a knowing glance, saying nothing. The final words of the song are the same as above, "That person I loved!" However, instead of ending on a powerful high note, the singer is instructed to speak the words relatively softly, *mp parlando*, unaccompanied by the piano. When Chong-p'il did so, even his speaking voice was marked by the raspy sound of swollen vocal cords that are not adducting normally. After the applause, Paul leaned over to me and whispered in English, "I was really worried for him. He doesn't have a clean sound, and he was pushing too much."

When the concert was over, I stood with Paul and a group of students in the lobby of the concert hall, waiting to congratulate the performers. A soprano held out the program and pointed to the song Chong-p'il had sung. She said to me, "That was my favorite. It had so much power [*him*]." Paul whispered to me, "See what I mean?" The different ideologies of vocal development and aesthetics were manifest in this event. Paul spoke from one end of the continuum, focused primarily on a notion of vocal health and cleanliness; Chong-p'il sang from the other end, focused primarily on vocal intensity and power.[20] And Chong-p'il had evidently stirred something in the young soprano who reported hearing power in the song. But why should these be the terms that frame this opposition? Why cleanliness in the first place? As I show below, this narrative of personal technical development and the aesthetic cleaning of the voice aligns with a broader ethnonational narrative of musical development and sanitary transformation in Korea.

BATHROOMS AND BEL CANTO

As I mentioned above, Max Noah's 1949 article, "Mission to Korea," reported that while certain infrastructural pieces of a "modern society" were visible in Korea, there was at the same time a lack of modern "behavior," specifically relating to hygiene and sanitation. He wrote: "The cities have electricity, paved streets, banks, post offices, and court houses, but no water or sewage systems. In the homes, women continue to cook in the most primitive manner, wash their clothes in the river, iron clothes by beating them with sticks, and serve their men and raise their children with little regard for the principles of sanitation."[21]

In chapter 3 I showed how Noah linked what he saw as the problems of cultural backwardness with musical backwardness, claiming that

Korean music educators did not know "the correct use of the child's voice" or how to achieve "voice blending" and only cultivated "forced singing and shouting tones." Similar characterizations can be heard today from the growing number of singers who have studied abroad and have returned to Korea. They generally use these phrases when describing three categories of singers of European-style classical music. One category is the group that Paul commented on: voice students who had not yet departed for studies abroad. The second category comprises singers who have studied abroad and returned but whose voices have begun to deteriorate. The final group includes older singers in Korea who are understood to belong to a different generation altogether. These singers seem to exhibit styles that are locatable somewhere along the continuum of development—not as rough as traditional singing, but not as clean as the contemporary classical singing found abroad.

For example, in one conversation with students about their professors of voice, a person praised a particular professor's unique kindness to and consideration of students. He also commented on the professor's appearance, saying he looked like a "Westerner" (sŏyang saram) because of his height and facial features. But when I asked about his voice, there was an awkward silence. The student asked me with a smile, "Have you heard his voice?" I replied that I hadn't. He went on, "Well, it's not a natural voice, not a clean voice." And he continued, "But he was trained long ago. He is from the old generation" (kusedae). This teacher's membership in an older cohort, not merely his age, was intended as an explanation for the sound of his voice. Like the voices of singers of flamenco, p'ansori, and even sometimes of opera, this singer's voice was perceived to be from an earlier stage of development.

One way that Koreans narrate the rapid transformation of Korea is by recalling how dirty their country used to be relative to the contemporary period. North American and European missionaries often viewed Korea in the same terms. In volume 2 of Isabella Bird's 1905 travelogue, *Korea and Her Neighbors: A Narrative of Travel, with an Account of the Vicissitudes and Position of the Country*, Bird, a traveling missionary, reported returning to Seoul in 1897, after her initial visit in 1894: "Old Seoul, with its festering alleys, its winter accumulations of every species of filth, its ankle-deep mud and its foulness, which lacked the redeeming elements of picturesqueness, is being fast-improved off the face of the earth." Thanks to the chief commissioner of customs, Mr. J. M'Leavy Brown, and the "capable and intelligent Governor of the city," Ye Cha Yun, "Seoul, from having been the foulest, is now on its way to being the cleanest city in the Far East!"[22] However, despite these visions of modern sanitation, Bruce Cumings reports that "most foreigners thought South Korea was irremediably filthy until the 1980s"—in contrast to North Korea's capital city, Pyongyang, which was supposed to have been extremely clean.[23]

Discourses of sanitation and cleanliness often form around the topic of bathrooms, in which they are linked to the broader sanitization and modernization of the country. There has been a push through organizations such as the Korea Toilet Association (KTA) to improve the "toilet culture" *(hwajangsil munhwa)* of Korea—a change it calls the "toilet revolution" *(hwajangsil hyŏngmyŏng)*. This organization gives out awards to particular bathrooms for meeting or exceeding certain standards of cleanliness. The motto for the Inaugural General Assembly of the World Toilet Association, which took place on November 22, 2007, was: "Toilet Revolution, Changing the Future of Mankind" *(Hwajangsil hyŏgmyŏng i illyu ŭi mirae rŭl pakkumnida)*. The KTA characterizes toilets as "the space for the culture of each country" (in English) and has even made statements in Korean such as "Toilets are our face" *(Hwajangsil ŭn uri ŭi ŏlgul imnida)*, in its goal of transforming what it calls the "toilet etiquette" *(hwajangsil et'ik'et)* of the country. They aim to make "beautiful toilets" that go beyond the purpose of such spaces in the past, when "toilets were just for meeting a simple physiological urge"; such toilets become "spaces for relaxation and living spaces where users can put on makeup, read, and think."[24] This seems quite clearly to depict bathrooms as undergoing the transition from "nature" to "culture"—a transition that is made clear by one of the newer features of public bathrooms: an "etiquette bell" *(et'ik'et pel)* or "manner bell" *(maenŏ pel)* that plays "cultured" classical music to cover up embarrassing but "naturally occurring" sounds. One occasionally even runs across a plaque mounted on the wall outside a public restroom announcing its having been awarded "Seoul Best Toilet" status by the city.

For many of my informants, this toilet revolution is linked to the explicit instructions posted in bathrooms, indicating that the bathroom should be a treated as a place of cleanliness, health, and beauty for clean, healthy, beautiful people (the same attributes, note, that one finds idealized in the *sŏngak* voice). When I asked people—from students to working professionals—why these signs exist, they usually said that they were intended to help change the etiquette of the older generation *(kusedae)*. These signs are aimed not only at keeping bathrooms clean but also at changing the bathroom "etiquette" *(et'ik'et)* from that of "backward nations" *(hujin'guk)* to that of "advanced nations" *(sŏnjin'guk)*—what has been called "toilet training" *(hwajangsil kyo-yuk)* for adults.[25]

As odd as this topic might seem for understanding the aesthetics of voice, the related categories of body, sociality, and sanitation intersect in a way that is highly relevant for the discussion. Even stories of *p'ansori* training make an implicit conceptual link between narratives of toilet culture and narratives of singing culture. For instance, after I had observed a *sŏngak* voice lesson for a few hours in a teacher's home studio, the teacher invited me, her accompanist (a close friend who also was a church choir director), and one of her students to stay for a dinner of spicy fish soup. After dinner, this voice teacher, who was both a church choir conductor and the wife of a Presbyterian minister, told me a story of how as a young woman she had gone with her mother to hear Kim So-hŭi, a famous *p'ansori* singer and "intangible cultural property" *(muhyŏng munhwajae)*. After the concert, members of the audience were allowed to ask questions. The teacher told me that she had asked the great singer if the stories she had heard of *p'ansori* training were true. She said she was not surprised that Kim So-hŭi admitted to training by a waterfall in order ultimately to learn how to sing "over" it. She was, however, surprised to hear something confirmed that is supposed to take place just before one makes the final vocal "breakthrough" to *tŭgŭm*. Before the teacher told me what she had heard, she turned to her friend and asked her if she knew what *p'ansori* singers drank before they reached the final stage of voice. The friend's eyes grew wide, and she smiled. She whispered something, and the teacher nodded. "No!" *(Aniyo!)*, the pianist said. The teacher nodded again. Then she told me.

According to the teacher, Kim So-hŭi had admitted that she had drunk excremental water *(ttongmul)* prior to achieving her final stage of voice. She said that before she made her vocal breakthrough, Kim had taken the rotten *(ssŏgŭn)* excrement from an outhouse (the teacher called it a "Korean traditional bathroom," *Han'guk chŏnt'ong hwajangsil*) and drunk it. This was supposed to have helped her achieve the voice that the teacher heard at the concert.

Despite this teacher's claim of hearing it directly from the source, some people argue that this, unlike training by the waterfall, is just a myth. When I took the question to a *kayagŭm* (Korean zither) player who teaches at the Kungnip Kugagwŏn (National Gugak Center, formerly the National Center for Korean Traditional Performing Arts), she told me that she had heard a radio broadcast in which Kim Soh-ŭi was asked the same question but had denied it adamantly. The *kayagŭm* teacher's opinion was that someone had characterized the strength and toughness of the *p'ansori* voice, the *han* of the *p'ansori* voice, as a voice that "could drink excremental water" *(ttongmul ŭl masil su innŭn moksori)* rather than a voice that was the result of drinking such a thing.

I later found an interview with Kim So-hŭi and Pak Tong-jin, in which Kim So-hŭi denied having drunk excrement—directly contradicting the story told to me by the classical voice teacher above. Pak had told the *Koreana* magazine that he had sung for "nine hours and forty minutes straight," to which Kim responded, "But please don't tell them you spit up blood or eat human excrement after performances! People spread these incredible rumors about *p'ansori*."[26] This is the conversation that followed (reproduced in English by the magazine):

> *Pak:* I never spat up blood, and, while I did drink some human excrement once, I did it because in the old days people believed it had medicinal effects. I would never recommend it to my students! It had nothing to do with my throat.
>
> You see, a long time ago my teacher boasted of singing for one hundred hours straight. That's how he mastered *p'ansori*. Of course, I believed him, so I went up into the mountains—that's the only place you could sing without bothering people—and tried doing the same thing. I was around thirty at the time, and I figured the more practice the better.
>
> *Kim:* A lot of people have ruined their voices that way.
>
> *Pak:* Well, I sang for eighteen hours a day for forty-five days, and my body swelled up and I couldn't even move my arms. Nowadays there are medicines to treat such conditions, but back then we had nothing. People drank human feces for swelling. It smelled disgusting but it worked![27]

I cannot be sure whether the classical voice teacher was bending the truth or simply misremembering Kim So-hŭi's statement. But what seems evident is that the teacher's story depended on an ethically charged qualitative framework of cleanliness that serves to differentiate Christian singers of European-style classical singing from their pagan forebears in Korea. And even in this stretch of interview, Pak Tong-jin, who admitted to having consumed *ttongmul*, characterized the belief in its medicinal usefulness as a thing of the past.

A detailed description of *ttongmul* as medicine appears in an interview with the *myŏngch'ang* (*p'ansori* master) Pak Ch'o-wŏl, conducted by Kim Myŏng-gon.[28] Kim was the screenwriter for Im Kwŏn-t'aek's 1993 film *Sŏp'yŏnje*, which tells the story of wandering *p'ansori* singers in South Chŏlla Province as Korea was modernizing. Kim came to the interview with questions regarding two legends *(chŏnsŏl):* Did *p'ansori* singers really drink excremental water? And did they really "vomit blood from their throats" *(mok esŏ p'i rŭl t'ohada)* as they progressed toward *tŭgŭm?* Pak responded that she herself had never vomited blood. Then Kim brought up the historical drama about Song Hŭng-ok, a master *p'ansori* singer, in which in one scene Song "gurglingly emitted red blood from his mouth" *(sippŏlgŏn p'i rŭl ip esŏ ulk'ŏk ulk'ŏk ssoda naenŭn changmyŏn i issŏtta).* Pak replied, "Has that man caught tuberculosis?" *(Chŏ saram p'yepyŏng e kŏllyŏnna?)* and argued that the writer or director of the drama had not done enough research on the actual life of Song.

Pak's response to the question of excremental waste, however, confirmed a variation of the story I had heard from another *p'ansori* singer residing in the United States regarding the method of *ttongmul* production. Pak clarified that *ttongmul* was not simply scooped from an outhouse but had a recipe for preparation and purification. This is the four-step recipe for excremental water *(ttongmul chejopŏp)* that she gave to Kim:

1. *Kulgŭn taenamu t'ong ttukkŏng ŭl mumyŏngch'ŏn ŭro kkok kkok kamssan taŭm, pyŏnsokan e nŏŏ tunda.*
2. *Myŏt kaewŏl twi taenamu t'ong ŭl kkŏnaemyŏn ch'ŏn sai ro sŭmyŏdŭn "malgŭn" ttongmul i kadŭk ch'a itke toenda.*
3. *Kŭ mul ŭl ttukpaegi e tama p'ŏl p'ŏl kkŭrinda. (kisaengch'ung pangmyŏl chakchŏn).*
4. *Mul i sigŭmyŏn k'o rŭl han son ŭro magŭn taŭm tansum e masinda.*

1. After you have tightly wrapped a thick bamboo stalk with canvas to make a lid, stick it into the toilet and leave it behind.
2. When you remove the bamboo stalk after a few months, it will be full of "clear" excremental water that has seeped through the gaps in the cloth.
3. Put that water into an earthen pot and bring it to a boil. (parasite extermination tactic).[29]
4. When the water has cooled, cover your nose with one hand and then gulp it down.

Pak explained that when a person practices every day for a few hours, the vocal cords become swollen, one develops a fever *(sŏngdae ka putko yŏl i saenggida),* and one's voice becomes "hoarse" *(chamgida).* She said that excremental water was a folk remedy *(min'gan ŭi soksŏl)* that was used to cure such wounded throats. She went on to say that it was actually efficacious and that she had heard of people taking it when their entire bodies were swollen *(on mom i puŭn saram)* in order to remove the poison in their bodies and reduce the swelling *(mom ŭi tokki rŭl ppaego pugi rŭl naerida)*. Pak admitted that she herself had drunk it a few times, and a few of her disciples had as well. But, she conceded, excremental water, like many other medicines, belongs to a "rare old story" *(kwihaettŏn yennal yaegi)*. Echoing Pak Tong-jin above, Pak Ch'o-wŏl said, "Because there is so much good medicine these days, no one drinks excremental water" *(chigŭm ŭn choŭn yak i manajyŏsŏ ttongmul masinŭn saram ŭn ŏpta)*.

The image of a suffering person drinking purified excremental water as both a medicine and a kind of magical potion that allows them to transcend the final stage of *p'ansori* training is, at minimum, a common notion of a *p'ansori* singer who creates art through suffering, who is strengthened through the kind of self-destruction that comes from trying to sing for eighteen hours a day, who achieves artistry through the emotional state known as *han*. The image also stands as a stark contrast to the middle- and upper-class Presbyterian Christian notions of purification, cleanliness, and sanitation that pervade discourse regarding *sŏngak* singing in Korea. And as Pak's own admission of medical advances indicates, excremental water is a medicine from the past, which lives on today only as a story.

In Korea, the *p'ansori* voice—whether positively or negatively valuated—conjures up a person, like the emotion of *han,* from an earlier time. A friend of mine in Korea called the *p'ansori* voice a "grandmother voice" *(halmŏni moksori)*—an endearing personification of the sound. Some emphasized the indigeneity of the *p'ansori* voice, particularly in contrast to the seeming foreignness of the *sŏngak* voice. In one of my earliest interviews on the subject in 2005, one informant, speaking for all Koreans, insisted, "We hear *p'ansori* as our voice, but we don't hear opera as our voice." However, for the Christians who are at the center of this study, the *p'ansori* voice conjures up an image of alterity: a singer whose vocal cords bleed and who ingests human excrement. Therefore it is not so surprising that the qualia of such a voice might be perceived by a younger generation in terms of a continuum of vocal cleanliness—especially one that is related to a narrative of cultural advancement seen in part through the toilet revolution: tracing a shift from outhouse, to dirty bathroom, to clean bathroom, to a space for cultural expression, from which no *ttongmul* could be gathered. This transformation of bathrooms is also a transformation of the qualia and behaviors of the bathroom: the kinesthetic qualia of using the bathroom (squatting or sitting, as it were), the environmental qualia of the bath-room (the smells, sounds, and appearances), and the social qualia of bathroom (behaviors or etiquette). It is within this framework of cultural change that the sound of the *p'ansori* singer comes to be heard as muddy and unclean, in direct contrast to the clean, pure sounds associated with contemporary singers of *sŏngak*.

CONCLUSION

In this chapter, I have brought together a number of strands of qualitative experience to explore the way in which members of a particular stratum of Korean Christian society view the voice in terms of a teleology of biographical and cultural development according to an overarching ideology of cleanliness. In particular, the phonosonic aspects of *sŏngak* are positioned at the clean end, and those of the more traditional styles are placed at its opposite. This continuum is organized in terms of a chronotope of ethnonational advancement and spiritual enlightenment, such that the *sŏngak* voice is heard as the clean, Christian voice, and voices generally considered to be traditional come to be heard as unclean, un- or pre-Christian voices.

Although various English phrases like Francis Bacon's "For cleanness of body was ever esteemed to proceed from a due reverence to God, to society, and to ourselves," in *The Advancement of Learning*, and John Wesley's famously simplified version, "Cleanliness is next to godliness," have been translated into Korean, I know of no common saying in Korean that connects cleanliness to Christian holiness.[30] However, it is precisely with this sentiment that Christian singers of *sŏngak* attempt, with the voice as their emblem, to align faith, sociality, and the cultivation of personhood via the clean voice. This Christian enlightenment project in Korea measures its ongoing progress in terms of the cleanliness of the voice as an extension not only of the body but also of the heart and mind.

Before a church service at Somang even begins, a series of prayers serves in the ritual purification of the choir members who will be singing in the service. Shortly after the choir arrives, the *ch'ongmu* (manager) opens the rehearsal with a prayer. Then the choir conductor takes over and rehearses the choir. The choir members put on their robes—out of sight of the congregation—and walk together to the sanctuary. They are instructed not to eat or drink with their robes on, not to carry bags over the shoulders while wearing their robes, not to use the bath-

room with their robes on, and so forth. When they arrive in the sanctuary and are assembled in their spaces, the *taejang* (chief representative)
of the choir says a prayer to open this stage of rehearsal. The conductor
again rehearses the choir until about ten minutes before the church service is to begin. Then a *moksa* (pastor) approaches the choir and offers
a final prayer. With that, the choir leaves the sanctuary and waits in a
small stairwell just out of site until they are called back into the sanctuary for the service.

In this ritual series of prayer, there is an ascending hierarchy of status
and authority of speech, moving from the *ch'ongmu*'s prayer, to the
taejang's prayer, to the *moksa*'s prayer. Yet each prayer is nearly identical to the others in form and style. The prayer is almost always delivered in a soft, hushed voice—sometimes so soft that some members of
the choir engaged in conversation do not realize that the prayer has
started. And at each step, the person offering the prayer usually thanks
God and asks God to give the choir *sarang hanŭn maŭm* (loving heart-
minds), *arŭmdaun maŭm* (beautiful heart-minds), and *kkaekkŭthan
maŭm* (clean heart-minds), so that their voices communicate God's
grace and express his will to the congregation.

Each step in this prayer ritual purifies both the *maŭm* and the voices
of choir for the next step: the *ch'ongmu*, elected by the choir, prepares
the way for the *taejang*, appointed by the elders, who prepares the way
for the *moksa*, hired by the elders and, presumably, chosen by God. It
is, then, the *moksa* who prepares the way for the congregation to experience their deity. The church service is a ritual that aligns the individual
voice with the individual *maŭm*, and multiple voices with multiple
*maŭm*s, in a softened acoustic environment that is felt and interpreted
as the qualitative representation of love, beauty, and cleanliness.

Just as cleaning the voice clears the way for productive emotional
expression and praise, cleaning the *maŭm* as a form of "ethical attunement" clears the perceptual channels used to experience the world.[31] A
sermon by Somang head pastor Kim Chi-ch'ŏl given on November 23,
2008, illustrates this perspective. The sermon was titled "God Who
Enlightens the Eyes of our *Maŭm*" *(Maŭm ŭi nun ŭl palk'isinŭn
Hananim)* and was based on Ephesians 1:15–23.[32] The sermon was
organized as a kind of response to non-Christians who are curious
about Christians. According to Kim, worldly people ask why people
spend so much time at church, give so much money to the church, and
seem to have a constant expression of happiness on their faces. These
outsiders criticize Christians for their formality and conservatism. Then

Kim explained that Christians are both happy and stubborn people because they "live their lives with attentiveness and anticipation, even though it might sometimes be dangerous" *(wihŏm hajiman kinjang kwa kidaegam ŭro insaeng ŭl sanŭn saram ida)*. They are people who "believe in the works of the Holy Spirit, have wonder and admiration, and are delighted by the adventure" *(sŏngnyŏng ŭi yŏksa rŭl mitko nollaum kwa kyŏngt'an ŭl katko mohŏm ŭl chŭlgŏwŏhanŭn saramdŭl ida)*. He explained all of this with a story about the purification of the *maŭm*.

Kim began by paraphrasing a story from a book on leadership *(lidŏsip)* by John Maxwell, a self-marketed "leadership expert." The story is about the perceptual experience of an old man. While the man was sleeping, his grandchildren rubbed some foul cheese into his moustache. When the stench finally woke him moments later, the entire world stank to him. No matter where he went, the smell would not go away. Kim's point was that the foul smell of the cheese from his dirty moustache affected the way he perceived the entire world. And then he told his audience, "When our *maŭm* is rotten *(ssŏkta)*, it seems as though the whole world is rotten. But when the work of God enters our *maŭm*, we see possibility in a seemingly rotten world."[33]

Notice here how the adjective used to describe the *maŭm* is the same as that which the voice teacher used to describe *ttongmul* and as that which *sŏngak* singers in general use to describe some of the voices of the past: rotten. Furthermore, this notion of seeing "possibility" *(kanŭngsŏng)* has resonances with the way Kim Chi-ch'ŏl and Lee Myung-bak jointly characterized the work of contemporary conservative politics. In chapter 2 I focused on President Lee Myung-bak's 2008 inaugural speech in relation to the sermon given one day earlier by the Somang Church head pastor Kim Chi-ch'ŏl. In both cases, the addressees are asked to cease dwelling on the past, to give up complaining about hardship, to shift focus away from struggle and suffering, and to look toward the future. In these speeches, both Lee and Kim asked their listeners to remove the metaphorical cheese from their moustaches—or the *ttongmul* from their throats or extra vibrations from their vocal cords—to perceive the world with an "enlightened *maŭm*" and presumably to display this perception with a clean voice.

Thus cleanliness, as a guiding principle within this particular Christian aesthetic of progress, operates as a cover term that can apply to many dimensions of social, psychological, and material life: the voice, the *maŭm*, social relations, the city, politics, and so on. In this manner, cleanliness becomes a conventional qualisign of advancement. The qualia of these corporeal, phonosonic and communicative, spiritual-psychological, and material and environmental dimensions become indexically linked one to another in ritual sites such as churches, from which qualitatively manifest values emanate into the broader social world. Under the cover term *cleanliness,* their qualia are not only indexically linked but also iconically linked; that is, they are perceived to be alike in some respect. Just as Christians in church should strive to clean their imperfect voices, they also should strive to clean their imperfect *маŭm* as well as their imperfect social relations. The qualia through which Korean Christians come to experience and conceptualize cleanliness of the voice, the heart, and their social relations are linked in a state of *qualic transitivity.*[34] Culturally regimented as conventional qualisigns of progress, relations among the qualia of Christian life in its various semiotic modalities are organized and perceived in terms of the overarching abstract quality of cleanliness, which takes the human voice as an anchoring emblem; the properties or features that apply to the phonosonic channel also apply transitively to the various other modalities to which the former is indexically and iconically linked.

The voice is a concrete qualic embodiment and expression of this abstract qualitative ideal. Yet its culturally sanctioned power to effect social change is not limited to personal cleanliness. A singer can express her own cleanliness, but making her audience feel clean requires a different kind of labor. One can phonosonically perform one's own advancement, but bringing others along using the qualia of voice is another thing altogether. In the second part of the book, I turn to the institutionalization of voice and the kinds of social relations that it mediates.

PART TWO

The Sociality of Voice

CHAPTER 5

Tuning the Voice

Sŏngak pervades many of the explicitly Christian semiotic genres that form the basis of church sociality in Korea (e.g., praise and worship, missionary activity and evangelism). Anchored to the church in this way, *sŏngak* also positions individuals in time and space. For most singers of *sŏngak,* the Korean present—the spatiotemporal *origō,* or deictic anchor point, from which they sing, so to speak—is understood in terms of a Christian narrative of the country's dramatic social, cultural, political, and material change. This change is perceived in part through a Christian aesthetic of progress. The aestheticized qualia of the vocal channel serve in the performance of a contemporary Korean Christian identity: a modern Korean Presbyterian who has moved beyond the suffering and hardship of the past to celebrate the health, wealth, and enlightened stability of Korea's Christian present. To sing *sŏngak* in Korea is to present oneself as a certain kind of person.

But the social world of the *sŏngak* singer in Korea also is anchored to another institution: the college of music, or, simply the "school" *(hakkyo).* When singers—both students and working professionals—are not at home, they are moving constantly between church and school, and nearly all of their social interactions in between are oriented to one or both institutions. Often, singers are affiliated with multiple churches and schools. On the surface, the church and the school seem to have a complementary relationship. The school authorizes performers through training and certification, and the church authorizes performances by providing an audience. However, because of their different institutional structures, many singers actually experience their movement between the two as an uncomfortable, sometimes incompatible contrast. This perception has to do with the different institutional social structures into which singers are socialized.

More than mere physical spaces in Seoul, the church and the school are social spaces that are distinguished by, among other things, their different models and structures of discipleship. At church, singers are considered to be privileged disciples of Jesus Christ, exemplifying Christian service and modeling a Christian persona through their voices. The specific qualia of their singing are supposed to manifest in practice the more abstract qualities of modern Korean Christianity. In contrast, singers in schools see themselves positioned within an old-fashioned educational system of discipleship, where students' vocalization always should be performed in emulation of and deference to their professors.[1] Although school is the authoritative site of specialization in European-style classical singing, students complain that the pedagogical framework is backward and destructive—more focused on teachers' status and income than on students' personal development or on the attainment of the evangelical ideal they hold for themselves, their peers, and their instructors. Despite a curriculum grounded in Western classical music, the school is seen as bearing an uncomfortable residue of the past—a feudal, hierarchical neo-Confucian training system requiring absolute submission to authority—that the church is supposed to have discarded in favor of a more egalitarian and progressive system of relations.[2] At church, singers see themselves cultivating their "God-given" voices as a form of Christian service. At school, where they compete over scant resources and recognition, they often see themselves emulating the voices of their teachers as a form of filial servitude.

This is not to say that these singers romanticize the church as perfect or problem-free. They view the church as a flawed, often-disappointing, earthly institution that is constantly threatened by the corruption and un-Christian motivations of its members and leadership. Nor, in fact, do they romanticize the lives of churchgoing persons. Many of these singers behave just like their more secular peers, consuming alcohol and having premarital sex, yet remain committed in speech and practice to their faith and to their obligation to the institution of the church (and generally prefer to break the rules with fellow Christians, if possible). Just as longstanding members of large, wealthy churches are sometimes suspicious of new adult members, who they suspect might have joined as a networking strategy rather than out of sincere faith, longstanding members of the church are sometimes suspicious of other longstanding members for what they call *"mot'ae sinang,"* literally, "faith from the mother's womb." This phrase is often used to describe persons who use their lifelong Christian affiliation as a cover for potentially scandalous sexual or financial activities. I heard numerous stories, rumors, and preemptive warnings about nominally Christian persons with *mot'ae sinang* duping and betraying their more gullible spiritual brothers and sisters.

Some Christians have little contact at all with the non-Christian social world and see any remotely secular leisure activity—singing at a *noraebang,* joining university classmates in "membership training" events, eating and drinking with colleagues, and so forth—as a threat to their faith. In general, singers view the church as an institution ideally organized around and oriented to the values of Christianity and therefore as the primary site, indeed the fundamental source, of ongoing social progress and change in Korea. While imperfect in the present, for *sŏngak* singers the social life of the church exists in stark positive contrast to the past, in part because of the idealized future potential that it projects. As an object of cultivation and continual striving, the church, like the voice itself, is, in a sense, "pitched" toward the future.[3] The school, on the other hand, is understood to be rigidly backward and thoroughly behind the times. And even though the vast majority of singers—both students and professors—are self-identified Christians, the structure of the school (and music education more generally) is understood to undermine the purported values of its Christian members. In this way, the chronotope of Christian progress discussed in chapter 2 is nested in the relation between school and church, with an outmoded past and progressing present playing out in the singers' very experiences of moving between them.

In the present chapter, I focus on the institutionalization of *sŏngak* by exploring the relationship between the church and the college of music as sites for the enregistered performance of institutional identities. I focus on the problem of discipleship to show how the relationship between church and school is a source of ideological confrontation that manifests itself in the voice as a kind of "grain." I argue that vocalization itself contributes both to the particular organizational structures of the different institutions and to the relationship of the institutions one to another. I do this by examining the way these specialists of voice—both students and professionals—make adjustments to their vocal qualia in both speech and song as they move between church and school and, in so doing, inhabit the appropriately differentiated discipleship roles. I call this process qualic tuning. The concept of qualic tuning highlights the malleability of the voice as an aspect and instrument of transformable personhood. The transformability of personhood is evident in the way singers adjust vocally to different models of discipleship when moving between the institutions. The voice is thereby calibrated differently to church and school through subtle qualitative shifts that are necessary in order to engage successfully in these different social environments. Qualic tuning shows how the *sŏngak* voice, despite its seemingly unified form, is actually a fractured register that positions individuals differently in different social spaces. Although *sŏngak* is central to the singing cultures of these two institutions, the singing cultures themselves are quite different. I want to emphasize that I am not merely talking about different performance contexts; rather, I am pointing out how the qualia of the voice phonosonically position these singers in different, sometimes contradictory frameworks of sociality.

I first show how relations among church members are organized ostensibly in terms of communal, familial deference to the Christian God, in contrast to the Confucianism-inflected Korean kinship system. Then I discuss the demographic and ideological relationship between churches and colleges of music and the role of these relationships in the development of an audience for vocal music in Seoul. After discussing local understandings of discipleship in the context of the school, I offer an analysis of the competing forms of discipleship that singers encounter as they move between church and school and the role their voices play in mediating this movement through social space. Focusing on the apperception of semiotic production, this chapter concentrates on the way in which normativities of vocal practice emergent in specific institutional centers put a kind of pervasive "pressure" on the voice by linking enregistered forms of vocally mediated discursive interaction to the immanent, higher-order ethnonational chronotope of Christian progress elaborated in chapter 2. From the school to the church, the chronotope of Christian progress is invoked and aestheticized as an ongoing departure from a derided past that lives on, stubbornly, in the present, threatening Korea's advancement.

CHRISTIAN KINSHIP

During my fieldwork, a number of people joined the church choir that I was singing with. After auditioning successfully with a hymn, newcomers would spend a probationary period of a few weeks attending regular rehearsals and participating in a few informational sessions during which they would learn the rules of the choir. Only then were they allowed to perform at services. Even so, new members were fully expected to advance through the probation period to become full participants in the choir. And on their first day of rehearsal, newcomers would stand in front of the choir and introduce themselves, and then they would be serenaded with a particular congratulatory song *(ch'ukpoksong)*, which choir members sing with palms turned upward toward the sky.[4] The song extols the addressee, describing the individual as having demonstrated true Christian virtues and the ability to lead others to worship God:

> *Ttaeronŭn nŏ ŭi ap e ŏryŏum kwa ap'ŭm itchiman*
> *tamdae hage Chu rŭl parabonŭn nŏ ŭi yŏnghon.*
> *Nŏ ŭi yŏnghon uri pol ttae ŏlmana arŭmdaunji*
> *Nŏ ŭi yŏnghon t'onghae k'ŭn yŏnggwang padŭsil Hananim ŭl ch'anyang*
> *O hallelluya.*
> *Nŏ nŭn t'aekhan choksok iyo. Wang kat'ŭn chesajang imyŏ*
> *kŏrukhan nara, Hananim ŭi soyu toen paeksŏng.*
> *Nŏ ŭi yŏnghon uri pol ttae ŏlmana sarang sŭrŏunji*
> *Nŏ ŭi yŏnghon t'onghae k'ŭn yŏnggwang padŭsil Hananim ŭl ch'anyang*
> *O hallelluya.*

> Although sometimes you face difficulty and pain,
> your soul confidently looks toward the Lord.
> When we look upon your soul, how beautiful it is,
> Through your soul, we praise God who will receive glory in the highest,
> O halleluiah.
> You are a chosen people. You are a royal priesthood, and
> a holy nation, a people belonging to God.
> When we look upon your soul, how beautiful it is,
> Through your soul we praise God who will receive glory in the highest,
> O halleluiah.

Drawing on a verse from 1 Peter 2:9, the song ritually congratulates the addressee for demonstrating strength of faith. In this particular instance, the choir, composed of legitimized evangelical leaders in the church, is a kind of special unit of this "people belonging to God," who draw on one another's faith to recognize and demonstrate for others the glory of their deity.

As with other group activities in Korea, leaders in the choir make great effort to build a sense of belonging and group identity among its members. In other contexts, this sense of interpersonal and group affection and intimacy is referred to as *chŏng*, but in the church people generally use the term *ch'in'gyo* (fellowship). The choir even has an individual person in charge of organizing fellowship-building activities *(ch'in'gyo pujang)*. To continually build fellowship, members eat together as a group, attend individual members' outside activities as a group, and participate in frequent "membership training" retreats (MT, or *suryŏnhoe*), where members sing, eat, and pray together—sometimes for days at a time. The retreats also are a chance for members to pray directly for their group leaders. On one such retreat that I attended, the choir manager, the chief representative to the elders, the conductor, the accompanist, and a soloist sat on their knees in a fetal position, while the choir members formed circles around each person, laid their hands on the person's back and head, and prayed out loud for their health and success.

It was always a sad affair when people had to leave the choir. If a person had to move away for work or could no longer give time to the choir, members were saddened by the absence of a beloved member of the group. If a person left because of conflict, choir members were saddened by the conflict itself. As people explained it to me, the sadness of the situation came from the belief that the choir, like the church, was a family and should not be broken up.[5]

While the "church as family" is a common tropic extension of kinship relations among Christians outside Korea, its ramifications have been quite intense for Korea in particular, where, as it was put nearly forty years ago, people "seem to have the tendency to regard almost any organized social institution as a type of family structure," and the Korean kinship structure itself has been inflected so thoroughly by the tenets of neo-Confucian sociality.[6] In the decades following the Korean War, as the country transformed from an almost completely rural population to an almost completely urban one, the social institution of the Korean family faced pressure from rapid and pervasive demographic, economic, and spatial change.[7]

Rural populations migrated en masse to cities from villages—many of them "clan villages," in which more than half the families had the same family name.[8] During this process, the social unit of the clan or lineage, which had been organized for centuries in terms of practices of ancestor worship and financial contributions to clan properties and activities, was weakened by distance, an increased focus on the immediate nuclear family, and the establishment of newer urban institutional—sometimes called "neotribal"—affiliations such as schools, churches, companies, and clubs.[9] As younger generations increasingly began to reflect on earlier forms of kinship obligation as "old-fashioned, outdated, and undemocratic," many envisioned the urbanizing transformation as a form of progress from social relations based on authority and submission to those based on "Western-style exploitation of individual talents and abilities."[10]

In early Korean Protestant writings, Christianity was often construed as directly confronting an outmoded neo-Confucian ethical system that sought to dictate proper relations among people. For example, Yun Ch'i-ho (1864–1945), a Christian intellectual, made the claim that "Christianity is the salvation and hope of Korea."[11] Kenneth Wells gives an account of the grounds on which Yun attacked the notion of filial piety *(hyo)* at the heart of the Confucian system of ordered social relations: "Yun charged that filial piety, while 'covering a host of sins,' freed one from the concern for the millions without food, homes, education or spiritual understanding. It permitted idle speculation on questions of infinity and non-infinity in a 'perpetual war . . . in regard to the priority of *ri* or *ki*,' and encouraged 'the doctrine of the inferiority of women, of absolute submission to kings' and of 'everlasting go-backism' . . . whereas Confucian ethics ended in moral elitism, Protestant ethics were a sort of 'everyman's' morality."[12]

When discussing filial piety, many informants explained to me that neo-Confucian social relations were idealized in terms of the three bonds *(samgang)* and the five relationships *(oryun)*. The three bonds refer to the authority of the ruler over the subject, of the father over the son, and of the husband over the wife. The five relationships (addressed in the Book of Mencius, IIIA.4) refer to the relationship between father and son, between ruler and subject, between husband and wife, between old and young, and between friend and friend. In such a framework, one is always positioned and classified according to not merely an institutional identity but also a relational identity with respect to other individuals.[13] My informants explained that interpersonal behavior, that is, microsociological interaction, is emphasized in one's performance of relational personhood, because one ideally is always orienting to the three bonds or the five relationships.[14]

Protestant Christianity presented an alternative to this model, the implications of which are still being worked out in the church. Although Korean Protestants view the church as a fundamentally modern institution, they often note that many vestiges of neo-Confucian sociality can be found in the church. Many of my informants complained about the hierarchical nature of Korean churches and their fellow church members' preoccupation with church-conferred titles, such as *chipsa* (deacon), *kwŏnsa* (exhorting deaconess or Bible woman), and *changno* (elder).[15] However, Korean Christians also emphasized their belief that all church members are part of one family *(kajok)*, as age-neutral brothers *(hyŏngje)* and sisters *(chamae)* under one father *(abŏji)*. Whereas neo-Confucianism has been shown to influence heavily the devotional culture of Korean churches, with special emphasis on institutional hierarchy and absolute submission to an all-powerful father, it nonetheless also often serves as a temporalized object of alterity—the "old-fashioned way"—to be contrasted with the idealized egalitarian and democratic principles of symmetrical siblinghood purportedly existent in contemporary Korean Christian sociality.[16]

In contrast to this simplified Christian model of brothers and sisters under God, my informants pointed out that Korean kin terms describing literal family relations are quite complex.[17] For example, kin terms are differentiated according to patrilineal and matrilineal lines (e.g., one's maternal aunt is referred to differently from one's paternal aunt), and sibling terms are differentiated according to relative age and speaker gender (e.g., boys and girls refer to their older sisters differently). However, in church, the basic unmarked form for referring to or addressing another Christian is ideally (but not usually in practice) the general term for male sibling *(hyŏngje-nim)* or female sibling *(chamae-nim)*. Furthermore, the titles that church members may carry—indeed, are expected to carry as they grow in age and stature within the church—are not relational per se but are rather positional within an institution explicitly oriented toward God. The introduction of a third factor (i.e., the Christian God) to which all participants are instructed to orient during interaction as a first-order relation governing their relation to others as Christians comes into tension with a system that emphasizes asymmetric sociocentric relationality based on the particular, often markedly uneven, relationship between two interactants. Some church members might be called *chipsa* or *kwŏnsa,* but all church members are *Hananim ŭi aidŭl* (children of God). Christian brothers and sisters are related insofar as they accept the Christian God as their father. The introduction of Christianity thus confronted a system of personhood defined by stratified sociocentric pair-part relations into an ostensibly egalitarian system of personhood defined by a joint relation to an omnipotent third ("brothers and sisters in Christ").

While the trope of the church as family is pervasive in Christianity, Somang Church puts a special emphasis on this point in ways that increase in significance over a person's life. Upon joining the church, new members receive a pen that reads "'Congratulations' Somang

Church New Family" *("Ch'uk" Somang Kyohoe sae kajok)* and take New Family Bible Study Classes *(Sae kajok sŏnggyŏng kongbu).* There is also Pastor Kim Chi-ch'ŏl's promise on the church website to "serve the disciples as sons and daughters of God" *(Hananim ŭi chanyŏdŭl in sŏngdodŭl ŭl sŏmginŭn mokhoe).* And Somang Church has even established a funerary and burial practice that further binds the members of the church as part of an institutional family.[18] Members of Somang Church may be buried together when they die.

In 1991, Somang built a retreat center *(suyanggwan)* just northwest of Seoul on a hill in a mountainous area of Kyŏnggi Province called Konjiam. Some church members' bodies have been buried there, but in general the bodies of the dead are cremated and their ashes are sprinkled around a single large gravestone next to the retreat center building.[19] Engraved into the large vertical gravestone are the words "Tomb of Somang Church Disciples" *(Somang Kyohoe sŏngdo ŭi myo)* and "I am the resurrection and the life" *(Na nŭn puhwal iyo saengmyŏng ini).* Engraved into the large horizontal slab of stone on which the gravestone rests is the familiar phrase from Genesis 3:19, "To dust you will return" *(nŏ nŭn hŭk ŭro toragal kŏt inira).*

In traditional Korean burial practice, family members are buried in burial mounds (tumulus, *pongbun*), one next to another, on a plot on a hill or mountain somewhere auspicious.[20] Somang Church has taken one large mound (the hill) and buried all of its members together. Whereas in traditional practice the different mounds relate each family member one to another by virtue of their proximity, in Somang's Christian practice, the single mound points to the single unifying Christian God as the principle of the church family. The Christian daily newspaper *Kungmin ilbo* reported that since the establishment of the gravesite in 1994, the number of "enshrinements" *(anch'i)* has increased 10 to 20 percent per year, with approximately a thousand church members having been "enshrined" there.[21]

Ostensibly, the blood relations and social positions that used to determine a person's status have been deemphasized in favor of a kind of lineage of faith, which connects living believers with those who have gone before. As a Christian disciple, one can join the church and become part of this family, accept the benefits and responsibilities of church life, and even receive a burial at Somang Hill. One is buried with one's Christian ancestors in a single ancestral plot. One is technically a member of the church family whether or not one holds an official position within the church. Although bloodlines, class status, and other forms of social distinction are important in shaping the kinds of relationships individuals can have in the church, the institutional and ideological promise is to treat everyone as equals—as brothers and sisters—under God.

It is through this promise, then, that a church like Somang, while complemented by institutions like the school in the cultivation of particular kinds of voices, nonetheless comes into ideological tension with what many singers saw as the school's residual neo-Confucian formula of social hierarchy. If trained singers in the context of the church were quintessential disciples or followers of Christ, in the context of the school they felt that they were quintessential disciples in a neo-Confucian system of apprenticeship.

TWO KINDS OF DISCIPLESHIP

Singers are important persons at Somang Church, occupying a vital position within the institution. They are exalted not only as musical evangelists but also as standard-bearers for the kind of voice that is perceived to best materialize the values of the institution and its qualitative attributes, for example, joy, advancement, purity, and faithfulness. The congregation looks to choir members as models of the ideal Christian disciple, as emerging leaders in the church, as contributing to the holiness of the institution and guiding others to become better Christian disciples. And the church choirs see themselves as fulfilling an indispensable ritual function by creating a sacred space in which the "Word of God" *(Hananim ŭi malssŭm)* can be revealed to members of the congregation. Alongside the sermons, the performances of the different choirs and soloists are broadcast online for all of the congregation and the public to view. Many soloists are known by name to the congregation because of these online broadcasts. They become institutional stars of sorts, with hit counts keeping record of the number of times their performances are viewed. Their offertory songs are featured separately from full-choir performances in a special dedicated section of the website. In these videos, the title screen lists their names and the songs they sing; web users can search the church website for the names of singers or for the names of songs.

In order for singers to audition for positions as soloists at the churches, they normally must be studying or have studied vocal music at one of the city's colleges of music. Many students are recruited through university networks to be soloists for church choirs. Professors at colleges of music play a important role in placing soloists in church choirs, either by bringing them into their own ensemble or by sending them to a colleague's or a subordinate's choir. Singers are often indebted to their professors for the opportunity to perform solos at church.

In the ideal model of this relationship, the professor takes responsibility for developing the student's career, and in return the student adheres to the principle of filial piety, serving and supporting one's teacher.[22] However, most students, graduates, lecturers, and quite a few professors complained that this system (at colleges of music in Korea) is corrupt, unfair, and ultimately destructive for the voices of young singers. These (mostly Christian) informants often characterized the voice departments in Korea as the "most Korean" of all university departments, by which they meant pejoratively the "most Confucian," by which they meant the most unjustly focused on the success, reputation, and absolute will of the professor.

People often spoke of a golden age of singing in Korea, sometime in the late 1980s or early 1990s, when a singer could train in Korea, study and perform abroad, and then return to Korea and gain employment on merit alone as a professor of voice at a local university. But things have changed. At the time of my fieldwork in 2008 and 2009, there were too many singers in Korea and too few paying performance opportunities. According to the Korean Education Statistics Service, there were more than three thousand college voice majors each year between 2005 and 2009, accounting for almost 10 percent of the total music majors.[23] *Sŏngak* voice majors alone outnumbered all students of traditional music combined. And a substantial portion of these singers now travel abroad for further study following graduation— what formerly had been a distinguishing opportunity for the privileged few.[24]

Family money is basically a prerequisite for studying voice in Korea. A number of people told me they had considered studying voice in college but were dissuaded by friends, family, and even university faculty after it was revealed that they came from modest means. The high costs come not from tuition directly but from the personal requirements beyond tuition, as I will explain shortly. First, I want to discuss briefly the backgrounds of the students who enter into this system.

The numbers of men and women in voice programs in Korea are more or less equal, but the paths that lead them to these programs are starkly differentiated by gender. For the most part, the women I met who pursue voice majors in college began their training at a young age (just like Yun-gyŏng, mentioned in chapter 3). Most of them entered one of the private performing arts junior high or high schools, such as Sŏnhwa Arts High School or Seoul Arts High School. Both schools have close ties to Christian organizations. Sŏnhwa Arts High School was founded as the Little Angels Art School in 1973 by the Reverend Moon Sun Myung (Mun Sŏn-myŏng), founder of the Unification Church. Seoul Arts High School, founded in 1953, is not explicitly linked to a specific church, but the very first image one sees when visiting the website is of a cross and a Bible at the pulpit. Messages from both its principal and its chaplain make explicit references to God.[25]

As my informants constantly reminded me, most of the women who study voice from an early age came from wealthy, educated, upper-class families. And indeed, the vast majority of the female voice students I interviewed had fathers who were physicians, lawyers, successful businessmen and entrepreneurs, or high-ranking pastors at large churches. Many of these students told me that their mothers had placed them in music schools before they themselves knew they wanted to sing. And quite often, they reported that their mothers made this decision because it would improve their chances for "marrying well" in the future.[26] With vocal studies at a top music school, they could become soloists at a place like Somang Church and be on display as attractive marriage partners for wealthy Christian men. When parents enter their young daughters into private music schools, few have plans for their daughters actually to work as professional singers when they graduate.

Men, on the other hand, have a somewhat different profile. Most of my male informants came from more middle-class families. If they did have money, it usually had been acquired more recently. One young tenor's mother sold bedding in a small store in Tongdaemun market; his father worked as a taxi driver and ran a snack bar in a sauna until he was able to open a liquor bar. Sending their son to the voice department at a top university was a very practical way not of reproducing their class status, as with the women, but of achieving upward social mobility. I also met a few male students who were from poorer families and lived together with other students, sometimes six to a room, in boarding houses run by Christian organizations.

College tuition varies according to the major, with the music major being among the most expensive a student can pursue (just behind dentistry, medicine, and veterinary medicine).[27] But it is not only tuition that demands family money. Before the university auditions actually take place, many students will take expensive lessons, often called "private tutoring" (kaein kyosŭp) from prospective professors at the university.

This is an illegal but widespread practice in Korea. For prospective voice students, this is an opportunity to demonstrate their potential discipleship by giving generous monetary gifts to the professor with whom they hope to study.[28] My informants rarely referred to these gifts as bribes *(noemul)*. If they did give them a name, they most simply referred to them euphemistically as gifts *(sŏnmul)*, gestures of gratitude *(insa)*, or tokens of thanks *(ch'onji)*.[29]

Giving money to a professor beyond the going rate for private voice lessons has two functions. One is simply to buy a place in a highly competitive university department. The other is to demonstrate one's potential for continued financial support of the teacher's performance career—that is, evidence of access to a wide enough social network and enough family money to guarantee ticket sales in the future. Hence, it is not simply a one-time payment but rather a kind of promise to establish a discipleship relation in which money flows upward toward the teacher and opportunities flow downward from the teacher. This relationship continues past college, determining the appointment of part-time lecturers to university departments and even the appointment of professors. In the latter case, the prospective professor is expected to give *insa* or *ch'onji* to the members of the selection committee. It is common knowledge among my informants that one usually can receive a position only at a university where one has studied and usually only under the auspices of the professor with whom one trained (often to take their place upon retirement). In 2008, I heard the going rate for a position at a university was around two hundred million *wŏn* (ca. $140,000 at the end of 2008).[30] As recently as 2012, I heard from a voice teacher that she was asked to pay nine hundred million *wŏn* to the university (to be split between the faculty and the university), plus "donation money" *(kibugŭm)* to individual faculty members and administrators. She refused.

There are certainly exceptions to these practices. Plenty of students, lecturers, and professors have entered voice departments without paying for it monetarily. Most say that about half of the faculty members are there on merit alone. People also say that many other students, professionals, and teachers have attempted to pay their way into departments but were ultimately not accepted (even though the money was not returned). Ultimately, younger singers and a few older ones complained that the combination of monetary obligation and a residual neo-Confucian emphasis on student-teacher filiality has created a kind of "feudal" *(ponggŏnjŏk in)* system among singers in Korea, which

many see as the "traditional" *(chŏnt'ongjŏk in)* structure of education.[31] In making this connection, some informants recited the old saying: "A disciple does not even step on the master's shadow" *(Cheja nŭn
sŭsŭng ŭi kŭrimja to papchi annŭnda),* which means that disciples
should always remain behind the teacher, never daring to approach, let
alone surpass, the teacher's status. Once I learned this expression, I
observed with a new perspective the common sight of a professor of
voice walking through a university building with fifteen or twenty students trailing behind him or her—knowing that not only the particular
professor but a number of the students as well had attained their positions in part through sufficiently generous gifts.

When I was able to speak candidly with students and professionals
of voice about the nature of discipleship relations in the university, most
made it clear that the values of the school often contradicted the values
of the church institutions, on which the school relied for both the students of and the audience for vocal music. Few if any classically trained
singers in Korea can earn a living from singing alone. There is practically no audience for European-style classical singing beyond Seoul's
churches and music schools.[32] In order to earn a living as a classically
trained singer in Seoul, one must teach lessons and participate in a
church. Many singers spend each Sunday running from one church to
another to sing, sometimes starting early in the morning and not finish-
ing until late at night. Soloists are paid between fifty thousand and one
hundred thousand *wŏn* per week but must attend weekly rehearsals,
services, trainings, special events, meals, and anything else for which
their presence is requested—which can add up to ten hours or more per
week. Although they receive payment, the emphasis is not on money.
Choristers expect that the soloists have joined the choir because they
love God and wish to help the congregation become closer to him. The
money they earn is understood as a mere gesture, some of which will be
returned to the church through tithing. One's living wages do not come
directly from these activities. Rather, they come from the relationships
that these activities make possible.

BUILDING AN AUDIENCE, MAKING A CAREER

The church provides a readymade audience for singers. The singer can
command the attention of the congregants during church services and
events and also draw members from the church into public settings
where they become audience members for secular art music or Chris-

tian-themed concerts with mostly secular content. The larger the church in which one sings, the larger the potential audience one can expect at any given concert beyond the church. One soloist at Somang Church emphasized for me the value of the church for a singer's performances outside the church. She said that when she gave her master's recital, church members formed the largest portion of her audience. She told me that this was due to *p'umasi*. *P'umasi* refers to a form of labor exchange, originating from a form of cooperative village organization.[33] This singer explained that *p'umasi* had been modified, honed, and strengthened in the churches and that her participation in a few different church organizations automatically guaranteed an audience at her recitals.

However, this example merely shows the role of the church in facilitating a volunteer audience. The church also can generate a paying audience. Professional singers in Korea give the majority of their performances for events related to a particular church or to Christian activity in general. There are benefit concerts, relief concerts, mission concerts, and other such concerts that are sponsored by churches, by the Christian Broadcasting Service (CBS), and by other Christian organizations. While singers might earn some money from these performances, the aim is generally to raise money for a Christian cause (e.g., a food drive or missionary efforts abroad). Instead of paying singers directly for a performance, a church might find other ways of compensating them.

A professor of voice at SNU told me of one such situation. Alongside her job at SNU, this professor was a prominent soprano soloist at Myŏngsŏng Presbyterian Church, which is reported to be the largest Presbyterian church in the world. She began singing there in the year 2000. The church was started in an eastern district of Seoul in 1980 by Kim Sam-hwan and has grown rapidly since then. Despite the size of the church, this professor said she received only seven hundred thousand *wŏn* per month for her singing. But after she recorded an album of sacred music, the head pastor called her and said the church would buy a copy of the album for each of its choir members. She told me there were almost five thousand choir members in the church.

On a smaller scale, churches often will subsidize tickets for members of a choir to attend the performances of one of the other choir members, for example, a group recital or an opera. But still, ticket sales mostly go to supporting the production itself, not to paying large sums of money to the performers. Those seeking to perform onstage must be able to guarantee ticket sales. Alongside being an active soloist in a large church, having a position as a lecturer or a professor at a local music college is extremely important for the opportunity to perform onstage in Seoul.

In many performance contexts outside Korea, a particular performer is chosen for some sort of artistic merit, technical skill, or fame that will generate ticket sales. An opera company will choose a singer in part because the singer will draw an audience. The same principle applies in Korea, but the particular calculus is different. As many students and professionals explained to me, most singers in Korea are not cast through an audition. Although auditions do take place, they are rarely the determining factor in casting decisions, because the arts market for classical music for the most part does not function according to a model of distinction or connoisseurship.[34] Concert audiences are populated primarily out of obligation, whether in the form of *p'umasi*, discipleship filiality, or some other form of reciprocity.

For any given opera stage in Seoul, whether the Korea National Opera (Kungnip Operadan, which performs at the Seoul Arts Center) or the Seoul Metropolitan Opera (Sŏul-si Operadan, which performs at the Sejong Center for the Performing Arts), there are a few different casts. Each cast gives one or two performances, and the opera runs for a few days at the most. The reason for this is simple: if there were only one cast, the opera company would not be able to fill enough seats for each performance. There simply are not enough opera fans to attend five performances of an opera in Seoul performed by the same cast, even the most famous operas such as *Madame Butterfly, Don Giovanni,* or *Rigoletto.* Singers are cast on the basis of the amount of ticket sales they themselves can generate, and this estimation is based on their church relations and the number of students (i.e., disciples) they have. Each cast is formed by estimating the total number of ticket sales the individual singers can generate for a given performance. The best show times (e.g., Friday and Saturday nights) are reserved for the faculty members of the largest and wealthiest voice departments, because their social influence and the reach of their social networks present the most potential for producing a paying audience.

While church relations are reliable in generating ticket sales, discipleship relations go further to actually guarantee ticket sales. Not only are the students of performing singers required to attend their teachers' concerts; they very often are also responsible for selling tickets to friends and family. In many cases, the performing singer acquires a role in the cast in exchange for purchasing a certain number of tickets ahead of time. Then the singer requires each of his or her students to purchase a portion of the tickets or to sell the tickets to friends and family on the teacher's behalf. If the student refuses or cannot follow through, the teacher might give low grades or withhold performance opportunities at the university. While I was doing fieldwork, there were even reports of corporeal abuse inflicted on students who failed to sell tickets for their university professors. And after I left the field, one of my own informants, a prominent soprano with a professorship in a prestigious department of voice, was fired on charges of extortion and violence against students.

Ticket sales are not income for the performers, however. Ticket sales only help singers secure a place in a cast. Church performances do not generate income either. They merely broaden the network of the singer's social relations. Professors' salaries in Korea are comparable to those in the United States and Europe, but this is not sufficient to pay the high cost of producing the frequent solo recitals that faculty members are expected to give. In a system of relations that informants sometimes described as a master-servant relationships *(chujong kwan'gye),* income is generated through an unofficial system of personal gift giving and reciprocity that rides along the entire chain of discipleship.

VOICING IN SERVICE AND SERVITUDE

In the Presbyterian Church context, you have, ostensibly, a communal orientation toward a single being to which the entire community is indebted. As the story goes, this being, God, has sacrificed his only son, Jesus Christ, for the sins of the world. One's position, title, or rank within the church represents an institutional position, but everyone is supposed to belong to one family, as brothers and sisters—as children of God. Although this is not always the way social relations actually play out, it is nonetheless the official, explicitly stated ideology. Discipleship in this case means the communal discipleship of Jesus Christ. Deference is made first and foremost to the Trinitarian figure of a singular, omnipotent, omniscient supernatural being. Although particular intimate relations within this community, generally among younger members, can be expressed by using asymmetric kinship terms for brother and sister that are differentiated by speaker gender (e.g., ŏnni for a female's older sister, *nuna* for a male's older sister, *oppa* for a female's older brother, *hyŏng* for a male's older brother), all members are supposed to be considered neutrally "brothers" *(hyŏngje-nim)* and "sisters" *(chamae-nim)*. In theory, the particular institutional titles merely communicate one's role in the church, not necessarily one's personal relations with others in the church. In practice, generational and network relationships among church members are still quite often hierarchical and structured in terms of institutional seniority and interpersonal asymmetries.

In the school context, no claim is made to the equality of the students. There are explicit vertical silos of orientation toward a particular professor. Although nearly all of the members of the voice department are practicing Presbyterian Christians, at the school the professor holds the highest rank, and all activity takes place in deference to him or her. Additionally, within and cutting across silos of what could be termed communal allocentric orientation to the professor, there is also what could be called a system of egocentric orientation based on seniority. *Sŏnbae,* those who arrived prior, are to be respected and deferred to by *hubae,* those who arrived subsequently. After one's first year, one is always *sŏnbae* to someone and *hubae* to someone else.[35] In a model similar to the teacher-disciple relationship, *sŏnbae* are responsible for helping and guiding *hubae* in whatever way they can, and *hubae* are expected to defer to and obey their *sŏnbae*.[36]

The two contexts of church and school are intimately linked, both demographically (with most singers attending Presbyterian churches) and ideologically (with the study of *sŏngak* understood to be in the service of Christianity, particularly of the Presbyterian sort). Students and professionals of voice move constantly between these two environments, and personal relationships between particular individuals are often present in both as well. And as I mentioned above, discipleship relations in school often play a large role in a singer's ability to obtain a position as a soloist or conductor in the church.

However, in moving between these two structures of discipleship, the nature of personal relations shifts—particularly among students and relatively junior professionals. Two students with a hierarchically inflected relationship at school (e.g., a second-year student and a fourth-year student in a voice department) might have a somewhat different relationship at church, where the second-year student might be the primary soloist in one choir and the fourth-year student might be the backup soloist in another. And whereas a student in the context of school might feel "beneath" a teacher and "behind" a long line of more senior students, that same student could find himself or herself a leader in the church, giving private lessons, helping to conduct a choir, and setting an example that inspires his or her Christian brothers and sisters, even those who are decades older. Whereas the singer's position in the school is perceived as relatively fixed (the school as an institution of training is organized around this fixedness), in the church the singer moves much more freely, inhabiting many different roles and contributing to the social life of the church in many different ways. Although they are generally always on stage "as Christians," they have much more freedom to shape the ways they engage with their fellow Christians "as singers" at church than they do at school, where their relations are more clearly determined by their status "as students" within the discipleship structure there.

I began to recognize the tension between these two seemingly complementary sites (church and school) when student informants described to me their best and worst experiences singing for an audience. Nearly all of their examples of great singing experiences had taken place at church or in church-related events. Students and professionals cited the audience's attentiveness and appreciation, a feeling of vocal freedom and relaxation and a sense of spiritual communion and joy as central elements of their best performances for Christian audiences. On the other hand, these same singers almost always told stories about failing exams, botching auditions, anxiety during competitions, and vocal fatigue during lessons as their worst singing experiences. They explained that singing in church or for Christian events, even if the music was not always as exciting or challenging as operatic music, was always focused on bringing the audience closer to God, which meant musical cathexis, affectively charged singing, and emotional communication with everyone present. They contrasted this with the challenges of singing in school, where performances were construed as events organized around critical judgment both by their peers and by their professors. Singing in school was not joyful as it was in church; more often than not, it produced anxiety and envy. Within the competitive context of the school, singers said, even devout Christians could become corrupt and envious; they might even attempt to sabotage the successes of their own Christian brothers and sisters. Just as students often talked about wanting to escape from the school to sing in the church, they also talked about how much they preferred the social environment of the church to that of the school. And in both of these realms of communicative interaction—everyday utterances and performances of singing—the tension between church and school emerged through the voice itself.

The School

As I mentioned above, singers often told me that departments of Western classical singing were paradoxically the "most Korean" or "most traditional"—meaning pejoratively the "most Confucian"—of all departments at a university. At school, one constantly is negotiating one's discipleship relation to one's teachers, as well as one's place in generational relation to one's cohort-relative seniors and juniors. This negotiation can manifest in the way singers adjust the qualia of their voices—in both speech and song—in relation to the person with whom they are interacting.

For example, I accompanied a group of fourth-year students from the SNU Department of Voice to the Seoul Arts Center to attend a joint performance by a member of SNU's faculty and a member of Ehwa Women's University's faculty. Many students, faculty, and staff of the department were in attendance that evening. As we strolled past the fountains and through the center's large concrete plaza, I heard a chorus of loud, high-pitched, nasalized voices calling out from behind us: "*Annyŏng haseyo!*" ("Hello!" with the relatively "polite" -*yo* sentence ending). We turned around and saw a group of young people approximately ten meters away, smiling and bowing quickly. The students I was with acknowledged the other group's presence with a soft, low-pitched "*ne*" (yes) and an almost labored smile and turned back around. I asked the student next to me who the others had been, and she answered, "*Il hangnyŏn haksaengdŭl*" (first-year students). Within minutes, one of the fourth-year students remarked to the others in a whisper, "*Ŏ, sŏnsaengnim!*" (Oh, teacher!), and all of the students straightened their bodies, began to smile and bow quickly, and called out "*Annyŏng haseyo sŏnsaengnim!*" in a high-pitched, nasalized tone. A professor from the department turned around and acknowledged the students' presence with barely a smile and then turned back to the people she was walking with, not uttering a sound.

I had seen the students I was with transform through the qualic tuning of the voice from being my peers (signaled by the unmarked pitch and timbre of their speech), into the superiors of junior students (signaled by the markedly lower pitch of their faucalized voices and by their slow, labored responses), into the inferiors of a professor (signaled by the markedly higher, nasalized pitch of their ventriculated voices and by their sharp, quick bows)—all by coordinating the signals in various modalities surrounding the relatively terse denotational content.[37] This first order of systematic prosodic contrasts further indexed a second indexical order of asymmetric role relations positioned within the stratified social structure of the school.[38] By tuning the qualia of the voice along with the visible channel of bodily comportment, the individuals signaled their relatively deferential or authoritative roles as contextually contingent stances. This particular event alerted me to the constant attention students must pay to their place within the hierarchy of the department and to the malleability of the voice in the process of inhabiting these different relational roles.

So conscious are students of the importance of their duties to their professors that the topic often arises as jokes or complaints in relatively public settings. Throughout my fieldwork in Seoul, I observed the weekly meetings of an English repertoire and diction course at SNU. The lecturer *(kangsa)*, Ms. Kim, invited me to participate in her class of approximately thirty students in their fourth and final year of vocal study. In late November, a tenor stood before the class and attempted to sing "O Mistress Mine," by Roger Quilter. As he ascended in pitch, his voice began to crack *(ppiksari)*, and he had to stop often to clear the phlegm from his throat. After a particularly bad crack, Ms. Kim stopped the singer and turned to the class and asked in English, "If you have an audition or a concert, but your voice is in a bad condition, what do you do?" The class was silent. "What do you do? How do you fix the problem?" she continued. A student in the front row mumbled in English, "Just do it." Ms. Kim responded that he still needed a strategy. Another student said, "Pray to the Lord" in Korean *(Chunim kke kido hamnida)*. A number of students nodded. Ms. Kim responded in English, "Yes, praying is good. I'm not against that. But what else should you do?" Then a student sitting in the rear of the classroom, who was much appreciated for making others laugh, called out in Korean, "Make a disciple sing" *(Cheja ege norae rŭl sik'imnida)*. The room erupted into laughter. Ms. Kim responded that this strategy had indeed become very popular, but that wasn't what she had in mind. As the room quieted down, she proceeded to explain a form of vocal warm-up that would remove phlegm from the throat and prepare a singer for a performance.

This anecdote illustrates a number of dimensions of studying *sŏngak* in Korea. First, it shows that even in the fourth year of their study, most students still do not have a basic grasp of vocal warm-ups or technique—even in one of the most prestigious departments in the country. None of the students were able to offer any sort of technical solution to the problem faced by the tenor in front of them. Second, it shows how

Christian religiosity is shared and expressed freely in the class. And third, it shows the commonly held assumptions about the kind of service that teachers expect from their disciples.

One way in which a disciple can serve a teacher is by adopting the teacher's method of vocal sound production and emulating it in performance. Despite the pervasive discourse in European and North American vocal pedagogy (not to mention literature and other forms of semiotic production) around "finding one's own voice," students in Korea usually are expected to reproduce the method and sound of their teacher's voices. The disciple is supposed to be of service to the teacher, and likewise the disciple's voice should replicate qualia of the teacher's voice.[39] By doing so, students index the teacher's authority through the qualia of the voice itself.

One of my key informants, Su-jin, was caught in a very difficult place when she returned from abroad to begin working as a singer and lecturer in Seoul. When a part-time teaching position opened up at her alma mater, Su-jin began to take private lessons with her former teacher, a professor at the university, to prepare for the audition. The teacher was on the audition panel that would decide which applicant would be hired. Su-jin often complained to me that the lessons and the entire structure of the application process forced her back into submission to her teacher. She attended weekly lessons for more than two months, each time bringing five hundred thousand *wŏn* in a white envelope for the teacher. They had not discussed a price, but she knew what the teacher expected. Money, however, was not enough. On one occasion we were having coffee when Su-jin's phone rang. The conversation was brief, and I only heard Su-jin respond deferentially, *"Ye, ye sŏnsaengnim"* (Yes, yes, teacher). After hanging up, Su-jin told me she needed to leave right away. Her teacher had called and demanded that she come to the university to take over the teacher's lessons for the day. But she was not surprised. This sort of thing had happened before, and she expected that it would happen again—especially if she received the lecturer position.[40]

As the audition drew nearer, Su-jin began to complain about vocal fatigue. She told me that her teacher had chosen a piece for the audition that was too heavy for her light soprano voice and was also pushing her to sing it in a manner that Su-jin felt was "not good for her vocal cords" *(sŏngdae e an chot'a)*. While studying abroad in Europe, Su-jin's vocal technique had undergone a major transformation, which she herself saw as far "healthier" *(kŏn'gang hada)* and more "natural" *(chayŏnsŭrŏpta)* than what she had learned originally in Korea. Most singers in Korea reported to me that loudness *(k'ŭn sori)* was still the most prized attribute of voices in Korea and also cited this as the reason why so many singers in Korea lost their voices so early in their careers. They saw this as a residual aesthetic value that was slowly being replaced by a focus on health and beauty. While in Europe, Su-jin had worked very hard to remove tension from her throat, jaw, and tongue, and to reduce the air pressure beneath her glottis. But her former teacher in Seoul insisted that she use more air pressure, make the tongue rigid, and tighten the jaw to produce what Su-jin perceived to be a more "piercing" *(tchijŏjinŭn)* sound. When I asked Su-jin why she didn't just ignore the teacher's guidance and sing in the audition as she wished to, she told me flatly that it would be impossible. It would show obvious disrespect to the teacher, and she would never be hired. For the remaining weeks leading up to the audition, she sang as her teacher demanded during lessons and likewise instructed students to do so in the lessons she taught on behalf of her teacher. But in church, onstage, or when teaching lessons at other universities, she sang and instructed as she felt was actually correct and healthy.

Su-jin passed the audition and became a lecturer for her alma mater. More than thirty singers auditioned for the position. The day she received the news, she invited me to dinner to talk about the audition. Over barbecued pork, she explained to me how happy she was that she had passed the audition but how worried she was about the demands of being a lecturer under her teacher. It meant that she would need to continue to adjust her vocal style while at the university, especially when her teacher called on her to take over her lessons. It might also mean that her teacher would ask Su-jin to continue training with her—a subtle directive to hand over part of her paycheck each week to the teacher in the form of reciprocal payment for helping her win the position.[41] It was obvious that the position, while necessary for Su-jin's own career, was also strengthening her role as disciple of her teacher and expanding the kinds of services she would be expected to provide.

In the contexts of Su-jin's situation, we had discussed the qualic tuning that goes on when students speak to their teachers. So I asked Su-jin how she had answered her phone when her teacher called to give her the news. She smiled and said, *"Choesonghamnida sŏnsaengnim"* (Forgive me, teacher), in a high-pitched, nasal voice, like the students I had seen bowing before their teacher. Her preemptive self-lowering apology (for not having met her teacher's expectations), the timbre and pitch at which it was delivered, the singing method she used during lessons and her audition, and her numerous tokens of generosity all signaled her commitment to the kind of discipleship filiality that makes Christian singers in Korea refer to voice departments as "the most Korean," "the most traditional," and the "the most Confucian" of all.

Between Church and School

Singers of classical music move constantly between the church and the school. A story about a young singer, Sang-u, will help illustrate how two institutions sometimes have a complementary relationship and sometimes come into tension with one another. Sang-u, a tenor in his fourth year of study at a university in Seoul, often described himself as someone caught between multiple worlds. His mother was a devout Christian, a *kwŏnsa* in a Presbyterian church. His father owned a *t'ŭrot'ŭ* bar that sold whisky and was frequented by shamans. His family had made its money recently as a result of his father's entrepreneurial success but still lived in the house that his father and uncle had built with their own hands. His girlfriend, a student of piano at the same university, whom he said he loved and planned to marry, came from a very wealthy, educated family. And when I met him in early 2008, he was struggling between two possible career paths: one as a local singer of Christian music, the other as an international singer of opera.

Sang-u had never taken a voice lesson before auditioning for university voice departments, but he had grown up singing hymns and gospel music with his mother in church and *t'ŭrot'ŭ* songs with his father at home and in the bar. His father often would call on him to stop by the bar and perform for the guests. He described having a natural attraction to Italian opera arias; the melodrama and theatricality reminded him of the songs he had grown up singing. In college he was recruited to sing with an all-male Christian vocal ensemble. He told me they were looking for a tall, good-looking tenor. Standing six feet one inch tall and described by others as "attractive" *(chal saenggida)* and "stylish" *(mŏt itta),* Sang-u was perfect for the part.

The ensemble was sponsored by a major Korean corporation. The leader of the group, who doubled as the piano accompanist, was the wife of the CEO. She formed the group with the explicit aim of bringing both the gospel and high culture to the poor and uneducated. They toured Korea, Asia, and even the United States, singing both classical music and gospel music. They released albums in which each of the five members sang at least one aria or art song. And they were paid well.

The ensemble had even agreed to pay for Sang-u's master's program in Korea if he kept singing with them. When I met him, Sang-u was trying to choose between staying in Korea to sing with the group and attend the master's program at his university on the one hand and focusing his energy on auditioning for conservatories abroad on the other. If he chose the former, he would most certainly become a local Christian singer—a career that his parents favored because of the possibility of making a living singing more popular music. This would mean eventually becoming a full-time singer of CCM *(ssissiem,* contemporary Christian music), which many classically trained singers in Korea pursue when their *sŏngak* voices begin to deteriorate. If he chose the latter, he would be committing to the life of a professional opera singer and all of the risks and insecurities that came with it. It would also mean putting off professional employment and continuing to pay for vocal study. He prayed for months, hoping to receive a signal from God guiding him one way or another.

Then Sang-u faced a crisis. When we met late in the summer of 2008 to have lunch at the school cafeteria, he told me that earlier in the summer he had gone to a doctor because he kept losing his voice. The doctor told him to rest his vocal cords, but, with auditions for the university opera production approaching, he disregarded the advice and continued to practice every day, to sing in classes, and to perform with his ensemble. He landed a leading role in one of the casts, but a month after the audition his condition had grown so dire that he could no longer sing. He returned to the doctor, who told him that he had developed nodes on his vocal cords and that his throat was effectively bleeding. The doctor told Sang-u that there was a possibility he would never sing again. He completely quit singing and tried not to speak, but kept the issue a secret from almost everyone. He was ashamed and fearful—ashamed because of what his peers would think about him and his future and fearful that he would bring shame to his professor, who had had a long career in opera and was generally seen as a great singer (but not teacher) in the department. The day after we met for lunch, he went back to the doctor for a checkup and was told that he had healed a great deal but was still in danger.

Sang-u was at a loss. He was planning a large concert with his singing ensemble, and he had been cast to sing a leading role in the university opera production. But he knew that his university professor could not help him prepare for either of them without further damaging his voice. He knew that his teacher's instruction actually was responsible for his having developed nodes on his vocal cords in the first place. Yet he could not go elsewhere for instruction. Students caught taking unsanctioned private lessons were severely punished and publicly shamed by their teachers. But Sang-u's own problems had grown so severe that he accepted the risk and asked a singer known for her knowledge of vocal pedagogy to give him a few private lessons, just to get him back on track. The person, Mi-jin, refused and apologized, citing the obvious professional risks involved.

Then, a few weeks later, Mi-jin ran into a friend of Sang-u's and inquired after his condition. The friend, breaking the promise of secrecy out of concern for Sang-u, told Mi-jin just how poor Sang-u's voice had become and explained that Sang-u was considering leaving school to let his voice heal completely. Mi-jin explained to me that when she heard this, she decided it would be unchristian to let Sang-u suffer. She said she thought of the missionaries and early Christian martyrs who had risked themselves for the sake of her ancestors. She said she also considered the contemporary Korean missionaries who were putting themselves in danger to save the unbaptized around the world. So she called Sang-u and asked him to come to her home studio to discuss the issue. She also asked me to join them. After talking for a couple of hours about his professional aspirations and his Christian faith, Mi-jin suggested that Sang-u take three lessons per week from her. She assured him that she was not concerned with the money and that he would not have to pay her the going rate for hourly lessons. Once they had agreed, they prayed together.

Sang-u's voice began to change after only a few lessons. He developed what singers call a "dome" on the sound, or "height" to the sound. This sonic phenomenon generally corresponds to the phonic process of focusing the overtones of the voice via the articulators, rather than attempting to reinforce the fundamental pitch through increased subglottal pressure and laryngeal tension. He reported feeling "space" inside his vocal chamber. Mi-jin encouraged him when she heard what she called his "natural" technique *(chayŏn palsŏng)* allowing his natural or "inborn" voice *(t'agonan moksori)* to come out. At first, she had to stop him from trying "too hard" *(nŏmu yŏlsimhi)*. But after a few weeks of lessons, both Mi-jin and Sang-u reported that he was finding the voice that God had given him *(Hananim kkesŏ chusin moksori)*.

Sang-u began to conceptualize his vocal practice in terms of two voices: one given by his university professor and the other given by God, which Mi-jin was secretly helping him find. He experienced these two voices as standing in competition with each other. The vocal methods he was learning from his professor were oriented to the professor's own standards and particularities. It was "his way." And like Su-jin above, Sang-u was obliged to pay deference to his teacher by reproducing the vocal qualia of the teacher's method of sound production. And he did so whenever he attended voice lessons with the professor. However, when practicing alone or singing with Mi-jin, with his vocal ensemble, or at church, he tried to sing with his natural or "God-given" voice. He decided that his professor's status was not sufficient to warrant destroying his own vocal cords and secretly worked with Mi-jin to continue to find and develop the voice that the two of them agreed was truly his.

Finally, Sang-u said he felt comfortable enough with his God-given voice that he began to use it at school. He sang in the university opera production using the voice. He performed his graduation recital using that voice. He complained, however, that when he sang for his university professor in one-on-one lessons, so strong was his feeling of discipleship and filial loyalty that his old habits seemed to come back—even when he tried to sing with his newly discovered technique. In this case, the enregisterment of his voice in the institutional context of the lesson extended out from the pure material of communication (i.e., "sound") into his corporeally embodied action. This dimension of semiotic action, via the phonosonic nexus, linked communicative practice to bodily "hexis" as "a practical way of experiencing and expressing [his] own sense of social value."[42]

Through this process, he had concluded that God had given him this voice to be an opera singer and wanted him to leave Korea for further study. While he and Mi-jin worked together to prepare his audition materials for conservatories in the United States, Sang-u sometimes practiced his repertoire as a soloist for the church choir that Mi-jin conducted on Sundays. He submitted a recording of himself and was granted auditions at all of the schools to which he had applied. After the live auditions, he was accepted at two U.S. conservatories, both with generous financial aid packages. For Sang-u, a focus on serving God, on the church, on Christian relationships, and on a notion of God's plan for his life ultimately led him to strengthen his conviction that he should continue to study vocal technique and sing operatic music. He decided that if he sang with his God-given voice, then he could both sing opera and bring God to his audience. As his voice and career became more aligned to his faith, more and more he began to see the school as a hindrance and the church as a help to all singers in Korea. He came to believe that the discipleship structure within the school often impeded the singer's progress by orienting the voice to the teacher rather than to God. In the church, he said, a singer could practice one's God-given voice away from the watchful eye of the teacher (even if it was another teacher who helped him realize this).

The Church

Like Sang-u, many singers take private lessons in secret and use their performances at church to practice their technique outside school. Their secret teachers often are fellow church members or at least have been introduced to them through a church connection. Many of the singers who admitted this to me also told me that they had prayed with their secret teachers and had agreed that it was God's plan to hold secret meetings. Furthermore, most of them kept it from their peers at school. Only a few close friends outside the voice department knew of their secret training. And as they noticed the sound of their voices changing and felt their technique grow more stable and less labored, they grew more and more thankful to God.

One final anecdote will help to illustrate how the church is perceived as a place in which the voice is freed from the constraints and discipleship structure of the school. In Ms. Kim's repertoire and diction class, students were required to choose two songs during the semester to perform for the class, one of which they would sing in the final class concert. On the final day of class in December, a baritone walked to the front of the class to perform his selection. He had chosen the "The Birds," by Benjamin Britten. The lines of the first verse, penned by Hilaire Belloc, are "When Jesus Christ was four years old/The angels brought Him toys of gold/Which no man ever had bought or sold." After the student had finished the song, Ms. Kim told him he needed to correct the pronunciation of a very important word. Admitting that it was not easy for native speakers of Korean to pronounce "Jesus" in English, she told the student that he had been pronouncing the word as "[ʑidzɔs]" instead of "[dʒiːzəs]."[43] After directing him to repeat the word numerous times, she turned to the class and asked the students to pronounce it. Many in the class reproduced the same phonological pattern as the student standing before the class had done.

After trying to explain the difference in phonetic terms, Ms. Kim asked me to stand up and pronounce the word. I did so, awkwardly—I had never called out "Jesus!" before. Then she asked me to say it louder. I repeated the word. Then she went through the students, one by one, asking them to stand up and call out "Jesus" in full voice. This went on for approximately seven minutes. At first, the students were hesitant and shy, and their words were almost inaudible. But after each student took a turn, more and more students joined in, repeating the word together like a chorus after the person standing had spoken. Every so often, Ms. Kim would ask me to repeat the word, and then she herself would repeat the word. After all the students had taken their turns, Ms. Kim asked me to stand one last time and pronounce the word. She instructed the students to observe my mouth and jaw as I spoke. Although I was not used to doing such things, I called out the word *Jesus* as clearly as I could, accenting and elongating the first syllable. Then a chorus of students repeated the word after me, matching my accentuation and intonational contour more closely than my pronunciation of the consonants and vowels. More students joined in for a second repetition. And on the third repetition even more students joined, this time reversing the accentuation and elongating the second syllable. A rhythmic representation would look something like this:

>   /   ˇ
>
> *NH:*   Je: sus!
>
>   /   ˇ
>
> *Class:* Je: sus!
>
>   /   ˇ
>
> *Class:* Je: sus!
>
>   ˇ   /
>
> *Class:* Je su:::::s!

Then some of them called out "O my God!" in English. Others began to laugh. And others still continued to repeat the word individually. As the room erupted into a cacophony of individually uttered tokens of "Jesus," I recognized the text that had just made its way into the classroom. The triplicate chant of "Jesus" here resembled the triplicate chant of "Chu yŏ!" that I had heard at the services at the Yoido Full Gospel Church, a Pentecostal church in Seoul that claims a membership of more than eight hundred thousand. The chant of "Chu yŏ," an honorific vocative for "Lord," serves as a transition between stages of a church service. An assistant pastor usually begins the service by leading the congregants gathered in the main sanctuary in singing gospel songs, accompanied by a rock band. After approximately thirty minutes of singing (beginning before the actual service), the assistant pastor asks the congregation to call out "Chu yŏ!" Together, they repeat "Chu yŏ" three times. The pastor holds the final vowel of the final repetition of "Chu yŏ!" while the congregation breaks into audible group prayer.[44]

Although the students in the diction and repertoire class did not start praying together, they had made an important transition. Seven minutes earlier, there had been a sense of anxiety and insecurity in the room. Now the students seemed comfortable and relaxed. Seconds after they chanted, the accompanist played the first notes of the Britten, and the baritone once again began to sing. To many of the students, the chanting of "Jesus" seemed funny, hence the shouting out in English of "O my God!" and laughter. But even though most of the students attended churches that were differentiated starkly from the Yoido Full Gospel Church in terms of class, ritual aesthetics, and theology (they were mostly middle- and upper-class Presbyterians, not Pentecostals), chanting "Jesus!" together still indexed the shared belief in Christianity among nearly all of them. In this moment of reorientation, the qualia of their voices were also recalibrated. For the remainder of the class, they vocalized more boldly, with more animation, with more obvious conviction and expression. And, also important, they did so with a measure of sincerity. In this event, I observed not only the interdiscursivity between events of entextualization in church and school (i.e., that they appeared to "move" from the church to the classroom) but also an intertextual linkage between the two, through which the iconically related texts (the triplicate chant) "incorporat[ed] aspects of context, such that the resultant text carrie[d] elements of its history of use within it."[45] In this case, the school did not become the church, nor did the classroom transform into a sanctuary, nor did the students transform into a congregation, nor did Ms. Kim transform into a pastor. However, the qualia of the school—of the social relations between the teacher and the students, of the social relations among the students themselves, of the sensation of vocalization before competing peers, of the qualitative dimensions of the voice itself—momentarily approached the qualia of the church, which brought the more abstract feeling of the qualities of Christianity into the immediate sensory and emotional experience of the event.

The students admired, appreciated, and trusted Ms. Kim for constantly reminding them of why they were singing in the first place. Earlier in the year, she had stopped the class to make an announcement.

It had come to her attention that many of the students were concerned about auditioning abroad. They feared that their voices were not "big" enough, that they would be rejected for looking and sounding "too Korean." Ms. Kim told them in Korean, "If you do not have a big voice, if you are not tall, if you do not have a great body, that is ok. What is important? Not music. Not money. God is the most important." One of the students called out in English, "Faith!" Kim responded affirmatively, repeating the word *faith* in English, and then switched back to Korean "The Lord is most important." She then switched back into English and said, "I'm telling you the truth."

Throughout the semester, Ms. Kim continually reminded them of this sentiment, particularly during moments of heightened anxiety or shame. And in that final class, through the chanting of "Jesus!" in a familiar poetic form, the students shifted their focus from the scholastic pronunciation of English words—a major source of anxiety among Korean speakers of English—to the contexts in which such words would be spoken and sung.[46] In this shift, they tuned the qualia of their voices from the school setting to the church setting, cuing up an apperceptive background different from the one they had started with.[47] This realignment of semiotic text to context effectively remapped the discipleship structure from one of neo-Confucian discipleship to one of Christian discipleship.

CONCLUSION

In this chapter, I have dealt with the vocal mediation of two related forms of personhood: the disciple in a school and the disciple in a church. I have shown how the qualia of the voice—in both its phonic and sonic dimensions—can be calibrated or tuned to these different institutional structures of discipleship, even beyond the physical boundaries of the institution. For most Christians and singers of *sŏngak,* these synchronically existing structures of discipleship are positioned diachronically within a Christian chronotope of ethnonational advancement: from the neo-Confucian sociality of premodern Korea to the Christian sociality of a developed, modern, and enlightened country. In the specific examples I have presented, the voice itself becomes a medium through which one's discipleship under and service to either a university teacher or Jesus Christ are expressed and embodied.

In both instances, the disciple pays deference to a higher authority and tunes the qualia of the voice to that figure. In speech, this is often done by lowering oneself through raised pitch, thus differentiating one's own voice from that of the addressee (as sometimes happens with other honorifics forms). This is precisely what took place in my description of how the younger students addressed the older students and how the older students addressed their professor. While this was common in person-to-person interactions (e.g., between a student and a teacher), I rarely observed a similar kind of nasality or ventriculation in direct prayer to God. Prayer often becomes more emphatic and animated than "normal" speech, occasionally rising in pitch and in some cases even softening in phonation, but it never seems to take on the same phono-sonic qualia of deference observable in person-to-person interactions. Even though God and Jesus are addressed and referred to using honorifics in Korean speech (unlike, for example, German, in which one addresses God using the intimate *Du* form), it does not seem to be necessary to infantilize oneself to be humble before God.

The formula is different in singing. The singer pays tribute to the higher authority by incorporating the ascribed attributes of the higher authority into the qualia of the voice itself. Rather than differentiating one's own voice from that of the higher figure (as in speech), the singer attempts to reproduce the higher authority's voice (in the case of a professor) or the perceived attributes of the higher authority more generally as a means of showing deference and respect to that authority. Some older students who had studied in the 1980s told stories of their professors' forbidding them to make any gestures or displays of emotion while singing, because, as the professors put it, they were mere students and had no right to command the attention of their professors; they sang only at their professors' pleasure. Because most students of *sŏngak* in Korea consider their God to be above their professors and value their relationship with the former over the relationship with the latter, they tend to view the higher form of vocalization as that which confirms their Christian discipleship in the church, regardless of what they are taught by their professors. Their natural or God-given voice is, in a sense, the voice of God.

The voice is a salient medium through which one practices one's faith—both in the treatment of the body and in the production of vocal sound. Often, the school is seen as the place where one's vocal expression of Christian discipleship is undermined by the demands of student-teacher filiality. At church, singers are charged with being disciples of Jesus Christ and with bringing others into the same system of relationships. At school, singers are socialized into a residual educational system of discipleship, where students' vocalization should always be performed in emulation of and deference to their professors. Singers point to this practice of emulation when a young voice seems increasingly defective. Even for those like Sang-u who manage to avoid vocal damage as they move between the church and the school and make adjustments to their voices accordingly, the constant threat that the school presents to their voices reminds them of a residual cultural past that seems stubbornly to live on in the present.

Despite the competing structures of discipleship, the school and the church are intimately linked in Seoul's musical culture. There remains the necessary flow of students and teachers between the two social realms and the interlocking of the two social networks in the city's performance contexts. Colleges of music, and the power vested in their faculty, form a whole authorizing realm of certification beyond the church, which determines which people can become soloists in Seoul's megachurches. And so the lives of Christian singers in Korea are institutionally anchored to both the church and the school. Qualic adjustments are being made constantly by tuning the voice to the array of inhabitable identities cued up by different contexts of interaction, utilizing the malleability of the voice as an aspect—and instrument—of transformable personhood.[48]

These two institutions are so powerful in the social life of *sŏngak* singing in Korea that the handful of singers who were not Christian consistently reported feeling oppressed by and isolated from the careers they chose. I met few singers who had been raised in Buddhist or irreligious households and wanted seriously to pursue a career (i.e., few who were not prospecting for marriage or other social opportunities not directly related to singing). These students consistently reported to me their desire to leave Korea and never return except to visit their families. While many Christian singers complained of the lack of a general public for their craft and lamented having to insert themselves into the discipleship structure of the school in order to work at all, they saw Christian culture in Korea as a viable and attractive performance scene for *sŏngak*. Non-Christian singers, however, realized that beyond the church there really was no *sŏngak* singing at all. No matter how good they were, without the church they would have no career. They said that *sŏngak* singing in Korea was Christian singing, and as non-Christians they simply wouldn't have an opportunity to sing.

And so, while *sŏngak* in Korea appears at first to be a unified communicative register, we can see now that it actually is a fractured register, a site of contestation, oriented differently toward different institutions according to their competing regimes of qualic evaluation.[49] Much of the striving to unify the register by the students and professionals I have discussed in this chapter—the desire to sing one way all the time—is an attempt to unify the institutions and to overcome the "audience segregation" that emerges from competing forms of institutionalized role recruitment.[50] This unification is viewed as the spread of Christian social relations from the ritual site of the church to other institutions and out into the world. In the following chapter, I discuss how a particular genre of vocal performance, the homecoming recital, does precisely this kind of unifying work by drawing on the authorizing forces of both church and school to create the public singer in Seoul. The ritual effect is to Christianize an ostensibly secular performance and to treat *sŏngak* as a thoroughly Christian semiotic register in Korea.

CHAPTER 6

The Voice of Homecoming

AN OSTENSIBLY PUBLIC PERFORMANCE

During one of my first visits to South Korea to conduct early fieldwork on cultural conceptualizations and practices of voice, I traveled around Seoul to visit various colleges of music and performance halls. At both I found rows of glossy fliers and professionally designed posters advertising the solo recitals of musicians who recently had returned home from study and professional work abroad. Most of these posters were for singers of *sŏngak*. The ubiquity of these fliers and the frequency of these recitals seemed to suggest a robust, thriving audience for this type of music.

As I mentioned in the introduction, I had originally traveled to Seoul to find out why Korea was producing so many successful singers of European-style classical music. Since Korean singers regularly swept conservatory auditions and competitions in the United States and Europe, I assumed that in Korea there must be some sort of thriving culture of connoisseurship for *sŏngak* singing and perhaps classical music more broadly. But I would discover that the social life of *sŏngak* singing in Korea, far more so than the social life of classical orchestral or piano music, was most centrally located in and anchored to the church. I found that the *sŏngak* voice itself served as an emblem of Korean Christian personhood framed by a specifically Christian aesthetic of progress. This pervasive Christianization of *sŏngak* as a semiotic register—a cultural model of social action associated with stereotypical persons and values—was reflected in the professed religious beliefs of my informants in Seoul. They perceived the practice of *sŏngak* in Korea as basically—or ideally—a Christian practice, even when the music was secular and it took place beyond the institutional boundaries of the church. But at the time of this early fieldwork in 2006, my awareness of the important sociocultural link between seemingly secular *sŏngak* performances and the cultivation of the *sŏngak* voice in Korean Christianity was still only developing.

I finally attended my first homecoming recital in early 2008. The week of the performance, I went to the box office of the Sejong Center for the Performing Arts, one of Seoul's premiere performance spaces, to purchase a ticket. The young woman behind the counter was noticeably surprised to see me there, but she happily sold me a ticket to a recital for the coming weekend. When I told her that it was my first time buying a ticket for a homecoming recital, she laughed and responded that it was her first time selling a single ticket for a homecoming recital. I asked her how could that be, since there were as many as four or five each week at the Sejong Center's recital hall alone. She explained that in the few months that she had been working at the center no one had come in to buy an individual ticket for a homecoming recital. Rather, right after scheduling a recital, usually a few people—the performer among them— bought up rows of tickets in advance.

When I arrived at the chamber hall later that week, the ticket seller's surprise made more sense to me. Many of the people waiting in the lobby seemed to know one another. Most of them stood in large groups and greeted the people who arrived (not me, however), and many addressed or referred to one another with kin terms or other institutional titles. When I walked into the lobby, it was clear that I had entered not a public event, exactly, but something more intimate and closed. And as I sat in the auditorium, waiting for the seats to fill up and finally realizing that they would not, I noticed something else: with fewer than a hundred people in a hall that seated at least three or four hundred, this was not the event that the marketing materials seemed to me to have been selling. The performance was not presented as the aesthetic object of a connoisseur's attention or as a public display of art music for anyone inclined to hear it. The singer had not simply thought to "put on a show and see who shows up."[1] This was a more intimate performance, in which a returning singer presented herself to her family, friends, and institutional relations as a professional singer.

At the intermission, I asked some teenagers seated nearby how they knew the performer. They responded that they did not know her personally but that someone who did know her had given them tickets. Others responded that they knew the singer through church, that they were acquainted with one of her parents, or that they were studying with the singer's former voice teacher. It seemed that most members of the audience were there because they either knew the singer or had been given free tickets by someone who did.

During the performance, older adults talked loudly with one another, teens texted on their mobile phones and giggled, and some small children even crawled around in the aisles—much to the irritation of the ushers who pleaded with the parents to take control of their kids. For approximately one hour, the sparse audience seemed to suffer patiently through the recital of European works in four languages by composers such as Handel, Meyerbeer, Berg, Poulenc, and Tchaikovsky, paying little attention to the events onstage.

Until the end, that is. After the singer had finished the final piece in her program, members of the audience stood from their seats and shouted "Encore!" at the top of their lungs.[2] Others whistled and yelled "Bravo!" [sic]. The singer remained onstage and, after the noise died down, began to sing a twentieth-century Korean melody composed by Im Kŭng-su (b. 1949) to a poem by Song Kil-cha (b. 1942) titled "As If Spring Were Coming across the River" (Kang kŏnnŏ pom i odŭt). After she had sung the final phrases, the crowd again broke into animated applause and called for another encore. This time the soprano sang a Christian hymn, "Nae yŏnghon ŭi kŭŭkhi kip'ŭn tesŏ," translated from the nineteenth-century American hymn by Warren D. Cornell, "Far Away in the Depths of My Spirit." The refrain went as follows:

> P'yŏnghwa, p'yŏnghwa roda
> Hanŭl wi esŏ naeryŏ one,
> Kŭ sarang ŭi mulkyŏl i yŏngwŏn t'orok
> Nae yŏnghon ŭl tŏp'ŭsosŏ.

> Peace, O Peace
> Coming down from Heaven,
> With waves of love forever,
> Cover my soul.[3]

A hush came over the audience. Adults stopped talking, teenagers stopped texting, parents embraced their children. The audience's full attention was on the singer. Some people closed their eyes, bowed their heads, and clasped their hands together. After the hymn, the audience again broke into ecstatic applause, but this time without any calls for another encore. It was as if they knew that this was the end, as if the Christian hymn obviously signaled the end of the event.

The audience filed out into the lobby and waited for the singer to emerge. People waited to greet her, to bestow flowers upon her, and to have their picture taken with her by a man in a dark suit, who appeared to be a professional photographer hired to document the event. Before leaving, each of us was instructed to take a small pink bag from the ticket counter. Inside was a small piece of chewy rice cake *(ttŏk)*, wrapped in a ribbon, a gift to thank us for attending.

As I would come to realize, everything about this particular homecoming recital was representative of the performance genre overall, from the location of the performance, to the selection of repertoire, to the extensive publicity, to the Christian hymn offered (and expected) as an encore. Of the numerous recitals I attended in 2008 and of the dozens of recitals described by my informants, I saw only one and heard of only a few in which a Christian hymn was not sung at the end. So I asked myself: Why the professional show for an event that was so clearly personal? And why a Christian hymn as an encore for a seemingly secular event?

This apparent contradiction is the starting point for this chapter. In the analysis that follows, I show how these various aspects of the performance event—both personal and professional, both religious and secular—are intertwined and mutually reinforcing for the ritual function of the recital. To do so, I give an ethnographically grounded account of the sociocultural work that goes into creating and maintaining an audience for such performances of *sŏngak* in Seoul. I follow by addressing the problem of "homecoming" itself and discussing the kinds of biographical transformations that take place as these singers train and work abroad. Finally, I draw on a semiotically informed anthropology of communication to "read" the ritual as a poetically structured text that brings together these two kinds of groups—performers and audiences—to produce transformative effects for both.[4]

My analysis hinges on the role and placement of the Christian encore sung in Korean in a public performance hall. By ritually mapping the transition from abroad to home, from foreign to familiar, and from secular to Christian, the hymn as an encore in this setting casts the entire event as thoroughly Christian and thoroughly Korean. In fact, *sŏngak* singing in Korea *is* Christian, in the sense that the vast majority of performers and audiences are linked one to another through churches.

The homecoming recital highlights this basic sociocultural fact by presenting the performer as a public professional and presenting the mostly Christian audience of intimate and institutional relations to itself as the general Korean public for this kind of music.

THE PROFESSIONAL SINGER

As any classical musician working in Korea will tell you, Korea really does not have a classical music market comparable to what one would find in Europe or the United States. Despite the large number of Korean musicians represented in conservatories and performing arts organizations around the world, concert halls in Seoul are often empty. So why were these events advertised if no one bought tickets from the box office? Why were there so many concerts if the audience seemed only to consist of family and friends? Why did they take place in large, public recitals halls if the audience did not fill even half of the seats? Why did the whole event have the show of an overtly public occasion if this was so clearly not the case?

At one level, the recital serves as a fairly straightforward ritual reincorporation of a singer into Korean society after an extended period of socially enforced separation and transition abroad. Singers have to study abroad partly in order to find steady employment at home. The homecoming recital is, in itself, an originary act in the biographical life of an individual singer: by aiding in the transition from student to professional, the recital is a practical enactment of the social permission granted to the returning singer to present his or her individual self as the primary focus of public performance. As Protestant Christians, the vast majority of students and professionals of *sŏngak* give most of their early performance opportunities in the context of the various churches where they sing. Before leaving Korea, a singer's personhood qua singer is defined primarily by the singer's place in the discipleship structures of church and school, and the use of the singing voice is more or less restricted to these institutions and oriented to these institutional interests. In both of these sites, the singer sings "through" an institution, or the institution "through" the singer, as it were; the personhood of the singer is inhabitable in terms of the particular institutional models of discipleship. In churches and music schools, singers vocalize for captive audiences, where attention is presupposed by participation in events such as practical exams or church services. More than merely celebrating the return of a musician to Korea following advanced study or work abroad, the homecoming recital inaugurates an individual into the professional music circuit of the city.[5] In so doing, it effectively baptizes singers as professionals in Korea by presenting them as authorized to perform beyond these two institutions. This baptism thus delivers singers into a role in Korean society different from the one they occupied when they left.

At another level, the recital transforms not only the singer but also the audience. The recital brings members of explicit institutions—especially families, schools, and churches—into a public space and recruits them to a public ritual that, in its organization prima facie, does not seem to address an institutional or subcultural audience.[6] However, people usually show up to a homecoming recital out of personal obligation to the performer and wait patiently until it is over. And through the structuring of the recital, members in attendance become engaged in a ritual performance as members of an emergent sociological grouping. For a durationally restricted period, it transforms a grouping of individuals—who may be strangers to one another but are related socially to the performer through institutional ties—into an idealized public for *sŏngak* singing in Korea. However, as I will show, this is achieved not through the scripted portion of the recital (i.e., what is listed in the program) but rather through the audience's participation in and reception of an encore. A Christian encore—usually a hymn—is offered to the audience as a performance explicitly for them, in which they, as a specific subgroup, can participate, while the performance context is presented as potentially for everyone, to which the general public is invited.

The programmed portion of the recital features little, if any, Christian content. Programmed Christian content in homecoming recitals is thoroughly secularized as "academic music" or "art music" and, with the exception of selections from Handel's *Messiah* and a few other pieces, is rarely performed in Korean churches or other religious settings. But during the encore, the Christian hymn is understood to be deeply and completely Christian, relevant to the faith and religious practices of the singer and most of the audience and framed as the culmination of the performance. Unlike the rest of the recital, the encore presents precisely those songs that one does hear in churches throughout Korea. The use of public performance halls for homecoming recitals allows the performer to use the encore to characterize the secular content of the recital as a form of music that is ultimately in the service of Christianity, while presenting a group of Christians to itself as the general public for this secular music. In so doing, the ritual performance surreptitiously characterizes modern Korean Christianity as an inherent quality of modern Korean publicity. That is, from the perspective of Korean Christianity and some of their most public representatives, *sŏngak* singers, the homecoming recital ritually enacts a contemporary Korean public as it should be: unmarked, generalized, normative, and thoroughly Christian.

BUILDING AN AUDIENCE

The homecoming recital is a big deal. For most singers, it will be the first time they have ever given a solo recital in their home country. If a singer had completed a master's degree in Korea before going abroad, he or she would have given a solo graduation recital on campus for family and friends. But homecoming recitals take place outside universities, in one of the professional recital halls in Seoul, usually the Sejong Center, the Seoul Arts Center, or Yongsan Art Hall. Unlike graduation recitals, homecoming recitals have the appearance of "real" concerts, with the full package of tickets, ushers, programs, and marketing materials. Although the concert generates no revenue for the singer, because singers purchase their own tickets from the concert hall and give them away as gifts (which are actually requests for attendance), the performance is treated as a real professional recital. If the homecoming recital does not appear to be of professional quality, the singer is not considered a professional, and the performance loses its legitimacy.

Seasoned professional singers in Korea, like many other performers, know that they must have a dense and expansive network of social relations in order to perform onstage. While artistic experience and accomplishments are important for receiving roles in operas and recitals, the most important factor is the guarantee that a singer can generate an audience by ensuring that someone will purchase tickets. Because there is virtually no consumer market for vocal performances of secular classical music, soloists are usually hired on the basis of their own ability to generate ticket sales. This comes down to two main factors: their social relations and their personal finances. Singers who perform widely in Korea therefore usually have faculty positions, are affiliated with large churches (with tens of thousands of members), and have family money. As Chi-yŏng, a mezzo-soprano, who had studied in Italy and also happened to be my neighbor, put it plainly: since the differences between singers' abilities in Korea are "paper-thin" *(chongi han chang ch'ai)*, if someone wants to reach the "A-class" *(eigŭp eik'ŭllaesŭ)*, there are only two methods: have either extremely powerful connections or extremely large amounts of money.

Singers who have just returned to Seoul are expected to fund their own homecoming recitals, which can cost as much as ten million *wŏn*. They rent the space, which can cost upward of five million *wŏn* depending on the day and time of the recital. They guarantee ticket sales by purchasing the tickets themselves and giving them to family and friends. Attendees are not expected to purchase tickets. An accompanist in the music department at SNU gasped when I told her I had purchased tickets to attend the homecoming recitals of people I did not know personally. She said she had never purchased a ticket for a homecoming recital and suggested that in the future I go to the box office and simply announce that I had been invited. (Another singer actually tried to pay me back for the ticket I had purchased for his recital. I refused his money, of course.) The point, she said, is not to make money; the point is to give a recital. When I asked why homecoming recitals were not simply free, she told me that it would be impossible because it would not seem professional.

Although a sufficient amount of money is a prerequisite for putting on a homecoming recital, money alone does not guarantee a place in a concert hall. One must supply credentials to the booking office to prove one is certified to perform in the space. Singers have to prove their qualifications by listing all of their institutions of training, degrees, and competitions won. This information is also included on the marketing materials and concert programs, which list the achievements of singers like professional curricula vitae. Singers also have to supply the names of faculty members and other established singers to the concert hall as references.

In addition to renting the hall and purchasing the tickets, singers pay a service to prepare the materials (a photo shoot, posters, and program design) for the recital and to distribute the marketing collateral to appropriate spaces (in the concert hall itself, in the respective schools the singer might have attended, mailers to friends and family, etc.). This portion of the recital can also cost around five million *wŏn*. The name of the service usually is listed on the posters and program as an "arts management" agency, such as Youngeum Arts Management (Yŏngŭm Yesul Kihoek).

If a singer has been gone for many years, much is expected of his or her return. The production of the recital—which indexes the enormous price tag of the event and of the singer's education as a whole—presents the constant threat of what Goffman called a "false front."[7] That is, before the actual recital, the marketing materials depict singers dressed in tuxedos and ball gowns, display the names of famous European composers in elegant Romanized fonts, and feature other images of luxury and grandeur, suggesting a personal history of professional accomplishment in the world that may or may not be based on reality. The homecoming recital is a ritual of authorization, and the attendees, particularly other singers, are continually asking themselves and one another "whether or not the performer is authorized to give the performance in question, and are not [always] primarily concerned with the actual performance itself."[8] There is the persistent danger of singers appearing as imposters if they do not meet the vocal standards commensurate with the event design.

This is exactly what happened on one occasion in May 2008. I accompanied a group of fourth-year students from a prominent voice department to the homecoming recital of a soprano, their *sŏnbae*, who had graduated from the department many years before. The recital took place at Seoul Arts Center, in Kangnam, and was highly anticipated by all of the attendees with whom I spoke. More people were in attendance for this recital than I had ever seen at any other. Unlike most homecoming recitals, which generally fill fewer than half the seats of a recital hall, all of the seats were filled. I found it curious at the time that a number of members of the faculty had also shown up, including the head of the department. Presumably, not all of these professors could have been the recitalist's instructors. A part-time lecturer in the department took me aside as we were congregating in the lobby and said, "She [the singer] has attended the most expensive schools, the Paris Conservatory, the Milan Conservatory, Peabody. She had better be good."

The soprano's performance failed to please the students. They whispered that the performer was "holding" her voice *(moksori rŭl chapta)* and that her tongue seemed to be "stiff" *(ttakttakhada)*. After a stretch of English songs, some of these students were critical of her diction and questioned, jokingly, whether she was really singing in English at all. Soon, students took out their phones and began texting their friends out of boredom. However, after the recital ended and the singer had emerged from the hall into the lobby to greet her audience, the professors were first in line to congratulate her. One professor cut through the crowd to introduce a visiting professor from the Eastman School of Music (in the United States), who was in Seoul to give master classes (for which the students would pay a great deal of money). I left the concert with a bass in his fourth year of college. As soon as we had left the performing arts complex and crossed the street, he looked around carefully and then began to criticize the performance. I asked him why everyone—not just family but students and faculty as well—had given her such warm and generous praise. He answered that she was very rich and therefore powerful. I asked him how he knew. He chuckled and replied, "Because there were so many people at her recital."

Of course, not all singers have the kind of power mentioned above. After years of private payments to voice teachers, master classes, competition entry fees, self-funded mission trips overseas, summer workshops in Europe, extended study abroad, and monetary gifts to teachers, the homecoming recital is in some sense a final payment for the right to be a professional singer in Korea. But its cost, after all of that payment, is sometimes too much for the singer or the singer's family to afford out-of-pocket. This is where a different kind of relationship of debt-obligation comes in, specifically anchored in gift exchange.

As with other areas of Korean society, the most common intersection of gift exchange with the recital is manifest in the informal favors that friends and acquaintances do for one another. For example, a person who works in a company or owns a store might buy a handful of tickets for the recital of a friend's son or daughter and invite (or oblige) his or her employees to attend the recital. Another person might buy a floral wreath (hwahwan) to be displayed in front of the recital hall. These wreaths are congratulatory flower displays that are endemic to recitals, store openings, funerals, and other major life transitions. The parents of the singer will be expected to reciprocate in the future with a similar kind of gift or simply by compelling their singer-child to perform in some capacity for the person on the receiving end, such as at a private function.

The extent and form of reciprocation depend on the relations of the persons involved and their capacity to reciprocate.[9] Given that the vast majority of classically trained sŏngak singers in Korea belongs to and sings in Christian churches, reciprocal relations are commonly established through the church. Many of my informants talked about the role of p'umasi among church consociates. As discussed in chapter 5, p'umasi refers to a form of labor exchange, originating from a form of cooperative village organization. Church members might be able to recruit the singer to perform for a church function, give lessons, or supply the labor of his or her own student disciples for some evangelical activity. This term p'umasi would generally come up when singers explained how the majority of the audience at their own or others' recitals was made up of fellow church members.[10] As I will show in the following section, the influence of the church does not end at its social relations; Christianity itself is in fact central to the way the homecoming recital functions.

On the one hand, this has to do with the associations most audience members make between *sŏngak* and Christianity, and, on the other, it has to do with the singer's own feeling of "return" as being a transition from being a performer of secular art music abroad and also a Christian to being at home as a Christian singer of vocal music trained in *sŏngak*. It is to this biographical transformation of the singer abroad that I now turn.

TRANSFORMATIONS ABROAD

What does it mean to come home? The homecoming recital does not merely mark the end of study or work abroad; it is an event in which one must have something to show for the time spent abroad. With all of the money and labor that goes into the recital, the stakes are high to convince an audience of its merit and legitimacy. Furthermore, it is absolutely necessary for making an appropriate transition home, just as going abroad is absolutely necessary for being able to work at home at all.

When students begin university studies in voice, they know they will have to go abroad.[11] As I was told repeatedly, it is practically impossible to gain employment as a voice teacher at a university—whether as full-time faculty or part-time lecturer—without a degree from a conservatory abroad. It is practically impossible to reserve performance space in a concert hall or to successfully audition for a professional solo part without a degree from abroad. Indeed, it is practically impossible to be treated as a professional without a foreign degree.[12]

Although numerous vocal performances take place at music departments all over Seoul, a central purpose of schools of music is to generate and regiment disciple relationships between students and their teachers. The role of vocal cultivation at school has two basic functions. First, the pedagogical mission of the college of music is focused on reproducing the faculty's vocal technique and style in the students. Second, its vocational purpose is to prepare students to audition for further study and performance abroad. Often, students use their disciple relationships at school to gain part-time work at churches, whether through a professor's recommendation or under the auspices of the professor him- or herself. But the vocal training that one receives in Seoul—even from its most prestigious departments—does not qualify one to be a public singer of *sŏngak*.

While the church operates as an important site of training for young singers and exposure for older singers, singing in church is nonetheless not considered serious professional work. Paid engagements taking place in, or explicitly facilitated by, the church are understood to be "work" *(il)* but are clearly marked as "part-time" work *(arŭbait'ŭ),* not professional work. Unlike in the United States and Europe, churches are not usually viewed as potential recital spaces for secular performances of classical music, so professional recitals almost never take place there. While secular music might be performed in a church, it is presented as a part of a church-oriented event (a fundraiser or church talent show) and is usually framed by a sermon and group prayer.

Abroad, classically trained Korean singers far exceed other foreign singers in number and prestige at many conservatories and international competitions. Yet despite achieving success at conservatories and competitions that could propel them into an international career, most classically trained Korean singers return to Seoul—which quite often is their plan from the beginning. In Seoul's local performing arts industry, adequate certification takes precedence in qualifying a singer for a job in performance or teaching. The conservatory name and the number and prestige of competitions won can make an enormous difference in a singer's employability in Korea.[13]

Singers who have studied and worked professionally abroad generally describe two simultaneous developments taking place during this time: technical and affective development. Su-yŏn, a key informant, worked as a lecturer in voice at a few universities in Seoul and as a conductor of a church choir. When I met her, she had recently returned to Seoul from Germany, where she had spent four years studying and working as a singer. Su-yŏn had originally gone to Germany to be with her husband, who was at that time also studying voice in Berlin. Before going to Germany, she had been a top soprano in a prominent voice department in Seoul. However, when she arrived in Germany, the faculty at conservatories there told her that her singing method would ruin her voice. She explained to me how she spent one year in Germany studying privately with a teacher before she auditioned again for conservatories there. During the first six months of these private lessons, the teacher would not allow her to sing anything except glissandi (smooth glides from one pitch to another) on "pure" Italian vowels ([e], [i], [a], [o], [u]). This, she explained, helped her "let go" of her dependence on hearing the sound of her own voice, which she had been taught to do in Korea, and to focus instead on the processual "feeling" of singing. After auditioning successfully, Su-yŏn spent the rest of her time in Münster and Freiburg studying and practicing the physiological and acoustic aspects of vocal sound production to ensure that she could "protect" her own voice and the voices of her students.

Singers usually describe the affective dimensions of vocal transition abroad as a transition from "singing notes" *(ŭmjŏng ŭl naeda)* to "making music" *(ŭmak ŭl yŏnju hada)*. They cite as fundamental their increased attention to the harmonic structure of a musical composition and their role within it, their more intense emotional commitment to the denotational text being sung in a foreign language, their feeling of close connection to others in an ensemble, and especially their newly formed relationship to an audience based on a common appreciation for music being performed in a secular context. Singers attribute the success of this transition to interaction with new teachers and peers and also give a great deal of credit to the audiences composed of eager fans of classical vocal music—something they had not experienced before leaving Korea.

Singers often told me that there were three kinds of audiences in Korea: one group comprising nonsingers who are brought to a performance via other social relations and therefore indifferent to the classical vocal music being performed; the "masses" who are only interested in hearing the "hits" and tend to resist anything new or different; and another, smaller group comprising trained singers who are likely to be critical of others' voices. In contrast, they told me that audiences in Europe and the United States comprised grateful music lovers with whom they could form an artistic, affectively charged relationship through performance.

Singers often described their own process of becoming music lovers themselves by recognizing the presence of and singing for audiences of connoisseurs. In an interview I conducted in Berlin in 2007, the world-famous Korean bass Youn Kwangchul (Yŏn Kwang-ch'ŏl) himself admitted to me that until the year 2000, well after he had started his professional international music career, he still continued to think mostly about the technical aspects of the voice during performances. He said that after singing with many professional colleagues and for many appreciative audiences in Germany and throughout the world, he finally realized that "the voice is really just pure material. You have to make music with it" *(Die Stimme ist ja ein reines Material. Damit muss man musizieren).*[14]

Singers also often report that their voices deteriorate or suffer when they return to Korea. As the mezzo-soprano Chi-yŏng explained:

EXCERPT 6.1

Taebubun yuhak kattaga wagajigo chŏngmal chal handago haesŏ tŭrŏwannŭnde kŭ chung e p'alsip p'ŭrodŭl i, isamnyŏn i chinamyŏn chŏmjŏm chŏmjŏm mok i taun i toenŭn ke irŏn yosodŭl ieyo. Ye. Kŭrŏk'i ttaemune chŏngsin ch'aryŏya twaeyo.

Mostly we went abroad and returned after being recognized for excellence, but eighty percent of us, after two or three years pass, find our throats gradually worn "down" *[taun]* because of these factors. Yes. So we have to be cautious.

My informants attributed the deterioration of voices to numerous causes. They complained that singers must also teach in Korea in order to earn a living and build a network of disciples and that teaching wears out the voice. They told me that most performance spaces have poor acoustics, so singers need a microphone to sing, which negatively affects a technique honed to amplify without a microphone in the proper acoustic environment. If singers want to perform, they said, they have to sing the same repertoire over and over again, which makes the voice "stiff" and restricts development; singers "tune" their voices to the expectations of their audiences, and Korean audiences want "big," "loud" voices *(k'ŭn sori)* regardless of the repertoire and despite the poor acoustics. And the very culture of the stage is also an issue: they told me that colleagues on Korean stages often try to sing over one another, despite the singer's dictum that the biggest voices onstage often resonate the least well in a theater.

Su-yŏn also described her experience of involuntarily shifting back to vocal habits she thought she had left behind in Seoul. For example, in the spring of 2008, Su-yŏn was involved in a concert at the Sŏngnam Arts Center, a massive arts complex in Bundang, a wealthy suburb south of Seoul. The program consisted of Gustav Mahler's "Das irdische Leben" for soprano and orchestra and his Fourth Symphony. "Das Irdische Leben" is sung in the voice of a starving child calling out to his mother for bread. The child dies. The fourth movement of the symphony contains "Das Himmlische Leben," a poem written from the perspective of a child who describes heaven and a feast of saints. As is common in Seoul, the concert itself was presented as a cross between an educational event and a musical performance, and the young conductor, who had recently studied in Austria, gave a thirty-minute lecture about Mahler before the concert.[15]

For weeks before the concert Su-yŏn expressed doubts and anxiety regarding the performance. Mahler orchestras are usually large and demand a very powerful, heavy voice to penetrate the thick orchestration. A soubrette or light soprano of her type is not normally cast to sing such music, even if the part represents the voice of a child. But the conductor had asked her to do it, and she accepted, feeling unable to turn down such a request. At the concert, the audience occupied, at most, a hundred of the approximately thousand seats in the hall. Su-yŏn and I had been singing together for months by this point, and we knew each other's voice well. I noticed that the timbre of her voice was different from what I had heard on earlier occasions. Throughout most of her singing, she was able to project enough to be audible above the orchestra, and her German diction was extremely clear, but her voice seemed tense and strained. When she was not singing, her face expressed discomfort, and I saw her rotating her jaw and tongue to moisten her mouth and throat.

About ten members from the church choir attended the concert. The day following the performance, when Su-yŏn arrived at choir rehearsal, she was obviously upset. She spoke to the choir about the concert and lamented the poor acoustics and the lack of rehearsal time. On my way home, I received a text message from her, thanking me for coming to the concert. She wrote that she had not been able to manage the performance well because the tempo had been too quick. Despite the obvious mismatch between her voice and the repertoire, I wrote back and told her how touched I had been by her delivery of the pieces. Then she wrote back with the following:

EXCERPT 6.2

Komapta. h h h Togil esŏnŭn nŭl kamjŏng, ŭmak ŭl saenggak haennŭnde Han'guk esŏnŭn sori put'ŏ saenggak hage toenda.

Thank you. [Han'gŭl letter representing laughter] In Germany I always thought about emotions, about music, but in Korea I have begun to think first about the sound.

Through many long discussions about this topic following the concert, I came to understand that Su-yŏn saw her role as a singer and her voice itself as different when she sang in Germany and in Korea. When she sang classical music in Germany, she told me she felt she was communicating emotion and musicality to her audience. She said she felt one of two things when she sang secular classical music in Korea: she was either bringing "culture" to an audience as part of an education model or was auditioning for critics whom she saw as powerful judges in a competition.

For singers returning to Korea, homecoming can be bittersweet. Despite celebrating their reunion with family and friends, they often report feeling let down by the sense that few people around them appreciate what they have accomplished overseas and what they are bringing back with them. The homecoming recital is supposed to be a triumphant concert that stands as a testament to their labors abroad. Yet few in the audience will judge the performance by the same aesthetic standards as the singer. Returning singers see themselves as having undergone intense, sometimes painful psychological transitions: having been marked as cultural outsiders; having been told that the techniques learned in Korea were backward and destructive; having been told that their pronunciation of Italian or German or English was poor and ethnically marked; having been told that they were not expressing the emotions required for the performance. Yet when they return home, they find that members of the audience have little appreciation for their training or experience. Rather, it is their certification and social connections that will draw a crowd.

Singers describe "abroad" as a place where, in the end, they were treated as professionals, as experts in their field, and worked independently among colleagues. They describe the homecoming as a return to a local hierarchy that has little to do with the craft of singing itself; they are "behind" (as *hubae*, relative juniors) or "prior to" (as *sŏnbae*, relative seniors) other singers by virtue of the year they entered the university. They are also reinserted once again into the role of disciple *(cheja)* of their former teachers and must assume the duties of this role. They describe abroad as the place where audiences are quiet, attentive, and willing to pay, where concert halls are designed acoustically to support the unamplified vocal sound production methods of classical singing. They describe homecoming as a return to singing with microphones, over a chattering audience, in acoustically "dead" concert halls. One singer described her frustrating experience of having to sing for a luncheon of mostly-male church elders while they slurped beef-rib soup *(kalbit'ang)*. Despite the many positive things reported by my informants about the return home—the food, the family, the language, the general feeling of home—they bemoaned the practical challenges of being singers in Korea and often cited the homecoming recital as their first experience of this difference.

Performances in Korea can feel downright out-of-place for singers. For example, in 2008 Pak Chi-yŏng gave a solo performance at Seoul Station, the major railway station in Seoul. Her program consisted of both the classical Italian repertoire and Christian hymns. As she sang, dressed in a floor-length blue gown, her voice amplified by a microphone to cut through the din of her environment, passersby gathered around her to observe the spectacle. Some members of the impromptu audience approached her and, standing just feet away, pointed cameras at her open mouth.[16] Public, free performances resembling variety shows tend to be the only places where strangers actually congregate on their own as an audience for classical music. And they serve as a stark contrast to the kind of performances Chi-yŏng and her husband, the tenor Chŏng Chung-sun, were used to in Italy, where they both studied and worked. Chi-yŏng graduated from Kyung Hee University, in Seoul, and went on to study at the Conservatorio di Musica G. B. Martini, in Bologna. Chung-sun graduated from Ch'ongsin University, a Presbyterian Christian college in Seoul, and then studied at the Conservatorio di Musica "Licinio Refice," in Frosinone, Italy. They spent nearly ten years studying and singing professionally in Italy and Germany before returning to Korea. Abroad, they sang in resonant churches and concert halls, before appreciative audiences, where tuxedos and gowns were appropriate not merely to the music being performed but also to the context of the performance. Chi-yŏng's performance in Seoul Station was a kind of transposition of the figure of the classical singer—and classical song—into a Korean context, where it underwent a semiotic transformation of cultural meaning. Both her voice as phonosonic nexus and her voicing of professional perspective were out of place.

When I asked Chung-sun and Chi-yŏng about singing in Korea after the homecoming, they cited the same problems others had raised and characterized performance contexts in Korea as one of the main causes for "ruining," "spoiling," or "wasting" *(ssŏkhida)* good voices. Chi-yŏng had explained to me that there are only three sites beyond church or school where singers could perform classical music beyond one's own self-funded recitals: a public hall run by a government agency, an invitation-only party hosted by a corporation or private organization, or a music event organized by a private agency for which tickets are sold. If members of government or agencies put on a performance and publicize the event, then one has to sing what is requested of them. The sponsors of invitation-only events also have very clear expectations for repertoire. And musical events organized and publicized by private agencies, while providing the most flexibility of repertoire, often have the lowest turnout. Ticket prices are high, the music is often unfamiliar to "the masses" *(taejung),* and, Chi-yŏng explained to me, members of the cast often have to sell or simply give away tickets to their friends and family.

The problem of audience *(kwan'gaek)* is recurrent in singers' lamentations about the performance culture of Seoul. Even with well-publicized events, the performers have to hand out tickets with the hope that some will purchase their tickets out of courtesy. If one hopes to capture and hold an audience's attention, he or she has to sing something familiar—which means having to sing the same thing on almost every occasion:

EXCERPT 6.3

Ye rŭl tŭrŏsŏ mejosop'ŭrano ka. Mejosop'ŭrano kok chung esŏ saramdŭl i hŭnhi anŭn ke Habanera channayo. kŭrŏnikka yŏnju chuch'oech'ŭk esŏnŭn Habanera pullŏ talla kŭraeyo.... kyesok kat'ŭn norae rŭl purŭnŭn ke kat'ŭn rep'at'ori rŭl purŭnŭn ke mank'i ttaemune wagajigo sŏngakchŏk in palchŏn i andoenŭn kŏeyo.... Togil yesul kagok, It'aeri yesul kagok ŭl purŭmyŏnyo kwan'gaek i ŏpsŏyo.

For example, the case of the mezzo-soprano.... Among the songs for mezzo-soprano, "Habanera" is well known to people, you know. Therefore the sponsors of the performance request "Habanera." ... Constantly singing the same song and singing the same repertoire a lot hinder the development of classical singing after a singer's return.... If you sing German art songs or Italian art songs, you won't have an audience.

If these singers are to have an audience, they must cater to the demands of their audiences. And so a number of contradictions have to be overcome in the homecoming recital. For the homecoming recital, the singer must, first of all, convince the audience of the legitimacy of the performance and its material. This means that the event must be presented as fully professional and public, consisting of foreign and somewhat inaccessible music, as well as something familiar, accessible, and locally authorized, for which the Christian encore is intended. But the performer must also manage the emotional conflict between the intimacy and comfort of home and the feeling of a professional "downgrade" that comes with leaving the performance contexts of Europe and the United States. This feeling is often first experienced in the affective distance singers feel from Korean audiences, who are not easily moved by most classical European repertoire. It is further strengthened by the sense that one's voice is deteriorating through the repertoire demands and performance spaces of Korea. The Christian encore helps resolve this dissonance. It is a semiotic genre that is comfortable to sing and deeply meaningful to both audience and performer—often expressing the very evangelical goals that lead singers to study and perform *sŏngak* in the first place. Thus, the Christian encore, as an affective meeting place for both performer and audience, is emblematic of the "home" in homecoming, out of the wilderness and into the safe, familiar realm of intimate spirituality. In the final section, I examine to the transformative effects that this ritual arrangement has on both audience and performer.

THE RECITAL'S RITUAL FUNCTION

The homecoming recital can be seen as a semiotic text formed out of multiple intersections of time and space. Rituals that mark the passage from one life stage to another are framed by chronotopes. If the internal sequencing of a story of personhood can be narrated as a biography with a chronotope of its own, some rituals marking major transition points will foreground the more temporal aspects and others the more spatial aspects of these shifts. Some, like the homecoming recital, highlight both. The biography of the individual singer is organized and presented in the recital program in terms of intersections of time and space that follow a remarkably consistent pattern. These intersections usually are invoked by the names of music schools, competitions, and performance contracts listed in the program. The dates and places begin in Korea, where singers are prepared for separation from home and for further studies and careers abroad. Then there is usually an extended period in Europe or the United States, where singers undergo dramatic and sometimes painful transitions, which are usually guided by their *sŏnbae*, their institutional seniors, abroad. After some time away, the singers return and are reincorporated into Korean society.

The university years for a singer in Korea are focused almost solely on preparing for auditions abroad.[17] These programs are designed around the successful separation of the singer from Korean social life, even as they put immense pressure on the student singer to orient to and participate in the local discipleship structure of the school. One professor explained to me that the numerous mission trips student singers take with their church choirs and Christian groups on campus help to prepare them to go abroad for study and work. Life abroad, then, is a period of transition that can last from one to ten or more years, depending on the singer's career success and financial resources. In many cases, the perceived liminality of this period can create fear and anxiety for the singer's family back home. Kim Yŏng-mi explained to me that while she was studying in Rome in the late 1970s, her mother came to Italy and took her to Philadelphia to live with her sister, because, as she put it, she "was becoming just like an Italian girl." But she, too, returned home a decade or so later. And when she did, she held a recital that announced her return to the social life of Seoul.

The organization of the sung portion of the homecoming recital looks very similar to a graduation recital for a singer completing a master's program in Korea. The pieces consist of songs or arias in more than one language, normally Italian and German, but often also include French or English. The recital is usually organized chronologically, beginning with baroque pieces by Bach, Handel, Purcell, or Vivaldi and then moving to art songs of the classical, romantic, and modern periods. Opera arias are often reserved for after the intermission. This temporal sequencing invokes a vector of vocal development that is understood to parallel an imagined progression of difficulty from earlier to later compositions. Students of voice usually begin their studies with bel canto arias from the eighteenth century, then move to art songs, and then to lighter opera arias, and finally to romantic Italian and French opera arias. This is often the case in Europe and the United States, but it is a pedagogical absolute in Korea. University students are expected to make a steady progression through the repertoire during college so that they can perform arias from Italian operas by Verdi and Puccini at their graduation recitals. I observed numerous graduation recitals in Korea at which undergraduate students sang arias that singers trained abroad would not sing publicly until they were more seasoned.

There actually are two histories aligned within the structure of the recital itself: a history of the development of European musical composition, and a history of individual-biographical development punctuated by shifts in repertoire. For example, Su-yŏn's homecoming recital was organized in precisely this manner. The history of European musical composition lined up with Su-yŏn's biographical history as a student of singing, progressing first through oratorio arias and art songs and then circling back for a second temporal progression through opera and operetta arias. The emphasis on German repertoire in her program indexed Germany as the site of her most recent vocal training, putting her past studies as a student in relation to the present event of the recital. And just as singers will most likely never again return abroad to study or perform for an extended period of time, most will never again sing music from their homecoming recital. Of the sixteen songs performed in her recital, Su-yŏn sang only two of them again in Korea: a piece by

Bach, "Schafe können sicher weiden," which she sang at church (to the irritation of some, since it was in German and not immediately recognizable as Christian), and "Les oiseaux dans la charmille," also known as "The Doll's Song," from Offenbach's opera *Les contes d'Hoffmann* (The Tales of Hoffmann). She sang this aria at numerous musical events outside the church.

Built into the structure of the recital, but not represented in the program itself, is a break with these earlier stages of development. This break is marked and managed by the inclusion of an encore following the programmed performance. Initially, my informants had general things to say about the encore. An encore—which takes place regardless of the quality of the singing—should, at the most basic level, consist of one song accessible on some level to the entire audience. However, it probably should not be taken from the standard "classical" repertoire; it should not resemble the rest of the recital or performances of classical music abroad. Informants said that the encore should be sung in Korean, possibly a Korean art song or a folk song set to a new accompaniment. If a singer chooses an encore in another language, it should be a very well-known composition, such as "O sole mio." Most important for the encore is that it be enjoyable, accessible, and meaningful to the audience, so that it can serve as a kind of reward to the vast majority of attendees who have sat politely through one hour of music in a language and form to which they have little intellectual or affective attraction.

Despite these generally stated guidelines for the encore, in practice encores at homecoming recitals overwhelmingly, almost absolutely, feature a Christian song sung in Korean. As I mentioned above, I saw only one recital in which the encore was not a Christian song. (It was "Gentle Annie," by Robert Foster, and later it was met with criticism from members of the audience.) Commonly heard songs include Christian songs such as "Chu ŭi kido" (The Lord's Prayer), hymns such as "Chu Hananim chiŭsin modŭn segye" (How Great Thou Art) and "O sinsil hasin Chu" (Great Is Thy Faithfulness), as well as more recent Korean Christian lyric songs such as "Ch'am choŭsin Chunim" (Truly Great Lord) and "Hananim ŭi ŭnhye" (The Grace of God). Su-yŏn sang "Amazing Grace" for her encore. She sang the first verse in English and the rest in Korean, again diagramming the shift from abroad to home via a shift in codes. And in just this way, as the singer returns home from abroad, the encore marks the transition from a repertoire of inaccessible foreign languages and increasingly "difficult" secular music in the singer's past, to familiar, personal, generally Christian songs sung in Korean, which will form the basis of the singer's professional career in the future. That is, the performance of a homecoming recital that culminates in the singing of a Korean hymn is a tropic figuration of the time and space that lead up to it: it links a history of classical music composition starting in Europe and ending in Korea with a biography of a classical singer that is returning from Europe to Korea in a single culminating point.

The homecoming recital's ritual text—its metricalized, poetic structure that gives it coherence and allows it to be reproduced in more or less similar form by singers throughout Korea—diagrams (via iconicity) and invokes (via indexicality) both the temporal progression of a singer in terms of professional "development" and the spatial movement of a singer through different environments, namely, "home" and "abroad." The recital is therefore a self-grounding "indexical icon" of the very social transformation that it narrates. The durational dimension of the recital has the features of Charles S. Peirce's famous example of indexical iconicity, a spatial image of a detailed map of a country scratched in the soil of that same country.[18] The recital presents a diagram of the biographical development of the singer, which is "scratched," so to speak, directly into the person's own personal biographical trajectory (the recital itself forming a major nodal point in the biography it narrates). When the performance is successful—felicitous in its ritual function—the singer passes from one life stage to another, from student to professional.

Despite the ubiquity of the form, a few singers, all of them Christians, told me they disapproved of the practice of performing explicitly Christian music in the encore. While the Christian encore is nearly always present at the recitals of more locally established singers (singers who are not just returning home), some of these same singers argued that the homecoming recital's role of establishing a singer as "professional" means, ideally, that it should be entirely secular, even "academic"[19]—even if, as they well know, "professional" implies "Christian" in the Korean context of *sŏngak*. While they could understand how it would be important to give back to their audience and express their gratitude to God, those who wanted to reproduce in Korea the recital culture from abroad also found it strange to include the Christian encore at the end of a basically secular performance. Still, in almost every case, these singers succumbed to social pressure and ended their recitals with a hymn or some other Christian song.

This disagreement points to the different conceptualizations of the function of the recital as a ritual of reincorporation, whether it should emphasize the events prior to the return (secular academic) or the performance contexts that most certainly will take place after it (Christian). However, as all singers in Korea become more aware that the professional singer's largest audience will consist of people who view classically trained vocal arts as part and parcel of Korean Christianity, the Christian encore is becoming more of an explicit and predictable commentary on the recital as a whole. The encore announces that the singer individually and the musical development of the populace generally are in the service of the Korean Christian God and that the recital is a kind of reciprocal act—a dedication—for all that this particular god is understood to have done for Korea (and for the performer). The recital accomplishes through specifically Christian encores what the tenor Yi Sŏng-ŭn did with words and money after he won the 2009 Metropolitan Opera National Council auditions. He announced to the press, "I want to become a world-famous singer so that I can reveal the glory of God," and gave all his winnings away to support missionary activities.[20] In the homecoming recital, the Christian encore makes explicit the metapragmatics of the recital; that is, it frames the social action accomplished by the recital by regimenting and guiding the interpretation of its pragmatic, indexical signs. Among Korean singers of *sŏngak,* the cultivation of the classical voice in Korea is understood to express and embody the strivings of Korean Christian personhood.

Thus the programmed portion of the recital is not the heart of the performance; the program represents a past-life stage of singers to which they will most likely not return (musically or biographically). In the shift from the programmed academic recital to the unprogrammed (but expected) encore consisting almost always of a Christian hymn, the audience transitions from gazing at the spectacle of a foreign semiotic form transposed into a Korean context (recall Chi-yŏng's performance in the train station) to ratifying a specifically local performance genre that fits into their cultural worship practices. The most consequential aspects of performance—those that accomplish the social transformation of both the singer and the audience—begin at the applause, reach full saturation during the performance of an encore, and continue to structure the event as the singer emerges from the theater into the lobby to greet her family and friends as fans.

In one sense, homecoming recitals like these train attendees to be an audience. They are instructed when to clap. They are asked not to speak during the performance. They are told not to eat in the auditorium. And they learn when and for how long to shout "encore!" For most in attendance, however, it is unlikely that the homecoming recital provides their first opportunity to shout to the stage. Like saying "amen" at church or even offering calls of encouragement *(ch'uimsae)* during a *p'ansori* performance, shouting "encore" is a form of participation and expressive ratification that is learned in multiple performance contexts and comes to be viewed as an expected and normal feature of performance in Korea. Attendees are aware of what form encores take in other contexts. But in the case of the homecoming vocal recital, the audience understands the Christian hymn or song to signal the real and absolute end of the recital. This piece creates the space in which the audience can participate and feel that the performance is for them and not merely for the performer. It is their emotional release as much as it is the performer's. At the moment when members of the audience clap at will, perhaps even rise to their feet while calling out "encore," the audience itself performs as a participating public for Christianized classical singing and does not act merely as a group formed out of personal relations.

At this moment, the singer is no longer a student showing the work he or she has accomplished—in one way to peers, in another to professors, and in yet another to family and friends—but a local artist meeting the demands of a local public.[21] The Christian character of the encore is what accomplishes this. It performatively presents a devoted Christian singer who can now evangelize professionally—both individually and publicly—through song. The Christian encore means that the singer has finally come home.

CONCLUSION

In conclusion, I want to emphasize that the homecoming recital is not merely a celebration of return. In many cases, the singer might have been home for months, perhaps even more than a year, and will have had plenty of time to catch up with friends and family, distribute gifts, accept invitations, receive congratulations, and so on. The singer likely will have participated in numerous celebrations of return prior to the actual recital. In fact, the singer likely will have even performed prior to the recital. The recital's sociocultural importance for Korea lies in its function as a ritual of transformation that takes as its communicative channel the very object of transformation that it "recites": the human voice as phonosonic nexus and, by extension, the bearer of that voice in the form of a voicing of personhood. Furthermore, the recital is unlike other kinds of homecoming events—gatherings for soldiers recently discharged from the military or special worship events for evangelists returning from overseas—in which a particular institution is clearly present in and perhaps even presides over or officiates the event via its sanctioned representatives (parents, higher-ranking officers, *sŏnbae*, ministers). In its explicit format as a public performance of secular art music, the homecoming recital downplays its institutional linkages—church, family, school—and focuses on the professional singer herself as both the object of and the officiant of the transformation. But like testifying or witnessing in church, the final hymn points to the Christian God and his sanctioned representatives (Jesus Christ and the Holy Spirit) as the ultimate agents of the transformation. And the audience socially ratifies this transformation through their calls of "encore," which cease only with the performance of the hymn sung in Korean, with the musical and denotational expression of Korean Christianity as the endpoint of the journey abroad and the starting point for a singer's life back home. After the hymn, the audience may well replace calls of "encore" with "amen."

The homecoming recital thus integrates a returning singer, after having studied and worked professionally abroad, into the social life of Seoul. By recasting private relations within a public setting, singers are presented as professionals to an audience of intimates and institutional relations; in turn, the specificity of Christian faith and worship is presented as a generalized and thoroughly pervasive aspect of public life in Korea.[22] My aim in this chapter has been to offer a systematic and ethnographically informed account of how such specific, interested claims to general publicity subtly affect local conceptualizations of sociality.

But these claims to publicity are nonetheless fraught with challenges and contradictions in both their ritual presentation and their ongoing practice. To become a public, professional singer in Korea, one must accept the local performance conditions that facilitate the ritual enactment of publicity. Singers often characterize this as a kind of sacrifice of the education, experience, and commitments gained abroad, in return for readmission into Korean society. Homecoming recitals facilitate this delicate transition by subsuming the repertoire of "abroad" within the repertoire of "home."

Singers also described the transition from programmed recital to encore as the point at which they no longer felt like students taking a test. They described the encore—the Christian encore—as the moment when they could finally sing in a classical style to a Korean audience and try to move the audience's emotions *(kamdong)*—something they were unable to do through the "academic" repertoire of the program. In Korea, the performance of secular art or operatic music brings with it a nagging concern about vocal sound production. Singers like Su-yŏn reported feeling that the entire performance was judged in terms of the size (amplitude) of the voice, despite the poor acoustics of spaces in which such voices are heard. This anxiety is often audibly manifest as phonic tension or fatigue in the voice itself. Regarding the performance of Christian music, however, singers describe a sense of freedom, openness, and happiness connected to a feeling of finally being able to "express themselves" before an appreciative audience in Korea—just as they had been able to do with more secular repertoire (and for different audiences) abroad.

Implicit and explicit expressions of Christian faith contribute to the creation of an ostensible Korean public attuned to classically trained voices. By linking Christianity to the performance of secular art music or operatic music, homecoming recitals subtly insert Christian institutions into the public life of performance arts in Seoul. The singing of the Christian encore constitutes the "Korean" voice, which draws on but is differentiated from other ethnonationally categorized voices to which singers orient—the voices from abroad (the Italian voice, the German voice, the Russian voice). By ritually positioning the Christian encore, sung in Korean, as the unscripted, temporally and poetically final portion of the recital and presenting it in a nominally public space (whether privately owned or not), a student becomes a professional, and a network of social relations is presented to itself as the general public for the *sŏngak* voice—as a fully Christianized Korea that has arrived at home in the present.

CHAPTER 7

Feeling the Voice

In 2009, when I returned to Korea for a follow-up research trip, the choir conductor at Somang Church invited me to sing a duet with her during the offertory *(hŏn'gŭmsong)* one Sunday during my stay. She had chosen John Rutter's setting of "The Lord Bless You and Keep You." The conductor had studied voice in Germany, and I had majored in German as an undergraduate, so we often switched back and forth between German and Korean in our conversations. After we had practiced with the accompanist a few times until we both felt comfortable with our notes, the tempo, and the blend of our voices, she told me, in German, that we would sing the piece one last time. She began her next phrase in German, saying, *"jetzt"* (now), but then switched to Korean and said, *"maŭm ŭro"* (with the *maŭm*, or heart-mind). Although she could just as easily have continued her phrase in German, saying, *"mit dem Herz"* (with the heart), or, as is often noted in musical scores, *"mit Gefühl"* (with feeling), she switched into Korean and used the term *maŭm*.

In European-style classical music rehearsals of all sorts, one commonly encounters the phrase, "Once more, with feeling." This directive usually follows some emphasis on the technical aspects of a rehearsal and is intended as an instruction to perform a particular musical text as if one were in an actual live performance, that is, with an affective charge intended to "move" an audience.

What did it mean to sing "with the *maŭm*" in this context? What was this *"maŭm"* that she spoke of? And how were we to use it? As I have argued throughout this book, the cultivation of the *sŏngak* voice is intimately linked with a transformation of emotionality among Korean Christians, the new idealized qualities of the voice being signs of a joyful, peaceful present. Absent should be the suffering of the past. For many contemporary Korean Christians, old-fashioned, unclean voices have phonosonic qualia that evoke feelings of sadness, feelings of *han,* that seem to belong to an earlier time. The raspy sound is understood to signal struggle or discomfort in the actual phonic production of voice. Referring to this kind of sound and the manner of its application in music on Chindo Island, Keith Howard noted that sorrow and sad songs, which gave rise to the basic singing technique, reflect "poverty, disease, overwork, desertion and lost love."[1] My Christian informants often extended this attribute of sadness to traditional singing itself. They characterized older styles of vocal production as inherently sad, even if the denotational content of the song was humorous or lighthearted. The qualia of older voices can suggest for the younger generations, and especially for students of *sŏngak,* a singer whose general state of being is sad, who has endured pain and torment, even if he or she has found a subject that makes him or her laugh. They told me that even the dancing peasants one sees in paintings from the Chosŏn dynasty, who wore smiles on their faces and slapped their legs, were joyous only as a kind of exception to struggle and hardship. Their joy was not stable, and the voice that momentarily expressed joy was nonetheless produced with a timbre developed out of the difficult circumstances of life. The point was neither that all older musical styles are laments, nor that all older music was sad, but rather that these older-style vocal characteristics index the sorrow of the past.

In this chapter, I turn to the place where these singers say they experience feelings as they sing—the *maŭm*. Although this chapter is concerned in part with Korean Christian characterizations of "emotions," "feelings," and "affect," my central focus is on the *maŭm* as the medium through which or place in which these phenomenal states are experienced, not on the ontological status of the experiences themselves. Hence, my goal is not to contribute to a theorization of the utility of affect, to argue that emotions are culturally constructed, to determine whether such feelings are universal or culture-specific, or to reveal the political implications of such experiences and their representations.[2] Rather, I focus on the actual locus in or through which contemporary Korean Christians report experiencing these sensations to better understand the social significance of communicative behaviors that refer to or invoke this locus.[3]

I have used the term *maŭm* repeatedly in this book. In chapter 1, I discussed the care that singers must take to appropriately control the *maŭm* while singing, lest they lose control of their performance and fail to achieve their evangelical goals. I mentioned the term in chapter 2, when I commented on Lee Myung-bak's inaugural speech in 2008. In that speech, Lee said, "Within the heart-minds *[maŭm]* of the Korean people, there is a map of the Republic of Korea that will be spread through the world," and I related this statement to the stained-glass map on the western façade of Somang Church, where Lee is an elder. In the stained-glass image, Korea is depicted as sitting at the figurative heart of the map. I also raised the concept of the *maŭm* in chapter 4 when discussing the way Somang Church's head pastor Kim Chi-ch'ŏl asked his congregants to clean their *maŭm* in order to see opportunity in a seemingly rotten world. In the present chapter, I return to this concept to explore the way the expressive and embodied dimensions of vocalization are understood in terms of the Christian *maŭm,* both as a component of an individual person and as an instrument of Christian sociality.

The *maŭm* is culturally conceptualized in Korea as the place where personally felt emotional experiences meet the production of culturally recognizable emotionality. I am interested here in the role of explicitly Christian contexts and registers that contribute to the conceptualization of the *maŭm*. Viewing such discourse about the *maŭm* in relation to vocalization will further illuminate how the voice is used to create, maintain, and transform social spaces.[4] In Christian semiotic genres, affectively effective singing and other forms of vocalization are understood not only to align a healthy body with a clean voice but also to align each joyful, loving, grateful *maŭm* to God and thereby align members of a Christian community one to another.

I begin by locating the term in a specifically Christian discursive register, exploring its emergence as a religious term in Bible translation. I then turn to the way performances of secular music serve as a chance for the singer to commune personally with God. By having a *maŭm* that is stably directed toward God, one can emit a voice that is stably in the service of God and that God can use to communicate particular emotions to the world—even emotions that the singer him- or herself has not experienced before. This is understood to allow for a kind of calmness and maturity of presence within the singer, who nonetheless is able to stir the emotions of others. Through this spiritual alignment, even an act of secular performance takes on an evangelical character. Finally, I explore the way in which this personal transformation of *maŭm* is used in vocal performance to create a communal orientation toward God, intended to induce among participants in the performance (including the audience) the very sentiments communicated by the texts being sung.

As voices are oriented to the church as an authorizing ritual center of semiosis and emanate from the church in the form of ostensibly public recitals throughout Seoul, *sŏngak* as a semiotic register of evangelism itself serves to align multiple *maŭm*s in terms of a higher-order chronotope of ethnonational development and spiritual enlightenment. Through this practice of orienting and aligning sound, body, and *maŭm* in a manner that is understood to be Christian, these singers create a voicing relationship with an authoritative source that collapses the distance between a particular event of vocalization and the previous authorized events on which it is based. That is, to have a voice that expresses and embodies modern Christian personhood is to make one's "true voice" (i.e., the "natural" or "God-given voice") literally "the voice of God."

MAŬM AND ITS CHRISTIAN INFLECTION

Maŭm is a so-called native Korean word. Most translations of *maŭm* into English translate it, like the Sino-Korean word *sim* (심/心), as "heart" or "mind," if not the compound "heart-mind."[5] The difficulties of the translation of such "cardiocentric" terms for the seat of thought and feeling in Chinese, Japanese *(kokoro),* and Korean have been addressed in varying degrees of detail.[6] Although further detailing the dimensions of semantic similarity and difference is beyond the scope of this chapter, it is worth exploring briefly the particularity of this term for speakers of Korean to begin to understand the concept's role in specifically Christian forms of phonosonic expressivity.

If we first think of what might be termed the attributional space of the concept—its perceived qualities, properties, and characteristics— the *maŭm* is much like its Standard Average European (SAE) counterparts.[7] The *maŭm* is the location and experiential source or instrument of human emotions, feelings, morality, desire, and sincerity. The *maŭm* is a malleable container that can be manipulated, filled, and emptied. The *maŭm* and its contents are usually imperceptible to other persons directly. When combined with other terms, the *maŭm* forms the basis of personality traits and characteristics according to disposition or temper. The *maŭm* can be given or received metaphorically. The *maŭm* can have other attributes, such as weight or color, which may be valuated positively or negatively. The *maŭm* is intrinsically human but may be extended to other animate beings.[8] There are, however, two major factors in the attributional space that differentiate it from SAE glosses. The first is the clear fact that the *maŭm* can also contain and generate thoughts and visualizations.[9] The second is the fact that the *maŭm* is located in the chest but does not refer to a part of the human anatomy.[10]

If we now consider the indexical space of the *maŭm*—that is, the conceptual relations of contiguity and contrast within a larger cultural-conceptual framework of imaginable entities, based on what Michael Silverstein has called "-onomic" or schematic structures of knowledge—the concept appears far more differentiated from its SAE cardio-counterparts.[11] Although the *maŭm* is functionally differentiated from, and forms a counterpart to, the mental processes arising from the "head" *(mŏri)*, thus resembling the English word *heart,* it also forms a counterpart to the body *(mom),* thus resembling the English word *mind.* In order to refer to the anatomical heart or its associated cardiological conditions, one would need to switch into a Sino-Korean scientific register and use the term *simjang* (viscera or organ of the *sim*). And although pain and discomfort can be felt within or through the *maŭm,* physical metaphors related to emotional sensations of the heart (breaking, aching, fluttering, etc.) often are constructed using a metonym with a clear physical extension: the native Korean word *kasŭm* (chest, breast), which refers to the *maŭm*'s location and encasing.[12]

The native Korean complementary opposites, *maŭm* and *mom* (body), should be differentiated further from an analogous, but not synonymous, Sino-Korean complementary relation: *chŏngsin* (ethereal mind, spirit, consciousness, *Geist*) and *yukch'e* (material body, flesh, corpus). And again in this Sino-Korean scientific register, *chŏngsin* is used for the Korean gloss of "psychiatry" (*chŏngsin ŭihak* is the medical science of the *chŏngsin*), and *sim* is used for "psychology" (*simnihak* is the science of the logic of the *sim*). In its differentiation from the body, the *maŭm* is sometimes glossed as "soul" or "spirit." In general, however, the *maŭm* can be differentiated from more literal words for spirit or soul: the Sino-Korean *yŏnghon* (which is used in Christian churches to refer to the soul), or the native Korean *nŏk* (which my Christian informants insisted should *not* be used to refer to their souls).

For *maŭm,* the gloss as "soul" usually refers to the sincerity or commitment with which one is engaged in an activity or state of being or simply to one's overall disposition or outlook. For example, a Christian friend who was listing her reasons for wanting to break up with her boyfriend cited as one of her chief concerns the fact that he was not a Christian. We were speaking in Korean, but at one point she switched into English and said, "My soul and his soul are different." When I asked her to repeat the phrase in Korean, she used the term *maŭm* to describe the differentiation. When I followed by asking if her *yŏnghon* and his *yŏnghon* were different, she laughed and replied that of course they were, because they belonged to different people. She explained that what she meant was that their feelings and ways of viewing the world were different.

It is important emphasize that the term *maŭm* is a member of the native-Korean class of the lexicon, differentiated from the Sino-Korean class. Sino-Korean words not only form the greatest portion of the overall lexicon but also serve as the basis for scientific, technical, and "high" linguistic registers. The importance of differentiated native and Sino-Korean lexica was an early concern for the translators for the Bible into Korean. In 1886, the Scottish Presbyterian missionary John Ross completed his Korean translation of the New Testament.[13] Before embarking on the Korean translation, Ross had been a missionary to China, where he had encountered a strong preference among converts for a Bible written in literary language. Ross writes, pejoratively, "But even if the Scriptures were, as I would they were, translated by learned Chinese, the simplicity of the Bible, so dearly loved by us, is regarded as a sign of inferiority by men to whom style is much more than thought."[14] And so as he and his team worked through the Korean translation, he constantly referred back to the Chinese case when trying to tailor the language to the linguistic conventions of Korean speakers:

> In one particular, I have taken the liberty of introducing considerable change in my translations. Coreans in both speech and writing are punctilious in distinguishing the social position of persons. Equals in age or rank may employ the direct form of speech, but strangers or persons socially unequal could not use the direct "thou" or "you" of English and Greek. To them such use of the second personal pronoun is disrespectful in the extreme. This has influenced all the translations. When God is addressed I have always used the indirect mode of address, e.g. in the Lord's prayer every "Thy" is translated by "father's" the term with which the prayer commences. When the disciples address Jesus, they are translated as always using the indirect mode "Lord" or "Teacher." Even in Chinese, I always use the indirect mode in prayer as the direct is not reverential. Coreans attach much more importance to the form of address than do the Chinese; this change is essential to accurate translation."[15]

In this manner, Ross came to recognize the bifurcated "high" and "low" registers on the basis of lexical distinctions made between Sino-Korean and native Korean words.

In contemporary Korean dictionaries, this bifurcation is reproduced when the Sino-Korean term *sim* is offered as a synonym for *maŭm*. *Sim* was used in classical Confucian and Buddhist texts as a member of a Sino-Korean philosophico-religious register.[16] During the Chosŏn period, the term *maŭm* (or its dialectal equivalents) would have been used in everyday speech and, after the invention of Han'gŭl in the 1440s, written down in some poems or personal letters. Still, classical Chinese constituted the vast majority of official written documents during the Chosŏn period.[17] The linguistic authorities of the time viewed Han'gŭl as a "vulgar" or "vernacular" script *(ŏnmun)*, the opposite of the "true" writing *(chinmun)* of classical Chinese. Although Ross maintained the honorific markings of speech addressed to Jesus or God in the Bible, he decided to translate the Bible into everyday vernacular speech formed out of native Korean lexical items, not Sino-Korean, thus elevating vulgar speech (and the vulgar script) to the status of holy speech:

> Owing to its extensive borrowing from Chinese the Corean language has more synonyms than our English, not merely synonyms which approach each other in signification but such as are indistinguishable, such as *hanal* and *tiun*, heaven, *saram* and *in*, man. These can be at any time interchanged but except to avoid vulgarity of style. I have always leaned to the use of the native instead of the borrowed word, as Saxon rather than Latin words form our English Bibles.[18]

Using this approach, he translated *heart* not as *sim* or some related compound, but as *maŭm*. This was part of the creation of a more general Christian discursive register based on the use of Han'gŭl and native Korean terms for Bible translation.[19] Indeed, it was the emphasis on native Korean terms that led to the adoption of "Hananim" as the Protestant name for God, rather than imported Sino-Korean glosses like "Sangje" or "Ch'ŏnju," which were used by Catholics.[20]

One sees the establishment of this Protestant Christian discursive register using native Korean terms not only in the Bible translation but also in the everyday speech used by the missionaries in their interactions with Koreans.[21] In 1877, John Ross introduced a phrasebook for missionaries working in Korea. It was titled *Corean Primer: Being Lessons in Corean on All Ordinary Subjects, Transliterated on the Principles of the "Mandarin Primer" by the Same Author.*[22] It was the first textbook of the Korean language in English.[23] The book consists of an introduction to

Han'gŭl orthography and Korean phonology, followed by twenty-three lessons on different aspects of daily life. Each lesson contains thematically relevant sentences, organized into three lines consisting of the Han'gŭl, an interlinear transliteration, and a gloss of the words in Korean word order. The book begins with lessons titled "The Library" and "The School"—where first contact between missionaries and potential converts might have been made—and moves through various topics, such as the rooms of a house, farm animals, leisure activities (e.g., walking), directions and exchange, time, weather, the body, soldiers, criminals, and color. It ends with lessons titled "Moral" (#32) and "Soul" (#33).[24] The sentences contained in these final two chapters emphasize moral and spiritual behavior in terms of the *maŭm*, usually glossed by Ross as "heart" but also occasionally as "mind." After phrases communicating basic Christian principles (e.g., that there is no transmigration of souls, that the soul is defiled by the world, and that one must do business that the conscience does not oppose), the final phrase of the entire book is simply *"ŏjin maŭm"*—kindhearted, gentle, benevolent or virtuous *maŭm*—which Ross glossed simply as "conscience or virtue."[25]

Studies of missionary efforts and Bible translation have demonstrated the difficulty of an interlingual glossing of the term *heart* when moving between differently conceptualized sources and cultural frameworks of moral thinking and feeling.[26] If we now look briefly to a few Korean Bible translations, we can see similar cultural-conceptual dissonances arising from the translation of these ethnopsychological terms and their intensional, or "sense," categories for types of interiority. For example, cognition, decision making, mental reflection, and imagination without emotion are usually dealt with in terms of the head *(mŏri)* or thoughts *(saenggak)* and are therefore contrasted with something like the *maŭm*. Take, for example, the New Revised Korean Version's (NRKV, 1998) translation of these terms in Romans 8:27: "And he who searches our hearts [maŭm] knows the mind [saenggak] of the Spirit [sŏngnyŏng]." But then take Daniel 7:15: "I, Daniel, was troubled in spirit, and the visions that passed through my mind disturbed me." In the NRKV version of this passage, *spirit* is *chungsim* (center or middle) and *mind* is *mŏri* (head), whereas in the Common Translation (CTB, 1977), *mind* remains *mŏri*, but *spirit* is *maŭm*. In the Revised Han'gŭl Version (RHV, 1987), *spirit* is *chungsim*, and *mind* is *noe* (brain).

In Korean Bibles, raw emotions and feelings, voluntary or involuntary, are often described as taking place in the chest *(kasŭm)*. The emotions or feelings of or in the *kasŭm* are often interchangeable with other verbs of emotion or displays of mourning. Take, for example, 2 Samuel 19:1: "Joab was told, 'The king is weeping and mourning for Absalom.'" The NRKV depicts the king as "crying and sad" *(ulmyŏ sŭlp'ŏhasinaida)*, while the CTB depicts the king feeling as if his *kasŭm* were tearing *(miŏjida)*. Just as the *kasŭm* can be "torn" or "broken," it can also be beaten. Take, for example, Matthew 11:17: "We played the flute for you, and you did not dance; we sang a dirge and you did not mourn." The NRKV translates the phrase about mourning as "You did not beat your breasts" *(nŏhŭi ka kasŭm ŭl ch'iji anihayŏtta)*. However, across Bible translations, *kasŭm* also is often interchanged with *maŭm*, such as in Isaiah 60:5: "Your heart will throb and swell with joy." The NRKV translates *heart* as *maŭm*, and the CTB translates it as *kasŭm*.

Although *maŭm* often serves as an affective or spiritual counterpart to the cognitive realms of thought and understanding, when *kasŭm* and *maŭm* are used in the same verse, the latter takes on the more cognitive properties. This is evident in the Korean Easy Bible (EB, 2009) version of Job 38:36: "Who endowed the heart *[kasŭm]* with wisdom *[chihye]* or gave understanding *[ch'ongmyŏng]* to the mind *[maŭm]*?" In instances when there is an explicitly cerebral or rational distinction from the "spirit," *maŭm* can be the Korean gloss, as in the NRKV's version of 1 Corinthians 14:15: "I will pray with my spirit *[yŏng]*, but I will also pray with my mind *[maŭm]*." From these examples, it is obvious that the term is pervasive throughout a number of dimensions of both cognitive and affective Christian experience as modeled and prescribed by the Bible. At the same time, it is evident that *maŭm* as a Korean cultural concept does not neatly fit with the usages of *heart* and *mind* established through various SAE Bible translations.

In contemporary Korean usage, the term is emphasized among Christians in religious communicative registers. The specifically Christian significance of the term in Korea became even more apparent to me when I performed a Google image search for the terms *heart, mind, cuore, Herz,* 심장 *(simjang),* 心 *(sim),* and 마음 *(maŭm).*[27] My goal simply was to see what sorts of images would be associated with which terms by looking at the first page of search results. The results were striking. When I searched the English word *heart,* the search produced a combination of medical diagrams of the human heart and images of the heart symbol, suggesting an extensional overlap between the anatomical and the affective. When I searched the English word *mind,* the search produced images of the human brain and of variously diagramed mental operations, suggesting an extensional overlap between the anatomical and cognitive. Searches for the Italian *cuore* and the German *Herz* produced mostly images of the heart symbol and a few of the anatomical heart. When I searched for the Korean word 심장 (*simjang*/anatomical heart), the search produced only medical diagrams of the human anatomical heart. When I searched the Chinese character 心 (*sim*/heart-mind), the search produced mostly images of the heart symbol. But when I searched for 마음 (*maŭm*/heart-mind), the search generated a diverse collection of images and pages, some depicting the heart symbol, some suggesting poetry, some depicting positive emotional expressions on people's faces (cartoon or real), and, notably, some with obviously Christian images, such as the cross, pictures of Jesus, and hands clasped in prayer.

Whereas the other terms were consistently linked to representations of a cognitive mind, or a loving-heart symbol, or an anatomical heart diagram, or some combination of the last two, the results for *maŭm* depicted a number of different things. One important element that stood out was the inherently interpersonal nature of some of the images: two persons sharing a single object, two persons looking into each other's eyes, and so forth. On these websites, the *maŭm* was represented as a kind of instrument of socialization between individuals and entire groups. This would fit with earlier studies of Korean ethnopsychology on the concept of *chŏng* (as discussed in the introduction), which is often conceptualized as a kind of interpersonal bond of familiarity and affection between two or more individuals. *Chŏng* can either grow between individuals by "entering" their relationship as an independent agent *(chŏng i tŭlda),* or it can be actively "given" by the individuals *(chŏng ŭl chuda).*[28] So in this sense, as the *maŭm* goes, so does *chŏng*. However, it is important to note that while the notion of *chŏng* is still widely used among Korean speakers, within the Korean church this feeling is more appropriately described by the somewhat more formal spiritual terms, *sagwim* (communion) or *ch'in'gyo* (fellowship). The emergence of affective communion among believers is understood to be the result of the Holy Spirit *(sŏngnyŏng)* and assisted by specific individuals *(ch'in'gyo pujang)* who are tasked with helping with this process, that is, with creating an atmosphere of sociability in the form of Christian fellowship.

Still another factor differentiates the *maŭm* search from that of the other terms. Of all of these searches, only the search for *maŭm* generated explicitly Christian images on the first page of results. Among the search results for *маŭм* was an image of sheet music titled "Hananim abŏji ŭi maŭm" (God the Father's *Маŭм*), with words and music by Sŏl Kyŏng-uk. I clicked on the image and was taken to a website, the heading of which read, "My Vision Is = to Spread Jesus!" in English.[29] The page immediately played a version of the song, with the following lyrics, sung in a soft, breathy, pop-style voice:

> *Abŏji tangsin ŭi maŭm i innŭn kot e*
> *na ŭi maŭm i itki rŭl wŏn haeyo.*
> *Abŏji tangsin ŭi nunmul i koin kot e*
> *na ŭi nunmul i poigil wŏn haeyo.*
> *Abŏji tangsin i parabonŭn yŏnghon ege*
> *na ŭi tu nun i hyanghagil wŏn haeyo.*
> *Abŏji tangsin i ulgo ŏduun ttang e*
> *na ŭi tu pal i hyanghagil wŏn haeyo.*
> *Na ŭi maŭm i abŏji ŭi maŭm ara*
> *nae modŭn ttŭt abŏji ŭi ttŭt i toel su itkirŭl*
> *na ŭi on mom i abŏji ŭi maŭm ara*
> *nae modŭn sam tangsin ŭi sam toegirŭl. . . .*

Father, in the place where your *maŭm* is
I wish my *maŭm* to be.
Father, where your tears well up
I hope my tears are visible.
Father, to your expecting soul
I hope my two eyes will face.
Father, you cry, and to this dark earth
I hope my two feet will proceed.
That my *maŭm* knows the Father's *maŭm,*
And every wish of mine can become the Father's wishes[30]
That my whole body knows the Father's *maŭm*
And my whole life becomes your life. . . .

Маŭм is a recurrent term in Christian sermons and is a central concept for directing the moral behavior and introspective lives of congregants. It is understood to connect emotion and action, to operate within frameworks of ethics and morality, and to generate desire and repulsion. From my brief attributional and indexical analysis, the results of the Google search, and now from these lyrics, we can see that the Christian inflection of the Korean term is coupled with a clear function of the *maŭm*'s role in aligning the "feelings" and "thoughts," the affective states and cognitive processes, of multiple individuals with one another and with God—indeed mirroring the attributes of God through the attributes of the *maŭm*. I now turn to the role of the voice as it relates to the *maŭm* by bearing the features of an evangelical notion of Korean Christian personhood.

ALIGNING WITH GOD THROUGH *MAŬM* AND VOICE

Kim Yŏng-mi, in an interview with Paek Chi-yŏn on April 8, 2008, for a Christian show called *Int'ŏbyu,* described the difference between singing "worldly" *(sesang ŭi)* music and "praise" *(ch'anyang)* music.[31] Kim Yŏng-mi described an instance when she could not access the emotions necessary to sing the role of Violetta Valéry in Verdi's opera *La traviata.* Kim explained how God supplied her with the emotions by placing them directly into her realm of sensation. And from this experience, she said she came to learn that although there is a difference between singing "sacred" and "worldly" music, she must remain stably directed toward God, regardless of what she is singing. This statement was provoked by a question from the interviewer about the *maŭm* in relation to Christian and secular music:

EXCERPT 7.1

1. Paek: *Op'era hago ch'anyang ŭl purŭl ttae hago tarŭseyo?*
Is it different when you sing opera and when you sing praise?

2. Kim: *Tangyŏnhi tarŭjyo.*
Of course it's different.

3. Paek: *Maŭm i tarŭseyo? Mullon purŭsinŭn kŏt to tarŭsigetchiman—*
Is the *maŭm* different? Of course you sing it differently, but—

With this question, Kim Yŏng-mi began her biographical story of spiritual and emotional transformation. The narrative, it turns out, was neatly metricalized and symmetrically balanced to form a poetic structure that modeled, through tense and voicing contrasts, the very transformation that she describes having undergone. Although the climax of the narrative takes place in historical time and a foreign place—some years ago in Japan—it is transposed into the event of Kim's narration through these contrasts. In so doing, it emphasizes the thoroughly evangelical nature of Kim's transformation: she underwent the spiritual change performing secular music abroad (while performing for the former colonizer of her country). To highlight the importance of these metrical units for the performative dimension of her story, I have arranged them schematically from left to right, with the poetically intratextual segments aligned along four different vertical axes. Segments 4–5 and 13–14 are aligned with the first axis, segments 6–8 and 10 with the second, segments 9 and 12 with the third, and 11 with the fourth. My analysis of the relationship among these segments follows the excerpt.

EXCERPT 7.2

4. Kim: [Laughing] *Che ka Chunim ege k'ŭn ŭnhye rŭl ibŏttanŭn kŏt ŭl nŭkkigi chŏn ŭi ch'anyang hago Hananim egero put'ŏ k'ŭn ŭnhye rŭl ibŭn chada ranŭn kŏt ŭl kkaedarŭn ihu ŭi ch'anyang i nŏmu tarŭguyo.*

My singing of praise before I felt that I benefited from the Lord's great grace and my singing of praise after I realized[32] that this great grace had come from God were very different.

5. *Kŭraesŏ iltan ŭn che ka op'era kasu nikka op'era rŭl hal ttae enŭn op'era ŭi chŏnch'e ŭi sŭt'ori wa yŏja chuin'gong ŭi sŏngkyŏg ŭl inje p'aak hamyŏnsŏ ŭmak sok e much'yŏ tŭrŏ kaya twaeyo. Amugŏt to saenggag ŭl mothae.*

Having said that, first and foremost, because I am an opera singer, when I do opera I have to be completely immersed in the music, grasping the overall story of the opera and the personality of the heroine. I can't think about anything else.

6. *Kŭrŏnde, chintcharo che ka kyŏnghŏm han kŏt ŭn, mwŏnyahamyŏn ŭn, che ka Ilbon ŭi Hujiwara Op'era hago op'era ra t'ŭrabiat'a, Ch'un-hŭi kongyŏn i issŏssŏyo.*

But, something I truly experienced, if you ask what it is, I did the opera *La traviata* with the Fujiwara Opera of Japan; it was a performance of the Lady of the Camellias.

7. *Kŭraesŏ kŭ 3-mak e naonŭn ch'unhŭi ŭi aria ka issŏssŏyo. "Addio del passato," "na ŭi chinan nal iyŏ, annyŏng" hamyŏnsŏ norae hanŭnde, ŏhyu, kŭ kamjŏng i chap'ijil ant'ŏraguyo.*

And in the third act, there is an aria [sung by] the Lady of the Camellias.[33] While I was singing "Addio del passato," "Farewell, days of my past," whew! I couldn't get a hold of those emotions.[34]

8. *Ŏlmana ŏryŏunjil . . . norae hanŭn kŏt ŭn him i an tŭrŏyo. kŭrŏna kŭ norae sok e innŭn kŭ kamjŏng kwa ttohan kŭ ŏullim kwa, ige naojil anŭnikka kŭnyang kŏt ŭroman purŭnŭn kŏt kat'ŭn kŭrŏn nŭkkim i tŭrŏyo.*

How difficult . . . it wasn't just difficult to sing. But the emotions and harmonies that are contained within that song—because these things wouldn't come out, I got the feeling that I was just singing superficially.

9. *Kŭraesŏ nŏmu komin ŭl hamyŏnsŏ, kido rŭl tŭryŏssŏyo. "Hananim, che ka Hujiwara e wasŏ irŏn chŏngmal choŭn yŏkhal ŭl mat'annŭnde, i op'era aria ŭi chŏngmal haeksimjŏk*

in kamjŏng i naojil anssŭmnida. Towa chuseyo. Abŏji towa chuseyo." Irŏmyŏnsŏ kanjŏrhi kido rŭl haessŭmnida.

So, being very worried, I offered a prayer. "God, I came to Fujiwara and took on this great role, but the true core emotions of this opera aria will not come to me. Please help me. Father, please help me." I prayed earnestly like this.

10. *Kŭrigo kŭ nal rihŏsŏl ŭl, yŏnsŭp ŭl kassŏyo. hapch'angdan i tchwak tullŏsŏ itko hapch'angdan ŭn twi esŏ, na nŭn ap esŏ honja norae hamyŏnsŏ, ap'ŭn mom ŭl irŭk'imyŏnsŏ norae hanŭn kŭ changmyŏn inde, che ka kŏgi yŏnsŭp ŭl hadaga, kŭ norae rŭl hadaga urŏssŏyo.*

And that day I went to rehearsal, to practice. It is the scene where I am singing alone in front, trying to get up with my sick body, with the chorus standing in a wide circle behind me. During rehearsal there, while singing the song, I cried.

11. *Kamjŏng i mak naonŭnde, i mŏri kayo. I mŏri ka tchuppit tchuppit sŏyo. Chintcha sŏyo. Kŭrigo onmom e chŏnyul i onŭnde, igŏn nae ka aniguna. Ige al—kŭgŏl nŭkkyŏjige, kŭrŏk'e ttŭgŏpke kŭgŏl yŏksa hae chusidŏraguyo.*

The emotions come violently to me, and my hair, my hair stands on end. It really stands up. And when I get shivers all over my body, [I think] "this is not me." [God] lets me know—lets me feel, fervently, He is working [in me].[35]

12. *Che ka kŏgisŏ nŏmu nŏmu kamdong haetko, "A, Hananim, nŏmu kamsa haeyo, Hananim nŏmu mŏtchyŏyo, ŏttŏk'e irŏn kamjŏng kkaji mandŭrŏ naesimnikka?"*

I was very, very moved there, and "Ah, God, thank you so much. God, you are so wonderful. How do you even create these emotions?"

13. *Kŭttae put'ŏ chŏ nŭn i Hananim i sesang e norae to nae ka midŭm an e issŭmyŏn Hananim an e issŭmyŏn ta yŏksa hae chusinŭn'guna. Igŏt ŭl ch'ŏlchŏ hage kkaedarassŏyo.*

Since then I—God performs His works [in me] even in worldly songs when I remain in my faith, when I remain in God. I realized this thoroughly.

14. *Kŭraesŏ ch'anyang hal ttae nŭn mullon kŭ kasa ka Hananim e taehan sarang ŭl irŏk'e chŏndal hanŭn kŏjiman, sesang norae nŭn sesang ŭi kŭ sŭt'ori chimanŭn, i, i "na ŭi yŏnggam sok e Chunim i kyesinda," igŏn pyŏnham i ŏptŏraguyo.*

Therefore, when I sing praise, the lyrics convey a love for God this way, whereas when I sing worldly songs, they are about worldly stories. This, this "God exists within my inspiration," this thing remains unchanged.

The horizontal schematic layout of the different vertically aligned segments of Kim Yŏng-mi's story—clearly resembling the Christian genre of testimony—reveals a poetically balanced narrative that diagrams, via its voicing and tense structure, the very story of transformation that it narrates. Segments 4 and 5 form a basic couplet in which Kim first introduces a general biographical chronotope of her transformation in light of her ongoing professional life as an opera singer and secular performer (for which, recall from chapter 1, she feels she was "chosen by God"). Segments 6–8 then take us back to the actual events during which this transformation took place: a performance of *La traviata* in Japan, where she, as Violetta, was to sing a farewell aria in the face of imminent death. The conflict arose when she felt herself singing "superficially," without the emotional dimension demanded by her professional standards. Segment 9, in which she describes offering a prayer to God, links up the different temporalities of the event of her narration (in past tense) and the narrated event of her prayer itself (in present tense). The prayer is not embedded within quotative statements (she does not frame the prayer using the direct -*rago* or indirect -*[n]dago* reportative grammar patterns) but rather is framed by self-standing metapragmatic statements in the past tense. The prayer to God in segment 9 departs from the narrative voice not only by switching to the quoted present tense but also through a phonosonic contrast: Kim utters her supplication with a softer, higher-pitched voice that differs dramatically from the more animated and authoritative sounds of the rest of her narrative. By performing the prayer in a slightly higher-pitched, softer voice (but without the marked nasality of the self-infantilizing strategies I observed among students in chapter 5), Kim lowers herself before God as she reconstructs her humble request.

Aligned with segments 6–8, segment 10 brings us back to the narration briefly, in which Kim describes the arrangement of people, her place alone in front, and how she cried while singing. This emotional outburst of tears introduces the core climactic moment of the narrative: God "working" in her. In segment 11, then, the use of the historical present draws her listeners into the experiential time-space of the narrated event by transposing its deictic *origō*, the indexical center or anchor point of the narrative, into the time and space of its narration. As Kim switches entirely to present tense, her voice grows more animated, even producing an occasional fricative voice gesture, and we are brought into the realm of intense feeling that she herself experienced during that moment of God "working" in her. This is achieved through both the phonosonic shift toward a more emphatic vocal style and the deictic transition from past to present tense—the sensorial experience of the "there and then" of the spiritual event is brought into the "here and now" of the interview. In this utterance, the distantiation between the event of narration and the narrated event that had been maintained through contrasts in tense and phonosonic qualia collapses, just as the distance between Kim Yŏng-mi, the humble supplicant, and God, the omnipotent being, collapsed in the event that she narrates.

In segment 12, then, the contrast between the interview as the event of narration and her contact with God as the narrated event are again demarcated and contrasted, as before in segment 9, with a description of her feelings in the past tense followed by a prayer in the present tense. And again, she recites her words to God with the same self-lowering vocal qualia as before. And finally, in segments 13 and 14, she returns to the same couplet form with which she began the narrative in segments 4 and 5. Kim offers a chronotopic statement about the change that has taken place "since then," which we now understand to refer to her spiritual experience in Japan, followed by a general statement about her understanding of her calling as a singer. Only this time, the calling is not merely to be a professional opera singer as in segment 5 but to be a singer who relies on God in both praise and worldly songs. Her position is made concrete in a verbal cadence consisting of an achronic, generalizing, nomic statement as a basic and enduring truth built upon the "plain" sentence ending *[-(n)da]* that is addressed to everyone and no one (as in a newspaper or a diary). Introduced and objectified by a repeated proximal deictic, "this" *("i")*, her penultimate statement "God exists within my inspiration" serves as the resolution of the narrative. The role of this belief in unifying sung genres (praise vs. worldly songs), speech genres (prayers vs. interviews), and even spatiotemporal perspectives (there and then vs. here and now) is further emphasized by Kim's final statement, "this thing remains unchanged."

Kim Yŏng-mi is known in Korea as a devout Christian who is a regular soloist at Onnuri Church, who prays with her students, who participates in missionary activities, and who sent her daughter to a private Christian school. Although in her interviews with me she emphasized her debt to her teachers and professional mentors, she also emphasized prayer and devotion as central components of her development as a singer. In the explicitly Christian context of the interview above, she emphasized the direct intervention of God in her singing. And stories about her faith—images of her during her school days in Rome, living on one banana a day, kneeling by the piano at night and praying for hours—circulate among singers in Seoul. Many teachers instruct their students to take Kim Yŏng-mi as a model not only of a singer but also of a Christian. For these singers, her voice serves as an emblem of the intersection between these two identities. It is therefore understandable that such a person would have difficulty empathizing emotionally with the "the fallen one" of Verdi's opera, presumably because, being raised as a devout Christian, she had little chance to experience the life of a courtesan. Likewise, it is easy to see how a singer who, out of necessity for her profession had maintained as healthy and stable a lifestyle as possible, would struggle to conjure up proprioceptive memories of bodily pain and suffering brought about by tuberculosis. Furthermore, she explained to me that her family was relatively well off and that she had left Korea for Italy in 1973, at the age of seventeen, to study in Rome. As a truly privileged person living abroad and studying opera, Kim Yŏng-mi might have found it difficult, if only momentarily, to access and express the emotional and physical suffering of Violetta, regardless of her past performance experiences and the expectation of professional performers to communicate emotions of all kinds.

But Kim Yŏng-mi believes that her God both feels the emotions of all humans and has himself felt the pain of death by sacrificing his son (Jesus Christ). Basing her actions on this belief, she turned to prayer. Kim Yŏng-mi described being able to feel the emotions and sensations necessary not just to sing convincingly on the "outside" but to have emotions on the "inside" as well. In her story, these were not provided by her own experience but were rather created for her by God. This being the case, she could feel happy in her *maŭm* even as she brought her audience to tears with sincere, expressive, emotionally coded singing.

Although she began by stating that there was a difference between singing secular and praise music, she concluded by saying that they were actually similar, insofar as God was "within [her] inspiration" *(yŏnggam sok e)*. Although the denotational content of praise and worldly songs was different, the two worked together: the former expressing a love for God, and the latter, in Kim Yŏng-mi's case, effectively performed because of a gift from God, that is, because of the miraculous delivery into her *maŭm* of emotions and sensations to which Kim Yŏng-mi would not otherwise have had access. This act of reciprocity was catalyzed by her prayer, the sentiment of which remained throughout the song while her body experienced shivers and pain. Although Paek Chi-yŏn's presumption was that the *maŭm* would be different for each of the two genres, we see that in fact, for Kim Yŏng-mi, the *maŭm* remained the same, always stable, always oriented to God.

By maintaining a stable *maŭm* oriented toward God, Kim Yŏng-mi found that she could expect other gifts as well that would help her move the *maŭm* of others. Just such a thing happened to Kim Yŏng-mi at an early-dawn prayer meeting staged at the Sea of Galilee in July 2005. She told this story on September 21, 2005, in an interview with Pak Na-rim on a television program called *Hanŭlpit hyanggi* (The Fragrance of a Blue Sky).[36] Twenty-five hundred Korean Christians had gathered at 5:30 in the morning for the service. When Kim Yŏng-mi awoke that morning, she had "no voice" *(mŏksori ka ŏpsŏyo)*. As she looked out at the gray water and the golden tones of the morning light, she thought to herself, "Jesus walked here, Jesus met his disciples *[cheja]* here," and she felt "an energy" *(kiun)* come to her. But her throat continued to hurt. So she said a short prayer before going onstage. As soon as she began to sing, however, her voice broke *(kkŭnk'ida)*. She stopped singing and whispered the name of the song into the microphone: "This is the Grace of God" *(Hananim ŭi ŭnhye imnida),* she said.

EXCERPT 7.3

Kŭrŏnde kŏgisŏ wanjŏnhi mak sŏngdodŭl i urŭm pada ka toego chŏ to ulgo kŭ sŏngnyŏngnim ŭi imjae hasim ŭl t'onghaesŏ "A, igŏn nae ka norae hanŭn ke anigo, nae ka ch'anyang i anira sŏngnyŏngnim kkesŏ ta chugwan hasil ttae e kŭ ŭnhye ka naeryŏ onŭn'guna."[37]

But suddenly the disciples there completely turned into a sea of tears, and I too cried, and through the Holy Spirit's presence [I realized], "Ah, this thing is not me singing, nor is it my praise, but rather grace is descending when everything is controlled by the Holy Spirit."

As both a "vessel of the Holy Spirit" and a "tool of divine will," Kim Yŏng-mi's voice returned in full force, and she was able to perform the song.[38] In this event of Christian communion and fellowship, Kim Yŏng-mi experienced and quite literally emitted what Bakhtin called the "authoritative word," which ventriloquates speakers in the form of "'the voice of life itself,' 'the voice of nature,' 'the voice of the people,' 'the voice of God,' and so forth."[39] Her voice and words as a medium of expression were infused with the absolute. Transformed from a performer into a receiving member of the congregation, she too could be moved to tears.

In this example, crying and emotional communion with other Christians and with God became the basis for what ended up being a successful performance. In chapter 1, I described Chang-wŏn's account of not letting oneself cry during performance lest one find oneself unable to sing. In that case, it was the danger of emotions interfering with and botching vocal technique. In the instance described by Kim Yŏng-mi above, the Holy Spirit was felt to be at work, guiding her voice and her heart. The heart was crying, but the tears were not of sadness; rather, they were of joy and praise at the realization that Kim Yŏng-mi was walking "where Jesus had walked" as an instance of chronotopic alignment. Indeed, when Pak Na-rim directly followed this narrative by asking Kim Yŏng-mi what sorts of things she prayed for these days, Kim replied:

EXCERPT 7.4

Uri sikkudŭl i hanmaŭm i toeŏsŏ kŭrŏn sayŏk ŭl kach'i haessŭmyŏn hanŭn kŭrŏn param i issŏyo.

I hope that our [Christian] family members develop one *maŭm* and that we can do this ministry together.

In this final statement, which concluded the interview, Kim Yŏng-mi's personal narrative of spiritual enlightenment through a realization regarding the *maŭm* becomes the basis for hoping for a larger-scale narrative of spiritual enlightenment concerning the *maŭm* of the world—to be assisted in part through her vocal performance—with South Korea as the spiritual center.

The concept of the *maŭm* in Korea plays a central role in regulating and shaping the affective dimensions of emotional experience. For Korean Christians, it has a special significance and function in helping them commune with their God via the Holy Spirit, achieving communion with fellow believers, bringing others into their community of belief, and providing a framework through which to interpret vocal performance. And just as Kim Chi-ch'ŏl's and Lee Myung-bak's story of twentieth-century Korea is one of the transition from chaos to stability, from receiving help to providing future leadership, so is the cultivation of both voice and *maŭm* a narrative of developing and achieving composure and control, such that one can move the emotions of others as part of an evangelical project. Within this framework, one should have a *maŭm* that is stably oriented toward God, so that the voice can carry out the evangelical work for which it is understood to be intended—as a gift from God.

MAŬM, VOICE, AND CHRISTIAN VOICING

Kim Yŏng-mi is a personification of the fulfillment of a project of Christianization that many Christians see in various dimensions of their society. For the present analysis, it is important to see that this transformation is manifest in the voice—the phonosonic nexus—such that Kim's personal biography comes to stand for an ethnonational history. Her voice channels the authoritative voice of an advanced nation, an enlightened people, and a Christian God. Her *maŭm* becomes the model *maŭm* for achieving one *maŭm* throughout the land.[40]

Numerous singers, both in Korea and abroad, told me that one of the greatest challenges for Korean singers is to convince European and North American audiences of their affective commitment to the music they perform, of their linguistically fluent understanding of the words they sing, and of their complete and culturally aware transformation into the operatic characters they portray.[41] The March 2008 issue of the music magazine *Ŭmak Ch'unch'u* contained an interview with a soprano named Betty Ŏm (Pet'i Ŏm), the central theme of which focused on the role of moving an audience's emotions *(kamdong)*. Near the end of her interview, she is quoted as saying: "If you walk around the streets and look, Korean people's expressions look a bit gloomy. However, because I was able to quickly lead the life of an Italian person, I was naturally able to come into contact with these people and their lifestyle and perform it naturally."[42] She goes on to say that singers should be put into contact with Italian culture earlier, so that it is easier for them to portray Italians as they mature as singers.

Kim Yŏng-mi herself said a similar thing to me in our earliest interview in 2005. Speaking of her students she said, "They have to go to Italy to taste the pasta, just like you had to come here to taste the kimch'i." But in later conversations with me, as well as in her interviews with Pak Na-rim and Paek Chi-yŏn, which were delivered in an explicitly Christian context, she seemed to suggest that enculturation abroad is potentially becoming less and less necessary for the development of sincere, emotionally moving performances of *sŏngak* as a specifically Korean Christian form of vocal art. This, it seems, is directly related to the notion of a cultivated Christian *maŭm* as the channel through which one can receive and display emotions that one has not personally experienced in one's worldly life; what one lacks in experience, in cultivation, in mastery, can be delivered by God to the sincere believer. If Korean Christians understand the *maŭm* to be the main site of emotional experience and a direct channel for communicating with God, for an increasingly wealthy and educated population whose experiential access to the suffering of Korea's past is more and more limited, the *maŭm* becomes conceptualized as the place through which they receive emotions from God that they themselves have not had— emotions that, important to note, they themselves *should not* have. After all, as Su-yŏn said, Koreans have received God's grace. As Korea increasingly becomes a practical center for *sŏngak*, some Koreans entertain the notion that their country will also gain cultural authority for *sŏngak* performance. And this authority is directly linked to the authority of the church.

Chang-wŏn told me that in the early days of *sŏngak* singing in Korea, singers used to use the English loan word *hat'ŭ* (heart) or the Italian word *cuore* to talk about emotional expressivity in sung classical music. Now that *sŏngak* is more established in Korea, he said, they have shifted to using the word *maŭm*. Whether or not this is empirically accurate, I think his account of language change is directly related to the Christianization of European-style classical singing in Korea and the place of the church in its institutional and cultural development. *Sŏngak* is coded, sometimes explicitly and sometimes implicitly, as Korean Christian music, as a Korean Christian vocal style, with Korean Christian performers singing for Korean Christian audiences. Thus any affective goals for performing a secular composition—for example, "moving" an audience's emotions—can be construed as Christian goals, just as in the final hymn of a homecoming recital. These specifically Korean Christian goals need not be met abroad in other, seemingly more legitimate linguistic-cultural contexts (e.g., Europe or the United States), but rather can be met at home, among fellow Korean Christians, using a *maŭm* that is stably oriented toward God.

Lee Myung-bak, in his inaugural speech in 2008, described a future Korea as a place from which the values of the twenty-first century would emanate. The SNU Praise Missionary Chorus, formed entirely by majors in *sŏngak* singing at Seoul National University, understands itself to be just such a vehicle for bringing Korean Christian values to the world. And this is achieved by turning both *maŭm* and voice toward God.

When I asked Chang-wŏn about his favorite singing experiences, he was quick to mention his participation in the SNU Praise Missionary Chorus and the feeling that emerged out of such an experience.

EXCERPT 7.5

C: *Ŭm. kŭ, che ka, chŏ nŭn Kidokkyo tchok ŭro mani, irŏk'e, chal mani midŭm i chom kwaench'anŭn p'yŏn iŏsŏ kŭrŏn tongari hwaltong ŭl hago issŏyo. Kŭraesŏ Sŏul Taehakkyo Ch'anyang Sŏn'gyodan irago p'ŭreijŭ minisŭt'ŭri hago innŭnde.*

Mm. I, I have a lot, like this, really a lot of good Christian faith, and I am doing these kinds of club activities. So I do what is called the Seoul National University Praise Missionary, Praise Ministry.

N: *A, Esŭenyu p'ŭreijŭ misyŏn?*

Ah, SNU Praise Mission?

C: *Ne ne.*

Yes, yes.

N: *Sŏnggadae? Sŏnggadae anira hapch'angdan.*

Choir? Not choir, chorus.

C: *Ye-ryŏng nuna innŭn, ye.*

With older-sister Ye-ryŏng, yes.[43]

N: *Ye-ryŏng?*

Ye-ryŏng?

C: *Ne, Ch'oe Ye-ryŏng.*

Yes, Ch'oe Ye-ryŏng.

N: *A, Ch'oe Ye-ryŏng. Ne ne ne.*

Ah, Ch'oe Ye-ryŏng. Yes, yes, yes.

C: *Kŭ saram innŭn tongari. Chŏ kŭraesŏ chŏ to kŭraesŏ kach'i hapch'ang hago hanŭnde kŏgi e t'uŏ rŭl kayo.*

The club with that person. I, therefore, I also, therefore, sing with the chorus and go on tours there.

N: *Ŏdi e?*

Where?

C: *Mwŏ Amerik'a na Osŭt'ŭreillia mwŏ Chaep'aen, Ch'aina irŏk'e watta katta hamyŏnsŏ hanŭnde kŏgisŏ, ŭm. K'ŭllaesik song malgo, ŭm, k'waiŏ ŭmak ŭl hanŭnde kŭttae to ch'am choayo.*

Um, America or Australia or, um, Japan, or China. As we travel like this here and there, um, we don't sing classical songs, but rather, mm, choir music, and at that time it is really good.

N: *Ŭm, waeyo waeyo?*

Mm. Why? Why?

C: *Ŭm. Kŭ yŏngchŏk in kyogam. Kŭrŏn ke issŏyo.*

Mm. Spiritual communion of feeling. There is that type of thing.

N: *Chogŭm myosa haseyo.*

Please describe it a bit.

C: *Ŭm, laik'ŭ, ŏ, mudang? Mwŏ wich'i? Mwŏ.*

Mm. It's like, uh, shaman? Uh, witch? Uh.

N: *Mudang? Ne ne. Syamŏn.*

Shaman? Yes, yes. Shaman.

C: *Syamŏn, ne. Laik'ŭ syamŏn. Kyogam. Ai, Kat hant'e che ka mal hago t'ok'ŭ hago aensŏ tŭtko tasi t'ok'ŭ hamyŏn che ka aensŏ hago irŏn nŭkkim i issŏyo. Kŭrŏm kŭttae ch'am choayo.*

Shaman. Yes, like a shaman. Communion of feeling. I, I talk to God, I hear an answer, and if I talk again, I hear an answer, and there is this kind of feeling. When this happens it is really good.

N: *Yŏnju tongan?*

C: *Ne. pik'ojŭ it ijŭ, ŏ, kasŭp'el?*
Kasŭp'el song. Aendŭ, mwŏ, ye.
Kasŭp'el song ŭl k'waiŏ ro norae
hanŭnde kŭttae kŭrŏn nŭkkim i
itko kŭ taŭm e kach'i k'waiŏ rŭl
hanŭn saramdŭl kkiri kyogam
hanŭn kŏt to choayo.

During the performance?

Yes, Because it is, uh, gospel?
Gospel song. And, um, yes. We sing
gospel songs as a choir, and during
this time I have the feeling, and it is
good to have the communion of
feeling among people in the choir.

As with the encores of homecoming recitals in Seoul, Christian performance here is characterized as the highest form of personal expression. This performance genre is used not for the lone performer to experience and communicate individual feelings but for a group to join together in a feeling of spiritual communion, with a collective *maŭm* that yearns for worship. This feeling of communion is emotional and affective in nature, as indicated by the term *kyogam*, which is based on the Sino-Korean *kyo* (exchange) and *kam* (feeling, emotion). This genre and its feeling are compared with the Korean shaman's historical role of making a space for personal emotional "release."[44] And this space of spiritual and emotional communion is created through dialogue between the singers and their God, such that the alignment of all the voices in a choir, following a "natural" (i.e., God-given) technique, becomes the experience of the voice of God. The creation of monophony out of polyphony, of a unitary language out of heteroglossia, of one emotion out of many, is the manifestation of the authoritative voice.

CONCLUSION

Chang-wŏn's mention of shamanism illuminates an important point about perspectival alignment through semiotic alignment. In shamanic ritual, there is a distinction between the voicing structure of divination, in which a shaman might report on the words and status of an ancestral spirit via explicit metapragmatic framings, and possession, in which the shaman produces the spirit's voice without such framings.[45] In divination, the shaman remains the animator of the spirit's words by referring to the ancestral spirit's words and actions (the narrated event) in the form of ritual speech (the event of narration).[46] In possession, the narrated event and the event of narration collapse into a monologically voiced text-event, and both the roles of author and animator coincide in the single phonosonic medium of the shaman's voice as the spirit's voice. This "breakthrough" of the narrated event into the event of narration collapses the deictic and qualic differentiation between the two.

For Chang-wŏn, the collective production of song in an explicitly Christian performance event produces a similar kind of voicing structure: a collapse of the distance between the event of gospel performance and the events that are being described by the sung text of the gospel performance (joyful *maŭm,* loving *maŭm,* clean *maŭm,* etc.). In this case, the distance between the two is not necessarily a spatiotemporal one but an emotional, affective one. A Christian performance of this kind should bring into the event the emotional states that inspired the event and are described in the event, such that one *feels* the grace of God while one *sings* "The Grace of God" ("Hananim ŭi ŭnhye"). "Inside" and "outside" come into in perfect alignment.[47]

But for these singers, one's own internal, closed-circuit alignment to external, open-circuit communicative media is not the ultimate goal. While their own faith and connection to deity must constantly be reconfirmed, their "calling" as singers—as with Kim Yŏng-mi—is to bring others into a similar kind of alignment. Let us recall chapter 1, where I discussed Chong-ho's criticism of the soprano who cried onstage. He was dissatisfied with the performance, because the singer did not bring to the audience the experience of God that she sang about in the song "Ch'am choŭsin Chunim" (Truly Good Lord). She had failed to quicken *kyogam* among the members of her audience, instilling in them only ambivalent empathy.

When the singer does move an audience during these performances, the voice as phonosonic nexus becomes the medium for a markedly Christian voicing structure, and the feelings described by the denotational voicings penetrate and become the feelings expressed by and embodied in the phonosonic voices themselves. In the context of contemporary Christianity, the feelings should be of joy, peace, love, and other emotional states that differentiate the advanced, enlightened present from the suffering past. One's emotional transition from sadness or apathy to joy and enthusiasm through Christian performance becomes a diagram of the same narrated transition of Korean Christians over ethnonational time more generally. For Kim Yŏng-mi as for Chang-wŏn, a chronotope of Christian progress, teleologically placing a joyful, blessed Korea at the spiritual center of the Christian world, is cued up and becomes the very framework through which the qualia of the *maŭm* and the qualia of the voice can be felt *as Christian*.

For the choir conductor at Somang Church I mentioned at the beginning of this chapter, singing "with the *maŭm*" did not merely describe the emotive expression of some individual, psychological interior. Rather, it described the way the voice could establish a holy channel of social contact. It described the phatic function of vocalization within an explicitly Christian ideology of collective emotionality. This simple switch of codes from German to Korean is representative of, indeed performative of, the greater shift that I have discussed, namely, that Korean Christians are orienting toward a Korean Christian concept of the *maŭm* as the seat of emotional experience, a channel of communion with God and others, and a locus of sincere feeling that can be shared between believers via the voice. For a performance of that song—even though it was in English—for that audience, in that context, we were not supposed to sing with the heart or *das Herz,* with *il cuore* or the *simjang* or anything else. We were supposed to sing with the *maŭm.*

Conclusion

The focus of this ethnography has been on Christian singers in Korea who strive to embody cultural ideals and social values through semiotic practice. Through performance and professionalization, prayer and evangelism, manipulations of sound and body, singers of *sŏngak* in Korea try to exhibit the qualities of Korean Christian modernity in the qualia of their voices. Their voices become emblems of this state of striving, revealing both their successes and failures as they work toward this goal. As I have shown, this state of striving is organized by a chronotope of advancement. A voice, the emotions it expresses, the person in whom it is embodied, and the social relations that it mediates can be relatively more old-fashioned or modern, more marginal or central, more holy or less, relatively clean or unclean on the basis of phonosonic practice that is apperceived in terms of a Christian aesthetic of progress.

But under the powerful sorting influence of this chronotope of advancement, striving itself has come under scrutiny. Whereas to strive for modernity was once a valid, indeed desirable, aspiration, more and more this disposition is looked down upon as a relic of Korea's past. That is, for a country that purports to stand "shoulder-to-shoulder with advanced countries," to *try* to be a leader, to *try* to appear advanced, to *try* to be an equal is to admit that one is not yet a leader, not yet advanced, and not yet equal.

Still, the tendency to strive remains. When President Lee Myung-bak and Reverend Kim Chi-ch'ŏl make chronotopic claims about the arrival of South Korea at the table of advanced nations, it is done with some ambivalence, as if the propositional statements regarding what "is" are also directives, or pleas, regarding what "should be." Political speeches that describe Korea standing shoulder-to-shoulder with the advanced nations of the world or Christian sermons that describe social progress, situated beneath a glowing stained-glass window depicting the Korean peninsula highlighted and enlarged at the center of the map, also communicate concern about the residual elements of Korean society that seem so stubbornly to hold the country and its people back from fully realizing its bright future. While images of advancement and global leadership point to an idealized future, they also invoke a difficult past, often perceived as shameful, that lives on in the present. Narratives of Korea's destiny to emerge as a world leader are often couched in terms of a sorting exercise—like the effort of the early twentieth-century intellectual Yi Kwang-su to distinguish "unsatisfactory but correctable 'secondary' traits from a 'fundamental' Korean national character, which he regarded a composite of many outstanding qualities."[1] The question for many Koreans has been and continues to be: which qualities should be cultivated, and which should be left behind?

Among the singers whose voices are linked to the Christian version of this story of progress, the same question pertains. When I interviewed the internationally renowned bass Youn Kwangchul (Yŏn Kwang-ch'ŏl) in Berlin in 2007, he explained that most people in the world do not want to become opera singers, because it is hard work *(schwere Arbeit)* and takes a long time to build a singer *(einen Sänger aufzubauen)*. But Koreans, he said, have desire and voice *(Lust und Stimme)*.[2] Kim Yŏng-mi put it to me very simply: "Koreans just have the most beautiful voices." According to both of them, the challenge for Korean singers is not vocal beauty; it is the ability to temper the desire for rapid advancement long enough to let the inborn beauty of their voices emerge and mature "naturally"—neither to "push" nor to "hold" the voice.

One of the first things I learned from singers in Korea was that big, loud, powerful voices are most favored by audiences South Korea. Singers strive to develop this kind of voice from the time they are very young—especially for their auditions to music conservatories. Abroad, teachers and other international peers sometimes hear the sounds of "pushing" or "holding" in Korean voices as the effects of poor technique and underdeveloped aesthetic taste. While Korean singers also learn to associate this singing method with their home country, its institutions, and its audiences, they also sometimes hear it as the product of a deeper feature of Korean society. Among men in particular, these sounds—the phonic strain of the voice, the air pressure under the glottis, the tension of the throat, and the sonic roughness that can emerge from all of this—are sometimes interpreted as residual *han*. Abroad, Koreans sometimes construe these sounds not necessarily as the fault of Korea's education system or popular taste but as a specifically Korean style of emotionally coded expressivity. In the "cleaning" of their voices abroad, singers change not only their technique but also the emotional coding of all sorts of sensations, from the more sonic and expressive sounds of the voice to the more phonic and embodied forms of vocalization. Like Chang-wŏn, they work hard to erase the traces of sadness from their voices, just as they try to remove it from their *maŭm*.

Some of these sounds are not the effects of sadness, not the *han* of colonialism or war or poverty. Rather, they are the sounds of striving, of constantly trying to do as much as possible in the shortest amount of time. For example, when Sang-u began his secret training to save and repair his voice, one of the first things his teacher told him was not to try so hard, not to hold the voice so tightly, not to push so much. His secret teacher told him to be patient. She said that volume and color and power would come if he just had patience and tried to do the "right" thing, the "natural" thing, with his voice. When Sang-u and I discussed the problem of young tenors like himself trying to sing high Cs in their college recitals, Sang-u smiled and said, "Yes, but Koreans are like that. Always—," and then, instead of speaking, he pantomimed struggling to pull himself up onto a ledge far above his head. In the same manner, Paul, the Korean student who had returned from his studies at Juilliard to visit family in Seoul, insisted that singers in Korea simply cannot wait for their voices to "blossom." Because of the culture of singing in Korea, he said, they insist on trying to do too much to soon and hurt themselves in the process, sometimes irreparably. Another young baritone, in one of my first interviews on the subject, said plainly that Korean singers like himself want recognition (*injŏng*) right away, immediately, at all costs. These statements point to what is often called a culture of *"ppalli ppalli"* in Korea. *Ppalli ppalli* means, literally, "quickly, quickly." The phrase can be used as a directive to do things rapidly and was commonly heard during the decades of Korea's swift modernization, when everyone's sense was that there was no time to lose. Like a voice fatigued by too much pushing, many Koreans feel a general sense of exhaustion from decades of striving.

Part of what students of *sŏngak* say they learn when they leave Korea is to let their voices develop "naturally," to "blossom." But these changes do not take place in some abstract ether outside Korea called "abroad." They take place in particular places like Milan and New York, Berlin and London. Back in Korea, returned singers talk about other trained voices in terms of when and where they were trained. Trained voices take on a certain national character: they sound Italian or German, American or Russian. In these descriptions, the voice, like an accent or a style of dress, becomes an emblem of place—seeming both to point to a place and to exhibit some identifying feature or quality of the place. For those who listen carefully, in Seoul's singing culture one can hear a topography of other countries, other characteristics, other qualities. Each voice expresses specific kind of foreignness by the qualia it has acquired abroad.

But the collective project in which these singers are engaged is not organized around celebrating and perpetuating the vocal triumphs of other countries. These singers dream of using their voices to make Korea a productive world center. They dream of making Koreanness itself an influential quality that emanates abroad. Their aim is to make Somang Church's stained-glass map of the Korean peninsula, enlarged and colored to stand out from to the rest of the world, a map of reality. And Christianity in Korea, with the Korean Christianization of the *sŏngak* voice in particular, allows this kind of singing and these kinds of voices to be heard and experienced as thoroughly Korean. Through Christianity, the people of Chosŏn can become, as Korean pastors often put it, "a chosen people, a royal priesthood, a holy nation, a people belonging to God."[3] They can move from global periphery to spiritual center. They can make the Korean peninsula an axis mundi uniting heaven and earth.

But, as I have shown, this model does not apply to everyone, not even to all of those involved in European classical music or even *sŏngak*. For many of these people, admittedly not well-represented in this study, participation in classical music or singing triggers nostalgia for past forms and genres of expressivity. The taxi driver I discussed in chapter 1 explicitly felt left out of this transformation of voice and lamented the loss of the sounds of *han* in the voice. Whereas some singers arrive abroad and find that they have residual and undesirable *han* in their voices, which they attempt to clean according to the principles of *sŏngak*, other musicians of European classical music turn back toward the sounds they associate with the Korean past.

This was the case with a young pianist (not a Christian) from Seoul whom I met in 2006. She had practiced earnestly for years to prepare for conservatory auditions in Germany. All the time, she felt that the music she was playing—Bach, Beethoven, Brahms—fit naturally with her musical tastes and disposition. But when she arrived in Germany and found herself competing against other Koreans—more Koreans, sometimes, than any other nationality—she said she came to the realization that she was "one of them," one of those thousands of Koreans who had "lost" their own culture and traditions and "replaced" them with someone else's. She failed the entrance exams and, upon returning to Korea, switched her major to traditional music. So profound had her connection to Korean traditional become, she told me, that upon listening she could feel each drum, each symbol, each sound in various parts of her body. But she characterized her transformation as long and painful. Sometimes these realizations occur suddenly and unexpectedly. A professor of traditional Korean music—again, not a Protestant Christian, but a nonpracticing Catholic—told me stories of singers trained in *sŏngak* who, out of mere curiosity, decided to take a course in Korean traditional music. These singers were surprised to find how natural traditional Korean music felt to them, she said. They had sung *sŏngak* their entire lives until one day something changed and they felt happiest singing traditional music, in a traditional vocal style, in Korean. They felt that Korean music and the traditional voice had returned them to their proper place. They had come home to Korea and to the Korean voice.

However, the chronotope of Korean Christianity that frames the Christian aesthetic of progress in which the *sŏngak* voice is situated and exalted does not point back to the resuscitation of tradition. It points forward to the idealized future of an influential, internationally recognized Christian society. It leaves things behind. It buries them. It erases them. And some of these things, for some of these people, it turns out, are irrecoverable.

Chapter 1 contained a vignette of a well-known and respected soprano who serves as a local paragon of the Korean Christian *sŏngak* voice. This soprano waxed nostalgic about the disappearance of Korean customs when she found herself unable to sing a traditional song because of the way it hurt her throat. Hers is a story of success in the Christian aesthetic of progress, illustrating how certain aspects of a cultural past must be left behind in the cultivation of the clean voice. At stake are contested cultural chronotopes made concrete in the phonosonic practice of singing. Her past striving had placed her fully on the other side of the chronotope of advancement; her own voice *is* the Christian aesthetic of progress. And from the center of modern Korean Christianity, the idealized qualities of which she herself embodied and expressed through the voice, she could hear but not reproduce the fading sounds of the past.

Notes

INTRODUCTION

1. A literal translation would be "military unit stew." The dish is also sometimes referred to as *chonsŭnt'ang,* "Johnson soup." On the *kijich'on,* or camp town, especially regarding social relations between American GIs and Korean women, see K. Moon 1997; and Yuh 2004.

2. The original English lyrics are: I'm pressing on the upward way / New heights I'm gaining every day / Still praying as I onward bound / "Lord, plant my feet on higher ground."

3. Although the Sino-Korean word *sŏngak* itself simply refers to vocal music (*sŏng,* voice; *ak,* music) and has been used to refer to singing in more traditional Korean forms of music, the word has come to stand primarily for "Western classical vocal music" in contemporary South Korea.

4. Okon Hwang (2009: 27) notes that as early as 1996, 20 percent of the students in the college division of the Manhattan School of Music were Korean nationals. And in 2001, the Japan Economic Newswire reported, "At Juilliard ... about 31% of the 591 undergraduate and graduate music students are ethnically Asian. Students from Japan, South Korea, China and Taiwan account for more than half the foreign enrollment, with the largest number—48 of 213—from South Korea" (Fukada 2001). See also Yoshihara 2007.

5. Dr. Ute Schmidt, Akademisches Auslandsamt, Hochschule für Musik Hanns Eisler, e-mail communication, March 23, 2007.

6. www.roccadellemacie.com/sito/index.php?id_pagine=311&id_lang=2, accessed June 10, 2007.

7. www.neue-stimmen.de, accessed April 5, 2010.

8. See Abelmann 2003; Kendall 1996; and Nelson 2000 on class and gender in South Korea. See Yoshihara 2007 for a more general account of class, gender, and race among Asian and Asian American classical musicians. See Koo

2007 for a sociological view of inequality, consumption, and the middle class in the decade following the Asian financial crisis of the late 1990s.

9. Accounts of this transformation can be found in Cumings 2005: 299–366; and Lie 2000.

10. See C.-s. Park 2003 for a history of Protestantism in Korean social institutions and politics.

11. For a discussion of the various estimates, see Han 2009: 9–10. On the basis of ethnographic research conducted among Korean missionaries in Korea, northeast China, Tanzania, Uganda, and the United States, Ju Hui Judy Han has written extensively on this topic and has shown that the narrative of Korea's transformation from suffering to prosperity is interwoven with the way Korean Christians view the targets of their missions as societies and places that resemble their own country's past (Han 2008, 2010a, 2010b, 2011, n.d.).

12. Aesthetics are a specific form of ethnometapragmatics (Silverstein 1979: 207ff.), a native view of the social appropriateness and effectiveness of semiotic form contextually mobilized in (and as) social action, which is revealed in discourse with varying degrees of explicitness. Steven Feld (1994: 77), in the technical semiotic idiom of Charles S. Peirce, has suggested that aesthetics be seen as "iconicity of style," where ways of judging semiotic form as beautiful and as natural "become identical, intuitively inseparable in local imagination and practice." And style itself, if it is to be culturally meaningful and socially effective, must be seen as more than just a formal homology of structures or co-occurrence patterns—as Agha (2007: 186), Brenneis (1984, 1985, 1987), Feld (1994: 77), Irvine (2001), Turino (1999), and others have pointed out. Instead, we must view style as a form of semiotic enregisterment, where its structural features are indexical of stereotypic values and types of personae within a (often naturalized) metapragmatic model of social action.

13. See C. E. Park 2003 for an ethnographic study of *p'ansori* performance.

14. Regarding the polysemy of *voice* in English, two decades ago Steven Feld and Aaron Fox (1994: 26) linked two discourses on voice: "One is a more phenomenological concern with voice as the embodiment of spoken and sung performance, and the other is a more metaphoric sense of voice as a key representational trope for social position and power."

15. Sapir 1927: 898.

16. Sapir 1927: 895. For decades, anthropologists and ethnomusicologists have paid increasing attention to the role of the voice beyond "ordinary" linguistic communication. Such research has dealt with, for example, the relative prioritization of voice among different musical modes (Blacking 1973), the interdependence of vocal sound's aesthetic and broader cultural significance (Feld 1982), the role of voice in wailing and lament (Briggs 1993, 1996; Seremetakis 1991; Urban 1988), vocal mediation between music and language in ritual and other performance contexts (Fox 2004; Seeger 2004), and the voice as a sociohistorically produced political object (Weidman 2006).

17. Ladefoged 2006: 3.

18. Cf. Kiksht, where "the functional load of the voiced/voiceless distinction is low" (Silverstein 1994: 42).

19. See Laver 1980 for a technical account of voice quality. See Fox 2004; Sicoli 2010; and Urban 1991 for ethnographic treatments of voice quality. Sapir (1927: 893ff) came to the notion of the voice proper by observing that the "lowest level of speech" is "the voice itself," upon which were built what he called "levels of speech" (not to be confused with honorific or deferential speech "levels" or "styles"; see Agha 1993; Errington 1985; and Martin 1964). If the "voice proper" was understood by Sapir as the first of these levels, the second was "voice dynamics" (including intonation, the "musical handling" of the voice, timbre, rhythm, etc.), the third was "pronunciation" (the phonetic shaping of particular words, "expressive symbolic character" of such shapings, etc.), the fourth was "vocabulary" (the selection of particular words in speech), and the fifth was overall "style" ("arranging words into groups and working these up into larger units").

20. A quest to understand the anatomy of phonation was precisely what led Spanish singer and voice pedagogue Manuel Garcia to develop a laryngoscope with which he could view his own phonating vocal cords. He published his results in 1855 in the *Proceedings of the Royal Society of London* in an article titled "Observations on the Human Voice."

21. For a powerful example of the relation between the formants of a particular speaking voice and the acoustic frequencies reinforced by a space of vocalization, see Alvin Lucier's 1970 composition, "I Am Sitting in a Room," for voice and electromagnetic tape (Lucier [1970] 1981). For this piece, Lucier recorded his utterances on electromagnetic tape and then played them back into the room, recording the playback with another recorder, and repeating this act numerous times. The recorded utterance is itself the description of the act and its goals: "I am sitting in a room different from the one you are in now. I am recording the sound of my speaking voice and I am going to play it back into the room again and again until the resonant frequencies of the room reinforce themselves so that any semblance of my speech, with perhaps the exception of rhythm, is destroyed. What you will hear, then, are the natural resonant frequencies of the room articulated by speech. I regard this activity not so much as a demonstration of a physical fact, but, more as a way to smooth out any irregularities my speech might have." He does this by reallocating the acoustic energy from that of verbal phonation within the vocal tract to that of resonance of speech within the acoustic space of the room. Rather than the room being the acoustic space for the voice, the voice becomes the phonatory source for the room (i.e., the voice is to the room what the vocal cords are to the vocal tract). As we hear each new recording replayed into the specific acoustic space of the room, the features of Lucier's speech slowly dissolve into a ring of different overtones, pulsing on the accents of his obscured speech. The first recording features Lucier's voice, recognizable as such, with a sonic background littered by the static of the tape. The most intense energy of Lucier's speech is the fundamental intonation of his voice, which fluctuates between 100 and 150 Hz. By the fifth repetition, the fundamental pitch has transformed into a kind of ringing drone at around 2,000 Hz, with occasional pulses shooting up to 5,000 Hz, reinforced by the high frequencies of Lucier's sibilants in speech. In the final re-recording, the acoustic energy of Lucier's speech has settled into a

high-pitched drone at just under 2,000 Hz. This is heard as a 7th-octave A-sharp/B-flat (1,865 Hz). The dramatic acoustic change that takes place from the first recording to the last recording, in which the phrasing is completely opaque, can be revealed visually through spectrographic analysis, which displays graphically the intensity of different frequencies. As the verbal utterances of the artist are recorded, replayed, re-recorded, and replayed into the acoustic space of the room, the vocal sound that was originally emitted decomposes and transforms into the ringing acoustic frequencies favored by the shape of the physical space in which they are being emitted. Thus, "any semblance of [his] speech, with perhaps the exception of rhythm, is destroyed" (Lucier [1970] 1981). Lucier's original speech is heard as low tones, the residue of a fundamental pitch beneath the ring of higher frequencies. And so we are compelled to ask: If this is a recording of Alvin Lucier's voice, do we still hear his voice in the final sounds? If not, at what point does Lucier's voice cease to be?

22. See Miller 1986; and Stark 2003 for pedagogical and historical accounts of this process, respectively.

23. The acoustic phenomenon associated with this type of vocalization has been shown by Johan Sundberg (1972, 1977, 1987) to be a clustering of the 3rd, 4th, and 5th formants around 3,000 Hz. This "singer's formant" is perceptually associated with a "ring in the voice" heard by an audience and gives vocal sound the "power" to carry over an orchestra or throughout large halls, without necessarily sounding loud in a small room. Sundberg (1972, 1974) showed how this was assisted by shaping the aryepiglottic resonator to one-sixth of the area of the vocal tract, causing the two to act as separate resonators. See also Beeman 2005; and Feld et al. 2004: 335.

24. Barthes (1972) 1977. See Bergeron 2009: 62–64 on the pedagogical relationship between Barthes and Charles Panzéra. Simon Frith (1998: 191) discusses Barthes's argument that the "grain" is the mark of the body in the singing voice, because "different timbral qualities have differential bodily implications"; the "ungrained" voice is understood to "conceal its own means of physical production." See also Jakobson and Waugh (1979) 2002: 262 on "physiognomic features" and Turino 2008: 43 on the voice as a "sonic body." See Eidsheim 2011b for an exploration of the material body in vocal performance and Young 2006 for an account of the body in recordings of voice.

25. Feld et al. 2004: 341.

26. Feld et al. 2004: 341.

27. In recent anthropological literature, there has been an effort to move away from the "body" as a universal concept and object of analysis and toward "embodiment" as a field of investigation that accounts for the dynamic processes by which social life is experienced in terms of corporeal phenomena (Bourdieu 1977; Csordas 1993; Farquhar 2002; Geurts 2002; Hanks 1990; Lock and Farquhar 2007). The usage of the term *embodiment* is not restricted to the biological body as such. But as the morphological units of the term show, embedded here is a means by which the social becomes "bodily," "of the body," or "in the body." This derivational move does not so much skirt the issue of the body as push us to investigate further into what precisely is conceptualized or referred to in relation to the lexemic base *body* (see Kockelman 2005). Some-

times *embodiment* can simply mean something akin to the materialization, manifestation, or concrete expression of a more abstract principle or quality. That is, something (e.g., virtue, capitalism, the Holy Spirit, redness, etc.) appears to someone to be embodied as or in something else; that is, it is semiotically mediated. In this formulation, embodiment is an indexical icon—a sign that is both indexical of (i.e., signaling by virtue of a perceived contiguity, or relation of causality, with) and iconic of (i.e., signaling by virtue of perceived formal similarity to) its object (Peirce 1997: secs. 5.71, 8.122; Silverstein 2000: 117–18, 133n22; Tambiah 1985: 156). A highbrow example of "embodiment" used in this manner would be the following statement: "Beethoven's music embodied the transition from the classical to the romantic periods of European musical composition." Beethoven's music occurred during this transition (contiguity), and one can hear the transition in the formal elements of the music itself (similarity). Throughout this book, I have chosen to treat *embodiment, bodily hexis,* and similar terms as forming a general semiotic field of investigation that opens up for analysis broader dimensions of culture. See the similarly general usage of *expression* in Feld 1982, and likewise for both *expression* and *embodiment* in Fox 2004.

28. See Chumley and Harkness 2013; and Harkness 2013, for a theorization of qualia for anthropology. See Munn 1986 for an ethnographic study of quality and value. See Keane 2003; and Manning 2012 for examples of semiotic anthropology that engages with the problem of materiality and sensuous qualities.

29. See Bourdieu 1977: 94.

30. See Mead 1934:61-68 on the "vocal gesture" as a "significant symbol."

31. It is precisely this obscurity that has generated attempts at psychoanalytic theories of voice. See Poizat (1986) 1992 on the "pure object voice" and more recently Dolar 2006, who begins by discussing the limits of structural linguistics (cf. Agha 2007; Daylight 2011; Kockelman 2005; Lee 1997; and Monson 1996) in the attempt to reveal the voice—the voice proper—as "a paramount 'embodiment' of *objet petit a*" (11). Granted, Dolar's book is meant as a celebration of psychoanalysis via a reading of Western philosophical treatments of voice. But, ironically, his formulation of voice as that which "exceeds language and meaning" (11) exposes a "blind spot" or source of "lack" (to use his terms) in his own method: long-term ethnographic study of the pragmatics of communicative interaction where the "object voice" is actually pursued. Simply put, it is hard to take seriously any generalizing theory of voice that is not actually based on research on the voice that it posits. As Wayne Koestenbaum (1993: 155) put it (playfully describing himself but easily also describing a more general search for the voice proper): if he had "succeeded in demystifying voice, [he] would have no god left."

32. See, for example, Chion (1982) 1999: 1: "The voice is elusive. Once you've eliminated everything that is not the voice itself—the body that houses it, the words it carries, the notes it sings, the traits by which it defines a speaking person, and the timbres that color it, what's left?"

33. See Agha 2007: 80–83 on semiotic registers.

34. Invoking Jakobson's (1960) six functions of language (and, more distantly, Malinowski), Fox (2004: 272) reminds us that singing is a phatic form

of communication: it focuses our attention on the communicative channel itself (i.e., the voice), and the singer aims to establish and maintain social contact through the phonosonics of vocal performance. Phaticity generally refers both to the physical medium of communication (as in the sound of a voice transmitted through a telephone line, or the visual medium of a digitized screen, or the hapticity of a handshake or a hug) and to the psychological notion of social contact or connectivity (see, e.g., Lemon 2013 on "phatic experts").

35. See Silverstein 1976, 1979, and 1993 for foundational papers on the concept of *metapragmatics*.

36. Note that these labels also presuppose various interactional frameworks, from the explicitly intersubjective to the seemingly self-directed, as in "self-talk" (Goffman 1978).

37. We can see how Sapir's construction of what he called "levels of speech" (see n. 19 above), viewed this way, is really a scalar listing of different kinds of sonic frameworks into which phonic production and organization are supposed to fit: from classification of sounds as or as not "voice," to the multiple "supra-segmental" dimensions of vocalization, to the variable articulatory phonetics of speech vis-à-vis the standards of a phonological system, to the meaningful pho-nemic combinations of speech as denotation, and so on. The voice in all of these dimensions is really the practical realization of a culturally ordered dynamic relationship between the meaningful phonic organization of sound and sonic systems of meaning differentiated by form. The voice is a phonosonic nexus, whether we are talking about the more familiar and cross-cultural realms of phonological structure, sociophonetic variation, or musical aesthetics, or in more culturally specific arrangements, such as those relating birdsongs to affect and morality (Feld 1982), collective weeping to empathetic experiences of pain (Seremetakis 1991), or ensembles of sonic features to characterological types in an urban landscape (Weidman 2010). As Kockelman (2011: 437) points out, the margins of some of these various orders of meaningfulness in language are, for "linguists and lay folk alike, . . . a kind of locale where human voice is still mythologically entangled with animal sounds because of its alleged iconic trans-parency and indexical immediacy."

38. See, e.g., Agha 2005; Harkness 2011; and Irvine 1990 on speech; Eidsheim 2011a; and Olwage 2004 on song.

39. In a classic example, Sapir (1927: 895–96) observed how the qualities of voice come to stand for a type of person within a social system of typifiable personae: "A man has a strained or raucous voice, let us say, and we might infer that he is basically 'coarse-grained.' Such a judgment might be wide of the mark if the particular society in which he lives is an out-of-doors society that indulges in a good deal of swearing and rather rough handling of the voice." This is an instance of "downshifting" (Parmentier 1994: 18–19) of the metonymical to the metaphorical, an effect of what Gal and Irvine called *iconization* (1995: 973) and later *rhematization* (Gal 2005: 35n5; 2013). In such events, an index-ical relation is interpreted as an iconic one. Through this process, a type of voice comes to stand for a type of perspective by some perception of qualitative simi-larity. And the qualitative differentiation of voices becomes not only the quali-tative differentiation of persons and their bodies (recall Feld et al.'s [2004: 341]

observation that "voice is among the body's first mechanisms of difference") but also the qualitative differentiation of identifiable perspectives.

40. In this example, the pastor performs what Hastings and Manning (2004) called the "voices of exemplary others." Hastings and Manning (2004: 301) argue that such "embodied voices," condensed in Erving Goffman's ([1974] 1986) notion of the *figure,* anchor semiotic systems in terms of which people "index their own situational and social positions" and thereby their relationships to others. A focus on such systems then allows us as analysts to "locate voice in relation to both identity and alterity" (302).

41. See Bakhtin 1981: 275–336 (also Vološinov 1986) for a foundational theorization of voicing in novelistic discourse and reported speech. Bakhtin's use of the term *voice* pertained to the semiotic presentation of the perspective of a character or social type vis-à-vis other identifiable positions in the text, whether in the narrator's universe or the universe of narration. This concept comes from the terminology of musical polyphony, in which any given voice (an internally coherent musical part or strand) in a composition is always positioned in relation to others both melodically (i.e., "horizontally" or syntagmatically) and harmonically ("vertically" or paradigmatically). In this formulation, utterances in the sociolinguistic world operate in a manner similar to the voices of musical compositions: one musical voice can respond to (and be positioned in relation to) another by repeating it, repeating it in a different harmonic mode, altering it melodically, inverting aspects of it, embedding it in another musical form, or diverging from it altogether. (See Nakassis 2012 for a semiotic theorization of such citationality and performativity in branding and counterfeiting.) This is not an exhaustive list of compositional techniques, of course. The distinctive characteristics of denotational voicings are revealed by the metapragmatic (index-regimenting) function of the calibration of deictics (Silverstein 1993, 2000) between the narrated event and the event of narration. The collapse of deictics comes across as one voice "breaking through" into the discursive space of another, bringing with it its generalized attributes and social-indexical relations (Harkness 2011). And, as Silverstein (1988) has argued, there is an irony in Bakhtin's notion of voice (and, by extension, in the trope of voice taken as a metaphor or metonym of power and agency), because it is in the very "production of voicelessness"—that which is ideologically presupposed to stand outside of narration and prior to discursive interaction (such as a linguistic code in the Saussurean tradition of semiology)—"where authoritativeness seeks perforce to ground itself in a pre-semiotic authority" (10).

42. See Silverstein 2003 on the concept of indexical orders.

43. Not personal attributes but shared assumptions about generalized attributes (Keane 2000: 272).

44. See Agha 2005 on *role alignment;* and Goffman 1979 on *footing.*

45. See Hill 1995; and Keane 2011 on the morality of voicing.

46. Bakhtin 1981: 293; 1986: 92–93. An illustrative example of this phenomenon that is highly relevant to the present analysis is Miyako Inoue's account of the emergence of "schoolgirl speech" in Meiji Japan, which views voicing as a function of reported speech in relation to a particular typology of voices in historical and cultural context (2006: 37–74). Inoue's powerful analysis highlights reported speech as the structured distancing of voices through the

frame of "overhearing." Inoue showed how both the listener—as a type of intellectual male—and the listened-to—as a type of schoolgirl—were positioned as social figures, as interested perspectives embodied in a type, through this structure of narration and voice delineation. Through this structure of reported speech, types were ascribed characterological attributes that were understood to be exhibited in the expressive forms they produced. In Inoue's account, the voice, once identified *as voice* and not simply as "inarticulate noise, undifferentiated from other elements in the sonic landscape," became a voice of something, of someone, of some type, of some form, involved in the production of some kind of utterance—*as language* (2006: 38). The voice-as-heard became indexical of something. It pointed to some social entity. For this reason, the voice qua phonosonic nexus was metonymically linked to a perspective of some sort, and, through rhematization (i.e., downshifting from indexicality to iconicity), the utterances produced at the phonosonic nexus were metaphorically linked to the qualities that were understood to belong to that perspective. So it is through this kind of immanent structuring of sociolinguistic space—presuppositions about voices and their linked perspectives that figure in a higher-order arrangement of social values and cultural conceptualizations—that this "low, vulgar schoolgirl voice," marked by verb-ending forms such as *teyo, dawa,* or *noyo,* as well as prosodic features that were described as "fast," "contracting," "bouncing with a rising intonation," and "sugary and shallow," could later on become the ideal voice type for the "feminine, middle-class woman"(2006: 37). All of this took place through the positioning of a listening narrator in relation to quoted voices.

47. This points to an interesting tension between the appropriation of voice in the phonosonic sense and the appropriation of voice in the more tropic sense. Compare, for example: Frith 1998 on the phonosonic voice as an expression of the individualized body and, in some cases, as inalienable legal property that can be "stolen"; Fox 2004 on country singing and the cultivated skill of embodying other identifiable voices from the phonosonic scale to the more tropic scale of social voicing; Keane 1991: 312 on the "delegation" of voice in the more tropic sense of the term as "crucial to how local action comes to be identified with larger structures and orders, ratifying the social and value-laden character of the agency in question" in marriage negotiation in Anakalang (see also Keane 1997); and Kunreuther 2006, 2009, 2010 on voice in both the phonosonic and tropic senses as they relate to cultural notions of intimacy, subjectivity, and directness.

48. See Boas 1889 on apperception.

49. Sapir 1925: 40.

50. Bakhtin 1981: 281, insertions mine.

51. For ethnographic examples of the intersection of aesthetics and ethics, see Hirschkind 2009 on listening and "ethical attunement" among Muslims in Cairo; and Engelhardt 2009 on "right singing" in Estonian Orthodox Christianity.

52. Bakhtin 1986: 84.

CHAPTER I

1. Readers will recognize the sound change I describe as one loaded with linguistic, musical, and broader semiotic ideology. For studies of the way ideology

frames and influences semiotic variation and change by shaping cultural reflections on and ideas about the relationship between structures and practices of communication, interaction, and signification, see Blommaert 1999; P. Eckert 2008; Gal and Irvine 1995; Joseph and Taylor 1990; Keane 2007; Kroskrity 2000; Silverstein 1979, 1985; Schieffelin et al. 1998; and Woolard and Schieffelin 1994.

2. Conversations with taxi drivers no doubt have an important role in ethnography. Heather Willoughby's (2002) study of *p'ansori* also begins with a story about a ride in a Seoul taxi. She describes the cab driver giving a "rather typical commentary on Korean music and its relation to history" that emphasizes the fact that Koreans had to "endure many hardships" and that their music is therefore "filled with *han*" (2). See also Eleana Kim 2010: 187–89 on male taxi drivers as "retain[ing] curious power as representatives of Korean (patriarchal) ethnonationalism and gatekeepers to cultural authenticity."

3. See Grinker 1998: 73–98; and Willoughby 2002: 85–96 for literature reviews on the concept of *han*.

4. Ha (2001: 388) estimates that, during the rapid urbanization of the 1960s and 1970s, between 20 and 30 percent of the South Korean population lived in slums and squatter settlements.

5. *Chŏng* has been described as the basis of "we-ness" basic to Korean social group formation (Choi and Choi 1991), a "no-trade" zone of sharing (S.-W. Lee 1991), and simply an interpersonal bond of familiarity and affection that grows between two or more individuals (J.-H. Kim 1981, 1992). See Jager 2003: 20–40 for a brief intellectual history of the term.

6. See Pilzer 2012 for a study of the voices of *han* in the songs of Korean survivors of Japanese militarized sexual slavery during the Asia-Pacific war.

7. See Kendall 2009 on nostalgia in South Korea. See also Fox 2004, where "real country" is a pervasive expression of nostalgia in Lockhart, Texas, for sustainable rural existence, employment, and stable domestic life—the "moral world as it could be, which in the local, working-class idiom means a world in the image of life *as it was*" (42).

8. The term *minyo* actually is a Japanese calque of the German term *Volkslied,* which was introduced into Korean by the Japanese novelist Mori Ogai (1862–1922); in 1913 the Japanese colonial government in Korea began research on Korean *minyo* to better "understand" the Korean people (Howard 1999).

9. The Korea International Broadcasting Foundation even named its English-language TV channel after the songs.

10. The difficulty of this passage will be familiar to readers who have seen Im Kwŏn-t'aek's 1993 film *Sŏp'yŏnje.*

11. See Hill 1995 for an analysis of dysfluencies of voicing in narrative, and also Keane's (2011) reading of Hill, emphasizing the productivity of a "clash" of voices.

12. The title of Kim Yŏng-mi's (2010) memoir is telling: *P'ŭrimadonna Kim Yŏng-mi ch'ŏrŏm: Chejadŭl i kajang tamkko sip'ŏ hanŭn yesulga* (Just like prima donna Kim Yŏng-mi: The artist whom disciples most want to resemble).

13. For an ethnographic study of place making in Korea, see Oppenheim 2008 on Kyŏngju as Korea's "preeminent culture city." See also Basso 1996; Feld 1996; and Munn 2013 for other approaches to the semiotics of "sensing" or "making" place.

14. Pyotr Il'yich Tchaikovsky, op. 6, no. 6.

15. The concert took place at the Yongsan Art Hall in the basement of the CCMM Building (Center of Communications and Mass Media). The CCMM Building is also the headquarters of *Kungmin ilbo* (the Kukmin Daily), a Christian newspaper founded by David Yonggi Cho, founder and former head pastor of the Yoido Full Gospel Church, and run by his son. The church's headquarters are located just a few blocks away.

16. See Fox 2004: 152ff. on "feeling" and "relating" in country music performance.

17. In some respects, the encore resembled the final hymn of a Wednesday evening prayer service, during which Protestant congregations around Seoul stand together to sing Malotte's "The Lord's Prayer" in unison.

18. "*Chigŭm chŏ nŭn sŏngakka rosŏ kajang wansŏng toen sichŏm e issŭmnida. Ŭmak ŭl hal ttae ŭi yŏyuroum kwa kamjŏng ŭl chayujajae ro p'yohyŏn hal su innŭn kŭkch'i e irŭn kŏt katsŭmnida.*"

CHAPTER 2

1. Unlike at the English services at other large churches that minister to expats and ethnically Korean foreigners residing in Seoul, the audience at Somang's English service is formed almost entirely by Korean members of the church who wish to practice English. Despite the English-language sermon and repertoire, the choir rehearsals are conducted entirely in Korean, and only a few of the choir members are comfortable speaking in English.

2. See Chong 2008; and T. S. Lee 2010 on church growth in Korea.

3. See Osmer 2005.

4. Such as in S. Lee 2008.

5. C.-ŭ. Yi 2007.

6. According to Fackler (2009), Apkujŏng is home to more than half of South Korea's 627 registered cosmetic surgery clinics. See also Curley 2007.

7. See Harkness 2011 for an analysis of a phonosonic difference in religious language between Somang Church and the Yoido Full Gospel Church. Cf. Titon 1988: 195–96 on the qualia of religious speech in an Appalachian Baptist church.

8. See Baker 2006, 2008; Grayson 2006; and Ledyard 2006.

9. See H. Choi 2009; and Chong 2008.

10. The title of the sermon is based on Isaiah 55:1–5.

11. See Kendall 2009: 1–33 on the treatment of shamanism as superstition *(misin)*. See Keane 2007; and Robbins 2004 on missionaries and narratives of conversion.

12. The title of the sermon is based on Matthew 5:10–12.

13. See Beidelman 1982: 16; and Keane 2007: 133.

14. See Clark 1986: 10; and T.S. Lee 2010: 38–39. See Wells 2006 on nationalism and the newly converted in colonial Korea.

15. Bruce Cumings (2005: 155) describes one event in which Japanese colonial police "locked protesters inside a church and burned it to the ground." According to Japanese officials, 535 were killed and over 12,000 were arrested;

according to Korean nationalist sources, 7,500 were killed and 45,000 were arrested (Cumings 2005: 155).

16. The Japanese colonial term for Korea was *Chōsen,* after Chosŏn, the name used for the Yi dynasty, 1392–1910.

17. For "ancestor," or "predecessor," Kim uses both *chosang* and *sŏnjo.* Both are built from the Sino-Korean character term *cho,* meaning "ancestor." *Sŏnjo* combines *cho* with the *sŏn,* meaning "preceding" or "prior to." *Chosang* combines *cho* with the *sang,* meaning "above" or "supreme."

18. Scholars studying the sociocultural forms and practices of Korea have noted and described, repeatedly, the rich and pervasive system of ancestor worship *(chosang sungbae)* cultivated during the neo-Confucian government of the Chosŏn dynasty (Deuchler 1992; Janelli and Janelli 1982; Kendall 1985). Rituals of ancestor worship include *chesa,* a memorial service held on the day of the ancestor's death; *ch'arye,* performed in the eldest son's house for recent ancestors during the Harvest Moon Festival (Ch'usŏk) and Lunar New Year's Day (Sŏllal); *sŏngmyo,* memorial services performed in front of ancestors' tombs; and *myosa,* memorials performed at tombs in memory of older ancestors. Christian institutions in Korea have systematically suppressed practices of ancestor worship, labeling them "idolatrous," in favor of rituals that address the Christian God and celebrate Jesus Christ (Baker 2006; Ledyard 2006). While some churches still permit members of the congregation to perform ancestor worship, in general it has been replaced by Christianized forms of ancestor "recognition" or "memorialization," such as the *ch'udo yebae,* which is addressed to God (not directly to the ancestors' spirits) and is normally performed only for one's immediate ancestors (Grayson 2009; O. Moon 1998).

19. Martina Deuchler 1992: 133. Chu Hsi (Zhu Xi in Pinyin), who lived from 1130 to 1200, was a leading neo-Confucian scholar in China during the Song dynasty (960–1279). See Porkert's (1974) discussion of *ki* as "energetic configuration" and "configuration of energy." See also Farquhar 1994; and Scheid 2002. See Kim and Park 2010 on the increase of male adoption for family succession during the Chosŏn dynasty.

20. In this sense, these Christians, like others, learn, as Webb Keane (2007: 115) put it, "to place themselves in a history that includes ancient Israel, as well as, in many cases, the national homeland of those who missionized them."

21. See Grayson 2001 for an account of the Tan'gun myth and Korean Christianity. See also Schmid 2002: 171–98; and G.-W. Shin 2006 on ethnic nationalism in Korea.

22. For Bakhtin (1981: 84–258), the chronotope (literally, "time-space"), referred to "the intrinsic connectedness of the temporal and spatial relationships in literature" (84), providing the "organizing centers for the fundamental narrative events of the novel" (250). In anthropology (Basso 1984; Gal 2006; Silverstein 1996, 2000, 2005; Stasch 2011), the chronotope has come to refer to a cultural model of time, space, and person, immanent in discursive interaction and in terms of which the discursive production of, and stance taken in relation to, semiotic material becomes pragmatically contextualizable and interpretable. This time-space envelope organizes the temporal and spatial deictic anchors in

terms of which actions are narrativized and thus placed in some meaningful relation one to another. In the implicit narratives that structure the sequencing and relationship of events and people in discourse, notions of time and space are connected in specific ways, such that events and the actions of persons deictically index (point to) other events and persons and the very event of narration itself.

23. See Harkness 2010 on denominationally different chronotopes of the movement of "the Word" and the Holy Spirit in Korea.

24. According to the International Institute for Democracy and Electoral Assistance (www.idea.int), voter turnout in South Korea was 80.65 percent in 1997, 70.83 percent in 2002, and 63.01 percent in 2007.

25. BBC 2007.

26. This term invokes West Germany's "economic miracle" (Wirtschaftswunder) following the Second World War.

27. Lee's notion of "pragmatic" is basically a synonym for "practical" or "useful." It does not have the technical meaning of semiotic pragmatics, which pertains to the phenomenon of signs in context or, more generally, of indexicality. His notion of "ideology" is the pejorative sense of the term, that is, a sort of explicit philosophical, and often political, fundamentalism held stubbornly in spite of empirically available facts, rather than the more general analytical use of the term in semiotic and linguistic anthropology as an important variable in sociocultural continuity and change.

28. "Tŏrŏnŭn mŏmch'it kŏrigo chwajŏl hagido."

29. "Purhamni hagŏna sidae e matchi anŭmyŏn iksukhan kŏttŭl kwa kwagamhi heŏjyŏya hamnida."

30. "In'gan kwa chayŏn, mulchil kwa chŏngsin, kaein kwa kongdongch'e ka kŏn'gang hago arŭmdapke ŏurŏjinŭn sam ŭl kuhyŏn hanŭn sidae chŏngsin imnida."

31. For other accounts of modernist narratives of rupture, see Bauman and Briggs 2003; Chakrabarty 2000; Keane 2007; and Latour (1991) 1993. On the problem of specifically Christian narratives of individual conversion and social transformation, see Cannell 2006; and Robbins 2007.

32. Quoted in C. Eckert 2000: 133. See also Wells 1990 on the role of Christianity in Yi Kwang-su's writings. See Schmid 2002: 121–129 on negative images of the yangban from the late nineteenth century to the early twentieth century.

33. Quoted in C. Eckert 2000: 133. In 1972, Park Chung-hee implemented the oppressive Yusin system, which effectively made Park dictator for life (until his assassination in 1979). Bruce Cumings (2005: 358) notes that "Yusin" is based on the same Chinese characters as Meiji Japan's "Ishin" restoration, which was initiated approximately one century earlier. According to Carter Eckert (2000: 141), "Meiji Japan's success in building 'rich country, strong army' served as an important model for Park throughout his life." Park's "New Village movement" (Saemaŭl undong) in the 1970s was designed to replace "traditional" living conditions with "modern" ones in rural areas.

34. Although Roh Tae-woo (No T'ae-u, in office 1988–93), who preceded Kim Young-sam, was elected, he was a former army general who was named by Chun Doo-hwan (Chŏn Tu-hwan, in office 1980–88), also an army general, as Chun's successor (see Cumings 2005: 386–92).

35. Quoted in T. S. Lee 2006: 338. The Blue House, or Ch'ŏngwadae, is the office headquarters and official residence of the president of the Republic of Korea. Only a few years after Kim Young-sam was elected, his son, Kim Hyun-chul (Kim Hyŏn-ch'ŏl) was jailed for the "Hanbo incident." The Hanbo Group was South Korea's fourteenth-largest conglomerate before it disintegrated in January 1997. Kim Hyun-chul was arrested later that year for bribing public officials and abusing power in government.

36. "*Chunim kke nara wa taet'ongnyŏng ŭl wihaesŏ kido hamyŏnsŏ saeroun sidae rŭl yŏrŏ kanŭn Hananim ŭi saramdŭl i toege haopsosŏ.*"

37. Han'gyŏre 2004.

38. C. Eckert 2000: 119.

39. See Gal 2006: 174 on metamessages as "(clues) that indicate the imagined recipients, the imagined route of circulation of the message, while simultaneously hiding exactly this information"; see also Gal and Woolard 2001 on the semiotic constitution of publics.

40. "*Yaksok e taehan somang ŭl sangjing hanŭn mujigae ŭi ch'ukso toen p'yohyŏn imyŏ, sŏngbu, sŏngja, sŏngnyŏng ŭi samwi ilch'e rŭl ŭimi handa*" (www.somang.net/html/info_info8.asp, accessed June 3, 2013).

41. Both *somang* and *hŭimang* can be translated as "hope," "wish," or "desire."

42. See BBC 2008; and CNN 2003.

43. There were many errors in the reporting, which were pointed out by the conservative press. The cow was in fact not infected with BSE. The program also translated a quote from the mother of a deceased woman as saying that her daughter might have died from variant Creutzfeldt-Jakob disease (vCJD), the disease that results when BSE infects humans. Actually, the mother said that she had been told that there was a possibility of Creutzfeldt-Jakob Disease [CJD], which is classed as a "Prion disease" with vCJD but is epidemiologically unrelated. It was later reported that the woman died of Wernicke's encephalopathy, which is related to vitamin B1 deficiency (Park and Yoo 2009). And finally, *PD Such'ŏp* claimed that Koreans are more susceptible than other ethnic groups to BSE. It was later reported that Kim Yong-sŏn, the Hallym University professor whose paper the program cited, felt that *PD Such'ŏp* had distorted and exaggerated his thesis (Chosŏn Ilbo 2008).

44. See Choongang Ilbo 2008 on the issue of the translation.

45. Reuters 2008.

46. See N. Lee 2007 for a detailed study of the history of the conceptualization and institutionalization of *minjung*. See also Wells 1995.

47. Tonghak, glossed literally as "Eastern Learning," arose in the 1860s as a doctrine that combined Confucianism, Buddhism, Taoism, and shamanism. Peasants widely adopted it, inspired by its exaltation of the masses and its anti-Japanese, anti-Western slogans. For historical accounts, see Cumings 2005; C. Eckert et al 1990. For the mobilization of the memory of the uprising in twentieth-century Korean progressive politics, see Abelmann 1996; and N. Lee 2007.

48. The words for "people," "nation," and "democracy" all are built on the Sino-Korean term *min,* meaning "people." See Em 2005 for an intellectual

history of the term *minjok*. In the 1970s, Christian theologians developed a kind of Korean liberation theology called *minjung* theology *(minjung sinhak)*, which they characterized as "a development of the 'political hermeneutics' of the Gospel in terms of the Korean reality" (Suh 1983: 17). The hermeneutics of *Minjung* theology viewed the Old Testament Exodus account as a paradigmatic event (W. Kim 2006). Unlike an ancestral view of a Christian heritage based on the transmission of the gospels from one person to another, *minjung* theology treated the pre-Christian masses as spiritually related to Jesus Christ through their experience of *han*. This particular branch of theology eventually faded from mainstream Korean Christianity.

49. *"Kwangupyŏng pandae ch'otpul siwi—pulpŏp in'ga chinjŏnghan minjujuŭi in'ga"* (www.alltogether.or.kr/new/9_extra/080503.jsp, accessed July 1, 2009).

50. N. Lee 2007: 5.

51. According to the International Monetary Fund, Korea's 2008 GDP was 929,124 in millions of U.S. dollars.

52. For discussions of evenemential (i.e., "event-based") approaches to cultural and historical analysis and the theorization of social change, see Sahlins 2004; and also Handman 2010.

53. *"Sŭsŭro rŭl charang sŭrŏwŏ hanŭn hamsŏng i iŏjigo."*

54. *"Yŏgi chŏgisŏ oech'im i kyesok toeŏtta."*

55. See Kang 2009 for an in-depth study of a decade of candlelight vigils in South Korea.

56. *"Kŏri esŏ kkutkkusi yŏksa rŭl kŏrŏ wassŭmŭl kŭttae mada tangsindŭl ŭn pulpŏp iramyŏ uri rŭl wihyŏp haessŭmŭl hajiman yŏksa nŭn hangsang uri rŭl chŏngŭi ro kirok hae wassŭmŭl uri nŭn kiŏk handa."*

57. See Abelmann 1996: 14 for a discussion of dates as punctuating narratives of Korean political history.

58. Cumings 2005: 120.

59. Cumings 2002: 27.

60. Park Geun-hye narrowly lost to Lee Myung-bak for the Grand National Party nomination in 2008 but then won the national election in 2012 and was inaugurated in 2013 as the first woman president of South Korea. Not only is Park Geun-hye the daughter of the former military dictator; she also acted as the country's First Lady from 1974, when her mother was assassinated by a North Korean sympathizer, until 1979, when her father was assassinated by his own chief of intelligence.

61. The sermon is based on Luke 7:29–35. I have translated the Korean *t'ansik* as "sigh." This can also be translated as "groan" or even "lament."

62. *"Yesunim ŭn yŏngchŏk igo chŏngsinjŏk in pun iŏssŭmnida."*

63. *"Ch'odŭng haksaeng i taehak kyosu ŭi kangŭi rŭl shwipke ihae haji mothanŭn kŏt ŭn tangyŏn hamnida."*

64. One could characterize Kim's communicative style and carriage as reproducing a kind of contemporary Christian version of the *yangban*. When this is scaled to the institution of the church, upper-class Presbyterian Christianity becomes a kind of path to the "yangbanhood of all believers," in the way that the Pentecostal Yoido Full Gospel Church has been accused of perpetuating the

"shamanhood of all believers" (cf. the doctrine of the priesthood of all believers, attributed to Martin Luther). For more on the qualitative and ideological attributes of the yangban and its place in recent Korean political culture, see Kim K.-O. 1988, 1996, 1998.

65. For the performance of Jesus's utterances in excerpt 2.9, Kim drew on passages from the Gospels of Luke, Matthew, and Mark. Mention of the relation between eyes and sight and between ears and hearing can be found in Proverbs 20:12, Jeremiah 5:21, Ezekiel 12:2, and Mark 8:18.

66. See Judith Irvine's (1990) analysis of prosodic differentiation in the performance of personhood in her accounts of "noble" and "griot" speech registers in Wolof, which, through the various features of bifurcated enregisterment, communicate different affective states, different participant roles, and different persona types. In Irvine's examples, speech qualities—known by the qualia of vocalization—play a key role in identifying and differentiating contrastive affective registers.

67. See Silverstein 2003 on orders of indexicality.

68. See T.S. Lee 2006: 342–45 on corruption in the Korean Protestant church.

69. See Feld 1996 on the concept of acoustemology.

70. See Hirschkind 2006; and Thompson 2004 on ideologically loaded soundscapes.

71. The notion of Protestant spiritual enlightenment that forms the basis of Kim's sermon is linked directly to the way sŏngak singers in Korea see the human voice a God-given tool that must be revealed and cultivated "naturally," that is, in some cases, "scientifically" through the development of efficient, stable, advanced phonosonic practices. See van der Veer 2001: 25 on nineteenth-century Christian missionary "attempts at conversion through education that affirms a higher morality and a stronger conformity with natural science than the practices and beliefs of the unconverted." See also van der Veer 1996.

72. Howard 1990: 146.

73. The irony in all of this is that Lee Myung-bak has a voice that my informants have described as "scratchy," "hoarse," "husky," "like gravel," and "terrible." The communications professor Ch'oe Jin, of Korea University, in a presentation titled "Speech and Communication of National Leaders," even argued that the "high tone and husky voice of the president gives a friendly feeling and passion" (*Yi Taet'ongnyŏng ŭi hait'on kwa hŏsŭk'ihan moksori nŭn ch'in'gŭn'gam kwa yŏlchŏng ŭl nŭkkige [handa]*) (quoted in Koh 2009). Such descriptions seem to ascribe to his voice the sound of *han* and *chŏng*, which I mentioned in the introduction.

CHAPTER 3

1. See J.S.-Y. Park 2009: 52 on linguistic nationalism and English-language learning in South Korea.

2. See T.S. Lee 2006: 332.

3. See Whorf 1956: 113–17, 144–45 on nomic assertions as statements of general truth.

4. See Hwang 2009; Min 2001; and Yi 1985. Citing Yi 1985: 80, Hwang (2009: 53) notes, "Most musicians who specialized in Western art music and lived through that early period would readily acknowledge that their musical activities in Protestant churches led them to become musicians."

5. See S. Lee 1988. Joo (1997) explains that the first Korean hymnal—and the first printed score of Western music in Korea—was compiled by the Presbyterian missionary Horace G. Underwood as an 1894 edition titled *Ch'anyangga* (Hymns of Praise) containing 117 hymns; of these hymns, 9 were written by Koreans, and the rest were translations from English; it is estimated that only 3 percent of hymns currently in use were penned or composed by Koreans (Joo 1997).

6. See King 2004; and Silva 2008 on Han'gŭl, Bible translation, and Christian missionaries.

7. See Y.-S. Chang 1982; and Yun 2008.

8. See H. Choi 2009.

9. See Chong 2006, 2008; and Clark 2006. This should be contrasted with studies of a more indigenous form of emancipation for women through religion: shamanism (see, e.g., Harvey 1980; Kendall 1977, 1985; J. Lee 2009).

10. Presbyterian Church 2001. The Korean title of this bilingual volume is *Ch'ansongga yebae: Miguk Changnogyo Han-Yŏng Ch'ansongga.*

11. Presbyterian Church 2001: vi. The anonymous editors also included a Korean version of this statement, which differs slightly in emphasis: "*Hanin kyohoe kyoindŭl ŭn ch'ansong purŭgi rŭl choa handa. Kidokkyo ka Han'guk e chŏnp'a toen irae, ch'ansong ŭn kyohoe saenghwal esŏ taedanhi chungyohan hwallyŏkso ka toeŏ watta. Ch'ansong ŭn Hananim ŭi malssŭm ŭl saramdŭl ŭi maŭm e simŏ chunŭn maegaech'e yŏkhal ŭl haejuŏssŭl ppunman anira 1910-yŏn e Sin-Kuyak Han'gŭl sŏnggyŏng chŏnch'e ka pŏnyŏk toel ttae kkaji saramdŭl ege Kidokkyo ŭi karŭch'im ŭl chŏnp'a hanŭn yŏkhal ŭl hagido haetta*" (iv).

12. Quoted in H.-g. Kim 1997: 57. My informants sometimes attributed this report to the histories of the Chinese scholar Qian Sima (Ch'ŏn Sima) of the second and first century B.C.E., who wrote about the inhabitants of Chaoxian (Korea).

13. See Howard 1990; Y.-k. Kim 1967; Rutt and Pratt 1999; Sin 2003; and Song 2001.

14. Hulbert 1909: 318, 319.

15. Hulbert 1909: 319–20. Like the bow-wow, ding-dong, and pooh-pooh theories, the yo-heave-ho theory seeks to explain the origins of language. *Yo-heave-ho* refers to the emergence of language out of grunts emitted during physical toil, *bow-wow* refers to the onomatopoetic imitation of "natural" sounds in the environment, *ding-dong* refers to phonetic gestures that purportedly occur "naturally" when humans come into contact with certain entities and features of their environment, and *pooh-pooh* refers to "natural" emotive expressions.

16. Gifford 1898: 200.

17. Baker 2006: 292.

18. I am indebted to Kiho Kim for arranging this trip and this meeting.

19. Ling 1952.

20. Ling 1952: 25.

21. For example, singing in the *noraebang* is a widespread and often obligatory form of leisure and professional socialization.

22. For Koreans described as "a highly spiritual people," see Baker 2008: 1; for their description as "natural evangelists," see Moffett quoted in Lampman 2007.

23. Clark 2003.

24. T. Lee 2010: 85; Baker 2006: 283–84. Baker (2006: 303), however, reports that as of 2006, the "defection rate" of Protestants had been above 50 percent since 1984 and that there currently are more *former* Protestants than Protestants in South Korea. Citing a 1997 Gallup survey, Baker calculated the number of persons who claim to be Protestant versus the number of persons who claim to have been Protestant at some point in the past but are no longer. The "defection" here seems to be based on a sort of scripted "Gallup Credo," an individual self-proclamation of faith by denomination.

25. See Baker 2006; and W. Kim 2006. Harvie Conn, a missionary to Korea during the 1960s, attributes Korean church growth to the "Nevius" system of missionization, which emphasized "the Bible as the basis of all Christian work and [an] elaborate system of Bible classes by which that book could be studied and applied to the believer's heart" (Conn 1966: 29). Timothy Lee has argued that an "evangelical ethos suffused the Korean Protestant church" to such an extent that it is often taken as axiomatic that Korean Christianity is evangelical (T. S. Lee 2006: 332). He also argues that the intensive and extensive evangelistic campaigns from 1953 to 1988 played a "decisive role in evangelicalism's outpacing other Korean religions in this period" (T. S. Lee 2010: 90). In fact, Korea's history of self-evangelization contributes to an important narrative that spreads the idea that Koreans are predisposed to Christianity. This view is sometimes anchored by the fact that Christianity was originally brought to Korea by Koreans themselves (see chapter 2), when a Korean Confucian scholar who received a Catholic baptism in Beijing returned to Korea in 1784 to evangelize (Grayson 2006). And Kim Kwang-Ok (1990, 1993, 1998), in his anthropological analyses of religion in Korea, has argued that Christian churches serve as a site for neotribalism and displays of secular achievement.

26. Sociologist Song Chae-ryong pointed out that although the number of missionaries from a country has generally been closely correlated with a country's economic power, the number from South Korea "far exceeds" the country's economic standing (quoted in Choe 2007). The emphasis on evangelism is so great that, despite continued church growth, the size of congregations cannot match the output of new ministers. Timothy Lee (2006: 341) explains that in 1995 there were more than 310 theological institutions in Korea, of which only 38 were accredited by the Ministry of Education. These seminaries produced about eight thousand graduates a year during the 1990s, but only about one thousand graduated from well-established institutions. The remaining seven thousand graduates were "the products of accredited but poorly equipped seminaries or, worse, of unaccredited institutions . . . ill equipped to minister to a highly educated society. . . . Many seminarians, as a result, opted for overseas work as missionaries" (341).

27. At places like Somang Church and elsewhere, singers trained in *sŏngak* are absolutely central to the church liturgy as well as to missionary activity abroad. In Osmer's (2005: 87) study of the "teaching ministry of congregations," he characterizes Somang Presbyterian Church as a "congregation living under the word." The services, he notes, are designed to foster an "atmosphere of reverent expectation" that "God's Word will enter this space through the preaching and praying of the worship leader, who serves as a conduit of God's address to the congregation" (101). Osmer bases his claim in part on interviews with members of the choirs and the congregation. The choirs, he writes, are "outstanding, and most congregations would be exceptionally proud if they had even one choir as good as any of Somang's five" (102). Yet the choir members claimed humbly to "work to make wonderful music" only to "prepare the way for the proclamation of the word" (102).

28. Normally, singers are required to be members of the church for one year before being allowed to audition for a choir. A successful audition is then followed by a probationary period of a few weeks, during which the new choir member learns about the group and its music. This generally does not apply to soloists, who are usually brought in with the auspices of a conductor or on the recommendation of a professor. Nonetheless, once accepted, they are expected to behave as if they were longstanding members of the church. A singer should never appear as if to be simply working for pay. Having explicitly announced my intention to conduct research on the voice in South Korean Christianity for a restricted amount of time, I was allowed to audition without the one-year membership.

29. Three of the paid soloists in the Somang choir that I joined during my fieldwork were members of the SNU Praise Missionary Chorus.

30. Trotta 1998.

31. "Hananim ŭi sarang ŭl chŏnhanŭn mesinjŏ ka toeŏ."

32. In the past, families gathered for Sŏllal and Ch'usŏk, when the men would conduct ancestor-worship rites. For Korean Christians today, these holidays are still an event for family gathering, but instead of performing the *ch'arye* ritual to remember and worship one's ancestors, they perform the *ch'udo yebae,* usually according to a worship guide distributed by their church. At the heart of the *ch'udo yebae* is the singing of hymns. And as with the *ch'udo yebae,* traditional or pre-Christian elements of Korean culture are not completely erased from contemporary Christian church services. Protestant churches in Korea generally have been careful to distance their own worship practices from pre-Christian forms of worship, whether of the Buddhist, Confucian, or Shamanic sort. In order to guide church members in the proper Christian celebration of pre-Christian holidays, Somang Church distributes guides for celebrating these holidays in an appropriately Christian manner. These guides outline the proper procedures for Ch'usŏk, Sŏllal, and a family's first visit to an ancestors' grave *(ch'ŏt sŏngmyo),* deemphasizing the relationship between the living and the deceased, in favor of informal Christian worship, during which participants read scripture, sing hymns, and pray. God is addressed as "Father" *(Abŏji),* but ancestors are never addressed directly. See Grayson 2009 for more on the development of the *ch'udo yebae.* See Janelli and Janelli 1982 for a detailed study of ancestor worship in Korea.

33. There are many instances in which markedly traditional forms are used in Christian worship practice—attire, musical instruments, occasionally even contemporary musical compositions harmonically reminiscent of more traditional Korean compositions (e.g., using the pentatonic scale).

34. According to the WHO, South Korea's suicide rate in 2009 was nearly forty persons per hundred thousand. This is double the rate in 2000 and triple the rate in 1985. This gives South Korea one of the highest suicide rates (if not the highest) among the OECD countries. (www.who.int/mental_health/prevention/suicide/country_reports/en/index.html, accessed October 16, 2011).

35. "*Hananim ŭi ch'angjo segye e tongch'am hamyŏ in'gan kwan'gye ŭi kippŭm ŭl nurisipsio.*"

36. My informants usually described *t'ŭrot'ŭ* as a "Korean traditional pop song" even though it is clearly a twentieth-century invention. The name comes from the English loan word *trot*, a popular style of the 1960s and afterward that is related to Japanese *enka*. See Son 2004 on the politics of *t'ŭrot'ŭ* singing in Korea. See Yano 2002 (especially 91–123) on vocal style and emotionality in *enka*.

37. See Silverstein 2003: 212 on registers as "alternate ways of 'saying "the same" thing' considered 'appropriate to' particular contexts of usage."

38. The character of Eliza Doolittle, as performed by Audrey Hepburn in the film *My Fair Lady* (1964), provides an example of this contrast when singing the song "Just You Wait, Henry Higgins." As Miss Doolittle begins the song, her Cockney accent is matched by a strong, punctuated rhythm and a strident chest voice. As she dreams of how she will prove her skills to Henry Higgins, this style gives way to much more legato musical phrasing and a mixed head-chest voice register, the more "heady" end of which makes it starkly differentiated from the earlier style. The differentiated use of registers in this song serves as an icon of her sociological transformation over time, which is most strikingly exhibited (and catalyzed) by her linguistic shift as guided by Professor Higgins.

39. See Shim 2004; C. E. Park 2003; and Um 2007 for more detailed descriptions and technical terms in *p'ansori*.

40. These days, specialists of *sŏngak* almost always have been raised in the church and have sung in a Western style all their lives. Few of the older *sŏngak* professionals were not born into Christian families, and nearly all of the singers I interviewed were introduced to *sŏngak* through the church. If they were not born into Christian families, most ended up converting and joining a church no later than young adulthood (cf. Chong 2008 on middle-aged conversion).

41. Byungwon Lee 1997: 53.

42. Shim 2004: 53.

43. As a phonosonic ideal, the *p'ansori* voice provides an orientation point for other forms of singing. For example, Byungwon Lee (1997: 57) writes, "The majority of pop singers in the *ppongtchak* [*t'ŭrot'ŭ*] style . . . tend to use a characteristically powerful chest voice similar to the *p'ansori*." Like *p'ansori*, it is known for "restriction and manipulation of airflow through the throat" (Hwang 2006) and "breaking throat sounds" (*kkŏngnŭn sori, kkŏngnŭn mok*) (Son 2006), both of which are associated locally with traditional forms of Korean vocalization and contrasted with European-style classical singing.

44. Laukkanen et al. 2006: 36.

45. Shim 2004: 53.

46. *Tŭgŭm* in the title refers to the arrival of *p'ansori* singers at the level of vocal mastery (see Willoughby 2002: 125–36). For the film, see Pak 2008.

47. This singer likened the voice to a stringed instrument that requires a certain kind of sustained contact. For many European-style classical singers, the voice is imagined as more of a horn, as a resonating chamber through which air passes. The initial site of sound production—the vocal cords—is not emphasized as a site of contact or manipulation in the same way.

48. Shim 2004: 54.

49. E.g., Pihl 1994: 104–5; and Willoughby 2002: 129.

50. Shim 2004: 53.

51. Noah 1949: 14–15.

52. Noah 1949: 16.

53. Hulbert 1909: 318. See Olwage 2004 on Victorian choral instruction and "civilizing missions" in colonial South Africa.

54. See Harkness 2011, 2013 for more detailed discussions of the semiotics of the *ajŏssi* and stereotypes of his behavior.

55. Cho 2002: 177.

56. On gender and militarization in Korea, see S. Moon 2005. On the contradictions of womanhood during Korea's postwar modernization, see Cho 2002.

57. See Poedjosoedarmo 1993 for a study of mouth shape and aperture in the comparison of "Javanese Pesindhen, or traditional female vocalists . . . and the voices of singers trained in the style of Western classical singing" (124). See also Bourdieu (1979) 1984 on *la gueule* and *la bouche*.

58. *"Ch'anyang | Nŏ nŭn Isŭrael chason ŭi on hoejung ege mal hayŏ irŭra nŏhŭi nŭn kŏrukhara i nŭn na Yŏhowa nŏhŭi Hananim i kŏrukhaminira."* Despite scholarly concerns over the fidelity of the translation of the New International Version since its first release in 1973, I have used the NIV for Bible passages in English throughout this book, since Presbyterian Evangelicals in Korea normally use the NIV when referring to an English-language Bible.

59. See Feld and Brenneis 2004; Erlmann 2004; Helmreich 2007; Hirschkind 2006; and Sterne 2003 on cultures of listening. See Monson 2008 on "perceptual agency."

60. See Chong 2008: 82ff. on prayer in Korean Christianity. Korean Christian congregations are notable for their emphasis on group prayer *(t'ongsŏng kido),* which is captured most potently in the regular dawn prayer meetings *(saebyŏk kido)* undertaken by many of the churches.

CHAPTER 4

1. *"Im wunderschönen Monat Mai, als alle Knospen sprangen, da ist in meinem Herzen die Liebe aufgegangen."*

2. Munn 1986. For further theorization of conventional qualisigns, see Harkness 2013.

3. For ideologies of cleanliness in relation to narratives of progress, see, e.g., Barnes 2006; Burke 1996; Corbin (1982) 1986; Elias (1939) 2004; and Rogaski 2004.

4. See, e.g., Comaroff and Comaroff 1997: 323–65.

5. On Korea's pollution prohibitions and rituals of purification, see, e.g., Ch'oe 1987; and Kendall 1985. On Korea's missionary and colonial "cleansing," see, e.g., H. Choi 2009; Henry 2005; S.K. Kim 2008, and Oak 2010.

6. On qualic transitivity, see Harkness 2013.

7. Some of these responses were sent by e-mail and written in nonstandard Korean.

8. They heard Rodrigo del Pozo, a haute-contre, singing "Ach, daß ich Wassers g'nug hätte," by Johann Christoph Bach (recorded in 2000), and Suzanne Ryden, a soprano, singing "L'amante segreto: Voglio morire," by Barbara Strozzi (recorded in 2000).

9. "Early music" usually refers to European music from around 1500 to around 1750.

10. In acts of semiotic rhematization, my informants generally treated rough or harsh vocal qualia, which *index* the strain and hardship of the past, as qualic *icons* of sorrow. This should be contrasted with the more direct "icons of crying," such as cry breaks and voiced inhalations, discussed in Feld 1982; Fox 2004; and Urban 1988.

11. Maria Callas, a soprano, singing "Nume tutelar," from *La vestale,* by Gaspare Spontini (recorded 1955), and Jussi Björling, a tenor, singing "Nessun dorma," from *Turandot,* by Giacomo Puccini (recorded 1960).

12. As I explain in chapter 3, European-style classical singing is known for blending the registers. Their unification is the functional opposite of the *p'ansori* singer, who makes a break between chest voice and falsetto. The Korean word *t'akhada* describes something that is muddy, impure, or turbid. When used to describe the voice, it can refer to a voice that sounds raspy, dull, or in some way old, tired, and worn-out. Many informants mentioned old men and alcoholics as examples of people with a voice that was *t'akhada*. Others compared it to the hissing sound of wind blowing or air escaping through a seal.

13. The notion of a "flattened" sound here is not the same as the "flat" sound mentioned earlier in the response. *Flattened* does not refer to being below the desired pitch, as in "flat" or "sharp" intonation *(natta/nopta),* but rather refers to the quality of the sound as "dead" or lacking resonance or "brightness," as opposed to a "sharpened," "pointed," potentially shrill sound.

14. Among singers, the Italian word *maschera,* meaning mask, refers to proprioceptively felt resonance in the upper-half of the face. It is associated with "ring" or "power" in the voice and the "placing" of the voice "forward."

15. Although my informants occasionally described popular voices—generally of younger singers—as clean, they usually qualified this by explaining that the singing was "raw" or "without technique" and conjectured that it would only be a matter of time before the cleanliness of the voice was lost to vocal damage.

16. Although we were speaking Korean, Chong-pi'l used the English loan word *hŏsŭk'i*. Recall the taxi driver mentioned in chapter 1, who also used the

loan word to describe the *p'ansori* voice and the traditional voices of Koreans more generally.

17. Harkness 2011.

18. Cf. Willoughby 2002: 120, 129 on the necessity of losing and then regaining one's voice in *p'ansori*.

19. He also added that students in Korea have to worry about what he called "unrelated things," such has serving their teachers and seniors, which distracts them from their vocal studies. See more about this in chapter 5.

20. Of course, I do not mean to naturalize these two poles. I only wish to show how they are constituted in the very socialization and cultural reflection on vocal arts and expression among these primarily Christian singers in Seoul. Powerful voices are still prized in many areas of Korean life, particularly in the militaristic cultivation of manhood. This kind of training was the focus of a 2009 *Chicago Tribune* article on the Blue Dragon Marine Corps Training Camp, which aimed to turn pampered, video-game playing Korean boys into tough, strong young men. The retired drill sergeant who runs the camp noted that he could hear the transformation in the boys' voices: "On the first day, I might hear 10 voices out of [a] group of 200. By the last, I can hear every last one of them. It's a thundering chorus" (Glionna 2009; I am indebted to Judith Farquhar for directing me to this article). Such an aesthetic of the (often national) masculine body is common to the "muscular Christianity" one encounters in various forms (see, e.g., Coleman 2007; and van der Veer 2001). See also Erlmann 1996: 224–42 on the aesthetics of power and "singing as loud as your voice can take it" in isicathamiya performance practice in South Africa; and Caton 1986: 302, and Caton 1990: 42 on vocal stamina, virility, and manliness in Yemen.

21. Noah 1949: 14.

22. Bird 1905: 266. In a footnote, Bird explains: "The finances of Korea are now practically under British management, Mr. J M'Leavy Brown, LL.D., of the Chinese Imperial Maritime Customs and Chief Commissioner of Customs for Korea, having undertaken in addition the post of Financial Advisory to the Treasury, and a Royal Edict having been issued that every order for a payment out of the national purse, down to the smallest, should be countersigned by him" (Bird 1905: 200n1).

23. Cumings 2003: 144.

24. "*Kwagŏ enŭn tansunhan saengnijŏk in yokku rŭl haegyŏl hanŭn changso yŏssŭna, ije nŭn hwajang, toksŏ, sasaek tŭng ŭl hal su innŭn hyusik konggan imyŏ saehwal konggan ŭro hwaryong toeŏya hamnida*" (www.toilet.or.kr/toilet /beauty/beauty_01.htm, accessed February 1, 2009).

25. Corporal 2007; Pae 2000.

26. Pickering 1994: 60.

27. Pickering 1994: 60.

28. M.-g. Kim 2009.

29. A *ttukpaegi*, earthen or stone pot, can be placed directly over a flame and is used for the preparation and serving of stews and rice dishes.

30. Bacon's (1605) 1873: 142; Wesley 1872: 320.

31. See Hirschkind 2006 on "ethical attunement" as the shaping of the sensorium toward ideal Islamic practice.

32. See chapter 7 for a more detailed discussion of *maŭm*. Although the term *maŭm* is used for Ephesians 1:18 in all Korean Bible translations that I have consulted, there are lexical differences among the English, Latin, and Greek versions. In the King James Version it is "The eyes of your *understanding* being enlightened; that ye may know what is the hope of his calling, and what the riches of the glory of his inheritance in the saints." In the New International Version it is "I pray also that the eyes of your *heart* may be enlightened in order that you may know the hope to which he has called you, the riches of his glorious inheritance in the saints." In the Latin Vulgate it is "illuminatos oculos *cordis* [heart] vestri, ut sciatis quæ sit spes vocationis eius, et quæ divitiæ gloriæ hereditatis eius in sanctis." In the Byzantine Majority, Alexandrian, and Hort and Westcott Greek the word is *kardia* (heart). But in the Stephens 1550 Textus Receptus and Scrivener 1894 Textus Receptus Greek the word is *dianoia* (knowledge).

33. *"Uri maŭm i ssŏgŭmyŏn sesang i ssŏgŏ poimnida. Kŭrŏna uri maŭm sok e Hananim ŭi yŏksa ka tŭrŏgamyŏn ssŏgŭn kŏt kat'ŭn sesang sok esŏdo kanŭngsŏng i poimnida."*

34. See Harkness 2013.

CHAPTER 5

1. See Scheid 2002: 168–77 for an overview of similar discipleship arrangements in the field of Chinese medicine. On the role of the church in the lives of Korean American university students in the United States, see Abelmann 2009.

2. For example, see Y.-S. Park 2007 for a celebratory view of the Korean church as spiritually egalitarian and socially equalizing (cf. H. Choi 2009; and Chong 2008).

3. See Robbins 2004: 164.

4. This song was written by Song Chŏng-mi.

5. The common trope of the church as family is based on passages in the New Testament, for example, 2 Corinthians 6:18, "I will be a Father to you, and you will be my sons and daughters, says the Lord Almighty."

6. S.-H. Park 1975: 5. On neo-Confucianism in the foundations of Korean kinship practice, see Deuchler 1992; and Janelli and Janelli 1982. See also Janelli and Yim 1993 on the competing tropes of "family" and "military" as cultural models of social behavior in Korean companies.

7. Timothy Lee (2010: 88) summarizes this change from census data: "Between 1960 and 1990, South Korea's rapid industrialization was accompanied by an equally rapid urbanization. Whereas in 1960 only 28 percent of the population was considered urban, 74.4 percent was considered so by 1990. The administrative regions considered as cities rose from 27 to 73. During this thirty-year period, South Korea's total population grew from 25 million to 43.4 million, a 74 percent increase. But the urban population in the same period more than quadrupled, rising from 7 million to 32.3 million. As would be expected, this urban population growth was most significantly influenced by migration from the country, which accounted for 46.23 percent of the total increase; the next most important factor was birth rate, which accounted for 41.4 percent of the increase."

8. Deuchler 1992: 9; Kap and Gamble 1975.

9. See S.-C. Kim 1998; K.-O. Kim 1998a; Kweon 1998; and K.-k. Lee 1975.

10. K.-k. Lee 1975: 280; see also Chong 2008 on submission, authority, and patriarchy in the church.

11. Quoted in Wells 1990: 53.

12. Wells 1990: 53–54. During the 1960s, Park Chung-hee condemned filial piety (*hyo*) and elevated loyalty (*ch'ung*) to the nation as a principle of Korean modernization. Park changed his position in the late 1970s, arguing that filial piety and loyalty to the nation were complementary principles (see Moon and Jun 2011: 124-5).

13. See Carr 2009; Mehan 1996; and Mertz 1996 on institutional identities.

14. See Deuchler 1992: 108-111. See Brandt 1971: 161-65 on "dyadic relations" in Korean village life.

15. Non-Korean Christians complained as well. For example, when referring to Korean churches, an American professor of church history whom I met in Seoul in 2006 said to me, "This is Confucianism, not Christianity!"

16. On the influence of neo-Confucianism in the Korean church, see Chong 2008: 29–30 and passim; and Chung 2001. On the idealized symmetry of relationships among age-neutral "brothers" and "sisters" in Korean Christian sociality, see Harkness, n.d.

17. See King 2006 for a list of kin terms of personal reference and address. See Wang 2005 for more on terms of personal address and reference in South Korean society.

18. See Clark 1986: 30–31 on congregationalism in Korean churches.

19. Although cremation was once shunned by upper-class Koreans because of its association with Buddhist funerary rites, it has become increasingly popular in Korea because of the lack of available land for burial (see H. S. Lee 1996; and C.-W. Park 2005: 290).

20. Janelli and Janelli 1982.

21. Y. Yu 2006.

22. See Scheid 2002: 168-177 for a discussion of the filial model of discipleship in Chinese medicine.

23. Kyoyuk T'onggye Sŏbisŭ 2009. This includes all students enrolled in voice programs, even those who are temporarily out of school (e.g., for mandatory military service). This number suggests that between three hundred and five hundred students graduated each year with a degree in vocal performance. This should be contrasted with the United States: in the 2006–7 academic year, only 251 students, or 1.8 percent, graduated in voice or opera out of a total of 14,220 students graduating with music-related majors (U.S. Department of Education 2007).

24. On education and study abroad in Korea, see Abelmann et al. 2012; and Lo et al. 2014.

25. www.yego.or.kr, accessed July 23, 2009.

26. See S.-B. Choi 1999 for a sociological study of gender, Western classical music, and class reproduction in South Korea.

27. At SNU, a public institution, the 2008 tuition for the undergraduate music major was between 4,354,000 *wŏn* per semester in the first year, down to 3,702,000

per semester in fourth year. At Yonsei, a private institution, the 2009 tuition for the undergraduate music major was 5,267,000 *wŏn* per semester, every year.

28. S.-B. Choi (1999: 1–2) mentions a scandal in which the parents of prospective female music students at SNU and Ewha were prosecuted and given jail sentences for bribing professors before the entrance examination. More recent cases of allegedly illegal private lessons by voice professors have been exposed in the press (see, e.g., Chosŏn Ilbo 2011).

29. The word *insa* can also be glossed as "greetings," "bow," "introduction," and "farewell."

30. During my fieldwork in 2008, the Korean *wŏn* fell from 0.0011 to 0.0007 U.S. dollars.

31. See Palais 1996 for a study of Confucian institutions and feudalism during the Chosŏn dynasty.

32. In an article on prestige classical music concerts in Seoul, the *Korea Times* quoted a survey done by the Korean Ministry of Culture and Tourism, which reported that the percentage of concertgoers who attended classical music or opera dwindled from 6.7 percent in 2000 to 3.6 percent in 2006 (Seo 2007). The article did not list the other types of concerts involved in the study. These numbers provide a picture of the imbalance but cannot be taken too seriously, since they do not account for the expansion of particular sectors of the performance market or of the market overall. Concerts of traditional Korean music fare even worse in attendance. For example, as Okon Hwang (2009: 27) notes: "As of 1997, 93.1 percent of full-time professorships in music at universities and colleges in Korea are occupied by musicians specializing in Western art music, compared to 6.9 percent of musicians in traditional music. Not surprisingly in the same year, 90.2 percent of places for incoming freshpersons at college and university level were available to study Western art music, but only 9.8 percent for traditional music. At the end of the twentieth century, more than ninety four-year universities and colleges specialize in Western music performance, while only nineteen departments offer programs in Korean traditional music."

33. See Chun 1984; and J.-H. Kim 1981, 1992. *P'umasi* is often grouped with *ture* (mutual aid organization) and *kye* (cooperative banking) as traditional systems of village cooperation. See K.-O. Kim 1993 for more on *kye* among members of Christian congregations and prayer groups.

34. See Bourdieu (1979) 1984 on distinction; see Silverstein 2004, 2006 on connoisseurship.

35. See N. Lee 2007: 160–62 for discussion of the importance of these relationships in Korean student movements.

36. Korean social interactions are influenced deeply by the principle of elder reverence and cohort-based hierarchies. Dredge (1987: 73) argues, "Korean elders are respected not so much because they are wise as because everyone can agree on what an elder is and can therefore share the same concept of social hierarchy."

37. On voice quality in honorific and "polite" speech registers, see Irvine 1974, 1990; and Sicoli 2010.

38. See Silverstein 2003 on indexical orders.

39. Cf. *p'ansori* training, in which the student "receives" or "acquires" the sound *(sori)* from the teacher (C. E. Park 2003: 157–201). See Scheid 2002: 176 for a similar, if extreme, version of this phenomenon, in which "discipleship in contemporary Chinese Medicine thus seems to be geared toward turning disciples into copies of their masters."

40. The issue of indebtedness in the entertainment industry has received much attention in the news recently, mostly regarding the "slave contracts" *(noye kyeyak)* that aspiring pop musicians often sign at the start of their careers. In one of the top news stories of 2009, the actress Chang Cha-yŏn committed suicide after being forced into sexual relationships with corporate executives.

41. The expectation that the teacher will receive a portion of the earnings generated by the disciple under the teacher's auspices is similar to the expectation that the church will receive a portion (via tithing) of the earnings generated by the singer under the church's auspices.

42. Bourdieu (1979) 1984: 474.

43. See Harkness 2012 for a study of the influence of Korean's vowel-harmonic binary between ㅏ [a] and ㅓ [ŏ] on English loan word pronunciation and ideologies of standard speech.

44. See Yoon 2005 for a study of this prayer practice, called *t'ongsŏng kido,* among Korean-American Christians.

45. Bauman and Briggs 1990: 73. See also Silverstein 1996 for an analysis of "interactional residue" alongside repeated entextualizations. See Faudree 2013 for an ethnographic study of singing as a medium for the creation, circulation, and transformation of texts in Oaxaca, Mexico.

46. On ideologies of English-language learning in Korea, see J. S.-Y. Park 2009.

47. My use of the word *setting* comes from the "scene" or "psychological setting," discussed by Hymes 1974: 55–56; and "Einstellung," discussed by Jakobson 1960: 356.

48. Co-occurring signs in speech and paralinguistic elements of communicative interaction are organized according to the metapragmatic regimentation of discursive registers and genres. As an aspect of this process, qualic tuning can take place simply through the pitch and timbre of one's speaking voice, or it can consist of a more elaborate complex or "bundling" (Keane 2003) of phonosonic qualia that corresponds to one's overall expression of deference, as with Su-jin's and Sang-u's strategies of adjusting their methods of vocalization to the different contexts in which they sang.

49. See Chumley 2013 on evaluation regimes of fine art in Beijing.

50. According to Goffman (1959: 49), audience segregation takes place when an "individual ensures that those before whom he plays one of his parts will not be the same individuals before whom he plays a different part in another setting."

CHAPTER 6

1. See Warner 2002: 114.

2. While the word *encore* in Korean is written as *angk'orŭ,* most of those who shouted generally approximated the French pronunciation of the word.

3. The original lyrics read: "Peace, peace, wonderful peace/Coming down from the Father above!/Sweep over my spirit forever, I pray/In fathomless billows of love!"

4. For explanations of the concept of "entextualization" and a semiotic account of the notion of a "text" more generally, see Bauman and Briggs 1990; and Silverstein and Urban 1996.

5. My informants recall homecoming recitals as far back as the 1980s, when the first generation of Korean students who went abroad to study music began to return. Informants also said that these recitals have become increasingly popular—and professionally necessary—since the late 1990s, when Korean musicians abroad began returning to Seoul in droves during the Asian financial crisis. When the crisis hit, many parents could no longer support their children's study abroad. In 1997 and 1998, starting when two of Korea's top conglomerates went bankrupt, the value of the Korean *wŏn* plummeted to less than half its dollar value, and the composite stock price index almost crashed. In response to the financial crisis, the International Monetary Fund pledged South Korea a loan of fifty-seven billion U.S. dollars in November 1997 (see Cumings 2005: 333; see also J. Song 2009).

6. From my brief description of the recital format above, it should be clear that these groupings do not conform to the characterization of a public that "organizes itself independently of state institutions, laws, formal frameworks of citizenship, or preexisting institutions such as the church" (Warner 2002: 66). The audience for homecoming recitals in Korea is constituted precisely through explicit social and institutional relations. And as my experience purchasing a ticket for the performance demonstrates, true strangers with no personal connection to the performer or other members of the audience are not expected to attend. Despite the seemingly neutral publicity for the event—no concrete audience or preconstituted group appears to be targeted by the advertisements aside from their existence in places where people are listening to or making music— independent individuals usually do not purchase tickets and show up at Sejong Center for the Performing Arts for the homecoming recital of a singer whom they do not know. Recent anthropological research has critiqued the notion of a "neutral" public as an instantiation of an idealized Habermasian public sphere, enabled by the circulating forms of print capitalism. These critiques have focused in large part on the way the constitution of so-called publics actually depends on their specific cultural conceptualization and institutional authorization (see Gal 2005, 2006; and Gal and Woolard 2001). See Bauman and Briggs 2003 on the relationship between John Locke's program of language purification and the modern notion of the public sphere. See van der Veer 2001 on Christianity in the bourgeois public sphere in Britain and India. See Cody 2011 for a comprehensive review of the anthropological theorization of publics.

7. Goffman 1959: 59.

8. Goffman 1959: 59.

9. Weddings in Korea are a good example of the role of money and ritual gift-exchange among acquaintances. Laurel Kendall (1996: 29) describes people entering a wedding, handing over envelopes of cash, the attendants opening the envelopes, counting the money, and logging the number next to the beneficiary's

name in a book. I myself have also stood in such lines and handed over such envelopes. Parents often finance the wedding and can use it to "cash in" on all of the weddings they themselves have attended. The more weddings people attend, the greater their social network and the greater the potential to receive money when their own children marry.

10. Having attended numerous recitals with other church members from my field sites, I can attest to the visible presence of church members in the audience. I know well the feeling of standing in line waiting to purchase a ticket and being bumped rather roughly by an older woman rushing to the front of the line to pick up her reserved tickets. Moments later, I would hear this woman addressed as *"kwŏnsanim."* As an unordained but important leader in the church, the *kwŏnsa* (often translated as "exhorting deaconess" or "Bible woman") has the capacity to corral large groups from the church to engage in specific activities. If a singer's mother is a *kwŏnsa,* the singer can likely guarantee a large turnout for a recital. In this way, the church provides an important source of financial and social support for ritual events such as homecoming recitals.

11. Students choose a target country according to the guidance of their professors. This is often the same place their professors studied.

12. Those who graduate with a degree in voice but do not go abroad are limited in their professional options. Many students become music teachers at primary and secondary schools. A large number of women I spoke with had married and quit singing the moment they had children. Many others were waiting to marry and sang only in church. A few had changed careers or were planning to do so—usually to something music related, such as "arts management," which basically describes the services for which singers pay to audition for schools abroad and to perform at venues in Seoul.

13. Abroad, however, many institutions do not look charitably on this process. In 2007, a professor of voice at the Universität der Künste, in Berlin, after praising her Korean students' voices, especially their "strong vocal cords," told me that the voice department was "sick of" the number of Korean students who were accepted, never learned to speak German, and returned to Korea following their training. The department ultimately raised the level of German proficiency required for entrance and added to the application an essay question about professional motivation. In 1999, according to Okon Hwang (2009: 29), one voice competition in Italy actually banned Korean singers from entering on the grounds that they were suspected of not seeking to further their performance careers. They were accused of using international credentials to gain employment as teachers in Korea and thus not "fulfill[ing] the purpose of the competition."

14. Interview conducted in German. In my interviews and conversations with other singers in Europe and North America, I have heard some singers mention the problem of adequate expression in performance, but few, if any, ever cited it as a central challenge to their professional development. On the other hand, many Korean singers told me that it was a problem for students studying abroad. Voice teachers in Europe, North America, and Korea cited this as a common difficulty for their Korean students, but I heard it even more often from the Korean students themselves. The differences in focus between

performing in Korea and performing abroad became extremely clear to me when singers who had never studied singing abroad said they focused most centrally on not making mistakes *(t'ŭllida)*, and those who had studied abroad said they focused on "emotionally moving" *(kamdong sik'ida)* their audiences with their voices. It is important to clarify here that I am not merely reinforcing the various orientalist stereotypes, nor are my informants adopting a self-orientalizing position. The issue of affect and expression is connected directly to the performance of secular art music in a European language for unappreciative or uninformed audiences or for critical judges in a position of authority. It has to do with a contextually specific form of anxiety around vocal performance, not with a general lack of cathexis. There is no shortage of public affect or emotionality in other Korean performance genres, whether in *p'ansori* or church singing. In fact, as I will suggest at the end of this chapter, the church and other Christian contexts are sites where affective disposition and displays of emotionality are encouraged and cultivated—hence the Christian encore.

15. Arts institutions often initiate "music appreciation" events to recruit—and train—potential connoisseurs, and Korean newspapers occasionally comment on the audience's lack of "manners" or unrefined "etiquette" during live performances *(yepŏp* or y*ejŏl;* also often expressed as the English loan words *maenŏjŭ* and *et'ik'et).*

16. At the request of the singer, I have not published stills from the video recording.

17. As with all other fields within the education industry in Korea, as accounted, for example, in Abelmann 2003 and Abelmann et al. 2012, an aspect of professional music training targets the specific needs of students wishing to go abroad for musical study. Services for merely completing the application and writing or editing the various application essays can cost as much as three million *wŏn.* They also often include translating faculty recommendations into the target language. Students often need to submit an audio recording of their audition repertoire for the initial screening. As with the marketing materials for their recitals, the objective of the recording sessions is to present a professional, finished product. This often means hours in the recording studio and in the editing room. The application process is a truly expensive endeavor. While many students pay their application fees and related service fees with money earned from part-time work, most often the family pays. As I mentioned above, family wealth is often seen as a prerequisite for the study of vocal music at the university level in Korea.

18. Peirce 1997: secs. 5.71, 8.122. See also n. 27 in the introduction.

19. My informants use the English loan word *ak'ademik* here. Baroque and classical arias from oratorios and the like are generally considered to be secular, academic pieces. With the exception of a few famous compositions, Handel's *Messiah* or Mendelssohn's *Elias,* for example, this music is only rarely performed during church services.

20. *"Segyejŏk in sŏngakka ka twaesŏ Hananim kke yŏnggwang ŭl nat'anaenŭn saram i toego sipta"* (Kungmin Ilbo 2009).

21. The encore overcomes, if only momentarily, "audience segregation" (Goffman 1959: 49).

22. See Gal 2005; and Hill 2001 for discussions of folk conceptualizations of "public" and "private."

CHAPTER 7

1. Howard 1990: 145. Howard qualifies this statement by reminding us that "sadness alone suggests the wrong atmosphere for songs. A prime aesthetic of singers, like band members, was to increase the 'enthusiasm' *[hŭng]* of an audience" (146).

2. For scholarly interventions in these areas of research, see Lutz 1988; Lutz and Abu-Lughod 1990; Mazzarella 2009; and Wierzbicka 1986, 1999. For overviews of the anthropological theorization of emotion and affect, see Besnier 1990; Lutz 1986; and Wilce 2009.

3. See, e.g., Rosaldo 1980: 31–60 on cultural conceptualizations of the heart among the Ilongot, and Brenneis 1990 on the social aesthetics of feeling in Bhatgaon. As Kockelmann (2011: 449) points out, the point "is not to define 'what emotions really are,' but rather to map out the relevant semiotic and intersubjective dimensions of an otherwise seemingly psychological and subjective domain."

4. See, e.g., Feld 1982; Fox 2004; and Urban 1988.

5. *Sim* is usually offered as a synonym of *maŭm* in Korean-language dictionaries. The common English phrase "to win hearts and minds" is sometimes translated as "to capture the maŭm" *(maŭm ŭl saro chapta)*. In Korean speech, *maŭm* is a pervasive term that is used in many unremarkable situations. Aside from direct reference to the heart-mind, one can use it to say things like "I like something" *(maŭm e tŭlda,* literally, "it enters the heart") or "I intend to" *(maŭm mŏkta,* literally, "to eat/consume the heart").

6. See Ikegami 2008; Occhi 2008; K.-J. Yoon 2004, 2008; and N. Yu 2008, 2009.

7. Whorf 1956: 138.

8. The term for edible animal hearts, *yŏmt'ong,* generally cannot be used to describe a human person's heart.

9. Hence the translation for "mind." See N. Yu 2009 on the Chinese 心.

10. Kyung-Joo Yoon (2008) explains that it once did, but there is not enough historical evidence to tell when this usage disappeared. The same is said to be true for the Japanese *kokoro.*

11. Silverstein 2004.

12. See K.-J. Yoon 2008.

13. Grayson 1999: 169.

14. Ross (1877b) 1982: 171.

15. Ross 1883: 493–94. The spelling of *Koreans* as *Coreans* is in the original.

16. The Buddhist "Heart Sutra" in Korean is referred to as *panya simgyŏng.* And it was Mencius's understanding that *ren* (benevolence, humaneness), *yi* (propriety), *li* (observance of rites), and *zhi* (wisdom), stem from four "predispositions," "sprouts," or "beginnings" of the heart-mind (心): "commiseration, the sense of shame, a reverential attitude toward others, and the sense of right and wrong" (Shun 2010).

17. Ledyard (1965) 1998.

18. Ross 1883: 496.

19. See King 2004; Silva 2008.

20. See Baker 2002, 2006; Oak 2012. For a debate among scholars, especially James Grayson, Gari Ledyard, Don Baker, and Timothy Lee, over the status of *Hananim* as an indigenous word and its definition in nineteenth-century Korea, see http://koreaweb.ws/pipermail/koreanstudies_koreaweb.ws/2003-December/.

21. For his research on the use of *Hananim* (or the archaic *Hanŭnim*) in Korean Christianity, Don Baker (2002) consulted the first Korean-language dictionary, the *Dictionnaire Coréen-Français* (1880), prepared for the use of Catholic missionaries in Korea. There he found no entry for either native Korean term. Although there is an entry for *hanŭl* (the indigenous term for heaven), the only references to God are under the entries for *Sangje* and *Ch'ŏnju* (Baker 2002). I myself checked this source to see if the term *maŭm* appears. It appears in an alternate spelling. In James Scarth Gale's Korean-English dictionary of 1897, *Hanŭnim* and *maŭm* are both present.

22. Ross 1877a.

23. Grayson 1999.

24. The final chapter is misnumbered XXIII instead of XXXIII.

25. Ross 1877a: 89. Ross wrote *Ŏjin maŭm* in Han'gŭl as 이딘마음 *(idin maŭm)*, but romanized it as *udin maum*. The contemporary spelling of the term would be 어진마음 *(ŏjin maŭm)*, from 어질다 *(ŏjilda)*. Ross's spelling appears to combine a consonantal feature of P'yŏngan dialect (ㄷ/d rather than ㅈ/j) and a typographical error for the vowel (ㅣ/i rather than ㅓ/ŏ). On Protestants, Han'gŭl, and the P'yŏngan dialect, see King 2010.

26. For example, Schieffelin (2007) has discussed the difficulties missionaries faced when trying to reproduce the reflexive language of biblical scripture from a published Tok Pisin Bible into spoken Bosavi (Kaluli, one of four dialects used among the Bosavi people of Papua New Guinea) and a "cultural epistemology" of interiority and affect. Specifically, Schieffelin focused on the way new Christian speech registers were created in the process of translation: "One important shift was making explicit the source and location of private, affective and cognitive states, where previously no such designation was made" (147). For example, for the phrases, "I was troubled in my heart," the pre-Christian version was simply *"hida:yo:"* (I was worried; something was heavy in weight), but the missionaries calqued the Tok Pisin phrase *"bel hevi"* (literally, "stomach/heart heavy") as *"kufo: hida:yo:"* (literally, "stomach was heavy") (147). In addition to Schieffelin's observation of a new register in which thoughts and feelings were given an explicit source, we might add that this preexisting source—in this case the stomach—was endowed with new specifically Christian qualities and functions.

Robbins (2004: 185) explained how the Christianized Urapmin in Papua New Guinea locate both thought and feeling in the "heart" *(aget)*, which is understood to be located in the chest. However, thought and feeling are differentiated by the relatively agentive or patientive status of the experience and accordingly are marked grammatically. "Thinking" takes place when the heart is the subject; "feelings" arise in the heart. "Linguistically and experientially, [feelings] are agents that affect the heart, rather than operations that the heart carries out, and thus people have less control of them than they do their hearts" (185). The basis of "moral behavior" *(kukup tangbal)*, as it is constructed in the psychological discourse, is expressed as "good thinking" *(aget fukunin tangbal)*. Robbins used these observations to point to a broader cultural narrative of Christianization, in which the "Urapimin undertake the moral regulation of their inner lives" (226) by "suppressing the desires of the pre-Christian heart" (229) and "renouncing the will and cultivating a peaceful heart" (232).

27. I performed this search on October 13, 2009. I performed it a number of times, on different computers, and both logged in to my account and not logged in, to make sure that I was receiving consistent results. There was little variation from one search to the next, if any at all.

28. See J.-H. Kim 1981: 140–43.

29. http://ajskdlf2.tistory.com/547, accessed July 1, 2009.

30. A literal translation of *ttŭt* would be "meaning," but it can also be translated as "wish," "mind," and "intent."

31. The program name, *Int'ŏbyu,* is a loan word written as "人터뷰." Forming a pun, the first syllable is written with the Chinese character 人 (인,), which is pronounced as "in" and means "person." The interview aired on the Christian television station CGNTV (Christian Global Network Television).

32. *Kkaedatta* can mean "to be convinced or enlightened."

33. Named Violetta Valéry in Verdi's opera.

34. Literally, "Those emotions wouldn't be caught."

35. As another example of a Christian speech register, the rare verb *yŏksa hada,* referring to God working through someone, can be found in 1 Thessalonians 2:13:

> *Irŏmŭro uri ka Hananim kke kkŭnim ŏpsi kamsa hamŭn nŏhŭi ka uri ege tŭrŭn pa Hananim ŭi malssŭm ŭl padŭl ttae e saram ŭi mal ro patchi anihago Hananim ŭi malssŭm ŭro padŭmini chinsil ro kŭrŏhadoda i malssŭm i ttohan nŏhŭi minnŭn cha kaunde esŏ <u>yŏksa hanŭnira</u>.* (NRKV)

> And we also thank God continually because, when you received the word of God, which you heard from us, you accepted it not as the word of men, but as it actually is, the word of God, which <u>is at work</u> in you who believe. (NIV)

36. Kim Yŏng-mi also discussed this event in her interview with Paek Chi-yŏn above.

37. The construction of this portion of the Kim's statement is difficult to render in English. The verb *imjae hada* is rare but can be found in the *Kaeyŏk kaejŏng* translation in Ezekiel 37:1:

> *Yŏhowa kkesŏ kwŏnnŭng ŭro nae ke <u>imjae hasigo</u> kŭ ŭi yŏng ŭro na rŭl terigo kasŏ koltchagi kaunde tusyŏnnŭnde kŏgi ppyŏ ka kadŭkhadŏra.* (NRKV)

> The hand of the LORD <u>was upon me</u>, and he brought me out by the Spirit of the LORD and set me in the middle of a valley; it was full of bones. (NIV)

38. See Weber (1930) 1999: 113–14. For an ethnographic account of the role of the human voice in phonosonically materializing the divine for Apostolic

Christians in Zimbabwe, see Engelke 2007: 200–223. For an analysis of the technological reproduction of voice to facilitate feelings of closeness to the Prophet and spiritual immediacy among Mauritian Muslims, see Eisenlohr 2009. For a study of how American Evangelicals cultivate their hearts and learn to recognize the voice of God, see Luhrmann 2012.

39. Bakhtin 1986: 163. See Cavell 1994 on the "arrogation" of a universalizing use of voice in philosophy.

40. Note the interesting resonance of Kim's statement in excerpt 7.5 with the explicitly ideological complement to Park Chung-hee's Saemaŭl Undong (New Village movement) of the 1970s: the Saemaŭm Undong (New Heart-Mind movement), with Park Geun-hye as its spokesperson. Note as well the resonance of Kim's statement with the North Korean slogan Ilsim Tan'gyŏl (Unity in One Heart-Mind). The compound hanmaŭm is widespread in advertising and commercial naming practices throughout South Korea (e.g., Hanmaŭm Reality, Hanmaŭm Hospital, Hanmaŭm Kimbap, etc.).

41. See Yoshihara 2007 for first-person narratives of this experience.

42. Kilkŏri rŭl tanyŏ pomyŏn uri nara saramdŭl ŭn p'yojŏng i chogŭm ŏduwŏ poyŏyo. Hajiman It'allia saramdŭl ŭn sam i kot yŏn'gi rago hal su itki ttaemune kŭdŭl kwa saenghwal hanŭn kaunde sŏ chayŏn sŭrŏpke yŏn'gi rŭl chŏphal su issŏssŭmnida. Ŭmak Ch'unch'u, March 2008, 80–81.

43. The term nuna here is used tropically as a kin term, expressing intimacy between a younger man and an older woman (from the perspective of the man). Chang-wŏn knew that I knew Ye-ryŏng, because she was a soprano soloist for the choir I sang with at the time.

44. See Baker 2006: 293; and Chong 2008: 91–99 on prayer, emotional release, and "opening up" the self in Korean Protestant Christianity.

45. See Bruno 2002: 23–36 for a Korean case.

46. See Goffman (1974) 1986 on the role partials of animator, author, and principal.

47. See Trilling 1972; and Keane 2002 on "sincerity" and "authenticity." See Titon 1988: 252–56 on authenticity and "good singing," as well as Samuels 2004; and Fox 2004. See Wilf 2010, 2011, and 2012 for a series of articles dealing with the problem of sincerity, creativity, and expression in U.S. jazz education.

CONCLUSION

1. C. Eckert 2000: 134.

2. In the German word Stimme, we find a very clear referential overlap between the voice as phonosonic nexus and the voice as a semiotic enactment of differentiable perspective: eine Stimme can refer to both a human voice and a political vote.

3. From 1 Peter 2:9: "Kŭrŏna nŏhŭi nŭn t'aekhasin choksok iyo wang kat'ŭn chesajangdŭl iyo kŏrukhan nara yo kŭ ŭi soyu ka toen paeksŏng ini i nŭn nŏhŭi rŭl ŏduun tesŏ pullŏ naeŏ kŭ ŭi kiihan pit e tŭlŏgage hasin I ŭi arŭmdaun tŏk ŭl sŏnp'o hage haryŏ hasimira."

References Cited

Abelmann, Nancy. 1996. *Echoes of the Past, Epics of Dissent: A South Korean Social Movement*. Berkeley: University of California Press.

———. 2003. *Melodrama of Mobility: Women, Talk, and Class in Contemporary South Korea*. Honolulu: University of Hawai'i Press.

———. 2009. *The Intimate University: Korean American Students and the Problems of Segregation*. Durham, NC: Duke University Press.

Abelmann, Nancy, Jung-ah Choi, and So Jin Park, eds. 2012. *No Alternative? Experiments in South Korean Education*. Berkeley: University of California Press.

Agha, Asif. 1993. "Grammatical and Indexical Convention in Honorific Discourse." *Journal of Linguistic Anthropology* 3 (2): 131–63.

———. 1998. "Stereotypes and Registers of Honorific Language." *Language in Society* 27: 151–93.

———. 2005. "Voice, Footing, Enregisterment." *Journal of Linguistic Anthropology* 15 (1): 38–59.

———. 2007. *Language and Social Relations*. Cambridge: Cambridge University Press.

Bacon, Francis. (1605) 1873. *The Advancement of Learning*. Oxford: Clarendon Press.

Baker, Donald. 2002. "Hananim, Hanŭnim, Hanullim, and Hanŏllim: The Construction of Terminology for Korean Monotheism." *Review of Korean Studies* 5 (1): 105–31.

———. 2006. "Sibling Rivalry in Twentieth-Century Korea: Comparative Growth Rates of Catholic and Protestant Communities." In *Christianity in Korea*, edited by R. E. Buswell and T. S. Lee, 283–308. Honolulu: University of Hawai'i Press.

———. 2008. *Korean Spirituality*. Honolulu: University of Hawai'i Press.

Bakhtin, Mikhail M. 1981. *The Dialogic Imagination: Four Essays.* Austin: University of Texas Press.

———. 1986. *Speech Genres and Other Late Essays.* Translated by V. W. McGee. Austin: University of Texas Press.

Barnes, David. 2006. *The Great Stink of Paris and the Nineteenth-Century Struggle against Filth and Germs.* Baltimore: Johns Hopkins University Press.

Barthes, Roland. (1972) 1977. "The Grain of the Voice." In *Image-Music-Text,* 179–89. New York: Hill and Wang.

Basso, Keith. 1996. *Wisdom Sits in Places: Landscape and Language among the Western Apache.* Albuquerque: University of New Mexico Press.

Bauman, Richard, and Charles Briggs. 1990. "Poetics and Performance as Critical Perspectives on Language and Social Life." *Annual Review of Anthropology* 19: 59–88.

———. 2003. *Voices of Modernity: Language Ideologies and the Politics of Inequality.* Cambridge: Cambridge University Press.

BBC. 2007. "Lee Wins South Korea's Election." December 19. http://news.bbc.co.uk/2/hi/asia-pacific/7150806.stm.

———. 2008. "South Korea Relaxes US Beef Ban." April 18. http://news.bbc.co.uk/2/hi/business/7353767.stm.

Beeman, William O. 2005. "Making Grown Men Weep." In *Aesthetics in Performance: Formations of Symbolic Construction and Experience,* edited by A. Hobart and B. Kapferer, 24–42. New York: Berghahn Books.

Beidelman, Thomas O. 1982. *Colonial Evangelism: A Socio-Historical Study of an East African Mission at the Grassroots.* Bloomington: Indiana University Press.

Bergeron, Katherine. 2009. *Voice Lessons: French Mélodie in the Belle Epoque.* Oxford: Oxford Unviersity Press.

Besnier, Niko. 1990. "Language and Affect." *Annual Review of Anthropology* 19: 419–51.

Bird, Isabella. 1905. *Korea and Her Neighbors: A Narrative of Travel, with an Account of the Vicissitudes and Position of the Country.* 2 vols. London: John Murray.

Blacking, John. 1973. *How Musical Is Man?* Seattle: University of Washington Press.

Blommaert, Jan. 1999. *Language Ideological Debates.* New York: Mouton de Gruyter.

Boas, Franz. 1889. "On Alternating Sounds." *American Anthropologist* 2 (1): 47–54.

Bourdieu, Pierre. 1977. *Outline of a Theory of Practice.* Translated by R. Nice. Cambridge: Cambridge University Press.

———. (1979) 1984. *Distinction: A Social Critique of the Judgement of Taste.* Translated by R. Nice. Cambridge, MA: Harvard University Press.

Brandt, Vincent. 1971. *A Korean Village: Between Farm and Sea.* Cambridge, MA: Harvard University Press.

Brenneis, Donald. 1984. "Grog and Gossip in Bhatgaon: Style and Substance in Fiji Indian Conversation." *American Ethnologist* 11 (3): 487–506.

———. 1985. "Passion and Performance in Fiji Indian Vernacular Song." *Ethnomusicology* 29 (3): 397–408.

———. 1987. "Performing Passions: Aesthetics and Politics in an Occasionally Egalitarian Community." *American Ethnologist* 14 (2): 236–50.

———. 1990. "Shared and Solitary Sentiments: The Discourse of Friendship, Play, and Anger in Bhatgaon." In *Language and the Politics of Emotion*, edited by C. Lutz and L. Abu-Lughod, 113–25. New York: Cambridge University Press.

Briggs, Charles. 1993. "Personal Sentiments and Polyphonic Voices in Warao Women's Ritual Wailing: Music and Poetics in a Critical and Collective Discourse." *American Anthropologist* 95 (4): 929–57.

———. 1996. "The Meaning of Nonsense, the Poetics of Embodiment, and the Production of Power in Warao Healing." In *The Performance of Healing*, edited by C. Laderman and M. Roseman, 185–232. New York: Routledge.

Bruno, Antonetta Lucia. 2002. *The Gate of Words: Language in the Rituals of Korean Shamans*. Leiden: Research School of Asian, African, and Amerindian Studies, Universiteit Leiden.

Burke, Timothy. 1996. *Lifebuoy Men, Lux Women: Commodification, Consumption, and Cleanliness in Modern Zimbabwe*. Durham, NC: Duke University Press.

Cannell, Fenella. 2006. "The Anthropology of Christianity." In *The Anthropology of Christianity*, edited by Fenella Cannell, 1–50. Durham, NC: Duke University Press.

Carr, E. Summerson. 2009. "Anticipating and Inhabiting Institutional Identities." *American Ethnologist* 36 (2): 317–36.

Caton, Steven. 1986. "Salam Tahiya: Greetings from the Highlands of Yemen." *American Ethnologist* 13: 290–308.

———. 1990. *"Peaks of Yemen I Summon": Poetry as Cultural Practice in a North Yemeni Tribe*. Berkeley: University of California Press.

Cavell, Stanley. 1994. *A Pitch of Philosophy: Autobiographical Exercises*. Cambridge, MA: Harvard University Press.

Chakrabarty, Dipesh. 2000. *Deprovincializing Europe: Postcolonial Thought and Historical Difference*. Princeton, NJ: Princeton University Press.

Chang, Yun-Shik. 1982. "Women in a Confucian Society: The Case of Chosun Dynasty Korea (1392–1910)." *Asian and Pacific Quarterly of Cultural and Social Affairs* 14 (2): 24–42.

Chion, Michel. (1982) 1999. *The Voice in Cinema*. Translated by C. Gorbman. New York: Columbia University Press.

Cho, Haejoang. 2002. "Living with Conflicting Subjectivies: Mother, Motherly Wife, and Sexy Woman in the Transition from Colonial-Modern to Postmodern Korea." In *Under Construction: The Gendering of Modernity, Class, and Consumption in the Republic of Korea*, edited by L. Kendall, 165–95. Honolulu: University of Hawai'i Press.

Ch'oe, Kil-Sŏng. 1987. "The Meaning of Pollution in Korean Ritual Life." In *Religion and Ritual in Korean Society*, edited by L. Kendall and G. Dix, 139–48. Berkeley: University of California Press.

Choe, Sang-Hun. 2007. "Afghan Hostage Crisis Transfixes South Korea." *New York Times*, July 26.

Choi, Hyaeweol. 2009. *Gender and Mission Encounters in Korea: New Women, Old Ways*. Berkeley: University of California Press.

Choi, Sang-Chin, and Soo-Hyang Choi. 1991. "We-ness: A Korean Discourse of Collectivism." In *The Psychology of the Korean People: Individualism and Collectivism,* edited by G. Yoon and S.-C. Choi, 57–84. Seoul: Donga Publishing Corporation.

Choi, Set-Byol. 1999. "High-Class Women and Cultural Capital in Consolidating High-Class Boundary: Korean Case: Females Majoring in Western Classical Music." PhD dissertation, Department of Sociology, Yale University.

Chong, Kelly. 2006. "In Search of Healing: Evangelical Conversion of Women in Contemporary South Korea." In *Christianity in Korea,* edited by R. E. Buswell and T. S. Lee, 351–70. Honolulu: University of Hawai'i Press.

———. 2008. *Deliverance and Submission: Evangelical Women and the Negotiation of Patriarchy in South Korea.* Cambridge, MA: Harvard University Press.

Choongang, Ilbo. 2008. *"PD Such'ŏp* kongdong pŏnyŏkchadŭl 'Pangsong naeyong kwangupyŏng anin chul aratta'" (Co-translators for *PD Such'ŏp* 'thought broadcast content was not mad cow disease'"). June 28. http://article.joinsmsn.com/news/article/article.asp?total_id=3206521.

Chosŏn Ilbo. 2008. "Kwangupyŏng nonmun, midiŏ ka Pup'ulligo chŏngch'ikwŏn i agyong" (Media inflates and politicians abuse mad cow thesis). May 8. http://m.chosun.com/article.html?contid=2008050801749.

———. 2011. "Pak Mi-hye Kyosu, Kyujŏng ŏgigo 'sigandang 2 manwŏn' kaein lesŭn" (Professor Mi-hye Pak breaks the rules, "20,000 *wŏn* per hour" private lesson). March 7. http://m.chosun.com/article.html?contid=2011030700671.

Chumley, Lily Hope. 2013. "Evaluation Regimes and the Qualia of Quality." *Anthropological Theory* 13 (1/2): 169–83.

Chumley, Lily Hope, and Nicholas Harkness. 2013. "Introduction: Qualia." *Anthropological Theory* 13 (1/2): 3–11.

Chun, Kyung-soo. 1984. *Reciprocity and Korean Society: An Ethnography of Hasami.* Seoul: Seoul National University Press.

Chung, David. 2001. *Syncretism: The Religious Context of Christian Beginnings in Korea.* Albany: State University of New York Press.

Clark, Donald. 1986. *Christianity in Modern Korea.* Lanham, MD: University Press of America.

———. 2003. *Living Dangerously in Korea: The Western Experience, 1900–1950.* Norwalk, CT: EastBridge.

———. 2006. "Mothers, Daughters, Biblewomen, and Sisters: An Account of 'Women's Work' in the Korea Mission Field." In *Christianity in Korea,* edited by R. E. Buswell and T. S. Lee, 167–92. Honolulu: University of Hawai'i Press.

CNN. 2003. "First Apparent U.S. Case of Mad Cow Disease Discovered." December 24. http://edition.cnn.com/2003/US/12/23/mad.cow/.

Cody, Francis. 2011. "Publics and Politics." *Annual Review of Anthropology* 40: 37–52.

Coleman, Simon. 2007. "Of Metaphors and Muscles: Protestant 'Play' in the Disciplining of the Self." In *The Discipline of Leisure: Embodying Cultures of Recreation,* edited by S. Coleman and T. Kohn, 39–53. Oxford: Berghahn.

Comaroff, John, and Jean Comaroff. 1997. *Of Revelation and Revolution: Dialectics of Modernity on a South African Frontier.* Vol. 2. Chicago: University of Chicago Press.

Conn, Harvie H. 1966. "Studies in the Theology of the Korean Presbyterian Church: A Historical Outline, I." *Westminster Theological Journal* 29: 24–57.

Corbin, Alain. (1982) 1986. *The Foul and the Fragrant: Odor and the French Social Imagination.* Leamington Spa, UK: Berg.

Corporal, Lynette Lee. 2007. "'Toilet Training' for Adults Underway." November 13. http://ipsnews.net/news.asp?idnews = 40032.

Csordas, Thomas. 1993. "Somatic Modes of Attention." *Cultural Anthropology* 8 (2): 135–56.

Cumings, Bruce. 2002. "Civil Society in West and East." In *Korean Society: Civil Society, Democracy, and the State,* edited by C. Armstrong, 11–35. New York: Routledge.

———. 2003. *North Korea: Another Country.* New York: New Press.

———. 2005. *Korea's Place in the Sun: A Modern History.* Updated ed. New York: W. W. Norton.

Curley, Gregory. 2007. "Apgujeong: Seoul's Magnet for Stars." *Han'guk Ilbo,* July 19, 2007.

Daylight, Russel. 2011. *What If Derrida Was Wrong about Saussure?* Edinburgh: Edinburgh University Press.

Deuchler, Martina. 1992. *The Confucian Transformation of Korea: A Study of Society and Ideology.* Cambridge, MA: Harvard University Asia Center.

Dolar, Mladen. 2006. *A Voice and Nothing More.* Cambridge, MA: MIT Press.

Dredge, C. Paul. 1987. "Korean Funerals: Ritual as Process." In *Religion and Ritual in Korean Soceity,* edited by L. Kendall and G. Dix, 71–92. Berkeley: University of California Press.

Easy Bible Editorial Committee. 2009. *Shwiun Sŏnggyŏng* (Easy Bible). Seoul: Agap'e.

Eckert, Carter. 2000. "Korea's Transition to Modernity: A Will to Greatness." In *Historical Perspectives on Contemporary East Asia,* edited by M. Goldman and A. Gordon. Cambridge, MA: Harvard University Press.

Eckert, Carter, Ki-baik Lee, Young Ick Lew, Michael Robinson, and Edward W. Wagner. 1990. *Korea Old and New: A History.* Seoul: Ilchogak.

Eckert, Penelope. 2008. "Variation and the Indexical Field." *Journal of Sociolinguistics* 12 (4): 453–76.

Eidsheim, Nina Sun. 2011a. "Marian Anderson and 'Sonic Blackness' in American Opera." *American Quarterly* 63 (3): 641–71.

———. 2011b. "Sensing Voice: Materiality and the Lived Body in Singing and Listening." *Senses & Society* 6 (2): 133–55.

Eisenlohr, Patrick. 2009. "Technologies of the Spirit: Devotional Islam, Sound Reproduction and the Dialectics of Mediation and Immediacy in Mauritius." *Anthropological Theory* 9 (3): 273–96.

Elias, Norbert. (1939) 2004. *The Civilizing Process: Sociogenetic and Psychogenetic Investigations.* Oxford: Blackwell.

Engelhardt, Jeffers. 2009. "Right Singing in Estonian Orthodox Christianity: A Study of Music, Theology, and Religious Ideology." *Ethnomusicology* 53 (1): 32–57.

Engelke, Matthew. 2007. *A Problem of Presence: Beyond Scripture in an African Church*. Berkeley: University of California Press.

Erlmann, Veit. 1996. *Nightsong: Performance, Power, and Practice in South Africa*. Chicago: University of Chicago Press.

———. 2004. *Hearing Cultures: Essays on Sound, Listening, and Modernity*. Oxford: Berg.

Errington, Joseph. 1985. "On the Nature of the Sociolinguistic Sign: Describing the Javanese Speech Levels." In *Semiotic Mediation: Sociocultural and Psychological Perspectives*, edited by E. Mertz and R. Parmentier, 287–310. Orlando, FL: Academic Press.

Fackler, Martin. 2009. "In South Korea, Cosmetic Surgery Falters with Economy." *New York Times*, January 2.

Farquhar, Judith. 1994. *Knowing Practice: The Clinical Encounter of Chinese Medicine*. Boulder, CO: Westview Press.

———. 2002. *Appetites: Food and Sex in Postsocialist China*. Durham, NC: Duke University Press.

Faudree, Paja. 2013. *Singing for the Dead: The Politics of Indigenous Revival in Mexico*. Durham, NC: Duke University Press.

Feld, Steven. 1982. *Sound and Sentiment: Birds, Weeping, Poetics, and Song in Kaluli Expression*. Philadelphia: University of Pennsylvania Press.

———. 1990. "Wept Thoughts: The Voicing of Kaluli Memories." *Oral Tradition* 5 (2–3): 241–66.

———. 1994. "'Aesthetics as Iconicity of Style' (uptown title); or, (downtown title) 'Lift-up-over Sounding': Getting into the Kaluli Groove." In *Music Grooves*, edited by C. Keil and S. Feld, 109–50. Chicago: University of Chicago Press.

———. 1996. "Waterfalls of Song: An Acoustemology of Place Resounding in Bosavi, Papua New Guinea." In *Senses of Place*, edited by S. Feld and K. Basso, 91–135. Santa Fe, NM: School of American Research Press.

Feld, Steven, and Donald Brenneis. 2004. "Doing Anthropology in Sound." *American Ethnologist* 31 (4): 461–74.

Feld, Steven, and Aaron Fox. 1994. "Music and Language." *Annual Review of Anthropology* 23: 25–53.

Feld, Steven, Aaron Fox, Thomas Porcello, and David Samuels. 2004. "Vocal Anthropology: From the Music of Language to the Language of Song." In *Blackwell Companion to Linguistic Anthropology*, edited by A. Duranti, 321–45. Oxford: Basil Blackwell.

Fox, Aaron. 2004. *Real Country: Music and Language in Working-Class Culture*. Durham, NC: Duke University Press.

Frith, Simon. 1998. *Performing Rites: On the Value of Popular Music*. Cambridge, MA: Harvard University Press.

Fukada, Eiko. 2001. "Classical Music Looks to Asia for Talent." *Japan Economic Newswire*, January 1.

Gal, Susan. 2005. "Language Ideologies Compared: Metaphors of Public /Private." *Journal of Linguistic Anthropology* 15 (1): 23–37.

———. 2006. "Contradictions of Standard Language in Europe: Implications for the Study of Publics and Practices." *Social Anthropology* 14 (2): 163–81.

———. 2013. "Tastes of Talk: Qualia and the Moral Flavor of Signs." *Anthropological Theory* 13 (1/2): 31–48.

Gal, Susan, and Judith Irvine. 1995. "The Boundaries of Languages and Disciplines: How Ideologies Construct Difference." *Social Research* 62 (4): 966–1001.

Gal, Susan, and Kathryn Woolard, eds. 2001. *Languages and Publics: The Making of Authority.* Manchester, UK: St. Jerome Publishing.

Gale, James Scarth. 1897. *Korean-English Dictionary.* Yokohama, Shanghai: Kelby & Walsh.

Garcia, Manuel. 1855. "Observations on the Human Voice." *Proceedings of the Royal Society of London: 1854–55,* vol. 7: 399–410.

Geurts, Kathryn. 2002. *Culture and the Senses: Bodily Ways of Knowing in an African Community.* Berkeley: University of California Press.

Gifford, Daniel Lyman. 1898. *Every-Day Life in Korea: A Collection of Studies and Stories.* Chicago: Fleming H. Revell Company.

Glionna, John. 2009. "Kids Get a Taste of Toughness." *Chicago Tribune,* September 1.

Goffman, Erving. 1959. *The Presentation of Self in Everyday Life.* Garden City, NY: Doubleday.

———. (1974) 1986. *Frame Analysis: An Essay on the Organzation of Experience.* Boston: Northeastern University Press.

———. 1978. "Response Cries." *Language* 54 (4): 787–815.

———. 1979. "Footing." *Semiotica* 25 (1–2): 1–29.

Grayson, James Huntley. 1999. "The Legacy of John Ross: A Neglected Chapter in the History of Pan-East Asian Missions." *International Bulletin of Missionary Research* 23 (4): 167–72.

———. 2001. *Myths and Legends from Korea: An Annotated Compendium of Ancient and Modern Materials.* Richmond, Surrey, UK: Curzon Press.

———. 2006. "A Quarter-Millennium of Christianity in Korea." In *Christianity in Korea,* edited by R. E. Buswell and T. S. Lee, 7–25. Honolulu: University of Hawai'i Press.

———. 2009. "Ch'udo Yebae: A Case Study in the Early Emplantation of Protestant Christianity in Korea." *Journal of Asian Studies* 68: 413–34.

Grinker, Roy Richard. 1998. *Korea and Its Futures: Unification and the Unfinished War.* New York: Palgrave Macmillan.

Ha, Seong-Kyu. 2001. "Substandard Settlements and Joint Redevelopment Projects in Seoul." *Habitat International* 25: 385–97.

Han, Ju Hui Judy. 2008. "Missionary." *Aether: The Journal of Media Ethnography* 3: 58–83.

———. 2009. "Contemporary Korean/American Evangelical Missions: Politics of Space, Gender, and Difference." PhD dissertation, Department of Geography, University of California, Berkeley.

———. 2010a. "Neither Friends nor Foes: Thoughts on Ethnographic Distance." *Geoforum* 41 (1): 11–14.

———. 2010b. "Reaching the Unreached in the 10/40 Window: The Missionary Geoscience of Race, Difference and Distance." In *Mapping the End Times: American Evangelical Geopolitics and Apocalyptic Visions,* edited by J. Dittmer and T. Sturm, 183–207. Hampshire, UK: Ashgate Publishing.

———. 2011. "'If You Don't Work, You Don't Eat': Evangelizing Development in Africa." In *New Millennium South Korea: Neoliberal Capitalism and Transnational Movement,* edited by J. Song, 142–58. London: Routledge.

———. N.d. "Our Past, Your Future: Evangelical Missionaries and Memories of Development." In *Territories of Poverty,* edited by A. Roy and E. Shaw. Athens, GA: University of Georgia Press.

Handman, Courtney. 2010. "Events of Translation: Intertextuality and Christian Ethnotheologies of Change among Guhu-Samane, Papua New Guinea." *American Anthropologist* 112 (4): 576–88.

Hanks, William. 1990. *Referential Practice: Language and Lived Space among the Maya.* Chicago: University of Chicago Press.

Han'gyŏre. 2004. "Yi Myŏng-bak Sijang 'Hananim kke Sŏul ponghŏn' parŏn murŭi" (Public criticism of Mayor Lee Myung-bak's remark, "Dedicate Seoul to God"). July 2. http://legacy.www.hani.co.kr/section-005000000/2004/07/005000000200407021018001.html.

Harkness, Nicholas. 2010. "Words in Motion and the Semiotics of the Unseen in Two Korean Churches." *Language & Communication* 30 (2): 139–58.

———. 2011. "Culture and Interdiscursivity in Korean Fricative Voice Gestures." *Journal of Linguistic Anthropology* 21 (1): 99–123.

———. 2012. "Vowel Harmony Redux: Correct Sounds, English Loan Words, and the Sociocultural Life of a Phonological Structure." *Korean Journal of Sociolinguistics* 16 (3): 358–81.

———. 2013. "Softer Soju in South Korea." *Anthropological Theory* 13 (1/2): 12–30.

———. N.d. "Intimacy, Status, and the Contradictions of Christian Kinship in South Korea." Paper presented at the Annual Meeting of the American Anthropological Association, Montreal, Canada, November 17, 2011.

Harvey, Youngsook. 1980. "Possession Sickness and Women Shamans in Korea." In *Unspoken Worlds: Women's Religious Lives in Non-Western Cultures,* edited by N.A. Falk and R.M. Gross, 41–52. New York: Harper & Row.

Hastings, Adi, and Paul Manning. 2004. "Introduction: Acts of Alterity." *Language & Communication* 24 (4): 291–311.

Helmreich, Stefan. 2007. "An Anthropologist Underwater: Immersive Soundscapes, Submarine Cyborgs, and Transductive Ethnography." *American Ethnologist* 34 (2): 621–41.

Henry, Todd. 2005. "Sanitizing Empire: Japanese Articulations of Korean Otherness and the Construction of Early Colonial Seoul, 1905–1919." *Journal of Asian Studies* 64: 639–75.

Hill, Jane. 1995. "The Voices of Don Gabriel: Responsibility and Self in a Modern Mexicano Narrative." In *The Dialogic Emergence of Culture,* edited by D. Tedlock and B. Mannheim, 97–147. Urbana: University of Illinois Press.

———. 2001. "Mock Spanish, Covert Racisms and the (Leaky) Boundary between Public and Private Spheres." In *Languages and Publics: The Making of Authority,* edited by S. Gal and K. Woolard, 83–102. Manchester, UK: St. Jerome's Press.

Hirschkind, Charles. 2006. *The Ethical Soundscape: Cassette Sermons and Islamic Counterpublics.* New York: Columbia University Press.

Howard, Keith. 1990. *Bands, Songs, and Shamanistic Rituals: Folk Music in Korean Society.* Seoul: Royal Asiatic Society.

———. 1999. "Minyo in Korea: Songs of the People and Songs for the People." *Asian Music* 30 (2): 1–37.

Hulbert, Homer Bezaleel. 1909. *The Passing of Korea.* New York: Doubleday.

Hwang, Okon. 2006. "The Ascent and Politicization of Pop Music in Korea: From the 1960s to the 1980s." In *Korean Pop Music: Riding the Wave,* edited by K. Howard, 34–47. Folkestone, Kent: Global Oriental.

———. 2009. *Western Art Music in South Korea : Everyday Experience and Cultural Critique.* Saarbrücken, Germany: VDM Verlag Dr. Müller.

Hymes, Dell. 1974. *Foundations in Sociolinguistics: An Ethnographic Approach.* Philadelphia: University of Pennsylvania Press.

Ikegami, Yoshihiko. 2008. "The Heart: What It Means to the Japanese Speakers." In *Culture, Body, and Language: Conceptualizations of Internal Body Organs across Cultures and Languages,* edited by F. Sharifian, R. Dirven, N. Yu, and S. Niemeier, 169–90. Berlin: Mouton de Gruyter.

Inoue, Miyako. 2006. *Vicarious Language: Gender and Linguistic Modernity in Japan.* Berkeley: University of California Press.

Irvine, Judith. 1974. "Strategies of Status Manipulation in Wolof Greetings." In *Explorations in the Ethnography of Speaking,* edited by R. Bauman and J. Sherzer, 167–91. New York: Cambridge University Press.

———. 1990. "Registering Affect: Heteroglossia in the Linguistic Expression of Emotion." In *Language and the Politics of Emotion,* edited by C.A. Lutz and L. Abu-Lughod, 126–61. Cambridge: Cambridge University Press.

———. 2001. "'Style' as Distinctiveness: The Culture and Ideology of Linguistic Differentiation." In *Style and Sociolinguistic Variation,* edited by P. Eckert and J. Rickford, 21–43. Cambridge: Cambridge University Press.

Jager, Sheila Miyoshi. 2003. *Narratives of Nation Building in Korea: A Genealogy of Patriotism.* Armonk, NY: M.E. Sharpe.

Jakobson, Roman. 1960. "Closing Statement: Linguistics and Poetics." In *Style in Language,* edited by T.A. Sebeok, 350–77. Cambridge, MA: MIT Press.

Jakobson, Roman, and Linda R. Waugh. (1979) 2002. *The Sound Shape of Language.* Berlin: Mouton de Gruyter.

Janelli, Roger, and Dawnhee Yim Janelli. 1982. *Ancestor Worship and Korean Society.* Stanford, CA: Stanford University Press.

Janelli, Roger, and Dawnhee Yim. 1993. *Making Capitalism: The Social and Cultural Construction of a South Korean Conglomerate.* Stanford: Stanford University Press.

Joo, Sung-hee. 1997. "A Study of an Early Korean Hymnal Published by Rev. Horace G. Underwood in 1894." *Chongshin Review* 1: 344–87.

Joseph, John, and Talbot Taylor. 1990. *Ideologies of Language*. London: Routledge.

Kang, Jiyeon. 2009. "Netizenship Politics: Youth, Anti-Americanism, and Rhetorical Agency in South Korea's 2002 Candlelight Vigils." PhD dissertation, Department of Communications, University of Illinois.

Kap, Ki-Hyuk, and Sidney D. Gamble. 1975. *The Changing Korean Village*. Seoul: Royal Asiatic Society.

Keane, Webb. 1991. "Delegated Voice: Ritual Speech, Risk, and the Making of Marriage Alliances in Anakalang." *American Ethnologist* 18 (2): 311–30.

———. 1997. *Signs of Recognition: Powers and Hazards of Representation in an Indonesian Society*. Berkeley: University of California Press.

———. 2000. "Voice." *Journal of Linguistic Anthropology* 9 (1–2): 271–73.

———. 2002. "Sincerity, 'Modernity,' and the Protestants." *Cultural Anthropology* 17 (1): 65–92.

———. 2003. "Semiotics and the Social Analysis of Material Things." *Language & Communciation* 23 (3–4): 409–25.

———. 2007. *Christian Moderns: Freedom and Fetish in the Mission Encounter*. Berkeley: University of California Press.

———. 2011. "Indexing Voice: A Morality Tale." *Journal of Linguistic Anthropology* 21 (2): 166–78.

Kendall, Laurel. 1977. "Mugam: The Dance in Shaman's Clothing." *Korea Journal* 17 (12): 38–44.

———. 1985. *Shamans, Housewives and Other Restless Spirits: Women in Korean Ritual Life*. Honolulu: University of Hawai'i Press.

———. 1996. *Getting Married in Korea: Of Gender, Morality, and Modernity*. Berkeley: University of California Press.

———. 2009. *Shamans, Nostalgias, and the IMF: Korean Popular Religion in Motion*. Honolulu: University of Hawai'i Press.

Kim, Eleana J. 2010. *Adopted Territory: Transnational Korean Adoptees and the Politics of Belonging*. Durham, NC: Duke University Press.

Kim, Hŭng-gyu. 1997. *Understanding Korean Literature*. Translated by R. Fouser. Armonk, NY: M. E. Sharpe.

Kim, Joo-Hee. 1981. "P'umasi: Patterns of Interpersonal Relationships in a Korean Village." PhD dissertation, Department of Anthropology, Northwestern University.

———. 1992. *P'umasi wa chŏng*. Seoul: Chimmundang.

Kim, Kuentae, and Hyunjoon Park. 2010. "Family Succession through Adoption in the Chosun Dynasty." *The History of the Family* 15 (4): 443-452.

Kim, Kwang-Ok. 1988. "A Study on the Political Manipulation of Elite Culture: Confucian Culture in Local Level Politics." *Korea Journal* 28 (11): 4–16.

———. 1990. "Religion: Experience or Belief System? A Korean Case." In *Society and Culture in the Pacific Region*, edited by S. B. Han and K.-O. Kim, 237–61. Seoul: Seoul National University Press.

———. 1993. "The Religious Life of the Urban Middle Class." *Korea Journal* 33 (4): 5–33.

———. 1996. "The Reproduction of Confucian Culture in Contemporary Korea: An Anthropological Study." In *Confucian Traditions in East Asian*

Modernity: Moral Education and Economic Culture in Japan and the Four Mini-Dragons, edited by W.-M. Tu, 202–227 Cambridge, MA: Harvard University Press.

———. 1998. "The Communal Ideology and Its Reality: With Reference to the Emergence of Neo-Tribalism." *Korea Journal* 38 (3): 5–44.

Kim, Myŏng-gon. 2009. "Myŏngch'angdŭl ŭn chŏngmal mok esŏ p'i rŭl t'ohaessŭlkka?" (Did p'ansori masters really vomit blood from their throats?) May 11. http://dreamnet21.tistory.com/tag/%EB%98%A5%EB%AC%BC.

Kim, Shin K. 2008. "An Antiseptic Religion: Discovering a Hybridity on the Flux of Hygeine and Christianity." *Journal of Religion and Health* 47 (2): 253–62.

Kim, Song-Chul. 1998. "Kinship in Contemporary Korea: Normative Model versus Practice." *Korea Journal* 38 (3): 128–47.

Kim, Wonil. 2006. "Minjung Theology's Biblical Hermeneutics: An Examination of Minjung Theology's Appropriation of the Exodus Account." In *Christianity in Korea,* edited by R. E. Buswell and T. S. Lee, 221–37. Honolulu: University of Hawai'i Press.

Kim, Yang-kon. 1967. "Farmers Music and Dance." *Korea Journal* 7: 4–29.

Kim, Yŏng-mi. 2010. *P'ŭrimadonna Kim Yŏng-mi ch'ŏrŏm: Chejadŭl i kajang tamkko sip'ŏ hanŭn yesulga* (Just like prima donna Kim Yŏng-mi: The artist whom disciples most want to resemble). Seoul: Pijŏn kwa Lidŏsip.

King, Ross. 2004. "Western Protestant Missionaries and the Origins of Korean Language Modernization." *Journal of International and Area Studies* 11 (3): 7–38.

———. 2006. "Korean Kinship Terminology." In *Korean Language in Culture and Society,* edited by H.-m. Sohn, 101–7. Honolulu: University of Hawai'i Press.

———. 2010. "Dialect, Orthography, and Regional Identity: P'yongan Christians, Korean Spelling Reform, and Orthographic Fundamentalism." In *The Northern Region of Korea: History, Identity, and Culture,* edited by S.-J. Kim. Seattle: Center for Korean Studies, University of Washington.

Kockelman, Paul. 2005. "The Semiotic Stance." *Semiotica* 157: 233–304.

———. 2011. "A Mayan Ontology of Poultry: Selfhood, Affect, Animals, and Ethnography." *Language in Society* 40 (4): 427–54.

Koestenbaum, Wayne. 1993. *The Queen's Throat: Opera, Homosexuality, and the Mystery of Desire*. New York: Poseidon Press.

Koo, Hagen. 2007. "The Changing Faces of Inequality in South Korea in the Age of Globalization." *Korean Studies* 31 (1): 1–18.

Korean Bible Society. 1977. *Kongdong pŏnyŏk sŏngsŏ* (Common Translation Bible). Seoul: Korean Bible Society.

———. 1987. *Sŏnggyŏng chŏnsŏ: Kaeyŏk han'gŭlp'an* (Complete Bible: Revised Han'gŭl Edition). Seoul: Korean Bible Soceity.

———. 1998. *Kaeyŏk kaejŏng* (New Revised Korean Version). Seoul: Korean Bible Society.

Koh, Il-gwan. 2009. "Ch'oe Chin: 'MB, ŏnŏ ŭi chŏlcheryŏk parhwi haeya'" (Professor Ch'oe Chin: "MB, you must show the power of restraint in language"). *Han'guk Ilbo,* February 12. http://news.hankooki.com/lpage/politics/200902/h2009021216451421060.htm.

Kroskrity, Paul, ed. 2000. *Regimes of Language: Ideologies, Polities, and Identities*. Santa Fe, NM: School of American Research Press.

Kungmin Ilbo. 2009. "T'enŏ Yi Sŏng-ŭn Met'ŭ Op'era K'ongk'urŭ kongdong usŭng" (Tenor Yi Sŏng-ŭn is the co-winner of the Met Opera competition). February 24. http://news.kukinews.com/article/view.asp?page=1&gCode=cul&arcid=0921202820.

Kunreuther, Laura. 2006. "Technologies of the Voice: FM Radio, Telephone, and the Nepali Diaspora in Kathmandu." *Cultural Anthropology* 21(3): 323–353.

———. 2009. "Between Love and Property: Voice, Sentiment, and Subjectivity in the Reform of Daughter's Inheritance in Nepal." *American Ethnologist* 36 (3): 545–562.

———. 2010. "Transparent Media: Radio, Voice, and Ideologies of Directness in Post-Democratic Nepal." *Journal of Linguistic Anthropology* 20 (2): 334–351.

Kweon, Sug-In. 1998. "The Extended Family in Contemporary Korea: Changing Patterns of Co-Residence." *Korea Journal* 38 (3): 178–209.

Kyoyuk T'onggye Sŏbisŭ (Korean Education Statistics Services). 2009. "Ŭmak kyeyŏl chaejŏk haksaengsu" (Number of students enrolled in postsecondary departments of music). Seoul: Han'guk Kyoyuk Kaebalwŏn (Korea Education Development Institute). http://std.kedi.re.kr, accessed July 1, 2009.

Ladefoged, Peter. 2006. *A Course in Phonetics*. 5th ed. Boston: Thomas Wadsworth.

Lampman, Jane. 2007. "How Korea Embraced Christianity." March 7. www.csmonitor.com/2007/0307/p14s01-lire.html.

Latour, Bruno. (1991) 1993. *We Have Never Been Modern*. Translated by C. Porter. Cambridge, MA: Harvard University Press.

Laukkanen, Anne-Maria, Eva Björkner, and Johan Sundberg. 2006. "Throaty Voice Quality: Subglottal Pressure, Voice Source, and Formant Characteristics." *Journal of Voice* 20 (1): 25–37.

Laver, John. 1980. *The Phonetic Description of Voice Quality*. Cambridge: Cambridge University Press.

Ledyard, Gari. (1965) 1998. *The Korean Language Reform of 1446*. Seoul: Singu Munhwasa.

———. 2006. "Kollumba Kang Wansuk, an Early Catholic Activist and Martyr." In *Christianity in Korea*, edited by R. E. Buswell and T. S. Lee, 38–71. Honolulu: University of Hawai'i Press.

Lee, Benjamin. 1997. *Talking Heads: Language, Metalanguage, and the Semiotics of Subjectivity*. Durham, NC: Duke University Press.

Lee, Byungwon. 1997. *Styles and Esthetics in Korean Traditional Music*. Seoul: National Center for Korean Traditional Performing Arts, Ministry of Culture and Sports.

Lee, Hyun Song. 1996. "Change in Funeral Customs in Contemporary Korea." *Korea Journal* 36 (2): 49–60.

Lee, Jonghyun. 2009. "Shamanism and Its Emancipatory Power for Korean Women." *Affilia: Journal of Women and Social Work* 24 (2): 186–98.

Lee, Kwang-kyu. 1975. *Kinship System in Korea*. New Haven, CT: Human Relations Area Files.

Lee, Namhee. 2007. *The Making of Minjung: Democracy and the Politics of Representation in South Korea.* Ithica, NY: Cornell University Press.

Lee, Soo-Won. 1991. "The Cheong Space: A Zone of Non-Exchange in Korean Human Relationships." In *The Psychology of the Korean People: Individualism and Collectivism,* edited by G. Yoon and S.-C. C. Choi, 85–99. Seoul: Donga Publishing Corporation.

Lee, Timothy S. 2006. "Beleaguered Success: Korean Evangelicalism in the Last Decade of the Twentieth Century." In *Christianity in Korea,* edited by R. E. Buswell and T. S. Lee, 330–50. Honolulu: University of Hawai'i Press.

———. 2010. *Born Again: Evangelicalism in Korea.* Honolulu: University of Hawai'i Press.

Lee, Yu-sŏn. 1988. *Kidokkyo Eumaksa* (A history of church music). Seoul: Kidokkyo Munsa.

Lemon, Alaina. 2013. "Touching the Gap: Social Qualia and Cold War Contact." *Anthropological Theory* 13 (1/2): 67–88.

Lester, Rebecca. 2005. *Jesus in Our Wombs: Embodying Modernity in a Mexican Convent.* Berkeley: University of California Press.

Lie, John. 2000. *Han Unbound: The Political Economy of South Korea.* Stanford, CA: Stanford University Press.

Ling, Stuart. 1952. "Singing in Korea." *Music Educators Journal* 39 (2): 24–26.

Lo, Adrienne, Nancy Abelmann, Soo Ah Kwon, and Sumie Okazaki, eds. 2014. *South Korea's Education Exodus: The Life and Times of Early Study Abroad.* Seattle: Center for Korea Studies, University of Washington.

Lock, Margaret, and Judith Farquhar, eds. 2007. *Beyond the Body Proper: Reading the Anthropology of Material Life.* Durham, NC: Duke University Press.

Lucier, Alvin. (1970) 1981. *I Am Sitting in a Room: For Voice and Electromagnetic Tape.* Sound recording. New York: Lovely Music/Vital Records.

Luhrmann, Tanya. 2012. *When God Talks Back: Understanding the American Evangelical Relationship with God.* New York: Alfred A. Knopf.

Lutz, Catherine A. 1986. "The Anthropology of Emotions." *Annual Review of Anthropology* 15: 405–36.

———. 1988. *Unnatural Emotions: Everyday Sentiments on a Micronesian Atoll and Their Challenge to Western Theory.* Chicago: University of Chicago Press.

Lutz, Catherine A., and Lila Abu-Lughod, eds. 1990. *Langauge and the Politics of Emotion.* Cambridge: Cambridge University Press.

Manning, Paul. 2012. *The Semiotics of Drink and Drinking.* London: Continuum.

Martin, Sameul. 1964. "Speech Levels in Japan and Korea." In *Language in Culture and Society,* edited by D. Hymes, 407–15. New York: Harper & Row.

Mazzarella, William. 2009. "Affect: What Is It Good For?" In *Enchantments of Modernity: Empire, Nation, Globalization,* edited by S. Dube, 291–309. New Delhi: Routledge.

Mead, George Herbert. 1934. *Mind, Self, and Society from the Standpoint of a Social Behaviorist.* Chicago: University of Chicago.

Mehan, Hugh. 1996. "The Construction of an LD Student: A Case Study in the Politics of Representation." In *Natural Histories of Discourse,* edited by M. Silverstein and G. Urban, 253–76. Chicago: University of Chicago Press.

Mertz, Elizabeth. 1996. "Recontextualization as Socialization: Text and Pragmatics in the Law School Classroom." In *Natural Histories of Discourse,* edited by M. Silverstein and G. Urban, 229–52. Chicago: University of Chicago Press.

Miller, Richard. 1986. *The Structure of Singing: System and Art in Vocal Technique.* New York: Schirmer.

Min, In-Gi. 2001. "The Development of Korean Choral Music." PhD dissertation, Department of Music, University of Southern California.

Monson, Ingrid. 1996. *Saying Something: Jazz Improvization and Interaction.* Chicago: University of Chicago Press.

———. 2008. "Hearing, Seeing, and Perceptual Agency." *Critical Inquiry* 34 (Supp. 2): S36–S58.

Moon, Chung-in and Byung-joon Jun. 2011. "Modernization Strategy: Ideas and Influences." In *The Park Chung Hee Era: The Transformation of South Korea,* edited by B.-K. Kim and E. Vogel, 115–139. Cambridge, MA: Harvard University Press.

Moon, Katherine H. S. 1997. *Sex among Allies: Military Prostitution in U.S.-Korea Relations.* New York: Columbia University Press.

Moon, Okpyo. 1998. "Ancestors Becoming Children of God: Ritual Clashes between Confucian Tradition and Christianity in Contemporary Korea." *Korea Journal* 38 (3): 148–77.

Moon, Seungsook. 2005. *Militarized Modernity and Gendered Citizenship in South Korea.* Durham, NC: Duke University Press.

Munn, Nancy. 1986. *The Fame of Gawa: A Symbolic Study of Value Transformation in a Massim Society (Papua New Guinea).* Durham, NC: Duke University Press.

———. 2013. "The Decline and Fall of Richmond Hill: Commodification and Place-Change in Late 18th—Early 19th-Century New York." *Anthropological Theory* 13 (1/2): 137–68.

Nakassis, Constantine V. 2012. "Brand, Citationality, Performativity." *American Anthropologist* 114 (4): 624–38.

Nelson, Laura. 2000. *Measured Excess: Status, Gender, and Consumer Nationalism in South Korea.* New York: Columbia University Press.

Noah, Max. 1949. "Mission to Korea." *Music Educators Journal* 35 (6): 14–16.

Oak, Sung-Deuk. 2010. "Healing and Exorcism: Christian Encounters with Shamanism in Early Modern Korea." *Asian Ethnology* 69 (1): 95–128.

———. 2012. "Competing Chinese Names for God: The Chinese Term Question and Its Influence upon Korea." *Journal of Korean Religions* 3 (2): 1–27.

Occhi, Debra J. 2008. "How to Have a Heart in Japanese." In *Culture, Body, and Language: Conceptualizations of Internal Body Organs across Cultures and Languages,* edited by F. Sharifian, R. Dirven, N. Yu, and S. Niemeier, 191–212. Berlin: Mouton de Gruyter.

Olwage, Grant. 2004. "The Class and Colour of Tone: An Essay on the Social History of Vocal Timbre." *Ethnomusicology Forum* 13 (2): 203–26.

Oppenheim, Robert. 2008. *Kyŏngju Things: Assembling Place.* Ann Arbor: University of Michigan Press.

Osmer, Richard. 2005. *The Teaching Ministry of Congregations.* Louisville, KY: Westminster John Knox Press.

Pae, Ŭl-sŏn. 2000. "Arŭmdaun saram ŭn mŏmun chari to arŭmdapsŭmnida— Hwajangsil munhwa kaehyŏk haja" (The places where beautiful people stay are also beautiful—Let's reform the toilet culture). May 22. www.ohmynews.com/NWS_Web/view/at_pg.aspx?CNTN_CD = A0000008340.

Pak, T'ae-myŏng, dir. 2008. *Sori rŭl ŏtta, tŭgŭm* (Receiving the sound, *Tŭgŭm*). Kwangju Pangsong (Kwangju Broadcasting Company), South Korea.

Palais, James. 1996. *Confucian Statecraft and Korean Institutions: Yu Hyŏngwŏn and the Late Chosŏn Dynasty.* Seattle: University of Washington Press.

Park, Chan E. 2003. *Voices from the Straw Mat: Toward and Ethnography of Korean Story Singing.* Honolulu: University of Hawai'i Press.

Park, Chang-Won. 2005. "Korea." In *The Encyclopedia of Cremation,* edited by D. Davies and L. Mates. Aldershot, Hants, UK: Ashgate Publishing.

Park, Chung-shin. 2003. *Protestantism and Politics in Korea.* Seattle: University of Washington Press.

Park, Joseph Sung-Yul. 2009. *The Local Construction of a Global Language: Ideologies of English in South Korea.* Berlin: Mouton de Gruyter.

Park, Soon-Ham. 1975. "On Special Uses of Kinship Terms in Korea." *Korea Journal* 15 (5): 4–8.

Park, Yong-Shin. 2007. "The Church as a Public Space: Resources, Practices, and Communicative Culture in Korea." *International Journal of Korean History* 11: 61–81.

Park, Yu-mi, and Jee-ho Yoo. 2009. "Woman on 'PD Diary' Did Not Die of Mad Cow Disease." April 7. http://joongangdaily.joins.com/article/view.asp?aid = 2903230.

Parmentier, Richard. 1994. *Signs in Society: Studies in Semiotic Anthropology.* Bloomington: Indiana University Press.

Peirce, Charles S. 1997. *The Collected Papers of Charles Sanders Peirce.* Cambridge, MA: Harvard University Press. Electronic ed., Charlottesville, VA: InteLex Past Masters.

Pickering, Julie. 1994. "Kim Sohŭi and Pak Tongjin: P'ansori as a Way of Life." *Koreana* 8 (2): 58–61.

Pihl, Marshall. 1994. *The Korean Singer of Tales.* Cambridge, MA: Harvard University and the Harvard Yenching Institute.

Pilzer, Joshua. 2012. *Hearts of Pine: Songs in the Lives of Three Survivors of the Japanese "Comfort Women."* New York: Oxford University Press.

Poedjosoedarmo, Gloria R. 1993. "Uses of Phonation Type in Javanese." In *Tonality in Austronesian Languages,* edited by J. Edmondson and K. Gregerson, 123–32. Honolulu: University of Hawai'i Press.

Poizat, Michel. (1986) 1992. *The Angel's Cry: Beyond the Pleasure Principle in Opera.* Translated by A. Denner. Ithica, NY: Cornell University Press.

Porkert, Manfred. 1974. *The Theoretical Foundations of Chinese Medicine: Systems of Correspondence.* Cambridge, MA: MIT Press.

Presbyterian Church (USA). 2001. *Come, Let Us Worship: The Korean-English Presbyterian Hymnal and Service Book (Ch'ansongga yebae: Miguk Changnogyo Han-Yŏng ch'ansongga)*. Louisville, KY: Geneva Press.

Reuters. 2008. "Anti-U.S. Beef Protest Draws 100, 000 S. Koreans." May 31. www.reuters.com/article/topNews/idUSSEO21734120080531.

Robbins, Joel. 2004. *Becoming Sinners: Christianity and Moral Torment in a Papua New Guinea Society*. Berkeley: University of California Press.

———. 2007. "Continuity Thinking and the Problem of Christian Culture: Belief, Time, and the Anthropology of Christianity." *Current Anthropology* 48 (1): 5–38.

Rogaski, Ruth. 2004. *Hygienic Modernity: Meanings of Health and Disease in Treaty-Port China*. Berkeley: University of California Press.

Rosaldo, Michelle. 1980. *Knowledge and Passion: Ilongot Notions of Self and Social Life*. Cambridge: Cambridge University Press.

Ross, John. 1877a. *Corean Primer: Being Lessons in Corean on All Ordinary Subjects*. Transliterated on the Principles of the "Mandarin Primer," by the same author. Shanghai: American Presbyterian Mission Press.

———. (1877b) 1982. "Obstacles to the Gospel in China" (originally published in the United Presbyterian Missionary Record). In *Chon Rosŭ: Han'guk ŭi ch'ŏt sŏn'gyosa* (John Ross: Korea's first missionary), edited by J.H. Grayson, 166–73. Taegu: Kyemyŏng University Press.

———. 1883. "Corean New Testament." *Chinese Recorder and Missionary Journal* 14 (6): 491–97. Shanghai: American Presbyterian Mission Press.

Rutt, Richard, and Keith Pratt. 1999. *Korea: A Historical and Cultural Dictionary*. Richmond, Surrey, UK: Curzon Press.

Sahlins, Marshall. 2004. "Culture and Agency in History." In *Apologies to Thucydides: Understanding History as Culture and Vice Versa*, 125–94. Chicago: University of Chicago Press.

Samuels, David. 2004. *Putting a Song on Top of It: Expression and Identity on the San Carlos Apache Reservation*. Tuscon: University of Arizona Press.

Sapir, Edward. 1925. "Sound Patterns in Language." *Language* 1 (2): 37–51.

———. 1927. "Speech as Personality Trait." *American Journal of Sociology* 32 (6): 892–905.

Scheid, Volker. 2002. *Chinese Medicine in Contemporary China: Plurality and Synthesis*. Durham, NC: Duke University Press.

Schieffelin, Bambi. 2007. "Found in Translating: Reflexive Language across Time and Texts." In *Consequences of Contact: Language Ideologies and Sociocultural Transformations in Pacific Societies,* edited by M. Makihara and B. Schieffelin, 140–65. New York: Oxford University Press.

Schieffelin, Bambi, Kathryn Woolard, and Paul Kroskrity, eds. 1998. *Language Ideologies: Practice and Theory*. New York: Oxford University Press.

Schmid, Andre. 2002. *Korea between Empires, 1895–1919*. New York: Columbia University Press.

Seeger, Anthony. 2004. *Why Suyá Sing: A Musical Anthropology of an Amazonian People*. Urbana: University of Illinois Press.

Seo Dong-shin. 2007. "Expensive Vienna Concert Frustrates Fans." *Han'guk Ilbo*, July 22. www.koreatimes.co.kr/www/news/art/2011/08/143_6918.html.

Seremetakis, C. Nadia. 1991. *The Last Word: Women, Death, and Divination in Inner Mani.* Chicago: University of Chicago Press.

Shim, Joon Hee, ed. 2004. *Pansori: Commemorating Designation as a Masterpiece of Oral Tradition and Intangible Heritage of Humanity by UNESCO in 2003.* Seoul: National Center for Korean Traditional Performing Arts.

Shin, Gi-Wook. 2006. *Ethnic Nationalism in Korea: Genealogy, Politics, and Legacy.* Stanford, CA: Stanford University Press.

Shin, Youngok. 2007. *Hananim i sarang hasinŭn segye ŭi p'ŭrima donna: Sin Yŏng-ok ŭi ch'ansong* (The praise of Shin Youngok: The prima donna of the world whom God loves). Seoul: Saengmyŏng ŭi Malssŭmsa.

Shun, Kwong Lo. 2010. "Mencius." *Stanford Encyclopedia of Philosophy.* Edited by Edward N. Zalta. Stanford, CA: Stanford University. http://plato.stanford.edu/archives/win2010/entries/mencius/, accessed March 1, 2010.

Sicoli, Mark. 2010. "Shifting Voices with Participant Roles: Voice Qualities and Speech Registers in Mesoamerica." *Language in Society* 39: 521–53.

Silva, David. 2008. "Missionary Contributions toward the Revaluation of Hangeul in Late Nineteenth-Century Korea." *International Journal of the Sociology of Language* 192: 57–74.

Silverstein, Michael. 1976. "Shifters, Linguistic Categories, and Cultural Description." In *Meaning in Anthropology,* edited by K. Basso and K. Selby, 11–55. Albuquerque: School of American Research, University of New Mexico Press.

———. 1979. "Language Structure and Linguistic Ideology." In *The Elements: A Parasession on Linguistic Units and Levels,* edited by P. Cline, W. Hanks, and C. Hofbauer, 193–247. Chicago: Chicago Linguistic Society.

———. 1985. "Language and the Culture of Gender: At the Intersection of Structure, Usage, and Ideology." In *Semiotic Mediation: Sociocultural and Psychological Perspectives,* edited by Elizabeth Mertz and Richard A. Parmentier, 219–59. Orlando, FL: Academic Press.

———. 1988. "De-Voice of Authority." Paper presented at the Annual meeting of the American Anthropological Association, Phoenix, AZ.

———. 1993. "Metapragmatic Discourse and Metapragmatic Function." In *Reflexive Language: Reported Speech and Metapragmatic Function,* edited by J. Lucy, 33–58. Cambridge: Cambridge University Press.

———. 1994. "Relative Motivation in Denotational and Indexical Sound Symbolism of Wasco-Wishram Chinookan." In *Sound Symbolism,* edited by L. Hinton, J. Nicholas, and J. Ohala, 40–60. Cambridge: Cambridge University Press.

———. 1996. "The Secret Life of Texts." In *Natural Histories of Discourse,* edited by M. Silverstein and G. Urban, 81–105. Chicago: University of Chicago Press.

———. 2000. "Whorfianism and the Linguistic Imagination of Nationality." In *Regimes of Language: Ideologies, Polities, and Identities,* edited by P. Kroskrity, 85–138. Santa Fe, NM: School of American Research Press.

———. 2003. "Indexical Order and the Dialectics of Sociolinguistic Life." *Language & Communication* 23 (3–4): 193–229.

———. 2004. "'Cultural' Concepts and the Language-Culture Nexus." *Current Anthropology* 45 (5): 621–52.

———. 2005. "Axes of Evals: Token versus Type Interdiscursivity." *Journal of Linguistic Anthropology* 15 (1): 6–22.

———. 2006. "Old Wine, New Ethnographic Lexicography." *Annual Review of Anthropology* 25: 481–96.

Silverstein, Michael, and Greg Urban. 1996. *Natural Histories of Discourse.* Chicago: University of Chicago Press.

Sin, Yong-ha. 2003. *Essays in Korean Social History.* Seoul: Jisik-sanup.

Société des missions étrangéres de Paris. 1880. *Dictionnaire coréen-français.* Yokohama: C. Lévy.

Son, Min Jung. 2004. "The Politics of the Traditional Korean Popular Song Style T'ŭrot'ŭ." PhD dissertation, Department of Music, University of Texas.

———. 2006. "Regulating and Negotiating in T'ŭrot'ŭ, a Korean Popular Song Style." *Asian Music* 37 (1): 51–74.

Song, Bang-Song. 2001. "The Historical Development of Korean Folk Music." In *Contemporary Directions: Korean Folk Music Engaging the Twentieth Century and Beyond,* edited by N. Hesselink. Berkeley: Institute of East Asian Studies, University of California.

Song, Jesook. 2009. *South Koreans in the Debt Crisis: The Creation of a Neo-liberal Welfare Society.* Durham, NC: Duke University Press.

Stark, James. 2003. *Bel Canto: A History of Vocal Pedagogy.* Toronto: University of Toronto Press.

Stasch, Rupert. 2011. "Textual Iconicity and the Primitivist Cosmos: Chronotopes of Desire in Travel Writing about Korowai of West Papua." *Journal of Linguistic Anthropology* 21 (1): 1–21.

Sterne, Jonathan. 2003. *The Audible Past: Cultural Origins of Sound Reproduction.* Durham, NC: Duke University Press.

Suh, Kwang-Sun David. 1983. "A Biographical Sketch of an Asian Theological Consultation." In *Minjung Theology: People as the Subjects of History,* edited by the Commission on Theological Concerns of the Christian Conference of Asia, 15–38. Maryknoll, NY: Orbis Books.

Sundberg, Johan. 1972. "Production and Function of the Singing Formant." In *Report of the 11th Congress of the International Musicological Society,* vol. 2, edited by H. Glahn, S. Sorensen, and S. Ryom, 679–88. Copenhagen: Edition Wilhelm Hansen.

———. 1974. "Articulatory Interpretation of the 'Singing Formant.'" *Journal of the Acoustical Society of America* 55 (4): 838–44.

———. 1977. "Acoustics of the Singing Voice." *Scientific American* 236 (3): 82–100.

———. 1987. *The Science of the Singing Voice.* Dekalb: Northern Illinois University Press.

Tambiah, Stanley. 1985. *Culture, Thought, and Social Action: An Anthropological Perspective.* Cambridge, MA: Harvard University Press.

Thompson, Emily. 2004. *The Soundscape of Modernity: Architectural Acoustics and the Culture of Listening in America, 1900–1933.* Cambridge, MA: MIT Press.

Titon, Jeff Todd. 1988. *Powerhouse for God : Speech, Chant, and Song in an Appalachian Baptist Church.* Austin: University of Texas Press.

Trilling, Lionel. 1972. *Sincerity and Authenticity*. Cambridge, MA: Harvard University Press.

Trotta, Liz. 1998. "Why This Asian Opera Star Won't Become Entangled in Butterfly's Net." *Insight on the News* 14 (3, January 26).

Turino, Thomas. 1999. "Signs of Imagination, Identity, and Experience: A Peircean Semiotic Theory for Music." *Ethnomusicology* 43 (2): 221–55.

———. 2008. *Music as Social Life: The Politics of Participation*. Chicago: University of Chicago Press.

Um, Hae-kyung. 2007. "Professional Music: Vocal." In *Music of Korea,* edited by B. Lee and Y.-S. Lee, 104–26. Korean Musicology series 1. Seoul: National Center for Korean Traditional Performing Arts.

Urban, Greg. 1988. "Ritual Wailing in Amerindian Brazil." *American Anthropologist* 90 (2): 385–400.

———. 1991. *A Discourse-Centered Approach to Culture: Native South American Myths and Rituals*. Austin: University of Texas Press.

U.S. Department of Education, Institute of Education Sciences, National Center for Education Statistics. 2007. 2006–7 Integrated Postsecondary Education Data System (IPEDS). Aggregations by field of study derived from the Classification of Instructional Programs, developed by the National Center for Education Statistics, Washington DC. (Table prepared in June 2008.)

Vološinov, Valentin. 1986. *Marxism and the Philosophy of Language*. Translated by L. Matejka and I.R. Titunik. Cambridge, MA: Harvard University Press.

van der Veer, Peter, ed. 1996. *Conversion to Modernities: The Globalization of Christianity*. New York: Routledge.

———. 2001. *Imperial Encounters: Religion and Modernity in India and Britain*. Princeton, NJ: Princeton University Press.

Wang, Hahn-sok et al. 2005. *Han'guk sahoe wa hoch'ingŏ* (Korean society and terms of address). Seoul: Yŏngnak.

Warner, Michael. 2002. *Publics and Counterpublics*. New York: Zone Books.

Weber, Max. (1930) 1999. *The Protestant Ethic and the Spirit of Capitalism*. Translated by T. Parsons. London: Routledge.

Weidman, Amanda. 2006. *Singing the Classical, Voicing the Modern: The Postcolonial Politics of Music in South India*. Durham, NC: Duke University Press.

———. 2010. "Sound and the City: Mimicry and Media in South India." *Journal of Linguistic Anthropology* 20 (2): 294–313.

Wells, Kenneth. 1990. *New God, New Nation: Protestants and Self-Reconstruction Nationalism in Korea, 1896–1937*. Sydney: Allen & Unwin.

———, ed. 1995. *South Korea's Minjung Movement: The Culture and Politics of Dissidence*. Honolulu: University of Hawai'i Press.

———. 2006. "In God's Image: The Christian, the Individual, and the Nation in Colonial Korea." In *The Dignity of Nations: Equality, Competition, and Honor in East Asian Nationalism,* edited by S.Y.S. Chien and J. Fitzgerald. Hong Kong: Hong Kong University Press.

Wesley, John. 1872. *The Works of the Rev. John Wesley, A.M. Sometime Fellow of Lincoln College, Oxford*. Vol. 8. London: Wesleyan Conference Office.

Whorf, Benjamin Lee. 1956. *Language, Thought, and Reality: Selected Writings of Benjamin Lee Whorf*. Cambridge, MA: MIT Press.

Wierzbicka, Anna. 1986. "Human Emotions: Universal or Culture-Specific?" *American Anthropologist* 88 (3): 584–94.

———. 1999. *Emotions across Languages and Cultures: Diversity and Universals*. Cambridge: Cambridge University Press.

Wilce, James. 2009. *Language and Emotion*. Cambridge: Cambridge Unviersity Press.

Wilf, Eitan. 2010. "Swinging within the Iron Cage: Modernity, Creativity, and Embodied Practice in American Postsecondary Jazz Education." *American Ethnologist* 37 (3): 563–82.

———. 2011. "Sincerity versus Self-Expression: Modern Creative Agency and the Materiality of Semiotic Forms." *Cultural Anthropology* 26 (3): 462–84.

———. 2012. "Rituals of Creativity: Tradition, Modernity, and the 'Acoustic Unconscious' in a U.S. Collegiate Jazz Music Program." *American Anthropologist* 114 (1): 32–44.

Willoughby, Heather. 2002. "The Sound of Han: P'ansori, Timbre, and a Korean Ethos of Suffering and Lament." PhD dissertation, Department of Ethnomusicology, Columbia University.

Woolard, Kathryn, and Bambi Schieffelin. 1994. "Language Ideology." *Annual Review of Anthropology* 23: 55–82.

World Health Organization. 2011. "Mental Health." www.who.int/mental_health/prevention/suicide/country_reports/en/index.html, accessed October 16, 2011.

Yano, Christine. 2002. *Tears of Longing: Nostalgia and the Nation in Japanese Popular Song*. Cambridge, MA: Harvard University Asia Center.

Yi, Chi-ŭn. 2007. "Yi Myŏng-bak Tangsŏnja Kangnam 'Somang Kyohoe' inmaek kŭppusang" (President Elect Lee Myung-bak "Somang Church" network emerging). *Han'gyŏre*, December 26. www.hani.co.kr/arti/politics/politics_general/259250.html.

Yi, Yu-sŏn. 1985. *Han'guk yangak paengnyŏnsa* (The 100-year history of Western music in Korea). Seoul: Ŭmak Ch'unch'usa.

Yoon, Kyung-Joo. 2004. "Korean Maum vs. English Heart and Mind: Contrastive Semantics of Cultural Concepts." In *Proceedings of the 2003 Conference of the Australian Linguistic Society*. www.als.asn.au/proceedings/als2003.html, accessed February 8, 2008.

———. 2008. "The Korean Conceptualization of Heart: An Indigenous Perspective." In *Culture, Body, and Language: Conceptualizations of Internal Body Organs across Cultures and Languages,* edited by F. Sharifian, R. Dirven, N. Yu, and S. Niemeier, 213–43. Berlin: Mouton de Gruyter.

Yoon, Paul Chong-Chul. 2005. "Christian Identity, Ethnic Identity: Music Making and Prayer Practices among 1.5- and Second-Generation Korean American Christians." PhD dissertation, Department of Music, Columbia University.

Yoshihara, Mari. 2007. *Musicians from a Different Shore: Asians and Asian Americans in Classical Music*. Philadelphia: Temple University Press.

Young, Miriama. 2006. "Latent Body—Plastic, Malleable, Inscribed: The Human Voice, the Body and the Sound of Its Transformation through Technology." *Contemporary Music Review* 25 (1/2): 81–92.

Yu, Ning. 2008. "The Chinese Heart as the Central Faculty of Cognition." In *Culture, Body, and Language: Conceptualizations of Internal Body Organs across Cultures and Languages,* edited by F. Sharifian, R. Dirven, N. Yu, and S. Niemeier, 131–68. Berlin: Mouton de Gruyter.

———. 2009. *The Chinese Heart in a Cognitive Perspective.* Berlin: Mouton de Gruyter.

Yu, Yŏng-dae. 2006. "Ch'umobijang changnye munhwa sae taean ŭro ... kongdong pisŏk e kolbun ppuryŏ sŏnggyŏngjŏk ch'inhwan'gyŏngjŏk" (Memorial grave funeral culture as a new alternative: Sprinkling powdered bones at a communal gravestone, biblical and environmentally friendly). *Kungmin Ilbo,* July 7.

Yuh, Ji-Yeon. 2004. *Beyond the Shadow of Camptown: Korean Military Brides in America.* New York: New York Univeristy Press.

Yun, Theodore Jun. 2008. *The Politics of Gender in Colonial Korea: Education, Labor, and Health, 1910–1945.* Berkeley: University of California Press.

Index

acoustic spaces, 13, 16–17, 19, 21, 124, 135, 235n21; and homecoming recitals, 188–89, 200

advancement *(sŏnjin),* 226, 231; and church/music school relationship, 144, 150, 171; and clean voice, 114, 122–23, 129–130, 133, 137; and crying, 40, 45; and Kim Yŏng-mi, 37, 45; Korea as "advanced nation," 59, 61–64, 70, 90, 227; and Lee Myung-bak, 59, 61–64, 66, 226–27; and *maŭm* (heart-mind), 220, 226–27; and sanitation, 129–130; and Somang Presbyterian Church, 56, 59, 61–64, 66, 70–71, 77–78, 90, 150; and *sŏngak* as Christian voice, 100, 102, 109; and teleology, 115–122, 134; and vocal transformation in Korea, 32–33, 37, 40, 45, 47

aesthetics, 5–10, 14, 20–24, 49, 227; aesthetics of progress, 7–10, 21, 33, 111, 136, 141, 175, 230–31; and church/music school relationship, 141, 144, 163, 170; and clean voice, 33, 115, 123, 125, 127, 130, 136; defined, 9, 234n12; and homecoming recitals, 175–76; and Somang Presbyterian Church, 71, 78–79, 92, 111; and *sŏngak* as Christian voice, 81–82, 92, 97, 100, 102–3, 107, 109, 111

affect, 8, 41–42, 46–47, 247n66; and church/music school relationship, 159;

and clean voice, 119–120; and homecoming recitals, 186–87, 192–93; and *maŭm* (heart-mind), 201–3, 209–11, 220–21; and *sŏngak* as Christian voice, 102

alterity, 19, 106, 133, 148

ancestors/predecessors, 56–59, 243n17, 243n20, 246n48; and ancestor worship, 58, 89, 146, 243n18, 250n32; and burial practices, 149; and church/music school relationship, 166; and *sŏngak* as Christian voice, 89–90, 100

Apkujŏng, 51–52, 242n6

arirang, 35–40, 241n8, 241n10

art music, 13, 88, 125, 154, 164, 248n4, 257n32; and homecoming recitals, 176, 180, 185, 192, 194–96, 199–200

audiences, 2–3, 5, 8, 23–24, 227–28; attendance as obligation to performer, 5, 42–43, 156, 180; "audience segregation," 174, 258n50; and church/music school relationship, 5, 112, 141–42, 144, 154–57, 159, 167, 174, 180, 258n50; and clean voice, 112–13, 123, 137; and crying, 40–47; and homecoming recitals, 175–185, 187, 189, 191–93, 195, 197–200, 259n6, 259n10, 261n15; international, 187; and Kim Woo-Kyung, 112; and Kim Yŏng-mi, 44–46; and Lee Myung-bak, 62; and *maŭm* (heart-mind), 201, 204,

chronotope, 7, 33–34, 226, 230–31, 243n22; and ancestors/predecessors, 59, 90; and church/music school relationship, 141, 143–44, 171; and clean voice, 114–15, 118, 120–22, 134; and homecoming recitals, 193; and Lee Myung-bak, 64, 66, 70; and *maŭm* (heart-mind), 204, 215, 219; and *minjung* ("people"), 66–67, 69; and Somang Presbyterian Church, 59, 64, 66, 70, 77, 79, 90; and *sŏngak* as Christian voice, 105, 109

ch'udo yebae, 250n32

Chun Doo-hwan (Chŏn Tu-hwan), 68–70, 244n34

Ch'unhyannga, 119

churches, 3, 7–10, 23, 33, 50, 158; and audiences, 5, 112, 141–42, 144, 154–57; and Christian kinship, 144–150, 157, 15925nn4–5; and clean voice, 123, 137; and corruption, 142–43; and deacons *(chipsa)*, 147–48; and discipleship, 149–150, 171–72, 179; and elders *(changno)*, 147, 190; and exhorting deaconess *(kwŏnsa)*, 147–48, 164, 259n10; hierarchical nature of, 147–48, 158; and homecoming recitals, 174–181, 184–86, 191, 195, 198–99, 259n10, 261n19; and *maŭm* (heart-mind), 204, 221; and *"mot'ae sinang,"* 143; relationship with music schools, 141–44, 150–51, 154–59, 164–174, 257n41; and *sŏngak* as Christian voice, 96–97, 102, 251n40; and tithing, 154, 257n41. *See also names of churches*

Ch'usŏk, 89–90, 243n18, 250n32

classically trained instrumentalists, 5–6

classical vocal music, 2, 6, 9, 23, 85, 92, 175; and church/music school relationship, 156, 164–65; and clean voice, 113, 120–24, 128; and demographics, 257n32; and homecoming recitals, 179, 181, 184, 186–87, 191–92, 194–95, 197–200; and *maŭm* (heart-mind), 221. *See also* European-style classical voice; *sŏngak;* Western classical style

class status, 6, 87, 109, 149–152, 170. *See also* middle class; upper class; working class

clean voice *(kkaekkŭthan moksori)*, 6–10, 23–24, 112–137, 228; and "fuzz" sound, 9, 33, 115, 117; and Kim Woo-Kyung, 112–13; and Kim

Yŏng-mi, 37, 39, 46; and *maŭm* (heart-mind), 224; and modern sanitation, 23, 114–15, 127–134; phonosonic attributes of, 113–123, 125, 134, 137, 253nn8–15; and power/beauty, 113, 123–27; and *sŏngak* as Christian voice, 102, 104–5, 107; and vocal transformation in Korea, 33, 37, 39, 46–47, 120–24; and wobbly vibrato, 9, 33, 115–17

community: and *chŏng*, 32, 43, 145, 210, 241n5, 247n73; and church/music school relationship, 144, 157–58; communal singing, 84–85; and *maŭm* (heart-mind), 204

competitions, 3–4, 30, 34–35, 88, 122, 159; and homecoming recitals, 175, 182, 186, 193.

concert halls, 4, 112–13, 118, 127; and homecoming recitals, 179, 182, 185, 190.

concerts: benefit concerts, 155; and church/music school relationship, 50, 154–56, 161, 165, 168; and crying, 40–44, 242n15; demographics of, 257n32; and Kim Woo-Kyung, 112–13; and Kim Yŏng-mi, 44–46, 45*fig.;* Mahler concert, 188–89; mission concerts, 34, 88, 155; relief concerts, 155. *See also* vocal recitals

Confucianism, 8, 54, 86, 245n47, 249n25, 250n32; court music *(aak)*, 91; and filial piety *(hyo)*, 147–48; and *maŭm* (heart-mind), 207; and music schools, 151, 160. *See also* neo-Confucian dynastic rule

conservatives, 10; and beef protests, 65, 245n43; and clean voice, 135–36; and Lee Myung-bak, 59; and Somang Presbyterian Church, 52, 65, 135–36

conservatories abroad, 4, 30, 34, 86, 88, 165, 167, 191; and homecoming recitals, 175, 179, 183, 185–86; recordings for, 122.

conversions, 7, 54–55, 57, 59, 83, 87, 206, 251n40

corporations, Korean, 59–60, 164, 191, 257n40, 258n5

cosmetic surgery clinics, 52, 242n6

cosmopolitanism, 37, 39

cremation, 149, 256n19

crying: and clean voice, 113; and encores, 42–46, 242n15; and Kim Woo-Kyung, 113; and Kim Yŏng-mi, 44–46, 45*fig.;* and *maŭm* (heart-mind), 219; and vocal